God, Mammon, and the Japanese

Dr. Allen as He Appeared during His Later Years in Korea

GOD

MAMMON

and the

JAPANESE

DR. HORACE N. ALLEN and
Korean-American Relations, 1884-1905

FRED HARVEY HARRINGTON

1966
The University of Wisconsin Press
Madison • Milwaukee • London

Published by
The University of Wisconsin Press

Madison, Milwaukee, and London
P.O. Box 1379, Madison, Wisconsin 53701

to

Arthur Preston Whitaker

Preface

THIS is a tale of God, Mammon, and the Japanese—an account of missionary activity, economic enterprise, and political intrigue. The story concerns American relations with Korea (or Chosen), and revolves about the career of Dr. Horace N. Allen.

To most readers the name of Horace Allen has an unfamiliar ring. But, as the doctor himself said, "small men sometimes hold great stakes." Allen could not claim to be a great man nor an altogether noble one; but he lived in the midst of great events and left his mark upon the times. For two decades he labored in Korea, arriving as the Hermit Kingdom was thrown open to the outside world, departing as Japan established a protectorate. From 1884, "almost at the beginning," to 1905, nearly "to the end." Through those years he helped in the development of American interests in the Far East. There was a religious interest—Allen was the first Protestant missionary to reside in the kingdom of Korea. There was an economic interest—the doctor obtained for American business men the best of the franchises granted in the Land of Morning Calm. There was interest in the future of Chosen—Allen watched and participated in the diplomatic maneuvers which led to Japanese absorption of Korea, the first mainland colony of the Empire of the Rising Sun.

Preface

This volume is based principally upon an exhaustive study of the Horace N. Allen Manuscripts and the Korean material in the archives of the Department of State. These excellent collections supplement each other, the Allen Manuscripts emphasizing missionary and economic questions, the State Department records being strongest on the diplomatic side. The Foulk and Rockhill Manuscripts have also been used, as have the printed sources and secondary works; and I have corresponded with persons who knew Allen. The result, I trust, is a contribution to knowledge in an important and much neglected field. It is hoped, moreover, that this book will call attention to opportunities ahead. I was unable to secure access to the archives of certain missionary boards—archives that must contain a wealth of pertinent material. Equally valuable, when they become available, will be the records of American business concerns with interests in Korea. Finally, Asiatic and European diplomatic collections now closed to investigators will in time yield rich returns.

I have tried to emphasize those subjects that have received the least attention from other authors. Thus, it has been thought best to devote much space to the diplomatic and commercial aspects of missionary work, to the diplomacy of American investment projects, and to the relationship between Allen and the Korean court officials. On the other hand, there has been no effort to write a detailed history of Protestant endeavor in Korea; Paik and Rhodes have covered that ground. The story of the opening of Chosen and the accounts of the diplomacy of the Sino- and Russo-Japanese wars have been cut to a minimum because of studies already made by Treat, Dennett, Paullin, Vagts, Tsiang, and others.

To bring out the particular problems of each phase of American relations with Korea, I have adopted the topical approach. The first two chapters serve as introduction. The next five trace the missionary question through the years from 1884 to 1905. Then come four chapters covering the problem of investment diplomacy for the same period, the

remaining seven chapters being devoted to political developments in those years. Within each group of chapters, of
course, the treatment is chronological.

When reproducing Oriental names, it has seemed best to
follow the customary usage of American writers.

The title page bears a single name, my own. But no man
works alone when he recreates the past. I have had as my
collaborators those living and dead who have written in the
field in which this study falls. My footnotes and bibliography
are intended as an expression of appreciation. Nor does that
conclude my debt. I have received generous assistance from
persons who knew Dr. Allen—William Franklin Sands, Philip
Jaisohn, Alice Appenzeller. The National Archives, the
Library of Congress, the New York Public Library, the li-
braries of the Presbyterian Board of Foreign Missions, the
University of Wisconsin, Yale University, and the University
of Arkansas have aided me immeasurably. I have obtained
advice, encouragement, all manner of assistance from col-
leagues in a profession which has a strong tradition of co-
operation. I may mention in particular the late Professor
Robert B. Mowat of the University of Bristol; Professor John
D. Hicks of the University of California; Professor William
B. Hesseltine of the University of Wisconsin; Professor Henry
Steele Commager of Columbia University; Dean John Clark
Jordan and Professor Dorsey D. Jones of the University of
Arkansas; and Miss Livia Appel, managing editor of the
University of Wisconsin Press. My father, Arthur W. Har-
rington, has also made many valuable suggestions. The map
was prepared by Professor Ralph Hudson of the University
of Arkansas.

Whittlesey House has kindly granted me permission to
reproduce, from William Franklin Sands's *Undiplomatic
Memories,* the photograph of the monarch of Chosen. The
picture of Yuan Shih Kai is taken, by permission of The
Macmillan Company, from *The Re-Shaping of the Far East*
by B. L. Putnam Weale. The American Tract Society has

ix

Preface

allowed me to use the panoramic view of Seoul, which appeared in Lillias Underwood's *Fifteen Years among the Top-Knots*. The Seoul street scene is reproduced, with permission of the Page Company, from *The Spell of Japan* by Isabel Anderson. The photographs of Min Yong Ik and the palace entrance are from Rosalie von Moellendorff's biography of P. G. von Moellendorff, published by Otto Harrassowitz of Leipzig, copyright vested in the Alien Property Custodian, 1943, pursuant to law. The material is used by permission of the Alien Property Custodian in the public interest under License No. JA-189. The frontispiece portrait was supplied by Dr. Allen's son, Horace E. Allen of Toledo, Ohio. Mr. Bernard L. Holloway, president of the American Trading Company, provided me with the picture of James R. Morse. The photograph of the American legation is from the State Department files in the National Archives, the Korean decree from the Allen Collection in the New York Public Library.

The writing of this book was completed a year before the Japanese attack upon Pearl Harbor. Style and citations have been revised since then, and a few statements have been added in the light of recent publications; but emphasis and interpretations have been in no wise changed.

FRED HARVEY HARRINGTON

The University of Arkansas
Autumn, 1943

Table of Contents

Part IV: And the Japanese

List of Illustrations

Part I. The Stage is Set

I sneaked in by a ruse.—Horace N. Allen

Korea is the place . . . there you will see diplomacy in the raw; diplomacy without gloves, perfume or phrases.—William W. Rockhill

1

The Doctor Reaches Seoul

FUSAN, Korea's southern metropolis, was "wholly Japanese" when Horace Allen saw it first, in 1884. Chemulpo, the chief Korean seaport, had just one fine building—Japan's consulate. And in near-by Seoul, the capital, the sight to see was the legation of the Empire of the Rising Sun.[1]

As one looks back, these facts appear as signs of the coming conquest of Chosen. But few can read the future, and few in 1884 saw Korea as Japan's first mainland province. Why should Japan have been the conqueror? Might it not have been China? The Dragon Empire had settlers in Chosen, just as did the Japanese; and the Manchus had a suzerain claim that England recognized. Yes, and fifteen hundred soldiers in Seoul to support their stand, ten times the Japanese legation guard. Granted Chinese weakness, there still was Tsarist Russia, hovering over Korea at the north. And, finally, there was a possibility that Korea could stand alone. The country passed for independent in 1884. It had a king and court; it had what some have called an army; and, as it re-

[1] Horace N. Allen Diary, September 14, 1884, in the Allen Manuscripts in the New York Public Library; letter of Horace N. Allen published under the caption "Our First Letter from Korea" in the *Foreign Missionary*, 43 (1884):302–303.

3

linquished its hermit kingdom past, it was entering into relations with the great states of the world.

No one could guess the future when Horace Allen came to live in the Land of Morning Calm; and Allen, a tall, lean, red-haired doctor, did not even try. He had come to "grow up with the country."[2] Let it grow as Heaven willed.

He was eventually to be a diplomat, this six-foot traveller, and to match wits with the Japanese. He was to be a chief adviser of the Korean king and a skilful promoter of American economic interests. But that was in time to come. In 1884, as he jogged over the rough road to the capital of Chosen, Horace Allen was a savior of souls, the first Protestant missionary to take up residence in the kingdom of Korea.

"American all through,"[3] later on a power in the Sons of the American Revolution, Allen came of proud Yankee stock. There were other strains, of course, even a Pat Riley of Dublin among the doctor's grandparents; but the missionary preferred to talk of the New England strain: of his father, an Ohio pioneer; of granduncle Ethan Allen, Green Mountain Ethan, the hero of Ticonderoga; of another famous granduncle, Lyman Hall, a signer of the Declaration of Independence.

And properly did the missionary talk of these people. They were his kind. They gave to Allen his Calvinist creed, his stern Puritan theology. From them, too, came a pioneering instinct, a sense of duty, an urge to labor night and day. And also the overwhelming self-assurance, the quick temper, the sharp tongue, and the unforgiving spirit that were to cause the doctor trouble all his years.

Whence the missionary interest? Possibly environment; Allen was born (April 23, 1858), reared, and educated in Delaware, Ohio, where nestles the campus of mission-conscious Ohio Wesleyan. Then as now the town and college

[2] "The New American Minister," *Korean Repository*, 4 (1897):349.
[3] Draft of Allen's address to the Naval War College, 1905, in the Allen MSS. Facts concerning Allen's background and early life are drawn

seemed to slumber peacefully. But deep within there burned the spirit of the proselyting cause, the flame of piety fanned by the breath of humanitarian zeal. That selfsame fire had caused Americans to form a mission board as early as 1810 and had sent a steady stream of workers out to distant lands. And when Allen received his bachelor's degree, in 1881, reform crusades of one sort and another were arousing interest in mission work and in the opportunities for service which it offered.

At Ohio Wesleyan, Allen heard much of Christian labors overseas. The college paper carried news of alumni in the field and printed letters from far-off places. There was Thomas Jefferson Scott, for instance, who told of establishing the first Methodist theological college in Asia. There were George Davis and Hiram Lowry, who founded Yenching University in Peking. Gilruth and Janney wrote from India, Pilcher from China, McLaughlin and Gregg and Drees from Latin America.[4]

Other events left their impress. Lee Squier, one of Allen's friends in college, went out to Japan for the Methodists. And in 1883, soon after his graduation from the Miami Medical School, Allen married pretty Frances Messenger, a girl of a definitely religious turn of mind. Fannie was a quiet girl, lacking the pushing qualities of her aggressive husband, but still she often had a word to say when the occasion seemed to call for it.

There were doubts, of course, such doubts as torture many a youthful missionary as he leaves his native soil. When he was assigned to China by the Presbyterian Board of Foreign Missions, the young doctor "came near breaking out at the last," for "it seemed like such a plunge in the dark." Only his Puritan sense of responsibility saw the young man

largely from biographical notes in the Allen MSS. and the alumni records of Ohio Wesleyan University.

[4] Mrs. Bessie R. Beal, Associate Alumni Secretary, Ohio Wesleyan University, to the author, June 2, 1939.

5

through. "I had worked myself up to believe it to be my duty," he told his sister afterward, "and go I must."[5]

"Go I must." No pleasure there; and there was none in China for the Allens. They were "snubbed" by other missionaries on the outward voyage, the doctor lost some money, and Fannie's ill health prevented them from reaching their post in Peking. In Nanking, where they were stationed "temporarily at least," the couple found the people and the magistrates opposed to Christian effort. And, worst of all, there came a quarrel with a mission colleague. Whereupon the doctor took his bride and stormed off to Shanghai, completely miserable and thoroughly defiant.[6]

The quarrel? Allen was naturally nervous, upset by his wife's condition and his own disappointments. But there was more to it than that. Pious, kind, and generous though the young doctor was, he had never learned to get along with people. Thin-skinned, he often took offense where none was intended; short-tempered, he sometimes blurted out insults which he did not mean. And when his views were challenged, he neither yielded nor forgave. He himself tacitly admitted his shortcomings when he said, "I am not a society man and can't get along with people . . . I ought to be a farmer."[7]

Not that Allen was an ineffective missionary. His technical skill, his blunt sincerity, his willingness to work made him an asset to any mission colony. But quarrels do undermine prestige and hurt morale, and they have a way of bringing deep unhappiness to all concerned.

In Shanghai the Allens found their lot somewhat easier. Even so, the red-headed doctor was unhappy. He felt restless, superfluous, "rather disappointed as to the prospect for actual medical work." And, with Fannie expecting a baby,

[5] Allen to Jennie Everett, June 3, 1889, in the Allen MSS.

[6] Allen Diary, September 4, 1883, January 7, 1884, November 18, 1887; Allen to Jennie Everett, June 3, 1889, in the Allen MSS; Horace N. Allen, *Things Korean* (New York, 1908), 189–191.

[7] Allen Diary, November 6, 1887; William F. Sands to the author, May 28, 1939.

the climate was a cause of concern. With that in mind, Allen asked for transfer to the "healthy north." Chefoo he suggested first, and when that failed to stir his superiors, he suggested the more distant cities of Chosen.[8]

Had precedent been followed, the young man would have had another setback. For his Presbyterian board had already turned down a number of more impassioned "pleas for Korea."[9] Was it wise, asked the practical board secretaries, to start new stations when even the old were poorly manned? Why, anyway, Chosen? The French Catholics, who had been on the ground for three generations, had met with ghastly failures, culminating in the massacres of 1839 and 1866. An anti-Christian edict of the latter year stood unrepealed, and Korean treaties contained no guarantees for missionaries.

As it happened, though, the Presbyterians were shifting ground when Allen's bid arrived. One secretary, the Reverend Frank F. Ellinwood, had become convinced of Chosen's needs. And when presently the board received from philanthropists a gift of seven thousand dollars for work in the Land of Morning Calm, the question was settled. "God was plainly leading" now, and the cables flashed a one-word message of appointment to the waiting agent in Shanghai.[10]

The good news reached China late in July, 1884, a trying

[8] L. George Paik, *The History of Protestant Missions in Korea, 1832–1910* (Pyeng Yang, Korea, 1929), 76–77, quoting a statement made by Allen in 1909; Allen, *Things Korean*, 167; Allen to F. F. Ellinwood, January 29, June 9, 1884, and to Joseph Haas, June 6, 1884, in the Allen MSS.

[9] *Foreign Missionary*, 42 (1883–84):16–17, 246–249, 335–337; Lillias H. Underwood, *Underwood of Korea* (New York, 1918), 34. The background is covered in Harry A. Rhodes, *History of the Korea Mission, Presbyterian Church, U.S.A.* (Seoul [1935]); Paik, *Protestant Missions in Korea;* Arthur J. Brown, *One Hundred Years: A History of the Foreign Missionary Work of the Presbyterian Church in the U.S.A.* (New York, 1936); Charles Dallet, *Histoire de l'église de Corée* (2 vols., Paris, 1874); and Adrien Launay, *La Corée et les missionaires français* (Tours, 1899).

[10] Arthur J. Brown, *The Mastery of the Far East* (New York, 1919), 501; Arthur J. Brown, "A Reading Journey through Korea," *Chautau-*

time for the Allen family. Less than a fortnight earlier the Franco-Chinese war had driven Fannie and the doctor from their home. Hours more and their first baby came, an eight-pound boy who took his father's name. Allen, helping the physician in charge, saw his wife's face flush with fever, heard her cry out in delirium, watched her strength ebb with the hemorrhage that came when instruments were used. Those were anxious moments, and further trouble was expected by the four physicians present. But Fannie rallied, and Allen saw again the smile that meant so much to him. The danger was past when the cablegram arrived, but it was two months before the new appointee felt that he could leave his wife to make a tour of his new territory.[11]

From China, Korea had seemed a land of milk and honey. Viewed at closer range, it proved no garden of dreams. For all the efforts of the Japanese, Fusan lacked every up-to-date convenience. Chemulpo, Seoul's outlet on the Yellow Sea, was even worse. Sprawling beside a dreary mud-flat, it was a "motley place of slab shanties mud huts, sheds and fresh earth." To reach the capital city of Seoul, thirty miles inland, one chose between a treacherous fifty-mile watercourse and a rough mountain path. And when he arrived the traveller found little except sorry huts that suggested a "collection of haystacks that have 'wintered out.' "

The sight had discouraged many men before Allen; but he, remembering China, was determined to like what he saw. He praised the uninspiring scenery and rode a nasty native pony uncomplainingly. He found Oriental charm where others noticed only filth, he liked the people, "exceedingly lazy and dirty" though they were.[12] Perhaps he was already

quan, 41 (1905):566; Paik, *Protestant Missions in Korea,* 77, correcting Brown.

[11] Allen Diary, July 10, 1883; Allen to Ellinwood, July 22, 1884, in the Allen MSS.

[12] Allen Diary, September 14, 20, 22, 1884; Allen, "Our First Letter from Korea," *Foreign Missionary,* 43 (1884):302–303. Allen's impressions may be compared with those of Isabella L. Bishop, *Korea and Her*

counting on better days to come, though he could hardly have foreseen at this moment that he, Horace Allen, was to make possible Korea's first railroad, her first waterworks, her first city lighting and street car systems, her first modern mine.

Most Americans on reaching Seoul sought accommodations with the United States minister. Not Allen; he ate "dogmeat and rice" at a native inn. Having favors to ask at the legation, he feared to jeopardize his chances by piling up unnecessary obligations. America's representative, General Lucius Foote, was not noted for his hospitality; only two months before, the Reverend Robert S. Maclay, reconnoitering for the Methodists, had offended the envoy by outstaying a short welcome.[13]

Still, the handsome old politician was glad to see young Doctor Allen. Visitors were rare in 1884, and Seoul was a pretty tame place for a party hack indifferent to the diplomacy of China and Japan. It was pleasant, of course, to be the ranking Occidental representative in Chosen, but sixteen months of service had given Foote no great affection for the land. Dull, "filthy beyond endurance," it seemed no place for a Californian in his declining years.

Allen, ever quick to act, lost little time in stating his business. He was a Presbyterian medical missionary assigned to the kingdom of Korea. There could be no doubt as to the need. The foreign residents, for one thing; their morals were "shocking—all keep mistresses nearly." Then the natives. Mercilessly exploited by the upper classes, living in squalor and wracked by disease, the average Korean needed such attentions as a physician could provide. Christianity would

Neighbours (2 vols., London, 1898), 1:25, 30–31; John A. Cockerill, "To Seoul by Chair," *New York Herald,* December 1, 1895; Lillias H. Underwood, *Fifteen Years among the Top-Knots* (Boston, 1904), 1–5; Lucius Foote to the Secretary of State, May 23, 26, 1883, Dispatches, State Department Archives, in the National Archives.

[13] Allen to Ellinwood, April 3, 1885, in the Allen MSS. When Allen became United States minister, a European guidebook listed "Guest House, American Legation" among Seoul's hotels. Allen, *Things Korean,* 226.

follow. With Buddhism barred from the cities, with Confucianism in decay, the native faith was one of demons and earth spirits. And that, to a good Calvinist, was tantamount to no faith at all.[14]

Obviously, said Allen, the first Protestant station should be in Seoul. Fusan was "too Japanese," Chemulpo "too foreign" to be representative; and each contained a floating population hard for proselyting men to handle. The only other city "of much missionary importance" was the capital; from it "all work must radiate."[15]

Here, then, the legation's work began. Horace Allen was no diplomat, nor did he dream that he would one day represent his country's government in Seoul. What he did know, however, was that church and state go hand in hand in Oriental countries, that his soul-saving must have diplomatic sanction to be at all successful. Foote could protect and advise him, could help him get a mission building, could investigate the anti-Christian law. Would he do so?

Certainly, replied the general. Though he was a member of no church, he believed in missions "as a means of elevating the people" of Korea. And, though he did not say so, as a means of carrying out instructions from a State Department which had long aided missionaries. "Believing as this Government does," read the general's basic orders, "that the toleration of faiths is the true policy of all enlightened powers, this Department would be glad to see you extend your good offices within proper grounds and counsel the Coreans to treat all missionaries kindly."[16]

[14] Horace N. Allen, in an article on "Medical Work in Korea" in the *Foreign Missionary*, 44 (1885):76, speaks of the "absence of any faith." The actual situation is well described in Paik, *Protestant Missions in Korea*, 16–23; Bishop, *Korea*, 2:222–254; William W. Rockhill, *China's Intercourse with Korea* (London, 1895), 54–60; George W. Gilmore, *Korea from Its Capital* (Philadelphia, 1892), 185–198; and James S. Gale, *Korean Sketches* (Edinburgh and London, 1898), 213–218.

[15] Allen to Ellinwood, October 6, 1884, in the Allen MSS.

[16] Foote to the Secretary of State, September 1, 1884, Dispatches, State

The Doctor Reaches Seoul

Then, to clinch matters, there was Allen's scientific training. Foote would bend a little to obey instructions or to help a worthy cause; he would go much farther to keep a good physician near his ailing wife and his own aging frame. "I was gladly received," Allen noted bluntly in his diary, "because of the great need for a doctor."

The minister's aid began at once. Without him househunting would have been a dismal task. Renting was unknown in Chosen, purchase difficult: most natives were suspicious, and all transacted business with exasperating deliberation. Foote solved the problem instantly. True to an American tradition of mixing private gain with diplomatic service, he had dabbled in Korean realty. One of his houses served as United States legation and was to pay the general handsomely years after he had given up diplomacy. Another he would sell to Allen. Yes, he already had a purchaser, had indeed bought the house for someone else; but he preferred to sell to the Presbyterians. After buying, Allen found out why. The property had been earmarked for the Methodists. Foote's bad impression of Maclay, together with his need for a physician, had changed the course of mission history.[17]

The envoy did not stop with changing sects; he used his rank to help Allen break Korean law. Clearly, he observed, the doctor needed protection from the anti-Christian law, which, though unenforced in 1884, might one day be revived. Why not, then, adopt a disguise? The French Catholic priests did so; Foote had seen them garbed as native mourners. Allen could do better; being a physician, he could come to Seoul as American legation doctor. No pay, but a chance to be free from persecution while "preparing the way for the work

Department Archives; Secretary of State Frelinghuysen to Foote, October 23, 1883, Instructions, State Department Archives; Allen to Ellinwood, October 8, 1884, in the Allen MSS.

[17] Allen Diary, September 23, 24, 1884; Hugh A. Dinsmore to the Secretary of State, October 29, 1887, Dispatches, State Department Archives; Paik, *Protestant Missions in Korea,* 89, quoting a letter from Allen to Maclay.

which will soon begin."[18] Was such a ruse permissible under
the mission code of ethics? Allen thought so. Indeed, he was
delighted with the scheme and the way Foote saw it through.
The test came soon. Cornering the American minister,
Korea's king asked point-blank whether Allen was a missionary. "He is physician to the legation," replied the minister.
His Majesty appeared satisfied.[19]

It all seemed as simple as that to a fledgling mission agent
and a spoilsman diplomat. Actually, the clumsy camouflage
fooled no one. Even the muddle-minded monarch of Chosen
knew that Allen was a Christian worker[20]—and he was not the
first to hear the news. That Allen stayed in Seoul was due
not to the fumbling moves of Lucius Foote but to the state
of politics in the kingdom of Korea.[21]

Two forces worked on the missionary's side—the strength
of the progressive party of Chosen and the power of Japan.
Two forces that were really one, for the progressives of Korea

[18] Allen, "Our First Letter from Korea," *Foreign Missionary*, 43
(1884):303. On Catholic disguise measures, see Foote to the Secretary
of State, September 1, 1884, Dispatches, State Department Archives;
notes by Allen, written about November or December, 1888, in the Allen
MSS; Allen, *Things Korean*, 156; Gilmore, *Korea*, 140.

[19] Allen to Ellinwood, October 8, 1884, and to Mary Lee, February 18,
1903, in the Allen MSS.

[20] Allen to Ellinwood, June 2, 1885, in the Allen MSS; Allen, "Medical
Work in Korea," *Foreign Missionary*, 44 (1885):76.

[21] On the diplomatic background, see William L. Langer, *The Diplomacy of Imperialism, 1890–1912* (London and New York, 1935), 168–
171; T. F. Tsiang, "Sino-Japanese Diplomatic Relations, 1870–1894,"
Chinese Social and Political Science Review, 17 (1933):1–106; Payson J.
Treat, "China and Korea, 1885–1894," *Political Science Quarterly*, 49
(1933):506–543; Alfred Vagts, "Der Chinesische-Japanische Krieg, 1894–
95," *Europäische Gespräche*, 9 (1931):234–252; Nagao Ariga, "Diplomacy," in Alfred Stead, ed., *Japan by the Japanese* (New York and
London, 1904), 142–218; Shuhsi Hsü, *China and Her Political Entity*
(New York, 1926); Tyler Dennett, "Early American Policy in Korea,
1883–7," *Political Science Quarterly*, 38 (1923):82–103; Charles C. Tansill,
The Foreign Policy of Thomas F. Bayard, 1885–1897 (New York, 1940),
413–449; T. C. Lin, "Li Hung Chang: His Korean Policies, 1870–1885,"
Chinese Social and Political Science Review, 19 (1935):202–233; Seiji
G. Hishida, *The International Position of Japan as a Great Power*

preached a program they had learned from the Japanese, and Japan leaned heavily on her Seoul allies.

The Japanese and the progress party were agreed on missionary matters. Missions were a "civilizing" influence which would impel Korea toward the culture of the Western world and, consequently, toward the culture of the new Japan, rapidly adopting Western ways. Thus Kim Ok Kiun, the chief Korean progressive, had greeted the Reverend Maclay with open arms. Thus His Majesty, who relied on Kim and the Japanese, had promised to help support a Methodist school and hospital in Seoul.[22]

As with missions, so with the other enterprises in which Allen was soon to engage. Japan and the progressives wanted telegraph and railroad systems, posts and lighting plants, and other conveniences of the Occident. And since Japan had little capital, there was talk of giving some of the concessions to citizens of the United States.

(New York, 1905). At least three doctoral dissertations are of importance: Francis C. Jones, Foreign Diplomacy in Korea, 1886–1894, dated 1935, in the Harvard University library, an abstract of which appears in Summary of Theses, Harvard University, 1935, pp. 163–166; Harold J. Noble, Korea and Her Relations with the United States before 1895, dated 1931, in the library of the University of California, portions of which have been published as articles; Hong Sub Yoon, Korea in International Far Eastern Relations, dated 1935, in the American University library, Washington, D.C. I have examined the latter two of these theses. Korean domestic politics, discussed in all the works cited, receives particular attention in Allen's diary entries for December 26, 1884, and February 16, 1885; George C. Foulk, "Report of Information Relative to the Revolutionary Attempt in Seoul, Corea, December 4–7, 1884," Foreign Relations, 1885, pp. 335–343; Homer B. Hulbert, The History of Korea, vol. 2 (Seoul, 1905); Rosalie von Moellendorff, P. G. von Moellendorff (Leipzig, 1930); George H. Jones, "Historical Notes on the Reigning Dynasty," Korean Repository, 4 (1897):126–128, 220–228; George H. Jones, "The Tai Won Kun," Korean Repository, 5 (1898): 241–250; and Gordon Haddo, "The Rise and Fall of the Progressive Party of Korea," Chautauquan, 16 (1892):46–49.

[22] Foote to the Secretary of State, September 1, 8, 1884, Dispatches, State Department Archives; Allen to Ellinwood, February 23, April 3, 1885, in the Allen MSS; Paik, Protestant Missions in Korea, 73, quoting letters from Foote to Maclay.

All that looked well for Allen, but his backers had their weaknesses. For one thing, the progress party was still small. True, its youthful leader, Kim Ok Kiun, was a member of a mighty clan: the Kims had controlled the patronage of many kings. The Japanese were willing to finance the movement, and Kim Ok Kiun had won the royal confidence. Even so, the progressives were overshadowed by their foes—anti-foreign, non-progressive, anti-missionary politicians. This was natural; Chosen, having slumbered for many centuries, objected to sudden change, most of all when it was sponsored by ambitious, aspiring Japan. Koreans had traded with the islanders for generations, had conceded tributary obligations and Japanese claims in Fusan; but they had never learned to like their neighbor to the east. They could not forget that Hideyoshi had laid waste their land in 1592, and they were well aware that many Japanese still coveted their country —for security, supplies, and markets; as a steppingstone to China; and as an outlet for soldiers unemployed after Japan's liquidation of her feudal armies.

Distaste for the Japanese had deepened in Chosen in the years before the doctor came to Seoul. Her aping of Occidental ways made Japan seem a traitor to the Orient and— like the Westerners—an aggressor in Chosen. First notes, then gunboats, to force a treaty in 1876, establishing diplomatic intercourse and opening three Korean ports. The resentment this engendered, which showed itself in an anti-Japanese uprising six years later, still smouldered in 1884, despite the pro-Japanese progressives and Japanese subsidies of Seoul newspapers.

Conservative China, not Westernized Japan, was the favored nation in Chosen in 1884. Immigration, similarity of culture, and conquest had rooted Chinese institutions deep in the Korean soil. And that, for Allen, was bad news. For the Chinese in Korea disapproved of missionaries, fearing that Christian agents might disturb the Chinese-veneered patterns of the past; they disapproved also of the other forms of progress which the doctor was soon to promote.

Politically, China had long been suzerain in Chosen, the relationship resembling that of present-day dominion to the British crown. There was ceremonial deference and a very modest tribute, nothing more. Save for a trickling land trade, China valued Korea chiefly as a buffer and hence had interfered little in local matters.

But when Japan moved into action the Manchus began to see that safety of their eastern provinces depended on their domination of Chosen. Li Hung Chang, the leading Chinese statesman, therefore set out to strengthen the political and economic bonds between Korea and the Dragon Empire. When Japan insisted on the pact of 1876, he persuaded Seoul to offset the Japanese advantage by giving the same privileges to the United States, Great Britain, and Germany. Fight fire with fire.

Had all worked out as planned, China would have won complete control, and Horace Allen might not have been admitted to Chosen. But the Japanese would not be downed, and the Western powers did not give Li the aid he had counted on. England and Germany did half admit the suzerainty of China by sending consular rather than diplomatic agents to Seoul; but the United States felt otherwise. Brushing aside the special rights of the Dragon Empire, Washington accredited a diplomat of high rank to Chosen (minister plenipotentiary and envoy extraordinary) and thus lent weight to the Japanese contention that Korea was entirely independent of the Manchus and a fair field for Japan.

Nor did it stop with that. Americans in Chosen preferred the Island Empire, liked Japanese diplomatists, Japanese servants, Japanese mistresses better than the Chinese brands. Minister Foote disliked the Manchus with the intensity of a Californian who had seen the Chinese immigration problem at its height. His aide, Ensign George C. Foulk, knew and loved Japan and later took a Japanese girl for his bride. Both diplomats despised Manchu conservatism, both applauded the Japanese urge to progress. And both of them, Foulk in particular, overstepped diplomatic bounds to aid the pro-Nipponese progressives of Korea, receiving in return all manner of franchise promises.[23]

But important as it was, the American position checked the Manchus only temporarily. When Allen took up residence in the Land of Morning Calm, it was Li Hung Chang's program that was being carried out. True, the Korean king still favored Kim Ok Kiun, still leaned on Japan for advice, but most of the politicians in Seoul had come to support China openly. The queen, for example, and her relatives the Mins. They dominated the Korean government; and they were wedded to the Chinese-flavored past. Certainly there was no trace of progressivism in the superstition of the queen, in her belief, for example, that a necklace made of cats' vaginas would captivate her husband. And Min Yong Ik, nephew of Her Majesty, retained his Chinese conservatism even after a tour around the world.

Nothing there to encourage a young missionary; and the Chinese camp harbored still other foes of Christian labors. Anti-foreign as she was, Queen Min was mild as compared with her septuagenarian father-in-law, the Tai Wen Kun. No heir himself, this famous politician had made his twelve-year-old son a king in 1864 by having a dowager queen adopt the boy. As regent in his son's minority, as minority leader in the days of Min control, the royal parent proved a savage

[23] Letters to the Secretary of State from Foote, May 1, 18, July 19, October 23, 30, 1883, September 8, 1884, and from Foulk, February 20, 1886, Dispatches, State Department Archives; Secretary of State Frelinghuysen to Foote, March 9, 1883, Instructions, State Department Archives; Allen Diary, June 3, December 1, 1885; notes for an article, August, 1888, in the Allen MSS. The State Department attitude toward suzerain claims is well expressed by Assistant Secretary of State Adee (memorandum of July 30, 1895, quoted in Tansill, *Foreign Policy of Bayard*, 444, note): "we simply deal with the man we find in charge of the shop."

foe of all outsiders. The Christian massacre of 1866 was his, and it was he who had fought the French who came to ask for explanations. That same year he had let his people kill the crew of an American trading ship, the *General Sherman;* and four years later he met with arms an attempt by the Grant administration to obtain apologies and compensation. He snarled at the Japanese, attacked the treaties the Mins had made with the islanders, and organized the anti-Japanese revolt of 1882. The year 1884 saw the Tai Wen Kun in exile and his party persecuted by progressive king and conservative queen alike; but he still had followers, men who were to flock to aid him on his return in 1885.

China, the Mins, the Tai Wen Kun—singly or united, they meant grief for Allen. And to add another foe one could count in the Russians, who were also interested in Chosen and especially in her ports. Russia, like China, had an anti-missionary party in Seoul in 1884. Allen met its head, Paul G. von Moellendorff, a man of many masters. Germany claimed him as a national, Chosen as customs officer and king's adviser, China as an appointed Manchu agent, Russia in an undefined capacity. But not America; Allen found the strange Teuton hostile to American enterprise and "more anti-missionary than the Koreans themselves."[24]

Strong foes they were, and in the fall of 1884 the conservatives were making ready to eliminate the doctor's progressive backers. It irked reactionaries to see the king make Kim Ok Kiun a baron; it angered them to have His Majesty decide test cases in favor of the progressive minority. It was equally unpleasant to have the monarch deprive Moellendorff of power and cashier Chinese army instructors while bringing in technicians from Japan. Plainly, said the Chinese partisans, that must end, and soon.

A showdown, then, was bound to come, a test of strength between Japan and China, a fight between progressives

[24] Allen to Ellinwood, October 8, 1884, in the Allen MSS; Moellendorff, *Moellendorff,* 60–79 *passim,* 100–108.

and conservatives. Who could tell what that might bring—a Russian move for an ice-free port, an Oriental war, another Christian persecution? Certainly there would be a few bad days for the Americans, even if Japan and Kim Ok Kiun should win. And what if, as was more likely, China and the Mins should triumph? Or the Tai Wen Kun?

Allen did not bother to think along these lines. Foote, on whom he relied for counsel, believed that there would be no trouble.[25] And, anyway, there was no time to worry; the doctor was far too busy with details—preparing his Oriental house for Occidental occupancy, rushing back to Shanghai for his family, gathering supplies and hiring servants. Six weeks passed before these tasks were finished, and by then it was December 4, 1884, a fateful time for Allen and Korea.

[25] Paik, *Protestant Missions in Korea,* 73, quoting Foote; Allen, *Things Korean,* 167. See, however, Foote to Admiral John Lee Davis, November 18, 1884, Seoul Legation Files, State Department Archives.

2

First Clash of Empire

FOR the Allens December 4, 1884, was an ordinary day in Seoul. In the evening the doctor went to see a patient. As he tramped home through the deserted streets, he noted nothing extraordinary. Nothing to hear but the pounding rhythm of Korean laundry sticks and the howl of a dog or two; nothing to see but the snow-clad huts and the yellow moon, high and bright in the Oriental sky. Very lovely, very quiet and peaceful, Allen told his wife when he reached home. They must take a stroll one evening soon.

But there was more in store for Seoul's first mission family before the night was over. Along toward midnight Fannie and the doctor were roused from slumber by a great commotion just outside their residence. The gate bell clanged, there was the clamor of many voices, a voice called for Allen. And by the time the missionary had scrambled out of bed and reached his living room, Minister Foote's private secretary stood on the threshold, with a message and disturbing news.[1]

Scanning the note, listening to his visitor, the young physician must have foreseen that this would be a night to

[1] Allen Diary, December 5, 1884, in the Allen MSS; Allen, *Things Korean*, 68–72; Horace N. Allen, *Korea: Fact and Fancy* (Seoul, 1904), 21–22.

be remembered. Still, he could scarcely have had any idea how much it was to mean to him. How it was to turn him from a minor figure into a leading actor in the unfolding pageant of Korean history. How he was to combine intrigue with soul-saving and became a dollar diplomat; and how it would end, after twenty years, with the Allens ailing and prematurely old, harboring memories of much imperial blood-letting, of many clashes of the world's great powers, of the decline and fall of a kingdom that dated back more than a thousand years.

The message from Foote was a call for Allen's professional services. Min Yong Ik lay wounded unto death—Prince General Min Yong Ik, nephew to the queen and leader of the great Min clan. A bloody business, said Foote's secretary. And even bloodier than he knew; for the flowing wounds of Min Yong Ik set Koreans at one another's throats and brought China and Japan to blows for the first time in modern history.

The crisis, of course, stemmed from the major trends of the time—from a Japanese impulse toward expansion, from Chinese insistence on a buffer, from Korean greed for office.[2] The conservative Mins and their Manchu allies had decided that in self-defense they must eliminate the Japanese-progressive influence in Seoul; and simultaneously the Japanese and their Korean friends had resolved to make a bid for power while most of the Chinese troops were occupied against the French in Annam.

[2] The background of the émeute is best presented in Foulk's "Report," in *Foreign Relations,* 1885, pp. 335–343; Foulk had "exceptional means for obtaining useful information." Also useful are Tsiang, "Sino-Japanese Relations," *Chinese Social and Political Science Review,* 17 (1933): 79–81; Hulbert, *History of Korea,* 2:233–236; Moellendorff, *Moellendorff,* 69–72; Ariga, "Diplomacy," in Stead, *Japan by the Japanese,* 189–192; Haddo, "Progressive Party of Korea," *Chautauquan,* 16 (1892):47–48; and F. H. Mörsel, "Events Leading to the Emeute of 1884," *Korean Repository,* 4 (1897):95–98, 135–140. George N. Curzon, in his *Problems of the Far East* (London, 1894), 224, errs in suggesting that Russia was behind the revolt.

Until July, 1884, the progressives had more than held their own. Time after time the king had humbled Min Yong Ik and such Chinese agents as Moellendorff; repeatedly His Majesty had favored the progressive leader Kim Ok Kiun, Japanese Minister Takezoye, and pro-Japanese George Foulk of the United States legation. But in July the opposition struck. Min Yong Ik switched from civil to military office, purged the army of Japanese supporters, and reappointed Chinese aides who had been discharged by the progressives. His father, in control of royal revenues, froze the funds His Majesty had earmarked for "progressive contracts." Moellendorff reassumed advisory duties at the foreign office, and Chinese immigrants poured into Chosen. Perhaps a blood purge was in contemplation, for the queen's adherents and the Chinese began to treat the allies of Japan with a studied lack of courtesy.

Irritated and dismayed, the progressives planned a coup. Though weakened by the Min comeback, they still controlled the king, who trusted Kim Ok Kiun and was interested in the gold and arguments of Minister Takezoye. With His Majesty's cooperation, they reasoned, quick action might bring victory; delay was likely to mean complete elimination from the government. They must strike at once. "For the sake of Corea," one said to Foulk ("and his words did not seem empty"), the leading Chinese sympathizers "would have to be killed."

Preparing for their blow, the Japanese group spread unpleasant rumors. If the Mins prevailed, they whispered, China would swallow Chosen, Korean soldiers would be sent to help the Manchus fight the French. Concurrently, the Japanese legation guard drilled by night as well as by day, and Japan's partisans openly confessed their hatred of China. Japanese Minister Takezoye, formerly on good terms with Chinese scholars, became elaborately rude to friends of the Dragon Empire.

Finally, after five months of preparation, the thrust for

power came. On December 4, the day the Allens thought so peaceful, a banquet was held to celebrate the opening of Korea's postal service. The progressives, who controlled the post department, were out in force—keen, unscrupulous Kim Ok Kiun and his headstrong assistant Pak Yong Hyo, ambitious Hong Yong Sik, and clever So Kwang Pom; and at their side the spearhead of Japanese intrigue in Seoul—Shimamura, Japan's legation secretary. Only Takezoye was absent; the minister was reported to be "ill."[3]

The conservative opposition was present, too—their leader Min Yong Ik with two of his fellow generals; the scheming Moellendorff, pro-Russian Chinese agent clad as a Korean nobleman; Chinese Commissioner Chen Shu Tang. And there were the neutrals (or near-neutrals—Korea never begot impartiality), British Consul William G. Aston and Minister Foote from the United States, with his private secretary and interpreter. German Consul Zembsch was absent, indisposed; and Foote's helper Foulk was out of town, perhaps because he feared being drawn into the revolution which he sensed was coming.

From the start the banquet was different from the usual dull, formal state function. There was tension in the atmosphere, the strain that gathers when enemies break bread together. Moellendorff and Min Yong Ik did their best to

[3] For the outbreak and course of the revolt, Allen Diary, December 5, 11, 26, 1884; manuscript account by Foulk, and Foulk to the Secretary of the Navy, with report, December 20, 1884, in the Foulk Manuscripts in the New York Public Library; Foulk to the Secretary of the Navy, January 10, 1885, and Foote to the Secretary of State, December 5, 7, 17, 1884, Dispatches, State Department Archives; Tsiang, "Sino-Japanese Relations," *Chinese Social and Political Science Review*, 17 (1933): 81–85; Ariga, "Diplomacy," in Stead, *Japan by the Japanese*, 192–194; Moellendorff, *Moellendorff*, 72–75; Francis V. Dickins and Stanley Lane-Poole, *The Life of Sir Harry Parkes* (2 vols., London and New York, 1894), 2:217–224; Percival Lowell, "A Korean Coup d'Etat," *Atlantic*, 58 (1886):599–618; Frank A. McKenzie, *Korea's Fight for Freedom* (New York, 1920), 32–41; Hulbert, *History of Korea*, 2:236–242; F. H. Mörsel, "The Emeute of 1884," with correction, *Korean Repository*, 4 (1897): 212–219, 279–280.

whip up conversation, but to no avail. The progressives, plainly, had other matters on their minds—else why did Kim Ok Kiun leave the table so often during the meal?

The trouble broke at ten when the diners, finishing their food, were startled by the cry of "Fire!" There was no personal danger, they discovered as they rushed outdoors; the conflagration was not near at hand. But local custom required that there be a native general at every fire; so Min Yong Ik, most prominent Korean present, started up mindful of his duty. In so doing, he played directly into the hands of an enemy crouching just outside—probably a Japanese-trained Korean whom Min had drummed out of the army. As the prince stepped from the building, leaning upon the arms of lackeys, he was slashed down with a heavy sword. One blow lopped off the arm of a Min retainer, others cut the general again and again until he fell as one dead.

He was wounded badly, but not quite gone. As his assailant raced off into the night, Min dragged his bleeding body back indoors and staggered into the arms of Moellendorff, muttering, "An assassin has killed me."

After that, all was confusion. Moellendorff, Foote, and Aston stayed with Min; nearly all the others ran from the scene of horror. The progressives, elated over the success of the first steps in their insurrection, rushed off to find the king. Other Koreans, preferring life to valor, hastened to seek hiding places, casting off the telltale insignia of their rank as they did so. What of their leader, whom they had left behind? Well, he might die, as other Mins had died before him, at the hands of assassins. Why risk death by waiting to find out?

It was Moellendorff who took affairs in charge, though he was himself in danger. He called for chairs to take Min to a safer place. And when these were delayed an hour, as most things were in Seoul, the Chinese-Russian agent bandaged the lacerated prince with his own untrained hands. Finally it was possible to move Min to Moellendorff's headquarters; but even here there was no one to tend the wounded man.

None, that is, but a dozen perplexed and helpless native men of physic, trained in dog-soup therapy. Observing their incompetence, someone suggested calling the Japanese legation doctor; but who would trust a Min to the Japanese? Moellendorff, though anti-missionary, preferred to call on Allen. When Min failed to rally, he scribbled a note to the American: he had "a dying man on his hands"; would Allen come? In the hope that he would, Moellendorff was sending a guard of fifty native soldiers.

Had Allen stopped to think, he might have speculated that here was his chance to win over the Chinese partisans, the strongest group in Chosen and the major obstacle to his missionary labors. But he had no opportunity to speculate; he saw only the path of duty. He must go. And, to make sure that he would be on time, he drove his guard across the city at double quick, strange pace for Seoul soldiers when they were not retreating from a foe.

Arriving at Moellendorff's, Allen found his royal patient in very bad shape, "all blood and gore." The sword had inflicted no fewer than seven slashes. One had partly scalped the leader of the Mins. A second had cut a swath from eye to spine, three more had bared the bones of poor Min's arms.

Pushing aside the native doctors, Allen set to work. And, save for one hurried visit home, he labored all the night, sponging, cleansing, stitching, bandaging the gaping wounds. A few he barely touched because of Min's exhausted state; one he missed completely because of the darkness, the confusion, and the "matted hair dress." But by dawn there was improvement. Encouraged, the American decided to dress all the wounds, and asked the Japanese physician to come in to help him.

That made a curious scene: two practitioners of Western medicine bending over a major foe of Western institutions; a mission doctor working on an anti-Christian politician, a Japanese physician laboring with an anti-Japanese Korean—and in Moellendorff's establishment, center of opposition to both Japan and the United States! Yet the work was done, and well done. Twenty-seven sutures, a ligature, lint padding, and adhesive plaster. Then and only then did Allen feel that he was free to leave for home and rest.[4]

Rest—if one could in the midst of revolution. Counting Min eliminated, the progressives and their Japanese confederates had hurried to complete their anti-Chinese coup. Arriving at the palace, Kim Ok Kiun and others told the king that there was trouble. Under the circumstances, they said, His Majesty should ask Japanese envoy Takezoye to "protect" the royal family with his legation guard. To make defense the easier, the monarch should move to a smaller residence that could be easily defended.

Faith or fear (he had overmuch of both) forced the king to acquiesce to these suggestions. He went to a palace that served admirably as a prison, and allowed a note to be sent to Takezoye, imploring Japanese assistance. Acceptance had been prearranged, of course. The messenger found Nippon's minister, who had been "ill" at dinner time, now fully dressed and his troops in marching order. Japan, apparently, was ready and eager to "protect" the Korean king and queen if it meant curtailing Chinese influence.

With the king in their possession, and possession guaranteed by Takezoye's soldiers, the progressives were ready to snatch the governmental power from the pro-Manchu family of the queen. One by one Min officers were called before His Majesty. Obeying—no Korean could ignore a royal summons— these individuals were hacked to pieces by young progressives while the Japanese looked on approvingly. Min Thai Ho, father of Allen's patient, was among the men to go, as was Min Yong Mok, a mighty member of the clan; Cho Yong Ha, the queen's cousin; and the king's chief eunuch, butchered

[4] Allen Diary, December 5, 1884; Allen, *Things Korean,* 196; Mörsel, "Emeute of 1884," *Korean Repository,* 4 (1897):215; Mrs. F. Ohlinger, "The Beginnings of Medical Work in Korea," *ibid.,* 1 (1892):354–355. Moellendorff later claimed credit for having saved Min. See Moellendorff, *Moellendorff,* 77.

in His Majesty's presence for expressing distrust of the progressives and Japan. All these and more.

After the slaughter the spoils were parcelled out. A pro-
Japanese cabinet was quickly formed, with jobs for all the
faithful. Kim Ok Kiun, naturally, was the central figure in
the new government, though he preferred to work behind
the scenes in a modest treasury post. Glory-greedy Hong
Yong Sik was allowed to feed his vanity as prime minister.

News of the progress of the insurrection soon reached the
foreigners in Seoul. Allen, of course, learned more than most.
While tending Min he had heard Chinese reports, for Moellendorff's house was full of the queen's supporters. And on
his way home he had picked up another slant on the news
from the pro-Japanese United States legation.

Well might the American pay heed to every scrap of evidence. This was no beerhouse brawl that foreigners could
easily ignore; it was a fight that would affect them one and
all. A Japanese victory would mean the scrapping of tradi-
tions in Chosen and would provide new opportunities for
Western nations. A Japanese defeat, on the other hand—a
popular reaction against Japan and the progressives—might
make the white men targets of a Korean mob. For the natives,
antagonistic toward Europeanized Japan, might attack all
representatives of Western culture.

Allen's countrymen had most to fear from this possible
development. They had made the wrong kind of friends. The
Germans had Moellendorff as a friend in the Chinese camp.
The English were known as allies of the Dragon Empire.
America, on the other hand, was a bad offender against the
Manchus and Mins. She denied the Chinese suzerain claim,
her agents were close to the friends of Japan, her legation
sponsored Allen's mission work in spite of Chinese disapproval. Foote had been astute enough to evade an effort to
draw him into the insurrection, but his sympathies were
obvious. To secure protection for his legation, he turned not
to Korea (as diplomatic usage dictated), not to China (as

Min Yong Ik, Nephew of the Queen

The attempted assassination of this reactionary nobleman precipitated the Korean émeute of 1884, which set Japan and China at each other's throats and gave to Dr. Allen a reputation he later used to help American missionaries and investors.

prudence dictated), but to Japan. It was Takezoye that he asked for a detachment of Japanese soldiers to guard against the disturbances set in motion by Takezoye's own adherents.

The very next day, December 5, reaction set in. The Japanese group continued to command the royal premises—Foote, Zembsch, and Aston saw that when they visited his frightened majesty. But beyond the palace walls there was a growing opposition to the islanders. Here and there the people gathered, great crowds of them by sundown. Planless, leaderless, they surged through the streets of Seoul all night long. Excitement mounted to fury as they marched, and by the morning of the sixth the Occidentals could hear them bellowing for blood, the blood of the Japanese who had made a prisoner of Korea's king.

And the Japanese had others to fear. Dead or in hiding, the Mins could not resist Nippon; but the Chinese could. Poor soldiers they might be—Allen thought them "only fit . . . to be shot at."[5] Still, they had the big battalions in Seoul, fifteen hundred men and more Korean allies, against a scattering of opposing natives and about a hundred and fifty Japanese. What was more, the Manchus had an able leader on the spot, Yuan Shih Kai, young protégé of Viceroy Li Hung Chang and a future president of China.

At first Yuan was deaf to appeals for aid—one from the troubled queen, many from the lesser Mins, still more from the common people. He had instructions to avoid a clash with Japan. China was busy with France, and Viceroy Li knew all too well how feeble were his country's fighting forces. Better to appease the Japanese as China had done in 1876 and 1882 and as Foote and Zembsch and Aston said she ought to do again.

Appeasement, though, must stop a little short of suicide. Yuan could hardly let the Japanese control the person of the king. Nor could he accept the measures of the new progres-

---

[5] Allen Diary, February 7, 1885; Foulk to the Secretary of State, March 9, 1885, Dispatches, State Department Archives.

sive government, determined to repudiate Chinese suzerainty. No, Manchu rights would fade out completely if action was postponed. So, moving slowly, Yuan demanded explanations from Takezoye and requested an audience with the king. When he failed to get either, he marched, on December 6, against the Japanese legation guard. The two great empires of the Orient were driving toward war.

It was all a nightmare to the foreign residents of Seoul, most of whom sought refuge in the United States legation. Fannie went there with little Harry; but Allen stayed to do his work outside, to guard his mission property with a gun which he later found could not be fired, and to attend Min Yong Ik. It was no easy job to cross the city when the natives were running wild; and what if Min died when under his care? "I was shaking in my boots," so the doctor put it five years later, "and knew that if the Prince who was nearer dead than alive would not pull through I would be ruined and very likely killed by a mob."[6]

But on the sixth the white men still were safe—the Koreans were concerned only with the Japanese. Mobs gutted Japanese stores and residences, and when they came upon a citizen of the Island Empire, they tore the luckless individual limb from limb. Happy indeed were the twenty Japanese who reached the American legation; Foote gave instructions to grant them all asylum.

While blood flowed in the streets of Seoul, Yuan Shih Kai reached the larger palace, to which the royal family had returned at Queen Min's insistence. Still cautious, the Manchu general sent an ultimatum before he charged. When this brought no response, the guns began to roar, Korean against Korean, China against Japan.

Anticipating just such an attack, Korean progressive Pak

[6] Allen to Jennie Everett, June 3, 1889, in the Allen MSS ("I showed her [*Fannie*] how to use my revolver and she agreed to kill Harry first and then herself, if the mob came in my absence."); Allen, *Things Korean*, 72; Allen Diary, December 5, 1884.

Yong Hyo had suggested that the Japanese withdraw to the coast, taking His Majesty along. There, safe from the Seoul mobs, the progressives could conduct the government; and thence Japan could rush reinforcements to ward off attack by Yuan. But Pak had been overruled, and Takezoye stayed on at the palace to fight a most unequal battle. His men with too little ammunition were ordered to defend a palace with too many gates against a far too numerous foe.

Japan's Korean soldiers broke immediately, deserting to the offensive side the minute the Chinese entered the palace grounds. The Japanese fought on alone. They were untried warriors, those Japanese, local troops none too well thought of in their native land; but they showed no signs of terror. Calmly they turned their knapsacks into breastworks, laughingly they directed fire at the motto "Courage" emblazoned on the breasts of the Manchu soldiers. Resolutely they checked a frontal drive and beat back a three-way converging attack planned by General Yuan. And when forced to yield, they withdrew in good order.

The king, meanwhile, was also changing sides. As a progressive, two days before, he had been appalled at the slaughter of his wife's relatives, and dismayed to find himself a puppet of Japan. When the fighting began, His Majesty, expecting Chinese victory, decided to abandon the losing side.

But to shift now was far from easy. The king, always indecisive, was at his worst in an emergency. Guns disturbed him, the sound of firing threw him into panic, made him quiver like a gutter mongrel and scurry to cover in a most unregal manner. Takezoye, moreover, having clung to the monarch for two full days, did not intend to relax his hold in time of crisis. If Yuan was beaten off, possession of His Majesty meant continued domination of the government, and if the Chinese won, the king might be a useful shield, a cover for retreat. Once the monarch did elude his Japanese custodians, but he was soon found cowering in the rear of the palace grounds.

Still, the prisoner king was not altogether an asset to the Japanese. His pleas to be let alone made the pretense of "protection" pretty thin, and his undisguised terror affected the Japanese soldiers as Yuan's troops drew near. Even as a shield His Majesty was none too valuable: the Chinese fired regardless of the danger to the royal person.

Worried, driven back step by step, the Japanese decided to retreat. Once they tried it with the king to block their line of fire; but this attempt failed miserably, and the blood of an attendant spattered on His Majesty's clothing. Takezoye thereupon concluded that the Japanese could travel faster unencumbered by their royal burden. The trembling monarch was allowed to leave—to jump on a loyal servant and ride pickaback to safety in the Chinese camp. The Japanese and a handful of progressives then smashed their way through the Chinese forces and made for the Japanese legation.

Despite his great advantage, Yuan did not pursue the fleeing soldiers. He had the king and other members of the royal family; he had reasserted Manchu suzerainty. To go further would profit nothing, and it would mean certain war between China and Japan.

Yuan was satisfied, but not so the natives of Seoul, who took up where the Chinese had left off. They struck down vainglorious Prime Minister Hong Yong Sik, who would not flee with the Japanese. They stoned the Japanese warriors who were fighting their way to the Japanese legation. They wrecked the homes of the progressives, tore down the post office, and burned the barracks built for Japan's guard. And thrice during that eventful night of December 6–7 they stormed the Japanese legation stronghold.

By the seventh the Japanese saw the wisdom of evacuating Seoul. Provisions were running low; with a hundred and forty soldiers, half as many refugees, and thirty servants crowded into one legation compound, there was little rice for the fighting men and only flavored water for the others. And there seemed no prospect of relief. Yuan, apparently, intended to allow the natives to do their worst; the only friendly message reaching Takezoye was from a Korean who made the superfluous observation that there was "great opposition to Japan" in Seoul.

It was a gloomy afternoon on which the Japanese and their progressive friends sallied forth (December 7); a somber sky looked down on besiegers and besieged. The Japanese, who had destroyed their diplomatic correspondence and fired their legation, moved in perfect order, the soldiers protecting the Japanese and progressive civilians. It was not too difficult to hack a path through the unorganized Korean mob. The Korean army then was given a chance to demonstrate how bad was its equipment and how much worse its aim. After that the Nipponese forced the west gate and made off for Chemulpo and home.

Allen and the other foreigners heard the crack of rifles on the sixth and seventh and the rumble of artillery fire. They heard the shouts of angry natives, saw the flames of burning buildings etched against the sky. And they heard news of violence, enough to keep awake any person who was harboring Japanese.

The worst moment came as the Japanese were retiring from the city. Firing was heard from the direction of Japan's legation. Then it came nearer to the property of the United States, ever nearer, until Allen heard the whiz of bullets. And then the sounds went by and died away.

Twice during the night of the sixth messengers had come for Allen. Min Yong Ik was failing, his lacerated face was swelling badly. But Minister Foote said no, the doctor could not leave the vicinity of the legation—and Allen was not disappointed. Next morning he did go, escorted by two of Moellendorff's white officers through the densely crowded streets. Finding Min improved, he yielded to the king's request that the prince be moved to join his royal relatives in the camp of the Chinese.

That night, December 7, Allen mounted guard before the

United States legation. It was hard to keep awake, for in ninety-six strenuous hours he had had but eight for sleep. Comforting, though, to know that fighting had abated and that the people were quieting down; and that a good guard of Chinese soldiers had been obtained to replace the incompetent Koreans and the Japanese detachment which under the circumstances needed more protection than it gave.[7]

Busy, critical days lay ahead for Allen. On the eighth he was called to Yuan's camp to check on Min and help the wounded Chinese soldiers. And when he returned from that hard work, he was faced with a major question: should he leave Seoul or stay?

Leave or stay? Decision was forced by the other foreigners, who were leaving Seoul. Even Moellendorff departed with his European subordinates; and the diplomats soon followed. Unnerved by their four-day ordeal, the envoys fairly snatched at the king's suggestion that they go to Chemulpo to establish communication with Japan. By doing so, they might head off a Japanese-Korean war or one between Japan and China; and even if they failed, they would be out of Seoul, away from the capital's grim politics and anti-foreign mobs.[8]

Should the Allens go also? Their friends advised it, all but Foote at any rate. Politician to the core, the minister refrained from taking any stand. "If I advise you to stay," he told the missionary, "and harm comes to you I will be blamed. If I advise you to go and your property is destroyed as it must be if you leave, then in case of their [sic] being no danger you will blame me for the loss of your property."[9]

After talking it over, Fannie and her husband chose to stay.

[7] Allen Diary, December 11, 1884, January 28, 1885; address to the Naval War College, in the Allen MSS. This Japanese detachment and the other Japanese in the American legation had not left with the main group of their countrymen.

[8] Foote to the Secretary of State, December 17, 19, 25, 1884, October 19, 1885, May 13, 1886, Dispatches, State Department Archives; Mörsel, "Emeute of 1884," *Korean Repository*, 4 (1897):218–219.

[9] Allen Diary, December 20, 1884.

They added up all sorts of reasons, including the difficulty of getting transportation to Chemulpo and finding accommodations there when they arrived; but the chief consideration was missionary duty. "We had come here for just this very work," wrote Allen in his diary, "and could not leave when so needed . . . We decided to stay and trust all to God." And perhaps to Chinese and Korean gratitude for saving Min.[10]

High-minded though it was, this decision led to a mundane quarrel with Minister Foote. Hearing of Allen's plans, the general urged the physician to move to the legation. "But I soon learned from his remarks," observed the distrustful missionary, "that . . . he cared not a bit for our safety but simply desired some one to look after his own effects." Seeing Foote's selfish motive, Allen bristled with the temper that had caused him trouble in the Chinese missions—and both were very tired. Sharp words were exchanged, and the warm friendship of October was broken for all time.[11] Allen, as often before and after, was on his own.

[10] Allen Diary, December 11, 20, 1884; Allen to Ellinwood, February 4, 1885, in the Allen MSS; *Foreign Missionary*, 43 (1885):429, 525.

[11] Allen Diary, December 11, 1884, February 11, 1885; Allen to Ellinwood, February 4, 1885, in the Allen MSS.

Part II. For God

The door of Korea is open to the divine proclamation as the door of no nation was ever opened since the apostolic age.—Dr. Charles C. Vinton

Our missionary work in the coming decades, whether we will or not, and whether for good or bad, will be more and more closely related to the influence of diplomacy and commerce.—Reverend Frank F. Ellinwood

3

God's Lobbyist

JAPAN, said her foreign minister, was not yet ready to fight China for control of Chosen. Japan's warrior class might cry for revenge after the defeat of December, 1884—and cry it did. The refugee progressives from Korea might urge strong measures—and urge they did. But the government in Tokyo felt unprepared for war, especially in view of possible Russian intervention. And no war came.[1]

Until this stand became known, there were anxious moments for China and Korea. The Dragon Empire, already at grips with France, had no heart for taking on more enemies. True, in a Japanese campaign she would have Korea as an ally—but even amateurs like Allen knew that Korean troops were "of little use." Rusty rifles, some with stones and ramrods jammed in their barrels; defective artillery weapons manned by untrained crews and often supplied with nothing more than blanks; and, what counted most, a total lack of

---

[1] On the diplomatic situation at this time, see Foote to the Secretary of State, January 2, 4, 1885, and Foulk to the Secretary of State, March 9, July 10, 22, 1885, Dispatches, State Department Archives; Allen Diary, January 11, March 11, 1885; Jones, "Foreign Diplomacy in Korea," in *Summary of Theses, Harvard University*, 1935, p. 165; Ariga, "Diplomacy," in Stead, *Japan by the Japanese*, 195–199; Tsiang, "Sino-Japanese Relations," *Chinese Social and Political Science Review*,

any sort of military morale, and in its place a will to avoid fighting[2]—these were scarcely assets.

Well aware of their weakness, the Chinese and Koreans grabbed at Japanese offers of a settlement. Perhaps the Japanese *had* started all the trouble; no matter, it still behooved Korea to apologize, to rebuild the legation of the Island Empire, to pay a small indemnity. China, too, backed down. She waived her suzerain right to have a representative attend the Korean-Japanese negotiations and yielded further still by signing the celebrated Li-Ito agreement, by which both Japan and China promised to withdraw their troops from Chosen and not to send them back without serving notice on each other. Neither empire would dominate the Korean army, and Chosen would be encouraged to strengthen her defenses under supervision of military counsellors from Western nations.

That told the story. The American, German, and British representatives in Chosen—Foote, Zembsch, and Aston—eased the way by becoming intermediaries. Moellendorff, too, played the part of peace agent.[3] But even if these zealous Occidentals had been inactive, the result would have been the same. Though Japan had risked a skirmish, she did not as yet desire a fight to the finish.

That, of course, meant tragedy for Korean progressives.

17 (1933):84–85; Hsü, *China and Her Political Entity*, 117–120; Payson J. Treat, *Diplomatic Relations between the United States and Japan, 1853–1905* (3 vols., Stanford University, 1932–38), 2:199–200, 215–218; Lin, "Li Hung Chang: His Korean Policies," *Chinese Social and Political Science Review*, 19 (1935):230–232; Henri Cordier, *Histoire des relations de la Chine avec les puissances occidentales, 1860–1900* (3 vols., Paris, 1902), 2:589–590; George T. Ladd, *In Korea with Marquis Ito* (New York, 1908), 203–209; and Langer, *Diplomacy of Imperialism*, 169–171.

[2] Gilmore, *Korea*, 235–238; A. H. Savage-Landor, "A Visit to Corea," *Fortnightly Review*, 62 (1894):189–190; Curzon, *Problems of the Far East*, 164–168.

[3] Foote to the Secretary of State, December 7, 29, 31, 1884, January 2, 4, October 19, 1885, Dispatches, State Department Archives; Moellendorff, *Moellendorff*, 77.

Lacking Japanese support, those who stayed in Seoul were quickly liquidated by the conservatives. Those who escaped faced a life of exile. So Jay Pil, disgusted with Japanese refusal to take action, went to the United States. The others—Kim Ok Kiun, So Kwang Pom, Pak Yong Hyo—remained in the Empire of the Rising Sun, awaiting the pleasure of the Japanese and living out the words of one of Kim's own poems:

> *Bright youth with all its joy has flown,*
> *My locks are touched with gray,*
> *And when a few more years have gone,*
> *I too shall pass away.*[4]

Seoul, meantime, slipped back into its old routine. Yet there were signs aplenty of the events that had just taken place. Burned buildings and looted homes (including those of Foulk and Townsend) kept fresh the memory of violence; and in the streets the dogs gnawed at the bodies of executed rebels. The Mins, restored to power, persecuted relatives of the progressives and appointed assassins to deal with those in exile. The people turned from the Western culture of Kim and the Japanese back to Manchu conservatism. The government lumber yards, built by progressives, met the fate of the postal building, and one observer noted that "the whole mass of the people are so violently pro-Chinese in their sentiments, and so violently bitter in their hatred of the Japanese that it is impossible to obtain other than a volume of execrations and vituperations against them and the conspirators."[5]

[4] Gilmore, *Korea*, 73; Allen to Ellinwood, May 7, 1885, in the Allen MSS.

[5] Foulk to the Secretary of the Navy, December 20, 1884, to the President of the Korean Foreign Office, June 12, 1885, and to Commander McGlensy, April 29, 1885, in the Foulk MSS; letters to the Secretary of State from Foulk, January 31, April 2, May 30, December 12, 1885, and from Foote, December 7, 1884, Dispatches State Department Archives; Secretary of State Bayard to Foulk, March 19, 1885, Instructions, State Department Archives; Allen Diary, December 26, 1884, January 30, February 3, 25, 1885; Ariga, "Diplomacy," in Stead, *Japan by the Japanese*, 194–195; O. N. Denny, "China and Korea," *Congressional Record*,

This trend, naturally, hurt the Americans who had an interest in Chosen. Before the revolution, in Foulk's words, "the prospect of good work in all directions in Korea pointed to the springtime, but the late disturbances have dispelled all these." Franchise grants that Foote had planned with the progressives were forgotten, all the sooner as the general resigned his post in January, 1885. Foulk, becoming chargé d'affaires *ad interim,* did as badly; as a progressive counsellor, he was distrusted by the incumbent conservatives. Missionaries who itched to follow Allen's lead found their prospects most discouraging of all. No one, not a single officer, in Seoul, would listen to a plea for missions.[6]

Like the others, Allen was shocked to see the Westernizing process checked; and he had further reasons for unhappiness. A man used to emergencies, the doctor had found the strength to meet the problems of December. But, as both he and Fannie learned, it was much more difficult to face the letdown after crisis. So hard that they could "almost wish" they were out of the country.[7]

And Allen, being an impatient soul, found it very difficult to treat Prince Min Yong Ik. The royal patient whined with self-pity when the doctor failed to visit him three times a day. He grumbled at the slow rate of his recovery and once in Allen's absence tried a native remedy. Only once, and the queen his aunt apologized for that; but there were other things. Difficulty with Min's women, for example. In an un-

50 Congress, 1 session (1888), 8140; reply of Moellendorff, reprinted in Moellendorff, *Moellendorff,* 135.

[6] Paik, *Protestant Missions in Korea,* 106–107, quoting letter from Foulk to Maclay; Foulk to the Secretary of State, December 26, 1884, April 28, 1885, February 18, May 13, 1886, Dispatches, State Department Archives; Allen Diary, February 14, 18, October 22, December 1, 1885; Allen to Ellinwood, February 23, March 5, 1885, in the Allen MSS. Foote resigned because of the impending reduction in rank of the American legation at Seoul. Foote to the Secretary of State, September 17, 1884, Dispatches, State Department Archives.

[7] Allen Diary, February 20, May 12, December 11, 1885. Allen's continuing fear of revolution is indicated in his letter of January 5, 1893, to Ellinwood, in the Allen MSS.

guarded moment Allen had said the prince might have them in "to look at his wounds." An unwise concession: when the missionary called again, he found his patient in relapse. Easy to explain, babbled Min's attendants, the presence of women always contaminated wounds. "Yes," wrote Allen sadly in his diary, "they may have been the *indirect* cause of it but not simply from looking at the wound."[8]

Yet there were compensations. The doctor's cure of Min paid dividends, messages from the king and queen, Min's assurances that the white man was his "brother," money "to 'fill my belly and make me feel good.' "[9] And then, as a fitting climax, the young missionary received appointment as physician to Their Majesties.

Court etiquette screamed against the choice; as a commoner, as a foreigner unacquainted with his own head of state, the Presbyterian was automatically barred from the royal presence. But a start was made with proxy treatments. Queen Dowager Cho, daring more, invited the American to treat her at her apartments. Allen went, pleasantly reflecting that "no other male foreigner ever openly entered one of these places." He found the queen mother more than modest: ensconced behind a screen, she showed the doctor just one arm, carefully bandaged save for a tiny patch of wrist. Barely enough to feel the pulse, but quite enough to shatter all tradition.[10]

The king came next. Anxious to see His Majesty, Allen intimated that proxy medication had its limitations; and the monarch, just as eager to see Allen, managed to manipulate the royal precedents. Since a foreign commoner was regarded as an inferior, the American missionary was made a Korean

[8] Allen to Ellinwood, February 4, 1885, in the Allen MSS; Allen Diary, January 11, February 11, 25, March 11, December 11, 1885; Gilmore, *Korea*, 91.

[9] Allen Diary, January 27, 1885; Allen, *Things Korean*, 211–212.

[10] *Foreign Missionary*, 44 (1885):176; Allen Diary, March 27, April 3, June 3, 1885; Allen to Ellinwood, May 19, 1885, in the Allen MSS; Allen, *Things Korean*, 191; Underwood, *Fifteen Years among the Top-Knots*, 25.

nobleman, champan of the third degree. Special dispensation freed the new appointee from a champan's obligations under native law, though men as mighty as Moellendorff had been bound by these; but the privileges of the position were retained, including right of access to the throne.

So it was that the youthful Allen, no star student in America, no leading light in China, reached the peak in Seoul, stood face to face with royalty. Into the labyrinthine palace grounds the missionary marched, as one who had come to stay. Down the corridors he strode, past the slouching sentries in their comic opera uniforms. On into the royal rooms, rooms furnished with a splendor that had cost Korea dear. And then the missionary from America cast eyes upon the king and crown prince of Chosen.[11]

There is magic in a crown, so Allen felt humble in the royal presence. A fine ruler, he thought respectfully, and a splendid son, both worthy of the loyalty of all Korean people. Yet actually he, Allen, was the most forceful person present. He, an uncrowned citizen of a kingless land, had traits of character that were to enable him to hold this Oriental monarch in the palm of his Ohio hand.

Allen and the king furnished a striking contrast. The short Korean was dressed in silken finery, the tall American in the modest best of a small missionary wardrobe. In looks, too, royalty had the advantage. His Majesty's round boyish face, his kindly eyes and genial smile, made him almost handsome. This could not be said of Allen. Some liked the missionary's towering height, his vigorous appearance, and his glance of keen intelligence, but none ever called him handsome. A bony frame, receding reddish hair, sharp features stamped with a petulant expression, these did not combine into a pretty picture.

[11] Allen to Ellinwood, August 20, 1886, in the Allen MSS; Allen, *Korea: Fact and Fancy,* p. 24 and note, showing Allen's changing views on the magnificence of the reception; Allen Diary, March 3, 1885. In a letter to the Secretary of State, May 7, 1885, in the Foulk MSS, Foulk gives a detailed description of the ceremony of court presentations.

Still, dress and beauty do not make the man. The beaming countenance of His Korean Majesty masked only cowardice and confusion. Allen, on the other hand, possessed both courage and decision, enough for two.[12] As a medical call, the visit yielded little; the woes of Chosen's monarch were not woes of the body. But for religion and politics it was significant. For the lean doctor from America emerged as a recognized favorite of the king.

It pays to be court favorite in a state where royal rule is absolute. Saving Min had brought the doctor admiration; news of the king's confidence set him on a still higher plane. Politicians wishing power began to seek his influence. Japan felt it worth while to cultivate his friendship, to make him the Japanese legation doctor. And even the Tai Wen Kun, returning from exile in 1885, called on the young physician. The old conspirator had little reason to admire a Christian missionary, least of all one who had saved a Min; but politics is politics, and the stern-faced foreigner was a factor none could ignore.[13]

At first this prominence gave Allen and his wife a feeling of distress. It was best, they thought, to "stay out of politics," to concentrate on medical and missionary matters. And so the doctor stated, publicly, in a Presbyterian organ, the *Foreign Missionary*. He would not participate in politics, he had refused to head a welcoming committee organized on the occasion of British Consul Aston's return to Seoul.[14]

[12] For the king see Bishop, *Korea*, 2:39; Curzon, *Problems of the Far East*, 163; Brown, "Reading Journey through Korea," *Chautauquan*, 41 (1905):513–518; Max von Brandt, *Dreiunddreisig Jahre in Ost-Asien*, 3:253 (Leipzig, 1901); "His Majesty the King of Korea," *Korean Repository*, 3 (1896):427–430; William F. Sands, "Korea and the Korean Emperor," *Century*, 69 (1905):580–581; and William F. Sands, *Undiplomatic Memories* (New York, 1930), 59–61. For Allen, see *ibid.*, 47. Gilmore, in his *Korea*, 107–108, says Allen's baldish appearance helped, for age was respected in Korea.

[13] Allen Diary, October 5, 7, 11, 1885, indicating that Allen was favorably impressed by the king's father. The Tai Wen Kun returned as an ally of the Chinese.

[14] *Foreign Missionary*, 44 (1885):176, letter dated May 15, 1885; Allen

For God

But even as he took this stand Allen realized that his prestige might help the church. Why not use the court connection if it would aid the Christian cause? Why not spend a little time as missionary diplomat? The opportunity was far too tempting to be rejected by an eager young enthusiast. Long before the *Foreign Missionary* printed his "stay out of politics" declaration, Horace Allen had changed his mind. Stay out of politics? Rather he was spending half his time on court intrigue, centering all his proselyting hopes around his standing with the king.

That was in the spring of 1885. Twenty years were to pass before the doctor ceased to work in Chosen; but never did he forsake this basic policy. As a missionary, as a diplomat, he built his power on influence at court, influence that grew out of his successful patching of the wounds of Min Yong Ik. Other missionaries, other diplomats were to criticize him for it. Better to work with the common people, many said, or to persuade the United States government to use some form of diplomatic pressure. But Allen, gratified over what he won, stuck always to the path of royal favor.

There were defects in the policy. For Allen was resting faith in an untrustworthy heathen king who shifted favorites overnight, a feeble monarch who was soon to lose his power to the Japanese. Moreover, the hours he spent at the venal court reduced by just so much the time he could give the average citizen, the Korean Christian of the future.

Even so, there was much to say for the technique chosen by the first resident Protestant worker in Korea. Chosen's life revolved about Seoul, and Seoul life about the king. If the missionaries had not recognized that fact, persecution might have ensued. Could one "stay out of politics" with that thought running through one's mind? Some could; not Allen. He was a pioneer, and pioneers must break the ground for those who follow. Allen did just that, provided later workers

Diary, May 19, 1885; Allen to Ellinwood, October 15, 1897, in the Allen MSS.

with insurance against persecution. The tale of Catholic work in Chosen is one of blood and martyrdom; that of the Protestants contains but one such tragedy, and that before the Allens took up residence in Seoul.

As in religion, so in other fields. In political controversies, economic matters, Allen was to rely upon his power at the palace. He was to see his plans upset sometimes by gunboat tactics, by diplomatic threats and marching soldiers. But by and large he held his own.

In 1885, of course, the doctor's court maneuvers were solely for missionary purposes. That was enough for one man. The Christian cause faced opposition with the progressives gone, the Chinese party dominant, and the Tai Wen Kun back in town. Allen could count on bitter resistance to each move he made, and probable defeat.

To meet these obstacles the missionary had just two weapons—the indebtedness of the Mins to him and the still progressive inclination of the king. Even these might disappear with time. The king might turn against America when he heard that the rank of her legation in Seoul had been reduced. And, as Allen mourned, "in such a changeable Government your friends of today may be headless tomorrow."[15]

Hurrying lest he be too late, the Presbyterian made a bold request—for a mission-dominated hospital in which the Korean government was asked to become a partner. Allen and the other doctors would be furnished by the Presbyterian Board of Foreign Missions. Korea was to do the rest, to pay for drugs and food, for heat and light, to provide the nurses and the other helpers.[16] The missionary counted on his standing in Seoul to bring him what he asked; but lest etiquette be outraged, he decided to file his petition through the United States legation. Wherefore he sought out Chargé Foulk.

Foulk stands almost alone in Allen's story, a man with

[15] Allen to Ellinwood, February 4, 1885, in the Allen MSS.
[16] The petition, in the Allen MSS, has been reprinted in Paik, *Protestant Missions in Korea*, 429–430.

whom the missionary seldom quarreled. And Allen occupies a like position in the ensign's biography. Both fought with Foote, both had disputes with missionaries, diplomats, and naval officers. Neither was an easy man to live with, but they got on famously together. The chargé wrote to Washington of Allen's noble deeds and splendid character; and the doctor told his mission board that Foulk was one in a million, "one of those rare men sometimes met with whom while they have no especial religious conviction yet are so impressed with the idea of Right & Duty that they are powers for good."[17]

He was a strange man, Foulk, a curious combination of strength and weakness. Erect, well built, handsome with his curly hair and soft mustache, he looked the perfect picture of a healthy young naval officer. Actually he was a sick man who was soon to die, some forty years before the skeletonic Allen. Foulk could curse and outdrink any man, but at heart he was a gentle soul, easily wounded by any unkind word. He was a scholar, a linguist, a man with political and literary gifts that far surpassed Allen's; but he did not use his talents to advantage and left no mark behind him when he died.

Liking Allen, hoping to advance his country's interests, Foulk threw his whole weight behind the hospital proposal. He was hampered, of course, by his low rank and his record of association with the discredited progressives. But the king still held the ensign in the highest regard, and in a year of

---

[17] Allen to Ellinwood, February 4, 1885, in the Allen MSS. A quarrel between Foulk and Allen is mentioned by Allen in a letter to Ellinwood, October 28, 1886, in the Allen MSS; their more usual relations are seen in Allen, "Medical Work in Korea," *Foreign Missionary*, 44 (1885):74–76, and Foulk to the Secretary of State, March 5, 1885, Dispatches, State Department Archives. For Foulk, see the sketch by Harold J. Noble in the *Dictionary of American Biography;* "George C. Foulk," *Korea Review*, 1 (1901):344–349; Harold J. Noble, "The United States and Sino-Korean Relations, 1885–1887," *Pacific Historical Quarterly*, 2 (1933):292–304; Dennett, "Early American Policy in Korea," *Political Science Quarterly*, 38 (1923):82–103. Foulk's quarrels have left their trace in various documents: Foulk to Rear Admiral John Lee Davis, December 20, 1884, in the Foulk MSS; Foulk to the Secretary of State, April 28, July 16, 19, 22, November 13, 1885, Dispatches, State Depart-

palace plotting Foulk had learned how things were done in
Seoul.

The petition as submitted bore the stamp of that experience. Foulk saw to it that Allen made no mention of missionary motives. The Presbyterian board became "a benev-
olent society in America that . . . supports hospitals in Pekin
Tientsin Shanghai Canton and other Chinese cities."[18] The
stress on China, too, was hardly accidental. The Mins were
certain to reject a plea that seemed "progressive." They
might consider one that bore Chinese endorsement. Could
not one say that hospitals were quite "conservative" on hearing that Viceroy Li Hung Chang had furnished two inside
the Dragon Empire?

The petition was filed in January, 1885. On April 9 the
hospital was opened, and Horace Allen had become a veteran
at diplomacy and court intrigue. With Foulk to back and
guide him, he had wound his way to triumph.

Inertia had been Allen's greatest foe. Emeute and counterrevolution had demoralized the court. What government was
left was in a "wretched state," the officers unable or afraid to
perform their duties. Min Yong Ik, who could have helped
the most, thought of nothing but the safety of his own skin.
Others, prompted by the king and queen, promised aid and
then procrastinated, until nervous Dr. Allen ground his teeth
in rage. Nothing seemed to help, not even refusing patients
"until the hospital was opened."[19]

ment Archives; Secretary of the Navy W. C. Whitney to Admiral John
Lee Davis, September 25, 1885, Seoul Legation Files, State Department
Archives; Allen Diary, February 14, 1885; Allen to Ellinwood, January
17, 1887, in the Allen MSS.

[18] Allen Diary, January 22, 1885; Foulk to the President of the Korean
Foreign Office, January 27, 1885, with reply of February 18 ("establish-
ing a hospital here, as in other countries, should be our first work."),
Seoul Legation Files, State Department Archives.

[19] Allen Diary, February 14, 16, 18, 20, March 18, 1885. Korean weakness is amply demonstrated in Paik, *Protestant Missions in Korea*, 106,
quoting Foulk; in Foulk to the Secretary of State, December 26, 1884,
February 8, March 9, 1885, Dispatches, State Department Archives; and
in the Allen Diary, February 16, 1885.

In several quarters there was open opposition. Some came from the Hei Min So, a royal hospital created in the early years of Yi ascendancy. The Hei Min So had ceased to function in the eighteenth century, but its payroll had lived on. And now, if Allen had his way, there would be a new hospital, and a thousand "officials" of the old would lose a source of income.[20]

More important were the objections of the foreigners in Seoul. The Chinese, the German, and the Russian parties all set themselves against the Allen-Foulk petition. Naturally: it would strengthen pro-Japanese America, would put Allen in the government, where he could undermine the power of the other non-Koreans. The strongest words came from Hermann Budler, the German consul general. Having learned to dislike missionaries while in China, Budler called the Allen project a "proselyting scheme," and prophesied that the hospital would become a "hotbed of trouble." No, he had nothing against a hospital, he only meant to see that it did not get into missionary hands.[21] Much the same attitude was taken by the "Moellendorff crowd," which was riding high those days. "Regular snakes every one of them," stormed Allen, as he saw their plans unfold. They, too, approved of hospitals—if Moellendorff was in command. Not otherwise; an interloper might disturb the Chinese-Russian balance which the German adviser so carefully maintained.[22] "Quite a triumph," as Allen put it, to have whipped foes strong as these. Small wonder that his thin face glowed with pride; small wonder that he boasted in his missionary letters home, and planned new victories to come.

There was much he could do as court physician. The very title helped immeasurably. Natives flocked to Allen's hospital when they heard that the missionary was "doctor to the king."

[20] Allen Diary, April 13, 1885; Foulk to the Secretary of State, May 30, 1885, Dispatches, State Department Archives; Allen, "Medical Work in Korea," *Foreign Missionary*, 44 (1885):74–76.

[21] Allen Diary, March 31, 1885.

[22] Allen Diary, February 20, September 6, 7, 1885.

And no one listened to the anti-Allen forces, to the men who whispered that "no one would be treated unless promising to believe in Christ."[23]

Foulk said the 1884 revolution had crippled missionary chances for some time to come, but his red-headed friend soon proved him wrong. As a royal officer the doctor could work without great fear of persecution—and he could do more. By word and by example he could show that Christian missionaries were an asset, not a liability; and as a man with influence, he could bring other proselyting agents to Seoul.

Missionaries were distrusted, so Allen's colleagues came as court employees, as hirelings of the heathen government of Chosen. Three missionaries Allen introduced in just this way—Methodist Dr. William B. Scranton and Presbyterian Dr. John W. Heron, as royal hospital employees, and Nurse Annie Ellers, a Presbyterian woman missionary, as physician to the queen. Others he helped as best he could. For Horace G. Underwood and Henry G. Appenzeller, ordained missionaries, he won quasi-governmental status in educational capacities; and he rendered other aid to the Reverends D. A. Bunker, Homer B. Hulbert, and George W. Gilmore, imported through the American legation as teachers in the palace school.[24]

As one success followed on another, Allen planned and plotted more. In 1886 he won a new concession, authorization to start a medical and scientific school inside the hospital, with Presbyterian missionaries as the teachers. He pulled some wires when Underwood and Appenzeller were seeking governmental aid for other institutions. He induced the king to set aside a new and better building for the hospital. And,

[23] Allen, "Medical Work in Korea," *Foreign Missionary,* 44 (1885):75; Allen to Ellinwood, May 7, 1885, in the Allen MSS; Foulk to the Secretary of State, May 30, 1885, Dispatches, State Department Archives.

[24] Paik, *Protestant Missions in Korea,* 99–118 *passim.* Rhodes, *Korea Mission, Presbyterian Church,* contains interesting statistics on all Presbyterian work; see pp. 544–545, 636–638.

by every backstairs method possible, he built up sentiment for complete religious toleration.[25]

It was hard work, this paving of the way for missionary enterprise; but Allen gloried in it. It provided outlet for the young man's bursting energy and satisfied his urge for accomplishment as even medicine did not. Here, in an Oriental court that seethed with vile intrigues, the doctor felt at home; here, by mixing with pagan marplots, he could do more for the Lord than could any other missionary in the East.

To play this game of politics one had to maintain connection with the United States legation; the American representative was needed as an ally all along the line. Next, it was necessary to understand the moves of every other diplomat in town, lest one lose a friend or fail to spot a foe. And always the court had to be watched, the ever-changing pattern in the kaleidoscopic picture of Chosen's palace politics.

The missionary found his own legation easiest to handle. There he was aided by the diplomatic policy of the United States, ever on the side of Christian teaching. Also useful was the close friendship with Foulk, who was the sole American agent in Korea until the summer of 1886. The ensign helped at every turn, let his doctor friend use his native agents and spoke out when he was needed. Perhaps, indeed, the naval officer was influenced by Allen's zeal; a man "of no especial religious conviction" in 1885, he wrote in 1886 that missionary work "cannot to my mind, be too highly commended."[26] The sincerity of that observation tends to be borne out by the fact that his last years were spent on the faculty of a missionary college in Japan.

[25] Allen Diary, March 29, May 12, 1886; Allen to Ellinwood, October 28, 1886, in the Allen MSS; Foulk to the Secretary of State, February 20, 1886, Dispatches, State Department Archives; Foulk to the President of the Korean Foreign Office, February 13, 1886, Seoul Legation Files, State Department Archives.

[26] Foulk to the Secretary of State, February 20, June 3, 1886, Dispatches, State Department Archives; Foulk to the President of the Korean Foreign Office, January 25, 1885, Seoul Legation Files, State Department Archives; Foulk to the President of the Korean Foreign Office,

God's Lobbyist

The ensign's immediate successors were nearly as cooperative as he. William Parker, appointed minister resident by Cleveland in 1886, fulfilled Allen's hope that he would prove to be a "Christian gentleman." He turned his offices over to the missionaries Sundays, thus helping them to worship well within the law; and he might have helped in other ways had he not drunk himself into ineptitude and quick retirement. William W. Rockhill, chargé in the winter of 1886–87, was not pro-missionary to the same degree; but even he helped Allen in his court manipulations. Hugh A. Dinsmore, who followed as minister, impressed Allen as "a conscientious Christian gentleman" as well as a "cool, level-headed lawyer."[27]

It was quite the opposite with the diplomats from other countries. The progressive character of mission work appealed only to the Japanese—and Japan was temporarily inactive in Seoul, while building strength for the battles of the future. But in any case Japanese assistance would not have been an asset, for the islanders were loathed in Seoul.

The French, who first appeared in 1886, looked far more promising; like the Americans, they had mission interests in Korea. But Catholic clashed with Protestant. The French resented seeing Allen's people working in the open while the priests were forced to labor underground; and the Protestants were sure the "Romanists" were hatching plots to secure special rights and privileges.

Being Protestant contact man, Allen was directly in the line of fire. He liked the French proposal to include in any treaty between Chosen and France a clause providing mutual

June 19, 1885, February 13, 1886, in the Foulk MSS; Paik, *Protestant Missions in Korea,* quoting a letter from Foulk to Appenzeller; Allen Diary, February 4, 1885.

[27] Allen to Ellinwood, June 15, 1887, in the Allen MSS; Parker to the Secretary of State, August 3, 1886, and Rockhill to the Secretary of State, February 5, 1887, Dispatches, State Department Archives; Paik, *Protestant Missions in Korea,* 126–127. See also Secretary of State Bayard to Foulk, April 30, 1885, Instructions, State Department Archives ("commend your efforts in successfully promoting Dr. Allen's schemes").

toleration; the Protestants, covered by the most-favored-nation system, would benefit by that. At the same time, he disliked the open agitation of the question that ensued when the French appeared; the Protestants were doing handsomely and might well suffer if the public was aroused. Still more distressing was the rumor that the French negotiators, if they failed, would see that the Protestants were driven out, leaving the ground to the well-hidden Catholic workers.[28]

Such tales and a profound distaste for the teachings of Catholicism stirred the Presbyterian doctor to action. In May of 1886, the month the French arrived, the king's interpreter asked Allen a number of questions about the Catholics, "questions which I knew came from his Majesty." "I thought it my duty to deal at some length with the subject," the missionary noted that evening in his diary, "and . . . show the workings of Catholicism in China Japan Mexico & Spain." Then, to press home the point, the young physician stated impressively that "the Americans are an independent people and look with disfavor on anything that tends to curtail our power. Were we Catholics our President would be under the power of the Pope, a thing we cannot allow."

"There are three other points of Catholicism that we cannot accept," continued the Presbyterian. "First, we are opposed to praying to idols or any one but the Creator of the Universe. The Catholics worship and pray to the Virgin Mary, Mother of Christ, a woman. Secondly, we think no one but God can forgive sin, they give this power to corrupt priests to whom all Catholics must confess their most private thoughts. Third the priests are men with the same organs and passions as other men, they are not eunuchs, and we claim that it is not safe for women to go and confess to these men their secret thoughts and faults."

[28] Allen Diary, May 7, 12, 13, 1886; article dated June 16, 1886, and Allen to Ellinwood, June 20, 1886, in the Allen MSS; letter to the Secretary of State from Foulk, June 2, 1886, and from Augustine Heard, January 16, 1893, Dispatches, State Department Archives; Launay, *La Corée et les missionaires français*, 336–338.

All very telling, Allen thought, particularly the point that priests were "not eunuchs." The conversation, he believed, would "doubtless produce its effect."[29] Perhaps it did; it may have helped to keep religion out of the Franco-Korean treaty concluded one month later.

But the French, though troublesome, were never open enemies. The Russians were, however, and they were powerful in Seoul in 1885, or at least until the double-dealing Moellendorff was driven out of town. The Germans were hostile, too; but more hostile than any of the others were the Chinese agents, working with their British allies.[30]

By 1885 the Korean policy of Li Hung Chang had undergone a change. The viceroy's program of "opening Korea" had brought only grief to China; consequently Chosen must be closed once more. Manchu suzerainty or sovereignty must be established for all time, and every foreign nation must be encouraged to handle its Korean business through Li's office in Tientsin. Yuan Shih Kai was sent to Seoul with a brand new title—Resident, the title used by the British down in India.

Resident it was; Yuan claimed the right to rule Korea and he made it clear that China aimed "at something at least akin to incorporation of Korea into her own Empire."[31] Li's agent bullied the king, dominated the government offices, had a man decapitated on the Seoul streets.

Yuan, of course, could not approve of Allen. The hospital, the doctor's court position, stood in the way of the Resident's plans for the domination of the Land of Morning Calm. Indeed, all Occidental influence was bad, and missionary work particularly—it diverted Korean minds from the study

[29] Allen Diary, May 9, 1886. William F. Sands to the author, May 28, 1939: "Allen did not like . . . Catholics."
[30] Allen Diary, October 22, November 4, December 1, 1885; Foulk to the Secretary of State, November 25, 1885, Dispatches, State Department Archives; Foulk to Charles Denby, December 5, 1885, in the Foulk MSS.
[31] Foulk to the Secretary of State, April 23, May 29, 1885, Dispatches, State Department Archives.

of the Chinese classics. Americans ranked with the worst, for the United States insisted that Chosen was independent.

Allen did not underrate the strength of Yuan Shih Kai. To be sure, he did make private fun of the youthful Resident, with his imperious manner and his insatiable appetite for food and females. But the doctor knew that Yuan was his chief adversary in Seoul.[32]

Yuan made no frontal moves against the people from America. His blustering was for the natives; in dealing with the foreigners he donned the velvet glove. He complimented Foulk, whom he intended to destroy, and he smiled at Allen, whom he regarded as an enemy.[33]

That was the public side. Behind the scenes Allen felt the tightening grip of the viceroy's trusted agent. Korean girls assigned to the hospital as nurses were snatched away to be Yuan's concubines. Proposals under consideration at the palace often met with opposition that could be traced to the same source. There was talk that Korea might be induced to crack down on the missionaries, and in 1886 the little band of Christian workers learned that the Resident was close to the king's father, the Tai Wen Kun, who just twenty years before had drenched Chosen in Christian blood.

[32] Allen Diary, January 22, 1886; address to the Naval War College and Allen to Ellinwood, November 24, 1885, in the Allen MSS.

[33] Foulk to the Secretary of State, November 25, 1885, Dispatches, State Department Archives; Allen Diary, December 1, 1885. Gilmore, in his *Korea,* page 262, describes Yuan as "a typical Oriental, of no special ability, but with an abnormal amount of cunning and duplicity."

4

To Save Some Souls

WHILE Resident Yuan Shih Kai planned future moves, Seoul's missionary population grew. In 1884 there were just the Allens, plus, of course, the secret Catholic colonies. By 1887 the Protestant community had grown to twenty souls, and every one was certain that evangelical endeavor was firmly rooted in Korea. Doubters could be shown the royal hospital, the Methodist dispensary, the Presbyterian orphanage, the schools of various kinds.

As yet there were few converts, but that was not surprising: the missionaries had refrained from active preaching. As Allen interpreted the policy, it was better "to instruct a Govmt in these institutions of modern civilization . . . than to carry on a feeble proselyting concern—Christianity always goes with the missionary even if he be serving an institution where if not proscribed it is taught with more or less secrecy."[1]

There was plenty to do while waiting for the day when preaching should be authorized. The Allens, keeping house for the first time in their lives, found that getting settled was quite a task. Fannie called their home "delightful" on her first day in Seoul. "Picturesque" would have been a better

[1] Allen to Ellinwood, February 18, 1886, in the Allen MSS; Allen, "Medical Work in Korea," *Foreign Missionary*, 44 (1885):76.

word; Occidentals are not bred to paper walls and leaky roofs and heat flues in the floor. Incidental damage done in the 1884 émeute added to the problem, making repairs essential.[2] And repairs took time in Seoul. Allen could storm, Fannie could plead, but no one living could make a Chosen worker hurry. Servants puttered and refused to do more than one type of labor; and all the natives had a way of making one man's work take care of three.

Foreigners got used to that in time. Even the impatient Allen learned to smile at the deeds of the lazy, grafting houseboys, to joke about the need for hiring a whole gang of men to run one garden shovel. Fannie, too, soon felt exasperation fade, and helped her husband make the difficult adjustment to the slower tempo of Korea.

Every foreign resident faced problems of communication and supply. Letters and newspapers from the United States took a full month to reach Seoul, and packages could not be counted on at all. Forewarned, the Allens stocked up on their provisions, made their home look like a "country grocery store"; but even with careful planning they were often caught short. Which meant a hurry order to the American Trading Company's office in Chemulpo or Smith's Cash Store in San Francisco or Montgomery Ward—and after that a wait of weeks.

Some things could be bought in Seoul, but very few, considering the city's size. Chosen, having been a hermit kingdom for so long, produced few articles that suited Western tastes.

[2] For life in Korea, see Allen Diary, especially from October, 1884, to February, 1885; articles by Allen, sketches of Allen's inventions, and letters from Allen to Charles Allen, March 5, 1905, to Evans, June 17, 1886, and to C. S. Carnaghan, December 11, 1888, in the Allen MSS; letters to the Secretary of State from Foote, October 12, 1883, September 17, 1884, and from Foulk, December 6, 1885, Dispatches, State Department Archives; Foulk to the President of the Korean Foreign Office, December 6, 1885, Seoul Legation Files, State Department Archives; Underwood, *Underwood of Korea*, especially pp. 40-41, 59; Mary F. Scranton, "Woman's Work in Korea," *Korean Repository*, 3 (1896):3; Gale, *Korean Sketches*, 143-156; and Sands, *Undiplomatic Memories*, 98-105, 110-115.

To Save Some Souls

One could get eggs, poultry and fish, rice, and radishes, turnips, and tough lettuce. Beef was likely to be diseased, potatoes and other standard vegetables were unobtainable, and one ended by eating rice, eggs, and chicken "until they came out at our nostrils."

Nor was buying easy. Local purchases had to be made in local currency, in coins each worth a fifteen-hundredth of a dollar. The shopper needed a man to carry change, and the Allen "cash box" was a room fully eight feet square.

And the prices! Seoul, as a newly opened city, had the price scale of a boom mining town. Cotton goods that brought fifteen cents a yard in the United States sold for fifty in Chosen, and it cost a dollar a day (thirty per cent of Allen's salary) for wood alone. Servants entrusted with household funds stole some and spent the rest with utter recklessness; and the Allens, attempting to make ends meet, felt themselves slipping into debt.

Still, it was not so bad. Fannie and the doctor had each other, and they were very much in love. To colleagues and to courtiers Allen seemed a cold and scheming man; at home he was a kind young husband and devoted father. Fannie, he told his diary, "crimps her hair and looks delicious in her new attire," namely, a dressing gown her husband had obtained from Yokohama. And little Horace, too, was the object of some compliments, as was his younger brother Maurice (named to rhyme) when he came in 1886. One should be strict with children, the doctor thought; he would rule his with a hand of iron. But the gruff exterior would not hide the pleasure and the love inside, the endless thrill of fatherhood. Even money matters could have been much worse. Fannie and the doctor were as well off as Foulk, supporting the legation on a chargé's pay. The king and queen sent presents now and then—fish and game, eggs and fruit, bowls and mats and kettles, and dressing gowns. And Allen learned to earn some extra dollars by writing articles for papers in the United States.

For God

The luxuries of home were brought in one by one. And labor, inefficient though it was, could not be called expensive. The Allens, on their twelve-hundred-dollar income, managed to maintain a whole corps of servants. They had a nurse, a cook, a waiter, a gate boy, sedan chair carriers, and several other helpers. Indeed, the missionaries lived so well that they were criticized for extravagance. Then, as now, travellers alluded to the "soft life" of the Protestant workers in Chosen, commented on the contrast furnished by the Catholic teachers.

But there were reasons, first-rate reasons, for the high standards. Allen's mission gains and those of his colleagues had been made possible by favor at a court characterized by pomp and ceremony; had he chosen to live as did the common people, his cause would have lost prestige. The aristocrats and many of the poorer natives would have classed him with the humble Catholic workers and would have been less likely to be interested in what he had to say. "Koreans are fond of visiting the homes of foreigners," one of Allen's colleagues explained. "They admire the comforts—to them these comforts are the highest of luxuries—of the home life of the strangers. They go home to ponder on the religion which takes hold of the present life of man and makes it more enjoyable. They mark our cheerful faces and our enjoyment of life, and wonder at the cause. They listen to the tales of the achievements of Western science.... When they realize that all this is the outcome and development of our religion, the practical value of Christianity makes a powerful appeal to them. It is no disgrace therefore that our missionaries ... live sometimes in comfortable homes."[3]

"Getting settled" included studying the culture and cus-

[3] Gilmore, *Korea*, 316. An editorial statement in the *Foreign Missionary*, 44 (1886):404, implies the same, to which Brown, in his "Reading Journey through Korea," in the *Chautauquan*, 41 (1905):495 (quoting John B. Nevius), adds: "if a missionary is willing to spend his life in this country he is entitled to all the comforts he can secure from his salary of ten or twelve dollars a week." According to Sands, Allen

toms of Korea. As Sir Harry Parkes remarked in 1884, the missionary pioneers in Korea would be prepared for active preaching only when they had acquired a broad understanding of the history and literature, the language and religions, the social and economic status of every class that lived and labored in the Land of Morning Calm.

No one could say that the assignment was a simple one. There were few books on Chosen; to Westerners the state was a "remote, strange field," as far removed as Tibet seems today. Knowledge had to be obtained upon the ground, and under the most difficult of circumstances.

Allen, first on the ground, never did get down to study. Finding that there were no language books, he hired a teacher, Ye Ha Yong, later chargé in Korea's Washington legation. Ye was as dilatory as most Koreans, a man who had "too many friends" to want to spend much time with Allen. And concentrated study irritated the missionary, too; he never did take kindly to the scholar's ways.

How could he study? The 1884 revolt broke off all thought of language lessons; and after that the court and the hospital required attention. After six months in Seoul the doctor still could not understand the natives without the aid of an interpreter, and he never achieved more than a "fair proficiency in the spoken language." True, he did slap together a phrase book that helped newcomers a little, but the substantial linguistic studies came from calmer souls who had a penchant for research.[4]

As for art and literature, history, religion, and the rest, they, too, failed to arouse the doctor's interest, and in any event he had too much to do to probe into Korea's past.

disapproved of foreigners who lived among the Koreans. Letter to the author, May 28, 1939. The standard criticism of the missionaries can be found in Angus Hamilton, *Korea* (New York, 1904), 261–265, and H. B. Drake, *Korea of the Japanese* (London and New York, 1930), 163–168, 188–189.

[4] Paik, *Protestant Missions in Korea*, 90, 133–141; Allen Diary, November 27, 1884, March 18, December 23, 1885; notes by Allen, phrase book,

Being attentive, he picked up many tales at the Chosen court, and some of these he published, after expurgation. He also assembled a collection of Korean pottery, with an eye to the profit in the deal.[5] But his contribution was not great; apparently he never understood the culture of the land in which he labored.[6]

Yet William W. Rockhill, an able Orientalist, said Allen knew "more about Korea than any foreigner who ever put his foot there."[7] And that was so if one meant politics and diplomacy. Allen did not choose a sweeping canvas, made no attempt to learn "everything about Korea." Just the court as he found it, only the Seoul he knew. Scholars thought that not enough, felt Allen did not comprehend the background of the controversies in which he was engaged. Others believed that he was afflicted with court myopia and neglected the man he really hoped to aid, the oppressed Korean farmer tilling his tiny plot of land. All true, but no one man had time for everything. Had he been scholar, Allen could not

and letter from Allen to Ellinwood, February 4, 1885, in the Allen MSS; Allen, *Korea: Fact and Fancy*, 11, 13; letter to the Secretary of State from Foulk, November 21, 1886, and from Allen, October 5, 1897, Dispatches, State Department Archives; Hamilton, *Korea*, 151.

[6] Inventory and correspondence with officials of Smithsonian Institution, 1889–1890, in the Allen MSS; Allen to W. W. Rockhill, February 28, 1901, in the Rockhill Manuscripts, deposited in the Yale University Library; note in the Allen MSS stating that Allen bought twenty tons of Japanese curios in 1895 and sold them at a profit to V. S. Fischer of Washington, D. C. Walter Hough, "The Bernadou, Allen and Jouy Collections, in the U. S. National Museum," in *Report of the U. S. National Museum*, 1891, pp. 429–488.

[6] Allen's contribution to the literature on Korean culture is seen in his *Korean Tales* (New York, 1889), reprinted in his *Korea: Fact and Fancy;* and in his articles: "Legends of Chong Dang and Vicinity," *Korean Repository*, 2 (1895):103–110; "Places of Interest in Seoul," *ibid.*, 128–133, 182–187, 210–214; "Folk Lore," *ibid.*, 462–465; "The Mutang," *ibid.*, 3 (1896):163–165; "A Fortune Teller's Tale," *ibid.*, 273–280; "Some Korean Customs: Dancing Girls," *ibid.*, 383–386; and "An Old Book on Korea," *ibid.*, 4 (1897):14–17.

[7] See also "The New American Minister," *Korean Repository*, 4 (1897):348 (Allen "by common consent, has for years been recognized as the best authority on 'things Korean' in general, in the country.")

have worked so well as a man of affairs; had his view been broader, he might have been less influential in the Chosen court.

In any case, studies took almost none of Horace Allen's time. His day was spent in attending to his court connections and in his job as missionary doctor.

Part of the Presbyterian's practice was with the foreigners. Mission boards do not always approve of having their physicians treat those in the foreign colony; but in Seoul it seemed desirable. It served, as a church report expressed it, to form "a bond of sympathy and support between the mission [in] its tentative and rather critical period, and that foreign element which, when not conciliated to a proper degree, is apt to be hostile to the mission work."[8] Thus Allen took appointment as physician to the Chinese Resident, as Custom House surgeon, as American, Japanese, and Russian legation doctor, as consulate physician for Germany, France, and Great Britain. Thus he took care of trader Walter B. Townsend and adviser Moellendorff and even nursed the Catholic priests whom he had denounced so vigorously. All this brought in "more than a salary," but the fees were not for Fannie and the doctor to enjoy; they went into the mission treasury.

While working in this fashion, Allen continued to act as the king's physician. The return was good, but the work was hard. Night after night the missionary couple would be awakened by the squeak of their gate outside, a sign that soldiers were coming for the doctor. It did not mean emergency, some special illness making a midnight visit imperative. More than likely it was merely a routine call to a court that slept by day and met by night. Nocturnal noises disturbed Fannie and her husband for months after they left Seoul.[9]

Wearily climbing out of bed, the king's physician pulled

[8] Presbyterian Board of Foreign Missions, *Report*, 1887, p. 155; Allen Diary, April 10, 1885; article by Allen, dated April 29, 1886, in the Allen MSS.

[9] Gilmore, *Korea*, 95. On Allen's court practice, see Allen, *Things Korean*, 191–196; map of Seoul in Curzon, *Problems of the Far East*,

For God

on his court clothes—his one tuxedo. Bidding his wife good-
bye and taking care not to wake the babies, he was off, his
sloppy soldier escort tagging on behind. It took only a little
time to reach the court, for it was on the west side now—the
king and queen had been driven out of their east-side palace
by the wailing spirit voices of the relatives who had come to
grief in December, 1884.

Easy enough, as far as that; then came the trial that tortured Allen's soul. His Majesty might be ready for the doctor,
and then again he might not. If not, court etiquette required
that the missionary await the pleasure of the king. While
doing so, he could talk with courtiers and nibble at the dainty
food the palace servants set before him. That was some compensation—Allen liked to talk and eat. But neither food nor
conversation was a substitute for sleep.

Yet the doctor stood it. He frowned and fidgeted, he boiled
inside and exhausted his slender store of patience; but he
saw it through. And saw it pay out in the end. The king
awarded him new, higher rank in the nobility, giving him
the right to come to court without a summons. His Majesty
extended aid to the Presbyterian hospital and other mission
ventures. And both king and queen came to feel that their
first Occidental doctor was the ablest, finest medical prac-
titioner in all the world.

At first, as might have been expected, Their Majesties were
a bit suspicious of the Occidental doctor. There was a great
upset when Allen gave the queen an opiate that laid her out
for nineteen hours. A court official came stamping in to ask
for explanations, and Allen had some worries for a while. But
that soon passed and there were only loyal patients at the
palace.

Proof of that came when Allen was absent from Seoul. Feeling sick, the queen called on the mission doctors for some

127; Underwood, *Fifteen Years among the Top-Knots*, 120–121. Allen
obtained four decorations from the Korean government, the last,
awarded in 1904, being the highest obtainable for one not of royal
blood.

medicine. Analyzing the illness, they sent a drug on to the palace. Back it came. It would not do, Her Majesty had said with firmness. Good Dr. Allen had prescribed for her before; *his* medicine had had another taste and color and had come in a bottle of a different shape and size. "Please send some more of that."

No man could be averse to such compliments; Allen loved them. Few physicians can claim royal patients, yet he, at twenty-seven, watched over a whole royal family. Only Foulk of all the foreigners knew the king as well as did the missionary doctor, and no other foreign male was ever to know the queen as well as Allen.

Physician to the court and the foreign colony, and also founder and director of Seoul's new royal hospital. The last position mattered most from the missionary point of view; it was through the hospital that the Presbyterians hoped to reach the heart and conscience of Korea.

The institution was successful from the start. It occupied a large Korean building, the confiscated home of the dead progressive premier Hong Yong Sik. As the émeute had fizzled out, the Mins had turned the house into an execution chamber and had soaked the walls and floors with the blood of Hong's relatives and friends. Chosen noblemen would not have cared to dwell in a structure that had seen such wholesale slaughter; but Allen did not mind. The house was large and well situated, and cures would soon wipe out recollections of the building's gruesome past. To Allen the institution's very name suggested this. Chai Chung Won, the king had called the hospital, a term that Allen took to mean the House of Civilized Virtue. A pity that later translators pointed out that Royal Hospital was the proper translation!

Civilized virtue or not, the house was a handsome one. Korea's court had spent from six hundred to a thousand dollars in repair work, restoring rooms despoiled by the mobs and cleaning up the gore-stained furnishings. Everything was finished when Allen started work. The wards were equipped and ready, a dispensary and operating room had been prepared, and kitchens, halls, and closets were all in good order. Nor had beauty been forgotten. Working in his operating hall, Allen could look out on a well-tended court, neatly decorated with fancy stones. Tending his patients in the wards, the Presbyterian could see a smiling garden and wall-encircled yards dotted with pretty native trees.

Supplies and helpers were provided, too. The king had made an annual appropriation of three hundred dollars for drug purchases and had assigned nearly a score of workers to help Allen with his job. Three of these were high officers, native superintendents Allen had requested for the purpose of concealing the institution's mission character. Four were students, who were not only to help but to observe the technique of the Occident. Two were secretaries, two were orderlies, and five were mere servants to do the menial work.[10] Later a group of dancer-concubines was sent along. To act as nurses, Allen guessed. "At least," he stated solemnly, "I mean to insist upon this interpretation." And so he did, till Resident Yuan Shih Kai disturbed this policy of purity by taking the girls back to their old profession.[11]

When the hospital's doors were opened, on April 9, 1885, Seoul rushed to take advantage of the opportunity. Twenty were treated as outpatients on the very first day, and the building's forty beds were not long empty. Indeed, the natives came so fast that the young and inexperienced doctor became a trifle flustered, and told his diary that he often wished he "could get out of it."

In time Allen had some help, and the pressure eased a

[10] Allen, "Medical Work in Korea," *Foreign Missionary*, 44 (1885): 74–76; Allen Diary, March 1, April 4 (with hospital rules), 1885; Foulk to the Secretary of State, May 30, 1885, Dispatches, State Department Archives.

[11] Allen Diary, August 5, 1885; Allen to Ellinwood, May 19, 1885, in the Allen MSS. Allen, however, said that the girls were withdrawn at his request. See his article "Some Korean Customs: Dancing Girls," *Korean Repository*, 3 (1896):383–386.

little. Meeting Dr. Scranton in Chemulpo, Allen persuaded the Methodist physician to help him out for a time. And in June, when Scranton left to start his own dispensary, Presbyterian Dr. Heron stepped in to take on part of the growing burden. Allen and Heron, working together, managed to take care of all the wards and to handle as many as seventy outpatients daily. Ten thousand were treated in the first twelve months, and in later years the total was much higher.[12]

"Medical missions," said the Layman's Inquiry of 1930, "represent, in themselves, the essentials of the Christian enterprise."[13] Similar thoughts must have occurred to the sick of Seoul as they learned of Horace Allen's Chai Chung Won. For it was said that the Americans turned none away. There were charges—five thousand cash ($3.50) for a home call; a fifth as much per day for a private room inside the hospital, and three hundred cash for a day's care in a ward. But the poor were not charged at all, and bills, payable "only on recovery," could be paid in produce if one lacked the cash.[14]

Having worked in China, Allen knew what kind of patients he would have—poor suffering natives accustomed to physicians fully as ignorant as they. These were the medicine men who pressed red-hot coins against the forehead to cure convulsions. Acupuncture, poking with dirty needles, was a common form of treatment, and nearly everybody was cauterized for indigestion. Poultices of cow excrement were prescribed for sores, caterpillars for bronchitis, maggots for delirium. "General weakness" called for tiger bone, the strongest part of the strongest animal. A soup made from snakes, toads, and centi-

[12] Allen Diary, April 10, 1885; Allen, *Things Korean*, 189; Foulk to the Secretary of State, May 30, 1885, Dispatches, State Department Archives; Allen to Ellinwood, May 7, 1885, in the Allen MSS; Horace N. Allen and John W. Heron, *First Annual Report of the Government Hospital for the Year Ending April 10th, 1886* (Yokohama, 1886).

[13] *Re-Thinking Missions* (7 vols., New York and London, 1932–1933), 7:194–213, quotation from p. 199.

[14] Hospital rules, Allen Diary, April 3, 1885; Allen, *Things Korean*, 205.

pedes was guaranteed to kill or cure, and dog soup had even greater popularity. Drinking it made the Koreans cannibals, Allen thought; did they not eat the dogs who ate the rebels killed in 1884?[15]

One did not need to condemn the whole—Korean doctors did use ginseng and other healing herbs. But more was needed for the "horrible diseases" Allen saw, for the "almost universal" syphilis, the "common" leprosy, and the equally prevalent typhoid, smallpox, epilepsy, dysentery, malaria, and tuberculosis.

And cholera. That was the worst. The "rat in the stomach disease," the people called it. The muscular pain one felt at first, that was the rat gnawing its way up the leg; and when it reached the stomach, the end soon came. Foreigners like Allen explained it in other ways, saw the people "ripe for the harvest" because of bad eating habits, the hot, unhealthy summers, and the stinking filth of sewage-drenched Seoul. However it was to be explained, it was bad, and people died.

White people, too. There was a scare in 1885, when the scourge hit China and Japan. All Seoul shuddered, and the Allens bent over little Harry's bed, as the baby tossed with fever. But all was well for one more year.

Then the calamity struck, in the heart of a burning summer. The natives died like flies, so fast that those who lived had scarcely time to dig the needed graves. Five hundred a

[15] On Korean medicine and medical problems, see notes from Allen to John C. Lundberg, March 25, 1887, and to the Japanese consul, January 26, 1886, in the Allen MSS; Allen Diary, January 30, 1885; Allen to Rockhill, May 12, 1891, an astounding letter, in the Rockhill MSS; Allen, *Things Korean*, 198–199; C. C. Vinton, "A Surgeon's Experience in Korea," *Church at Home and Abroad*, 9 (1891):222–224; J. B. Busteed, "The Korean Doctor and His Methods," *Korean Repository*, 2 (1895):188–193; J. Hunter Wells, "Medical Impressions," *ibid.*, 3 (1896):238–239; O. R. Avison, "Disease in Korea," *ibid.*, 4 (1897): 90–93, 207–211; William E. Griffis, "Corean Medical Science," *Overland Monthly*, new series, 1:44–46; Underwood, *Underwood of Korea*, 41; Gale, *Korean Sketches*, 34–36; Gilmore, *Korea*, 92–94; Brown, *Mastery of the Far East*, 556–557; Rockhill, *China's Intercourse with Korea*, especially p. 56.

The Monarch of Chosen

*Ik Song, twenty-eighth ruler of the Yi Dynasty, king of Korea
from 1864 to 1897 and emperor from 1897 to 1907*

Fate made this man a monarch but denied him sense and courage.
Hence his was a story of dissipation and confusion. Caught as he
was between the Japanese and Chinese, he turned to Occidental
advisers, among them Dr. Allen. But even they could not save him.
In time he and his country fell prey to the ambitious Japanese.

day, wrote the American minister, seven thousand souls altogether in Chosen's capital. And nothing seemed to help, least of all the paper images and demon incantations that the frightened people strung across the fever-ridden alleys of Seoul.

Ever the man of emergency, Allen sprang to action. His court prestige helped greatly. The Korean king, terrified as always in a crisis, gave his approval to a proclamation that the doctor wanted issued. And out it went, to tell the natives that they should boil their water, burn sulphur, clean their premises, and sprinkle lime. Rather late, perhaps, for measures of prevention; but Allen also tended the stricken population. He handled all he could himself, and, discarding dogma, called on the Catholic priests to help him with the others. All in all, despite the many deaths, the end result could not be called discouraging. Many died, but others, reached in time, pulled through with the assistance of Occidental medicine and the ministrations of the Protestant and Catholic mission people.[16]

Knowing what had happened, the Koreans looked on Allen with an ever-greater admiration. This scowling man from the United States had saved more lives than all the magic men of Chosen. Grieving relatives brought corpses to the hospital: could the mighty doctor give the dead man breath again? They even brought watches that had "died," for it was said that the tall physician could cure anything.

So Allen worked, with Heron by his side. They had their troubles: the government transferred servants and forgot to supply the hospital with food. Female patients were always hard to handle, until a woman doctor arrived; they often thought that they would rather die than show their bodies to the white man. It was hard to get permission for operations,

[16] Allen Diary, September 20, 27, 1885; Allen, *Things Korean,* 207; Parker to the Secretary of State, July 20, August 1, 1886, Dispatches, State Department Archives; *Church at Home and Abroad,* 1 (1887):76, quoting Appenzeller; Underwood, *Underwood of Korea,* 56; Horace N. Allen, *Report on the Health of Seoul for the Year 1886,* a pamphlet

particularly amputations. Yuan Shih Kai, when asked about one for an injured soldier, flatly refused to have it done. But the man would die, protested Allen. Very well, came the cold reply of the Chinese officer, let him die. What use could one hope to make of a one-armed soldier?[17]

So much medical work, Allen found, could be done only "at the expense of the spiritual." But the work was Christian work, and the religious motive never out of mind. The *Foreign Missionary*, organ of Allen's sect, was justified in saying that in Chosen "the cause of the Gospel . . . *moves on.*"[18]

Fannie and the doctor did their part for that cause. They held family worship before there was a single ordained Protestant in Korea. "As we have daily prayers and religious observances," was Allen's comment at the time, "we think we may do a little good even in this way."[19] With the Reverend Underwood in residence, Sunday services began in the early summer of 1885. In October the Protestant communion was administered for the first time, with wine and a silver teapot furnished by the Allens. Baptismal ceremonies came on Easter Sunday, 1886. Methodist Reverend Appenzeller officiated, baptizing three new members of his church. One was his daughter Alice, whom Allen had delivered a few months earlier—the first white child born in Korea. The second was the Scranton baby, just a few days younger, and the third was a man whom Appenzeller had converted in Japan, now an interpreter at the Japanese legation in Seoul.

These services, of course, were privately conducted and were exclusively for foreigners, persons whom the treaties

published by the *Chinese Customs Gazette.* Underwood, *Fifteen Years among the Top-Knots*, 133–145, is an excellent account of a similar epidemic, in 1895.

[17] Allen, *Things Korean*, 72, 206; Allen Diary, December 11, 1884; address to the Naval War College, in the Allen MSS.

[18] Allen to Ellinwood, February 23, 1885, in the Allen MSS; *Foreign Missionary*, 44 (1886):483.

[19] Allen Diary, November 12, 1884. Early services noted in the Allen Diary, November 27, 1884, June 28, October 11, 1885, April 25, 1886; Paik, *Protestant Missions in Korea*, especially p. 129.

gave a right to worship as they pleased. Quite different was the ceremony of July 11, 1886, when an aged Korean, No Tah Sa, became a baptized convert to Protestant Christianity. He backslid later, but his acceptance of an Occidental faith put to test the "quasi-recognition"[20] Allen had secured for his mission brethren.

Though No became a Methodist, Allen had had a hand in the conversion. His curiosity aroused by references to Christianity in Chinese documents, No had sought the doctor out in the fall of 1884. On December 4, the day of the great émeute, he had visited the missionary's interpreter and borrowed Allen's Chinese translation of the gospels of Mark and Luke. The doctor "cautioned him thr'o an interpreter that he would have his head cut off if found reading it." But No was determined, "shook his head knowingly and took the risks."

In the excitement of the revolution, the Presbyterian quite forgot old No. But the Korean was reading of the white man's faith and liking it. He appeared again in January, 1885, and served a while as Allen's language teacher. The doctor, busy, would rush away with his lessons half undone—and No remained in the missionary's office, studying Christian doctrine. Convinced, he went to Underwood and Appenzeller, there to learn more.

Eventually—before conversion—No left the service of the Allens. But as he left he took along the doctor's Chinese Testament. Theft? Possibly, though the owner did not mind. It was only in jest that Allen wrote in later days that "the stolen Testament made this man just enough of a Christian to allow him to enter the Methodist Church and retain the goods, but not enough to get him into the Presbyterian Church."

In other ways, too, Allen used religion. He prayed for all

[20] Gilmore, *Korea*, 299. No's case can be traced in the Allen Diary, especially the entry for January 29, 1885; Allen, *Things Korean*, 77; address of September, 1900, on the occasion of the translation of the New Testament into Korean, in the Allen MSS; Horace G. Underwood, letter in the *Foreign Missionary*, 45 (1886):223–224; Horace G. Under-

his patients, mixed his medicine with prayer. Once when he found a noble who could not "pass water," he went home and "prayed over it earnestly"—whereupon a Korean came on the run, calling that the deed was done, that the noble was "passing water constantly."[21]

On another occasion the doctor tried his best to make a convert. In June of 1885 a native woman was brought to his hospital. Dying of a "chronic abscess," the poor creature was all skin and bones. Allen's skill could not cure her; she sank ever lower. He could only hope to save her pain, and pity her as the tears stood in her dark, tired eyes. As she continued to fail, he tried to turn her mind to thoughts of the bright Christian world beyond this earth of sorrow. Legend has it that she became a convert and died wreathed in smiles, exclaiming "joy for me." But that is only legend, though Allen came to believe it himself. At the time, he realized that he had not done much—she did not understand his tongue and he had not learned hers. It was true, as the experts said, that failure to learn the Oriental languages resulted "in crippling the missionary for his whole missionary life."[22]

Yet, though he failed to save this woman, Allen had done much for the missionary cause. As one of his colleagues observed, he had made the missionaries "spoiled darlings" of a court that had loathed and persecuted Christians. He had founded a hospital and made it a going concern. He had participated in the opening of Christian services in this Land

wood, *The Call of Korea* (New York, etc. [1908]), 105; Paik, *Protestant Missions in Korea*, 90–91, 127–129; Rhodes, *Korea Mission, Presbyterian Church*, 19.

[21] Allen Diary, March 22, 1885.

[22] Fennell P. Turner, "Missionary Personnel in India, Burma, China and Japan," in *Re-Thinking Missions*, 7:155–193; Allen Diary, March 27, 1885. The case is covered in a communication of Allen's dated June 2, 1885, and published under the caption "A Very Sad Case" in the *Foreign Missionary*, 44 (1885):176, and the editorial on pages 150–151. The legend appears in Lillias H. Underwood, "Women's Work in Korea," *Korean Repository*, 3 (1896):63, and a note by Allen in the Allen MSS.

of Morning Calm. That should have been a source of comfort to any Christian, especially one who felt that "the inducements for becoming a medical missionary would seem to be *nil* aside from a desire to do a work of charity to others and satisfaction to ones self." And Allen would have been quite satisfied, had all been well within the missionary ranks.

But all was not.

5

We Too Are Mortals

NEW missionaries arrived in Seoul in the eighties expecting to meet a smiling band of Christian workers, cooperating harmoniously in the service of their God. They found instead a wrangling group of ordinary mortals. The frowns outweighed the smiles, there was backbiting in place of harmony, and sulking selfishness instead of enthusiastic cooperation.

A sad situation it was, for it destroyed the happiness of every Protestant in Chosen. And to the Allens it did more—it drove them out of mission work. True, money was a factor in determining the doctor's action, but he surely would have stayed in the proselyting field had it not been for the quarrels in the Seoul colony. It was the tale of China all over again, and the Presbyterian pioneer could not endure it for the second time.

There are many quarrels in missionary ranks; indeed, they are a major problem of the boards at home.[1] But need one be surprised? Should one not ask why there are not more? After all, as one of Allen's associates expressed it, "mission-

---

[1] This subject has not received the attention it deserves. See, however, Trevor P. Bowen, "Causes for Withdrawal of Missionaries," in *Re-Thinking Missions*, 7:44–46, and Arthur Judson Brown, *The Foreign Missionary* (New York, 1907), especially pp. 355–372.

aries are like other real Christians, no better, no worse."[2]
Many are strong-minded persons who would disagree under
the best of circumstances—and circumstances are not the best
in mission areas. A few assorted workers are crowded together
in a station, the only foreigners in a sea of Oriental peoples.
The surroundings are drab, the men and women must live
and work and play and pray together. Is it strange that there
comes a "staleness in daily associations," a "feeling of having
entirely sounded the mental and spiritual possibilities" of
the others on the staff?[3] Is it odd that differences should lead
to bickering, and bickering to the sharpest animosities?

Consider Seoul in the pioneer decade. Every missionary
there longed for white companionship. Fannie Allen beamed
when the Heron, Scranton, and Appenzeller ladies came to
town, and her husband enjoyed a visit with their husbands
or with the bachelor preacher Underwood. Scranton, Allen
thought, was "sensible," Heron "pleasant," and Underwood
"smart and business like." And they liked him as well, wrote
without envy of his "wonderful success," publicly proclaimed
that his coming to Korea had been "a special Providence for
the opening and establishing, on a firm basis, [of] a mission
in this land."[4]

That for a while; then the everyday contacts lost their
freshness. Fannie and the doctor, who in June of 1885 had
said that Mrs. Heron was "very polite and pleasant . . . a
dainty pretty little lady," thought her a scheming, malicious

[2] Underwood, *Underwood of Korea*, 43, in a discussion of missionary
quarrels in Korea.

[3] Isabella L. Bishop, "Missionary Hardships," *Korean Repository*, 5
(1898):20–21.

[4] John W. Heron, letter dated June 26, 1885, in *Foreign Missionary*,
44 (1885):273. See the Allen Diary, April 6, May 12, June 21, September
1, 1885, and Allen to Ellinwood, July 4, 1887, in the Allen MSS, for
the first impressions. Paik, *Protestant Missions in Korea*, contains biographical statements on the early missionaries; see also Underwood,
Underwood of Korea; Rhodes, *Korea Mission, Presbyterian Church;*
Daniel L. Gifford, "John W. Heron, M.D.," *Korean Repository*, 4
(1897):441–443; and Wilbur Swearer, "Memoir of Henry G. Appenzeller," *Korea Review*, 2 (1902):254–261.

liar before a year had passed. Scranton now seemed "jealous," and Allen announced in mission meeting that Underwood was a "hypocrite & tattler," Heron a "pouting envious man." All this backbiting was returned with interest. Mrs. Heron told Allen that he was "unfit for a missionary." Fannie and her husband were "boycotted" for a time, and many bitter letters crossed the Pacific bearing details of the doctor's faults.[5]

A gloomy business, but not too surprising. It was partly explained, as Allen's Presbyterian Board of Foreign Missions saw, by the fact that "the pioneer missionaries in Korea were in a situation of peculiar loneliness, isolation and trial." Seoul's bleak hills weighed heavily on individuals accustomed to the tree-dotted landscape of the eastern United States; and the capital's drab streets chilled hearts that still responded to warmth and color. The city's filth, its stench and summer heat, kept all the foreigners on edge, made them impatient with little faults of colleagues which in happier circumstances they might have ignored.[6]

[5] Allen Diary, May 7, June 17, 21, September 1, 1885, March 29, October 10, 1886, and more of the same, although Allen claims to have removed from his papers "considerable material of a missionary character . . . as relating mostly to inter-mission wrangles due to petty jealousies, etc."

[6] Underwood, *Underwood of Korea*, 40; Charles Chaillé-Long, *My Life on Four Continents* (London, 1912), 343–344, describing Seoul as "monotonous beyond description," and "the most loathsome city in the world." A typical reaction is that expressed in the doggerel of Captain Bostwick of the *U.S.S. Palos*, quoted in Brown, "Reading Journey through Korea," *Chautauquan*, 41 (1905):510–511:

> There's a singular country far over the seas,
> Which is known to the world as Korea,
> Where there's nothing to charm and nothing to please,
> And of cleanliness not an idea.
> Where the houses they live in are mostly of dirt,
> With a tumble-down roof made of thatch;
> Where soap is unknown, it is safe to assert,
> And where vermin in myriads hatch;
> Where the streets are all reeking with odors more rife
> Than the smells from a hyena's den;
> One visit is surely enough for one life,
> In that far-away land of Chosen.

And little faults there certainly were. Allen's shortcomings were all too evident: his self-pride, his short temper, his lack of Christian charity. These had been revealed before. He regarded himself as the dean of the Seoul mission colony, ruler by right of seniority. Yet Underwood and Heron had exactly the same rank as he, and though he had been first on the ground, their appointments to Korea antedated his.

Having influence with royalty, Allen used it to get court favors for the missionary cause—but he never did it quietly. His mission colleagues had to know that *he* had done it—he, Horace Allen, through *his* connections at the palace. One can see the stern-faced doctor gloatingly dispensing his patronage, and his fellow workers succumbing to what one traveller to Seoul called the "natural temptation to envy the success given to the methods and work of others."

Naturally, the defects of disposition were not monopolized by Allen. Foulk and His Korean Majesty managed to get along with the doctor; the missionaries could have done the same had they been kind and patient. But they, too, were men who wanted to hold the reins, men who lacked a talent for adjustment. It was simply, to use a missionary's phrase, that "some people are so diverse in their dispositions that even the indwelling Christ cannot make them live together."

Heron, Allen's co-worker at the hospital, was far and away the worst. Even one of his friends could write that his "dislikes were as strong as his friendships";[7] enemies believed them infinitely stronger. Heron and Allen did not get on together, and it may be said that the early mission quarrels in Seoul were born of a standing war between these two staff physicians of the Chai Chung Won. The others sometimes played the neutral role and sometimes mixed in the arguments; but the Heron-Allen struggle did not cease until Heron died of dysentery in midsummer, 1890.

Heron, an English-born American, was a better-looking man than Allen. His delicate features, his long eyelashes, and his large shining eyes made him almost pretty, a man whom

[7] Gifford, "Heron," *Korean Repository,* 4 (1897):441–443.

women admired. Vanity went with that handsome face, a vanity that bred contempt for the raw-boned Allen. And Heron was a little older than his colleague, another reason for his feeling of superiority. Professionally, too, he probably outshone Allen—he had been offered a professorship of medicine before he came out to the Orient. Being (or feeling himself) a better physician, how could he endure to have Allen lord it over him and occupy a better place in the regard of all Koreans?

Underwood, too, was given to condescension. He came from a background of self-appreciative Presbyterians. He looked the fearless deacon in his tall pipe hat and black coat buttoned up to his white necktie. And his firm-set jaw, his high-tossed head showed that he, too, felt the urge to rule. Orders he would not take, advice he seldom heeded, and, as the only ordained Calvinist in Seoul, he was sure his word was the word of God, even when he disagreed with all the others.

The Methodists were not very different, but there is no need for details. Plainly, Allen's colleagues were not the sort to stand for a display of arrogance. Plainly, also, they were not much given to praise of others. And Allen needed praise— needed and deserved it. Churlish he might be; the fact remained that he had brought the missionaries into royal favor. His "wisdom," as a successor rightly stated, made the natives friendly and helped to keep "the country open to the gospel in the after years when reaction . . . set in and many officials would fain have closed the doors again."[8] For that the doctor merited some thanks, sour-tempered though he was.

Moreover, in common fairness one should consider their ages. The Allens, the Herons, the Scrantons, the Appenzellers, Underwood, Hulbert, Gilmore, Bunker, Miss Ellers, Miss Lillias Horton, all were in their twenties when they came to Chosen; all lacked the wisdom that is accumulated in a life-

[8] *Report of the Ecumenical Missionary Conference,* 1900, 1:537, speech of O. R. Avison.

time of missionary work. The Methodists did have the counsel of the veteran Maclay in near-by Japan; the Presbyterians lacked even that and made mistakes in consequence. "We youngsters," wrote Allen as the quarrels began, "need to be held in by some older more experienced head."[9]

Youth can manage if it has an outlet for its energies. But there was none in Seoul. Allen did skate and his colleagues rode and played a little tennis; but by and large the group was too straightlaced to regard entertainment as quite proper. In the language of a visiting board secretary, "the typical missionary of the first quarter century after the opening of the country was a man of the Puritan type. He kept the Sabbath as our New England forefathers did a century ago. He looked upon dancing, smoking, and card playing as sins in which no true follower of Christ should indulge."[10] Yet youth and personality, environment, and lack of emotional and physical outlets did not tell the whole story. There were basic differences in policy that split the Seoul colony into two warring camps.

Politics, for one thing. Some approved of Allen's method of seeking concessions at the court; others insisted that "nothing could be more uncalled for, or more injurious to our real missionary work, than for us to seem to take any part in the political factions of Korea."[11] The Methodists sneered at the Presbyterians for running a hospital financed by a pagan government, and Allen derided the Methodist Dr. Scranton for his reluctance to assist in the Chai Chung Won. A similar clash occurred inside Presbyterian ranks when

[9] Allen Diary, May 7, 1885. See, however, his diary entry for April 10, 1885, revealing a disagreement with the elder Maclay.

[10] Brown, *Mastery of the Far East*, 540; Underwood, *Fifteen Years among the Top-Knots*, 11–12; Drake, *Korea*, 175; Gilmore, *Korea*, 107–108; Horace N. Allen, "Bicycle Experiences in Korea," *Korean Repository*, 3 (1896):320–322. See Sands, *Undiplomatic Memories*, 94–115, 199–200, and Allen to James H. Sands, November 27, 1899, in the Allen MSS, for references to types of entertainment in which the missionaries seldom indulged.

[11] "The Hour for Korea," *Foreign Missionary*, 44 (1885):153–156.

For God

Heron and Underwood opposed Allen's proposal for a government scientific school within the hospital.

Choosing native factions caused further disagreements. Underwood and Heron were "progressive" to the core. While passing through Japan they had been enormously impressed by the partisans of Kim Ok Kiun. Heron had studied Korean there under Pak Yong Hyo, and Underwood came to Chosen bearing letters of endorsement from progressive leaders.

Allen was appalled by this. He, too, liked the progressives, hoped they would come to power in the "next social trouble." But, being practical, he played along with the incumbent Mins. He shuddered to think of Underwood carrying testimonials from men proscribed as murderers by the Korean court, of Heron sitting at the feet of the queen's sworn foe.[12] Such foolishness would undermine the structure he had built with so much care. Moreover, he did not think much of gospel preaching. His Christian creed revolved about the symbol of the good Samaritan; good deeds, he thought, were more important than good words. Not so the Methodists and Underwood, " 'the Methodist preacher' of the Presbyterian mission."[13] To them the spreading of the Word outweighed all thought of social betterment, and the Allen-Heron hospital, with proselyting barred, was hardly Christian. Dr. Scranton was eventually to abandon all thought of treating native bodies and to concentrate upon their souls. And a visiting missionary who asked, "what are you doing in the way of social reform?" was answered, "nothing, we are too busy preaching the gospel."[14]

The best of diplomats could not have reconciled those two divergent views; but the missionaries had to face the situation every day. Allen, working with the court, insisted that gospel

[12] Paik, *Protestant Missions in Korea,* 80; Allen Diary, May 7, 1885; Allen to Ellinwood, August 2, 1887, in the Allen MSS; Allen, "Medical Work in Korea," *Foreign Missionary,* 44 (1885):76.
[13] *Korean Repository,* 5 (1898):257, quoting Scranton; Underwood, *Underwood of Korea,* 71; Paik, *Protestant Missions in Korea,* 150.
[14] Brown, *Mastery of the Far East,* 541.

teaching be delayed until the king approved. At first the other party acquiesced. "It is the unanimous judgment of all the missionaries here," wrote one, "not to attempt open evangelical work."[15] But, to Allen's deep chagrin, the temptation proved too great for the would-be preachers. They proceeded "cautiously but without apology." Government or not, they assured each other, there existed a "duty to preach and take the consequences."[16]

Yes, preach and take the consequences, as Peter had commanded (Acts 4:19–20). Wherefore Underwood, instructed to proceed to Seoul quietly, participated in revival meetings in Japan while the Korean adviser Moellendorff was visiting the empire. Upon reaching the shores of Chosen, the young Presbyterian minister advertised his presence by bawling hymns in a Chemulpo hotel. He did the same in Seoul, increasing his offense by translating the words into Korean. He attacked Allen for not teaching Christianity inside the hospital. He began instructing natives and teaching them his songs. He passed out Bible pamphlets and, with his friend Appenzeller, planned preaching tours in the interior.[17]

"Rash," cried Allen to his colleague; "rash," he wrote home to his mission board. As the dispute broadened, the American diplomats came in, on Allen's side. Foulk "cautioned" zealous men like Underwood "against indiscreet impulsiveness in propagating doctrines." Foulk's successor Rockhill, sharper, said he "considered any evangelizing work here at least premature and as endangering their position and their popularity at the palace." Minister Dinsmore, who followed Rockhill,

---

[15] Appenzeller, quoted in Paik, *Protestant Missions in Korea*, 127; *Church at Home and Abroad*, 6 (1889):116–117.

[16] Underwood, *Fifteen Years among the Top-Knots*, 14; William B. Scranton, "Methodist Episcopal Mission," *Korean Repository*, 5 (1898): 257; Gilmore, *Korea*, 302–303; Horace G. Underwood, letter in *Church at Home and Abroad*, 12 (1892):140, stating that there was "no call for timidity in Korea."

[17] Allen Diary, April 6, 1885, March 29, 1886; Allen to Ellinwood, May 7, 1885, in the Allen MSS; Swearer, "Appenzeller," *Korea Review*, 2 (1902):256.

agreed. But it did no good, only fed the flame of controversy, made more wrangling, more dissatisfaction all around. Allen became more set in his position, and the preaching men in theirs, the latter becoming sure that the diplomats were now "enemies" of Christian work.[18]

So quarrel fed quarrel. The missionaries began to criticize one another's private lives. One visiting clergyman, after living with Allen for a fortnight, accused his host of living far too well—and then demanded ten cents postage when the doctor asked him to send an article on from Japan. Allen, complaining endlessly about his colleagues, was no different. They shirked work, he claimed, they played tennis far too frequently, they did not study, and took vacations during the unhealthy season in Seoul.

By 1887 conditions had become intolerable. The slightest spark set off a loud explosion, which was attended by all sorts of scenes and harsh recriminations. Nothing seemed to help, not even mutual prayers and appeals to church superiors in the United States.[19]

Foolish petty fights, many of them, quite irrelevant to the major issues. Heron turned his language teachers against the Allens and aroused their anger. Allen offended by getting permission for the Herons to attend a palace banquet—it was humiliating, taking favors from an enemy. The Herons went, infuriating Allen by their late arrival and desire to see the king. And they, in turn, were irked once more when His Majesty gave Allen a new decoration. So it was for two solid years. There was a quarrel over the hospital horses, another over the playing of the Presbyterian organ. There were dis-

[18] Allen Diary, April 6, 1885; Allen to Ellinwood, May 7, 1885, in the Allen MSS; letter to the Secretary of State from Foulk, June 3, 1886, and from Rockhill, February 5, 1887, Dispatches, State Department Archives.
[19] Notes by Allen and letters to Ellinwood, March 14, 1886, and to Heard, December 29, 1895, in the Allen MSS; Allen Diary, March 29, August 20, October 27, 1886.

putes over language study and medicine and the articles that Mrs. Heron published in the United States.[20]

What to do? Allen knew, had known for a long time. "I am sorry such a thing has occurred," he wrote after a run-in with the Scrantons, "and would rather leave than cause such squabbles for foreigners to cavill at." And as the Heron difficulties grew, he realized that he and the other Presbyterian doctor would "have to part." Else he would go mad, he thought, for he was already "in the most wretchedly unlucky fix a decent man could be in."

A transfer was possible. After the first "surprising and provoking disagreement" with the Herons, Allen requested to be sent to Fusan. True, a year before he had regarded the southern port as "too Japanese" for mission work, but now he seemed to see possibilities. In any case, it would "remove present difficulties." And it would show up "dainty" Mrs. Heron, who had announced that Allen meant to drop his missionary work to make more money in another field.[21] But the Fusan plan fell through—the New York board told Allen to stay on in Seoul. No way out now but to leave mission work.

Desert the field? In 1883 the doctor would not have considered that. In 1884 he had rejected an invitation to start private practice in Seoul. But then the private quarrels arose, and Allen's ideas changed. If missionaries were like the jealous "unchristianlike" Heron, how could he live among them? If missionary preachers thought more of ranting than of saving lives, did he want to be a missionary? Doubts arose, doubts which were to pass in time, but which were very real in those sad days. Allen accused himself of "backsliding" and confided to his diary that he was "of opinion that mission work is a farce. I am kept busy by various outside duties, yet

[20] Allen Diary, June 28, 1885, August 20, September 5, October 10, 25, 1886; Allen to Ellinwood, October 28, 1886, in the Allen MSS.
[21] Allen Diary, June 21, September 1, 1885, January 20, September 5, 1886; Allen to Ellinwood, June 15–19, 1887, in the Allen MSS.

have an easy time. Heron has every other week wholly to himself and all but 2–3 hours of other weeks. Yet he does not study. Underwood has as much leisure. So have the Methodists. I think it is a pretty soft thing."[22]

Thus disillusioned and feeling pinched for funds, Allen began to look around in 1886 for opportunities outside the mission field. One was in private practice; he could with profit leave the Presbyterians and live on fees from the legation people and the other foreigners in Chosen. This he considered seriously and might have done it had not a better opening presented itself.

The better chance was in diplomacy. Allen's missionary troubles had never cost him the good will of Seoul's politicians and the diplomatic corps. After an Allen-Scranton fight Foulk had termed the latter a "bad man," and when the Herons collided with his friend, the chargé said that the Herons were "going to kill the prospects for mission work here." As for Allen, Foulk promised to stand by him "till the skys fall."[23]

This friendship had its points. Foulk recommended Allen for appointment as American legation secretary in Seoul, and Rockhill and Dinsmore seconded the nomination. All the envoys used the warmest words in urging Allen's case; he was *the* man, no other should be chosen.[24]

[22] Allen Diary, September 5, October 10, 1886, November 7, 1887; Allen to Ellinwood, March 22, 1899, June 7, 1900, in the Allen MSS.

[23] Note by Allen, dated November, 1886, and letter to Ellinwood, June 15, 1887, in the Allen MSS; Allen Diary, May 29, June 21, 28, December 22, 1885, October 10, 1886; Foulk to Scranton, May 13, 1885, in the Foulk MSS; Paik, *Protestant Missions in Korea,* 120, quoting a letter from Foulk to Appenzeller.

[24] Letter to the Secretary of State from Foulk, November 12, 1886, and from Rockhill, December 20, 1886, Dispatches, State Department Archives, the latter calling Allen "the most respected of our countrymen here"; Allen to the Secretary of State, March 7, 1887, requesting the Chemulpo consulate, and Allen to Ellinwood, July 11, 1887, in the Allen MSS. See, however, Dinsmore to the Secretary of State, May 9, 1887, Dispatches, State Department Archives, recommending C. C. Gray of Fayetteville, Arkansas.

But their support did not come soon enough. Washington was slow to notice Korean problems, slower still to do anything for a young man who lacked political endorsement. Before the United States had appointed any secretary of legation in Seoul, Allen had been tendered two Korean posts, and had accepted one.

The first of these two offers came from Moellendorff. In 1885 that master of intrigue offered Allen a job in Chosen's customs service. A magnificent post, paying more than twice the doctor's mission salary. But the Presbyterian had refused, and wisely. The power of Moellendorff was on the wane, his double game had caught up with him at last. The offer he made to Allen was an effort to enlist the missionary's influence in support of a dying cause, and Allen realized it.[25]

The other opening was quite another matter. In 1887 the Korean king decided to establish resident legations overseas —one for Washington and one for all the European nations. To guide the diplomats who went to the United States, His Majesty chose Allen, his old friend. "Foreign Secretary of the Legation" was to be the doctor's title and the salary was three thousand dollars, more than double what the Presbyterians paid.

In accepting, Allen told his mission board that he was doing so reluctantly, that no one could defy the king's command. He would go for a little while, he said, and then return to Presbyterian mission work. But privately he rejoiced to be free from missionary quarrels. He told his sister that he had proposed the whole thing to the king just to get out of his unpleasant situation in Seoul.[26]

There was a ray of sunshine at the end; Heron sent a friendly note saying Allen had treated him "better than he deserved." But reconciliation was to be short-lived; a Heron

[25] Allen Diary, July 19, 29, 1885; the latter entry notes Moellendorff's fall from power.
[26] Allen to Jennie Everett, June 3, 1889, Allen to Ellinwood, August 2, October 25, 1887, letter of resignation, October 26, 1887, in the Allen MSS; Allen Diary, July 11, 1887.

partisan told a "base lie" about the Allens as they passed through Japan. And, to make discouragement complete, the doctor heard of the "horrible disgrace" of a missionary friend who had become involved with a woman doctor in a Methodist station in Japan. "Much missionary scandal," grumbled Allen; he would have no more to do with all that business.[27]

[27] Allen Diary, November 29, 1887; Allen to Ellinwood, October 29, 1887, and to Min Yong Ik, July 25, 1889, in the Allen MSS, the latter containing a violent attack upon Heron: "The King ought to stop calling them to the Palace or having anything to do with them."

6

My Missionary Character

TWO years as a Korean agent in the United States proved to Allen that he preferred diplomacy to mission work. But never once did he lose touch with religious labors. He corresponded with the Presbyterian board, he tried to convert his diplomatic colleagues. At first, until fear and suspicion had died away, his efforts failed. But at Eastertime, 1889, Allen was able to persuade the whole Korean staff in Washington to attend service. This, according to the doctor, was "an event of equal importance to the establishment of a permanent legation in a Christian country."[1]

When Allen left Chosen's employment, he re-enlisted as a missionary. This time, however, he did not consider his a "lifetime appointment." Rather it was a stopgap affair. He had resigned as Korean legation secretary because he was seeking appointment as American minister in Seoul. Congressman William McKinley told him he could not hope to qualify while serving a foreign power; hence the resignation and the acceptance of a mission post pending State Department action.

After rejoining the Presbyterians, Allen was dispatched to Chosen "with a view to opening a missionary station at the

[1] Allen to Dr. Hamlin, April 20, 1889, in the Allen MSS.

85

port of Fusan, if upon visiting the place such a step should be found feasible." This was in line with the doctor's own request. While serving as a missionary he had been criticized for mixing too enthusiastically in politics. Political activity could be avoided by staying out of Seoul. He had been censured, too, for putting his hospital before mission work—for selling medicine and putting body cures before salvation of the soul. In Fusan there would be no hospital, and the doctor would have a chance to demonstrate his house-to-house technique. Finally, Allen thought that the Seoul missionaries could get along without him, and knew that he could not get along with them.[2]

Such were Allen's plans, and none could doubt that they were wisely laid. For once the doctor had considered his less attractive personal traits. In addition, he had proposed a plan that fitted in with the Presbyterian plan of decentralizing Korean mission work.[3] And Fusan was worth occupying, though Allen had denied it a few years before. The second city of the kingdom, it had as hinterland much of south Chosen. More important, it was controlled by Japan. In Fusan one could see the future of Korea. For the Japanese, there was the trade and government and a tidy residential quarter; for the Koreans, congestion, filth, and subjugation.

The Catholics had worked in southern Korea before Allen's arrival in 1890. So had the Japanese colporteurs of the American Bible Institute and an Australian Presbyterian named Davies. But despite the groundwork of these predecessors, the Allens could not get established. No house, no land, was to be had.[4]

Still fighting shy of the country's capital, Fannie and her husband left inhospitable Fusan for Chemulpo. There, in

[2] Allen to Ellinwood, September 24, 1889, in the Allen MSS.
[3] Paik, *Protestant Missions in Korea*, 167–168.
[4] Allen to Ellinwood, January 11, 1892, in the Allen MSS. On Fusan as a mission station, see Paik, *Protestant Missions in Korea*, 195–196, and Brown, "Reading Journey through Korea," *Chautauquan*, 41 (1905):494–497.

that dreary port, they settled down. The doctor opened a dispensary and started making calls. Results were good, and Allen told the board that no "time or money was wasted." Indeed, he was sure that he was doing "more and better work . . . in the medical line" than Heron up in Seoul.[5]

But Chemulpo was not Fusan. Evangelical endeavor was hampered by the shifting character of the population. And the port was too near Seoul. Twenty-six miles was not a great enough distance to prevent renewal of the old political entanglements and the old missionary quarrels. Allen found himself involved in the capital's political intrigues, and in missionary matters he felt "constantly subject to Heron's insults."[6]

Then, to touch the whole thing off, the doctor was ordered to Seoul. Heron had fallen ill, and the royal hospital was without a guardian. One could of course be sent from the United States, but that would take much time. It was simpler for the board to transfer Allen. He was near at hand, he had experience in running the hospital; and Chemulpo, as a temporary station, could be abandoned easily.

Gloom filled Allen's heart as he prepared to obey the board's command. Seoul was quite all right if one were an adviser or a diplomat. But now he must be a missionary and work with erstwhile foes.

Trouble arose the moment Allen reached Seoul. Heron, ill to death, had not a gracious word to say. Others in the Presbyterian colony showed the "old Heron spirit right through." They refused to let the Allens live in a Presbyterian school building, though it was vacation time. They

[5] Allen to Ellinwood, August 13, 1890, in the Allen MSS. Paik, in his *Protestant Missions in Korea,* 196–197, comments on the missionary situation in Chemulpo. Brown's "Reading Journey through Korea," *Chautauquan,* 41 (1905):497–498, gives a typical picture of the town. Brandt's *Dreiunddreissig Jahre in Ost-Asien,* 3:335, and Hamilton's *Korea,* 16–18, are more favorable.

[6] Allen to Ellinwood, August 13, 1890, in the Allen MSS; Dinsmore to the Secretary of State, March 24, 1890, Dispatches, State Department Archives, enclosing clipping from the *Hong Kong Telegraph.*

"insulted" Fannie and the doctor, treated the latter as "one to be avoided totally." Allen stated that he had come unwillingly and produced his orders from the board; but his colleagues were suspicious and appeared to believe that he had come to run the Presbyterian show.

The capital's religious colony had grown in the years since 1887. New missions had been founded by the Anglicans and the Australian Presbyterians; and the Baptists, southern Presbyterians, and southern Methodists were soon to come. In the meantime the older groups had grown; Allen's northern Presbyterians had seven workers on the ground. Still more impressive were the figures of conversion. When Allen departed for America, there had been just one native Protestant in all Korea. When he returned to Seoul, there were nearly a hundred and fifty, and the number was increasing rapidly. There was reason to believe that the years of spadework were soon to yield a fine Christian harvest.

A movement toward union also offered ground for encouragement. As the Protestant missions multiplied, there was bound to be conflict and duplication. Forward-looking missionary leaders sought to end this by cooperation; and in 1890 a United Council of American and Victorian Presbyterian Churches was formed. Allen was a charter member of this council, Heron president, the Australian Davies secretary. Out of it grew a larger Presbyterian council in 1893 and eventually the union movement which resulted in a real division of territory in 1907.[7]

Despite these pleasant features there still were many fights. One raged between the Protestants and Catholics. After years of underground endeavor, the Catholics had cast off disguise in 1887 and walked the streets in their Jesuit garb. They did so under cover of Korea's treaty with the French Republic,

[7] Paik, *Protestant Missions in Korea*, especially pp. 188–193; Rhodes, *Korea Mission, Presbyterian Church*, 21–24. Compare report of Dinsmore to Assistant Secretary of State, January 1, 1888 (34 Americans) with Heard to the Assistant Secretary of State, December 31, 1892 (78 Americans), Consular Dispatches, State Department Archives.

a pact which, while it contained no toleration clause, provided that "Frenchmen resorting to Corea for the purpose of studying the written or spoken language, sciences, laws or arts" should "always receive aid and assistance" from the Seoul government. That was enough to bring the Catholic church of Korea "little by little from its tomb"[8] and to encourage the French fathers to lay plans for the erection of a "school building" on land they owned on South Mountain in Seoul.

Here was the seat of further trouble. The building would overlook a native tablet house and stand out above the palace. Vainly did the king suggest a sale or trade of land. Then, finding the monks unwilling to yield their site, His Majesty issued a sharp decree to "forbid severely" the teaching of Christianity in the capital.

This edict of 1888 worked in with the anti-foreign riots organized by Yuan Shih Kai. Both Catholics and Protestants were affected by the trend. Native Christians were "squeezed" and persecuted more than ever. Korean teachers were stoned, servants of the missionaries found themselves in trouble, and social pressure was brought to bear on all who sent their children to the mission schools. Seeing how things stood, Minister Dinsmore had called itinerating Americans back to Seoul and had told the missionaries that they would be expected to desist from proselyting "by any method whatever not sanctioned by the authorities of the Government." Worse still, America reacted in similar fashion. Enlistments for Korea dropped, and contributions earmarked for the kingdom likewise fell.[9] Alarmed and angered, the American colony blamed the affair on Catholic zeal, Catholic arrogance, Catholic treachery. "The Romanists," wrote one of

[8] "Father Coste," *Korean Repository,* 3 (1896):151; Launay, *La Corée et les missionaires français,* 342–344.

[9] Dinsmore to the Secretary of State, April 28, 1888, April 1, July 3, 1889, Dispatches, State Department Archives; Paik, *Protestant Missions in Korea,* especially p. 146; Rhodes, *Korea Mission, Presbyterian Church,* 22.

the Methodists later, "had committed acts which brought all foreigners into disfavor."[10]

Anti-Catholic though he was, Allen did not agree with this interpretation. If there was blame, he said, the Protestants should take their share. "It is unfair," he had written from Washington, "to place the whole blame upon the Jesuits. They have lived in Korea in the guise of mourners, I have tended them in sickness and know that they live as do the humble natives. They have worked long and patiently with none of the comforts which rob mission work of its trials." The Protestants, by contrast, had "voluntarily, unnecessarily and willfully blocked their [own] progress by rashness." Some might have acted wisely; others were the "biggest fools that ever attempted to teach men wisdom." While the Catholics had proceeded cautiously, these Protestants had plunged into the interior, in open defiance of the American legation and the Korean foreign office. And, far from pioneering in their building venture, the French monks had merely followed a Methodist precedent. Appenzeller had built a "schoolhouse," though Chargé Rockhill had advised against it.[11]

Holding such views, Allen was bound to be unpopular in Seoul. It was the same old quarrel. Most missionaries wanted action, quick results, and mass conversions. They sneered at Allen's contention that evangelizing should be the final step in the process. They were impatient with his plan to start by teaching American civilization and then to show that Christianity supplied the base for Western culture. And they continued to question his policy of close cooperation with the king. He saw in Chosen a unique opportunity "to work from the top down rather than from the bottom up." They preferred the latter method and after Allen had left the

[10] Scranton, "Woman's Work in Korea," *Korean Repository,* 3 (1896):6.

[11] Letters from Allen to Josiah Strong, general secretary of the Evangelical Alliance, August 30, 1888, in reply to Strong's appeal for intervention; to Ellinwood, August 30, 1888; to Dr. Gillespie, August 20, 1888; to Dinsmore, September 21, 1888, and notes by Allen. All these documents are in the Allen MSS.

colony in 1888 had expressed their view in a formal resolution: "It is better to aim at the conversion of the working classes than at the higher classes."[12]

Allen did have some slight support. Some of the less important missionaries backed him up. More surprisingly, his old opponent Heron appears to have swung over to the slow-but-sure philosophy. The riots of 1888 had made a great impression on the Herons, had left them quite conservative.[13] This, though, was little comfort to the Allens, for personal animosity still estranged the Presbyterian physicians.

If anything, the hatred had grown with time. While in America Allen had become convinced that the Herons were harming his chances of placing a Korean loan. He based this view on the appearance of two wild yarns in the American press. One depicted Mrs. Heron's death as a Christian martyr. The other, written by the lady herself, maintained that the king of Chosen had three hundred concubines. Neither story was likely to convince Wall Street that Korea had a sense of national responsibility, and Allen, enraged, wrote Min Yong Ik that the Herons should be kept out of the palace. Perhaps the Herons heard of this suggestion; in any case, they doubled their attacks on Allen.

Heron's death did not improve the situation. Even as he died the sick man turned down Allen's offer of medical assistance. Mrs. Heron, half hysterical, poured out her grief in bitter words against her husband's foe. Allen, responding, told his mission superiors that Heron's death seemed a "special reward for past conduct" and that Seoul's "disgraceful wrangle" would continue until the widow Heron was removed from the scene.[14]

In August, 1890, came a chance to leave this all behind—

[12] Allen to Strong, August 30, 1888, in the Allen MSS; Paik, *Protestant Missions in Korea,* 191, quoting resolution adopted by the Council of Missions Holding the Presbyterian Form of Government.

[13] Gifford, "Heron," *Korean Repository,* 4 (1897):443; Gilmore, *Korea,* 311.

[14] Allen to Ellinwood, August 13, 1890, in the Allen MSS.

the long hoped for appointment as American secretary of legation. Allen accepted with alacrity. No doubt he would have done the same in almost any circumstances; but the Heron matter made him fairly snatch the job. To Underwood he explained that he was withdrawing from the Seoul mission colony "in the interest of peace and harmony." Writing to the board, he used much plainer words. "I have made up my mind," he said, "that I cannot work with the Presbyterian mission of Seoul, and I send my resignation . . . I have been insulted by these new people with Mrs. Heron to guide them. It will continue and I don't propose to fritter away my time in any such tom foolery . . . Such a spirit is not missionary and I don't care to be connected with such people . . . I would starve rather than place myself under these people."[15]

So for the second time the Allens left the mission field, and left it in a rage. Time never wiped out the recollection of the 1890 quarrels. So vivid did they remain, indeed, that the doctor came to feel that they and not the diplomatic opportunity had caused him to leave his mission post. "Jealousy of certain missionaries," he wrote a generation later, "so hampered me that I accepted unasked appointment as Secretary US Legation." The boards, he said, sent out "too many untrained, ungentlemanly, crack brained fanatics . . . men who could not earn their salt at home."[16]

The disputes lived on; but so did other aspects of the missionary work. Even as he talked of the shortcomings of

[15] Allen to Ellinwood, August 13, 1890, and to Underwood, about the same date, in the Allen MSS; Heard to the Secretary of State, January 14, 1890, January 1, 1892, Dispatches, State Department Archives. The first Heard letter refers to a later quarrel involving Mrs. Heron, the second calls attention to the fact that the king desired Allen's appointment as legation secretary. For appointments and efforts to increase Allen's salary, see Assistant Secretary of State Adee to Heard, July 11, 1890, Assistant Secretary Wharton to Allen, July 25, 1890, Secretary Blaine to Heard, September 29, October 11, 14, 21, 22, 1890, Secretary Olney to Sill, May 5, 1896, Instructions, State Department Archives.

[16] Note by Allen and letters to William Dulles, October 10, 1889, and to Frank Carpenter, August 23, 1900, in the Allen MSS.

some proselyters, Allen admitted that some of the best persons he had ever met were missionaries. Later he was to echo the words of John M. B. Sill, one of Cleveland's ministers in Seoul: "The missionaries here are a strong, level-headed, efficient body of men. They are a remarkable lot. I have had the greatest pleasure in associating with them. Some people say missionaries are a troublesome lot, but I have never met men more sensible, more easy to get along with. I think highly of them." On another occasion he remarked, "I am glad I am out of it tho I can't lose my interest."[17]

It was natural that Allen should become a missionary diplomat. For five years he had served the cause as missionary doctor. Now he was to serve it for seven as American legation secretary and for eight as full-fledged minister from the United States. As he had said to a Presbyterian board member in 1889, "whether in your mission or that of the United States I will maintain my missionary character and as heretofore we will work in full sympathy."[18]

In the legation years it was sometimes difficult to separate the diplomat and the missionary. For months after he entered the legation Allen ran the Presbyterian hospital. At first he did so from day to day, expecting the Presbyterians to send out a new physician soon. But when weeks passed without relief, he still held on. For if he left, the Christian cause might be compromised. The Japanese desired the hospital, which could be used to build up other forms of influence. They might have won it, too, had there been no acting head. They had a physician on the ground, one good enough to get the foreign practice and win some influence at the court.[19]

More likely, Allen's withdrawal would have helped an-

[17] Allen to Ellinwood, July 16, 31, 1892, in the Allen MSS; Rhodes, *Korea Mission, Presbyterian Church,* 470.

[18] Allen to William Dulles, October 10, 1889, in the Allen MSS.

[19] Allen to Ellinwood, January 5, 1891, and to the Presbyterian Mission of Seoul, December 30, 1890, in the Allen MSS. Rhodes's *Korea Mission, Presbyterian Church,* contains a good treatment of the rela-

other Christian sect. The Catholics were ready to "give everything to possess" the hospital. The Anglicans, now "making a great spread," were soon to be "straining every nerve" in the same direction. A slip by the Presbyterians might have put them in.[20]

Relieved at last (but only after training a successor), Allen dropped his function as physician. He continued as a contact man, representing the hospital in its negotiations with the Korean government. And it was well that he did so, for his successors needed aid.

Dr. Charles C. Vinton ran into trouble the moment he arrived. Pious and enthusiastic, he sided with the missionaries who wanted the hospital transformed into a religious institution. Meeting with resistance on this issue, finding that the government would not allow a chapel, Vinton closed the hospital in protest.

This, as Allen said, was a "most unfortunate occurrence." Vinton was forcing an issue that could not possibly be decided in favor of the mission colony. And in doing so he was taking the risk of losing the hospital entirely. The Anglicans were quick to seize the opportunity; they asked that the institution be transferred to their control. And since the king was most disturbed, this might have happened had not Allen been in town.

As it was, the affair was straightened out. Approached by Vinton, Allen told the Presbyterian that he had been given "bad advice." "The Board," he added, "cannot possibly sustain you in this action." Vinton yielded, and when Minister Augustine Heard had pulled some foreign office wires, the hospital resumed its business. But, as Allen said, it had been saved "entirely by the action of the American Legation, against the machinations of the Presbyterian mission."[21]

tionship between the missionaries in Korea and the Presbyterian Board of Foreign Missions.

[20] Allen to Ellinwood, July 23, 1891, in the Allen MSS.

[21] Allen to Ellinwood, July 3, 31, 1891, in the Allen MSS; Heard to the Secretary of State, August 31, September 12, 1892, Dispatches, State

Vinton's successor, Dr. O. R. Avison, also clashed with the Koreans. This time the Presbyterians had a better case. Grafting native politicians were feasting on the hospital appropriations, living in the institution, earning salaries without working, and diverting funds earmarked for useful purposes. Distressed, Avison threatened to resign. And naturally he called in Horace Allen. The legation secretary quickly brought his "personal influence" to bear and won guarantees that theoretically gave Avison the "absolute direction" of the institution. So things remained until 1896, when the Presbyterians won final and complete control by assuming full financial responsibility.[22]

Allen was equally helpful in other matters. But for his "indefatigable efforts" dead missionaries (including the hated Heron) would have lacked a decent burial place. As Heron's health failed, the Protestants filed a request for a cemetery site. Bound by treaty to supply one, Chosen offered a low sandy stretch across the river from Seoul. When this was rejected as unsuitable, the government became defiant. It refused to let the missionaries use Heron's back yard or another piece of mission property. It even halted Heron's funeral and led the missionaries to wonder if they could ever put their dead physician underground. But Allen found a way, secured a perfect site—five miles out of town, on a bluff that overlooked the river Han. In similar fashion he helped the Presbyterians buy the Fusan site for missionary quarters that he had failed to get in 1890.[23]

Assisting at court, Allen also tried to work through the Presbyterian board. By using this approach he hoped to

Department Archives. Paik's *Protestant Missions in Korea*, 228, suggests an additional motive for Vinton's action, the dishonesty of Korean officials.

[22] Paik, *Protestant Missions in Korea*, 229, quoting Presbyterian document; President of the Korean Foreign Office to Sill, May 22, September 26, 1894, Seoul Legation Files, State Department Archives.

[23] Underwood, *Fifteen Years among the Top-Knots*, 99–101; letter to the Secretary of State from Foote, November 27, 1883, and from Heard, July 28, 1890 (in Allen's handwriting), Dispatches, State Department

improve the quality of missionaries sent to Chosen. Thus in 1892 he told his former superiors that the Presbyterian mission in Seoul was in a "most deplorable and ridiculous" condition. Those who manned the outposts were all right, but the capital crowd was a "queer lot." They were unbusinesslike, spent their money foolishly. They were lazy and devoted too much time to tennis playing. They went vacationing to Chefoo in the summer, leaving a "poor, hysterical . . . less than useless" female in command. They closed the hospital in the "season of greatest usefulness," and left the orphanage in charge of natives even after one had stolen the doors and windows.[24]

Simultaneously the doctor argued against too great aggressiveness. Evangelizing was well under way by now, and Underwood was "roaring" that there was "no call for timidity in Korea." Allen disagreed. He thought the missionaries should appreciate their blessings, not press for more. They should be content with native houses and live unostentatiously. As it was, their style of living was improper and annoyed the diplomats "by putting some of them to shame"; Underwood, who had outside means, was called the "millionaire missionary." Vinton was not content with a house as good as the American legation and better than the establishments of France and Germany. A missionary wife could write that "compared with the Vanderbilts we live in a humble, not to say mean, way. Compared with the bulk of our constituents at home we live in, to say the least, the greatest ease and comfort. Compared with the people who, we have come to serve, we live like princes and millionaires."[25]

Archives; Allen to the Korean Minister of Foreign Affairs, February 21, 1899, Seoul Legation Files, State Department Archives; *Korea Review,* 5 (1905):32; Brown, "Reading Journey through Korea," *Chautauquan,* 41 (1905):494–496.

[24] Allen to Ellinwood, July 16, 1892, January 5, 1893, July 10, 1898, January 5, 1899, in the Allen MSS.

[25] Mrs. William Baird, "The Relation of the Wives of Missionaries to Mission Work," *Korean Repository,* 2 (1895):418; Allen to Ellinwood, October 8, 1888, January 5, 1893, January 5, 1899, in the Allen MSS;

Some of that was very well, to attract converts; but perhaps it had been carried rather far.

Show called attention to the missionaries, who after all were still not tolerated legally. And in addition there was open proselyting and Bible-selling, church-building, and loud psalm-singing. The American legation secretary could not quite approve, and looked for a reaction. "These new people pooh pooh at . . . the idea of any necessity for protection," he wrote to the Presbyterians in New York. "They have not seen an émeute and think it cannot come. I have seen it and this very day I am in receipt of news reliably from the Palace, that if I told to Vinton he would be in Chemulpo with his family in 24 hours for fear. I don't expect the matter to culminate at once, but tis only a matter of time. And when it comes they will know I am not the old foggy they tho't me . . . in advocating their remaining within protecting distance of the legation.[26]

All this was of course done in private. Outwardly Allen did not indulge in criticism of the missionaries but appeared their perfect champion. He seemed to aid the cause at every turn, to speak with the voice of all the missionaries.

To make his mission moves effective, the doctor had to have the aid of his superiors at the legation. That he won with little trouble. For that matter, he dominated the legation during his seven years as secretary.[27] Augustine Heard, minister when Allen was appointed, gladly yielded to his vigorous

Underwood, *Underwood of Korea*, 217; *Church at Home and Abroad*, 12 (1892):140.

[26] Allen to Ellinwood, January 5, 1893, in the Allen MSS. Less than two months later, warnings were served on all Christians in Korea, probably by agents of the Tong Hak. Launay, *La Corée et les missionaires français*, 347–355, with account of the martyrdom of Père Jozeau.

[27] Allen to J. Sloat Fassett, September 15, 1896, in the Allen MSS. See Heard's high estimate of Allen in his letter to the Secretary of State, March 31, 1893, Dispatches, State Department Archives. Compare with the relations between Dinsmore and his secretary, Charles Chaillé-Long, revealed in letters to the Secretary of State from Chaillé-Long, July 31, August 2, 1888, and from Dinsmore, August 31, 1888, Dispatches, State Department Archives.

assistant. An estimable and intelligent veteran of the China trade, Heard had hit the downward trail before he reached Seoul. His appointment was a sop to Massachusetts rather than a recognition of ability, and the old man was quick to recognize that Allen knew more about Seoul than he would ever learn.

John M. B. Sill, the school superintendent who succeeded Heard in 1893, was even more inclined to lean on Allen. He too was a pious, aging individual who knew that he was deficient in a knowledge of Chosen. He had secured his appointment because a friend, Don Dickinson, had wanted to give the old man a rest and an opportunity to study the "flora and fauna of Korea." Having come for such purposes, he was hardly likely to oppose the lively and positive legation secretary in Seoul. Nor did he. Instead he echoed his subordinate, especially on religious matters. ("I did this work," said Allen, "but as it had to have the minister's sanction, naturally he got the credit."[28])

Similar support came in from Washington. The State Department championed the missionaries willingly, eagerly. Alvey A. Adee, the department's key career man, insisted that Heard use the most-favored-nation clause to claim for American missionaries every gain the French obtained for Catholics.[29] Heard, Sill, and Allen were praised whenever they helped the Christian cause. More than that; the powers at home occasionally outran their Seoul agents in pro-missionary zeal. Published volumes of the State Department reveal editing along this line. Rockhill's reference to "a restless dispo-

[28] Resolutions of the Methodist church in Korea, January 19, 1895, Presbyterian resolution of 1895, Allen to James R. Morse, November 20, 1896, in the Allen MSS; John A. Cockerill, article in the *New York Herald*, December 1, 1895; *Korean Repository*, 2 (1895):80; 4 (1897): 315. Chaillé-Long, *My Life*, 337, mentions a motive similar to that of Sill.

[29] Noble, Korea and Her Relations with the United States (manuscript dissertation), has an excellent discussion of this point. See also Allen T. Price, "American Missions and American Diplomacy in China, 1830–1900," in *Summary of Theses, Harvard University*, 1934, pp. 174–177.

sition on the part of the missionaries in Corea to exceed the bounds of prudence in the prosecution of evangelical work" became merely "the efforts on the part of the Missionaries in Corea in the prosecution of evangelical work." The sense of a Dinsmore dispatch was changed entirely by the elimination of the second half of the sentence, "my admonitions have been very kindly and respectfully received by [these] very worthy people, but it appears that under a conception of authority 'higher than mans' their zeal gets beyond restraint." Also stricken out were other phrases and passages that might have given offense to friends of evangelical endeavor. "There is a very strong feeling against Christian work in Korea," ran one such passage, "and which will be intensified by aggressiveness ... I have discouraged the building of a church and counselled against it ... [Premature mission efforts involve] a liability of engendering prejudice against Americans, and the more serious political results."[30]

But in Korea anti-missionary sentiment was becoming increasingly apparent. Seoul diplomats saw it occasionally among the foreign merchants; Allen was to have some trouble with them later on. Opposition was also manifest among the naval officers who visited Chosen. Disliking Korea, they did not care to be called upon to protect soul-savers who were working in the kingdom. Captain Theodore F. Jewell, who had been called in by Dinsmore during the riots of 1888, said repeatedly that it was "a damned shame to have to send a man of war here to protect half a dozen missionaries," and that if he were king of Korea he would "cut off the head of every damned missionary in the country." It is only fair to add that Jewell was not entirely representative. The American minister described him as being in his cups when in

---

[30] Letter to the Secretary of State from Rockhill, February 5, 1885, and from Dinsmore, April 21, 1888, Dispatches, State Department Archives; *Foreign Relations*, 1887, p. 258; 1888, pp. 444–445. See, however, Secretary of State Bayard to Dinsmore, June 15, 1888, opposing the occupation of the interior, and Acting Secretary Wharton to Heard, February 24, 1893, Instructions, State Department Archives.

Seoul, as one "sadly lacking in the qualities which make up a gentleman."[31]

The developments of the eighteen nineties modified the pro-missionary viewpoint of the State Department. War broke out in Chosen, involving China and Japan. Quick to take a neutral stand, the United States desired its nationals to do the same. But the missionaries in Korea would not follow Washington. They sympathized with the people whom they served and made no secret of it. First they supported the Koreans against the Chinese; then, when Japan won the war, they centered their attacks on the Japanese. In acting thus they brought upon themselves the censure of their State Department.

The reprimands were sharp and to the point, arousing Allen to the defense of the Christian workers. He doubted whether the charges were justified by the facts. Sill said the same, at tedious length. He found the Protestants unjustly exposed to a "red-hot fire of malignant criticism." Far from being meddlers, most of the missionaries were "exceptionally discreet and single-minded in their devotion to their legitimate work."[32]

But this was special pleading. The missionaries were obviously involved in politics. Allen's whole career had shown the trend in Seoul. War and its aftermath in 1894–96 had "unquestionably drawn [many] into the vortex of politics." In 1895 missionaries accused Japan of assassinating the

[31] Dinsmore to Foulk, July 31, 1887, in the Foulk MSS, indicating that Jewell also quarreled with American business men in the Orient. See also Jewell to Dinsmore, June 20, 1888, Seoul Legation Files, State Department Archives. Brown's *Mastery of the Far East*, 322, also mentions anti-missionary views of naval officers; but relations were generally good and Allen, in his address to the Naval War College, in the Allen MSS, says that he received important advice and aid from Admiral John Lee Davis. See R. Chandler to Dinsmore, July 7, 1888, indicating general fear that small detachments might be cut off.

[32] Allen to Ellinwood, October 15, 1897, in the Allen MSS; letter to the Secretary of State from Allen, October 1, 1897, and from Sill, July 21, 1897, Dispatches, State Department Archives; Hulbert, *History of Korea*, 2:326.

Korean queen. Simultaneously they offended by giving aid and comfort to the king and granting asylum to the foes of the Japanese. At least one anti-Japanese revolt was hatched in Underwood's establishment, the insurrection of November, 1895. It was easy to understand; the missionaries had considered it "common mercy . . . not . . . politics," to admit being outraged by the more brutal acts of the victorious Japanese.[33] But, understandable or not, their stand was not one of neutrality.

Anxious to clear up the situation, the State Department told Sill to calm the missionaries down. If they desired protection from the legation, they should "strictly confine themselves to the missionary work, whether it be teaching in schools, preaching the gospel, or attending to the sick." Anti-Japanese opinion should not be announced, and Sill should "stop, if possible, the habit which has steadily increased since the arrival of American citizens in Korea, of irresponsible persons advising and attempting to control, through irregular channels, the Government of that country."

These words clearly condemned the twelve-year record of Sill's legation secretary. But neither Sill nor Allen took them seriously. Sill did not even feel obliged to mention his instructions to the mission colony. They were "permissive," he thought, "or at most . . . hortative, and not . . . mandatory." Disabused by the Department, the old man still resisted. A circular of warning, he maintained, would give a false impression of the Department's views. Eventually he did advise the missionaries to be cautious (circular of May, 1897), but only after a sharp and specific command from Washington.[34]

[33] *Korean Repository*, 3 (1896):454, quoting the *Japan Daily Mail:* "there exists in the Korean capital a social coterie of which the leading members are the Russian Representative, certain American missionaries, the Secretary of the United States Legation, the editor of the INDEPENDENT and their wives"; Underwood, *Fifteen Years among the Top-Knots*, 154–160; Allen to the Secretary of State, November 4, 1896, Dispatches, State Department Archives; Paik, *Protestant Missions in Korea*, 234, note.

[34] Sill to the Secretary of State, February 23, May 15, 1897, Dispatches,

The warning naturally affected the position of the Protestants. It lessened their importance at the Seoul court; it was ammunition for Japanese and other snipers at missionary activities. Actually, however, little had been lost. So long as Allen stayed in Seoul, the missionaries had a champion who could present their case at court.

Moreover, the State Department had not deserted the religious workers. Allen blamed the circular of 1897 on the "unfortunate utterances" in the press of "one silly woman," Mrs. Underwood (the former Lillias Horton). Others more correctly saw the warning as an American effort to avoid controversies with Russia and Japan.[35] Obviously the United States still favored the spreading of the Word in Chosen. That was shown by Horace Allen's progress. Two months after issuance of the circular, the doctor was promoted to the ministerial post. He had been a missionary, he was known to be in contact with the Korean colony of proselyters, his appointment was urged by religious leaders. No country that desired to check the mission movement would have selected Horace Allen as its representative.

State Department Archives; Secretary of State Olney to Sill, January 11, 1896, Secretary Sherman to Sill, March 30, 1897, Instruction, State Department Archives, the circular of May 11, 1897, being enclosed with Sill's dispatch of May 15; Allen to Jennie Everett, February 15, 1897, in the Allen MSS.

[35] Allen to the Secretary of State, October 1, 1897, Dispatches, State Department Archives; Allen to Ellinwood, October 15, 1897, and to Morse, October 15, 1897, in the Allen MSS.

7

Christian Diplomat

"OUR missionary work in the coming decades," wrote Frank F. Ellinwood of the Presbyterian Board of Foreign Missions, "whether we will or not, and whether for good or bad, will be more and more closely related to the influence of diplomacy and commerce."[1]

These words, penned in 1905, apply as well to the eight preceding years, when Horace Allen represented the United States as minister in Seoul. The strands of trade were woven well into the rope of Protestant evangelism. And missionary matters far outnumbered all the others at the American legation. Allen's first dispatch as minister discussed the problems of the proselyters, as did his last before retirement.

As Allen saw it, the envoy's religious task was twofold. The missionaries must be protected from foes of every kind. They also needed counsel that would aid them in keeping free from harm. If either aspect had been neglected, the Christian cause might have bogged down in Chosen. Since both were handled skilfully, Korea lived up to her promise and became the "banner mission field of all the world."

From the standpoint of accomplishment, the protective func-

[1] Paik, *Protestant Missions in Korea*, 258, quoting a Presbyterian report.

tion may have been the more important; but most of Allen's time went to advising. In countless different ways he told the missionaries what to do. He took up political and economic matters and problems of psychology. He communicated with the proselyters directly and by circular. He reached them through the Presbyterian board, to which he still reported. Using the State Department as an intermediary, he forwarded his judgments to all the mission bodies.

One of his more unpleasant jobs was checking the extremists. Every mission colony has some of these, men whose lack of judgment imperils the whole cause. French Minister Frandin, guarding the Catholic missionaries in Korea, moaned that many of his charges "were carried away by zeal for their cause." So it was with the Americans. "Among a set of missionaries of particularly high class," Allen put it, "the Korean mission has a few men who could well be spared."[2]

Among these was Dr. Vinton, whose ill advised closing of the hospital had caused much trouble during Allen's first days as legation secretary. Vinton continued to be difficult, objecting to his quarters and otherwise arousing Allen's ire. Finally, in the fall of 1897, there came a crisis. Vinton found some coolies working on the Sabbath, building a dividing wall between his residence and the Russian legation grounds. Shocked to see the Lord's day thus profaned, the enthusiastic young physician attacked the workers and drove them into full retreat. Then he snatched up all their abandoned tools and locked them up.

In many sections of the globe this matter could have been adjusted quickly. In Seoul it created international complications. The confiscated tools were Russian-owned, the routed coolies were employees of the Tsarist minister. Russia was strong in Seoul; after 1895 she was Japan's leading rival

[2] Letter to the Secretary of State from Heard, February 10, 1893, and from Allen, January 5, 1901, Dispatches, State Department Archives. Sands, *Undiplomatic Memories*, 94: "one narrow theologian, crabbed or ignorant bigot or tactless zealot can do more damage than a dozen saints can overcome in a lifetime."

there. Alexis Speyer, the Russian representative, was anti-American, anti-missionary, and ever anxious to maintain Romanoff prestige and honor.

Only by quick action did Allen avoid a full-fledged fight. Hearing of what had happened, he sent a note to Vinton: "Please give up the Russian articles & come to see me."

The missionary soon reported.

"Have you given up the things?" asked Allen.

"No," was Vinton's answer, "& I won't so long as they persist in working on Sunday."

"Then," said Allen sharply, "I can do nothing for you & must compel you to give them up as you have no right to seize & lock up their property."

Faced with that ultimatum, Vinton yielded. The tools were placed near the point of seizure, and the missionary agreed to interfere no more if Speyer's coolies stayed off mission property.[3]

Irascible as Vinton was, he was tame in contrast with Frank S. Moore, Presbyterian agent. Moore proved absolutely unmanageable. He wrote "insolent" letters to the Korean king, calling upon His Majesty to repent of his sins. Terming himself a missionary from the Almighty, he demanded a royal audience and tried to force his way into the palace. And when a guest in a native temple, he set to smashing the Buddhist idols.

Such a person is likely to create an anti-Christian reaction in any Oriental land at any time. And this was 1900, the Boxer year. The Tong Hak might rise again in Chosen, with a program of opposition to Christianity. Allen felt that "the elements for exciting such opposition" were present in Chosen even then, and so he could not blame the British representative for favoring "drastic punishment" for Moore. He himself threatened to imprison the impulsive missionary in the legation jail. He also took the matter up with the State

[3] Allen Diary, September 26, 1897; Allen to Ellinwood, October 15, 1897, in the Allen MSS.

Department and the Presbyterian board, and Moore was finally calmed down.[4]

Better balanced than Moore, but equally troublesome, were the trading missionaries. Oriental trade, of course, is closely tied to proselyting. The missionaries themselves provide a market for Western goods, and by word and example they stimulate the natives' desire for these products. To that extent they are the trader's friends, and merchants have good reason to bless and subsidize the proselyting men. But some of the missionaries Allen knew were not content to open up new markets; they also wanted to supply them. A Won-san missionary developed a commercial orchard; one in Seoul took paying guests, to the "manifest loss" of the Station House. Others accepted agencies for American exporters, thereby cutting into the profits of Townsend and Company, the American trading firm. Vinton brought in a hundred sewing machines. Underwood imported kerosene, coal, and agricultural implements. And others followed suit.[5]

Defending their actions, the trading missionaries insisted that they were doing a service to humanity. Having little overhead, they could sell their products cheap. Indeed, they often disposed of their stock at cost, getting satisfaction in the knowledge that Koreans were obtaining the benefits of Western civilization. Allen admitted that they were, said the missionaries were responsible for introducing better farm equipment, with a "possible creation of a demand."[6]

[4] Allen to his mother, November 2, 1900, in the Allen MSS; Allen to the Secretary of State, September 15, 1900, January 5, 1901, Dispatches, State Department Archives; Allen, *Things Korean*, 173–174.

[5] Allen to Ellinwood, January 5, 1899, in the Allen MSS; Bishop, *Korea*, 1:viii–x, containing Walter C. Hillier's description of missionaries' "utility as explorers and pioneers of commerce"; Hamilton, *Korea*, 263–265; "Are Missionaries Worthy of Diplomatic Protection?" *Foreign Missionary*, 42 (1883):190: "no average class of citizens is more likely to promote the development of international commerce than those who go forth to preach the Gospel, and thus to enlighten and elevate the masses of the people."

[6] Allen to Ellinwood, June 7, 1900, in the Allen MSS; *Commercial Relations of the United States*, 1900, 1:1072.

But, granting this, the minister still had not solved the problem. As envoy he represented the merchants as well as the missionaries. And it was obvious that "the trading propensities of our missionaries . . . annoys our merchants exceedin[g]ly." Walter D. Townsend, in fact, was so irked that he prevailed upon his mother to cease contributing to mission bodies. Nor could Allen blame him; the missionaries were skimming off the cream and leaving little profit-bearing trade for others.

Hoping to straighten matters out, Allen carried the matter to the missionaries themselves. He met with no success and "broke" with Underwood on the question. Failing there, he resorted to public protest, airing the question in public reports. Apparently some missionaries yielded after that. But never all; Allen was plagued with the problem as long as he remained in Chosen.[7]

Ordinarily the trading quarrel was limited to citizens of the United States, but occasionally the field was broadened. This happened in 1904, when the British journalist Angus Hamilton attacked the commercial practices of American missionaries.[8] And it had happened the year before when the Yalu River crisis broke.

On that occasion Russia, Japan, Korea were all involved. Russians were moving into the Yalu area, in northwest Chosen. Korea, in her perplexed and feeble way, was attempting to halt the advance; and Japan looked on with quite apparent disapproval. It was not a pleasant situation, and the neutral United States would have done well had she

[7] Allen to Ellinwood, January 5, 1899, in the Allen MSS; Allen to the Assistant Secretary of State, August 27, 1898, Consular Dispatches, State Department Archives ("the better class of missionaries will frown upon and discountenance the custom"); Sands, *Undiplomatic Memories,* 94; Seoul *Independent,* August 16, 20, 23, 27, 1898, including answer of Underwood ("Christian work is not allowed to suffer by the giving of time to secular business"); *Korean Repository,* 5 (1898):305–308, labeling the practice of taking agencies "very reprehensible"; *Commercial Relations of the United States,* 1900, 1:1072.

[8] Hamilton, *Korea,* especially pp. 261–265.

stayed out. But in she went, partly because of the commercial operations of two Christian teachers.

Graham Lee and Samuel A. Moffett were the men. Both were members of Allen's old mission; and both were interested in Yalu timber. Using whatever influence they had, they obtained a contract to bring out lumber from that region. Their agents had soon cut almost three thousand trees. Then trouble started. Korea's authorities demanded payment of taxes which Lee insisted were illegal. And the Russians, moving in, had a conflicting claim to the forest products of the area.

Naturally the missionaries turned to Allen. But the doctor was unreceptive. He would support the proselyting cause, he would back concessionaires; but he was not disposed to defend what looked like "a quiet gospel speculation." Besides, international complications were involved; and the "illegal" tax was only half the customary charge.[9]

Allen was equally unsympathetic with missionaries who mixed in political affairs. That is, he found it best to repudiate the precedents that he had established years before. As a missionary he had wallowed in court intrigue; as American minister he thought it "certainly right that our [mission] people should not interfere in politics." As a missionary he had written articles for newspapers in the United States; as American minister he pronounced this practice "pernicious" and said it would be "a better day for us when the missionaries confine their writings for publication to the Boards which support them, as do we in the Gov'mt service."[10] As a missionary he had sought diplomatic office; as American minister he objected when a former colleague did the same.

[9] Allen to E. V. Morgan, May 29, 1903, in the Allen MSS; Allen to the Secretary of State, May 26, 1903, Dispatches, State Department Archives.

[10] Allen to Ellinwood, October 15, 1897, January 7, 1898, in the Allen MSS; Allen to Rockhill, January 30, 1898, in the Rockhill MSS. Rhodes, *Korea Mission, Presbyterian Church,* 493–497, deals with relations of missionaries to the government in Korea.

Knowing Oriental politics, the doctor could hardly have hoped to separate court intrigue entirely from mission work. In Seoul religion and politics touched at every point. The French legation and the Catholic missionaries, he wrote, "work together so openly that the typical priest is commonly believed to be a quasi-political French emissary."[11] The Catholics also helped France's ally Russia, as did the Orthodox missionaries who were introduced in 1899. Japan began using Buddhist preachers at the time of the Sino-Japanese war, and the Anglican mission was not altogether divorced from politics. Under the circumstances the Americans (who dominated the Protestant field) were not likely to stay out entirely.

Always a realist, Allen did not attempt the impossible. He concentrated on externals, seeing that there was no obvious evidence of political activity. He censured the Methodist editors of the *Korean Repository* for printing anti-Russian editorials. He urged the State Department to crack down on the writing of political articles. He endeavored to find new outlets for missionary energy. Thus he supported the establishment of the Korea branch of the Royal Asiatic Society. "For the honor and edification of our spouting missionaries," he said, "I encourage it, as it tends to keep them out of mischief."[12]

So Allen checked the missionaries, curbed those tendencies which he regarded as bad. But as he did so he made a constructive contribution to their cause. He threw the whole great weight of his court power behind them, gave them the aid and protection which they sorely needed. He did this,

[11] Paik, *Protestant Missions in Korea*, 254–255, quoting a statement made by Arthur J. Brown in 1901.
[12] Allen to Rockhill, February 28, 1901, in the Rockhill MSS; Allen to C. C. Vinton, August 24, 1896, and to Bishop Joyce, January 6, 1898, in the Allen MSS; Secretary of State Sherman to Allen, February 24, 1898, Instructions, State Department Archives; Allen to the Secretary of State, January 7, December 23, 1898, Dispatches, State Department Archives, the last enclosing a note from Allen to Appenzeller, December 9, 1898.

not on one occasion, but on many. "Scarce a day passes," he wrote in 1901, "in which I am not called upon to assist a missionary."[13]

The chief problem of protection related to the inland areas; but there were difficulties even in the capital. Some court officials still disliked the new religion. As late as 1896 a pro-Chinese cabinet member had published an anti-Christian tract. "The Christian religion is vulgar, shallow, and erroneous," runs a typical passage, "and is an instance of the vileness of Barbarian customs, which are not worthy of serious discussion."[14]

Even some of those who respected Christianity contributed to missionary woes. The emperor was one. He liked the Protestants, was grateful for the advice and comfort they had given him. But now and then he desired a piece of mission property and insisted on his right to buy. In 1903 His Majesty's eye fell on the Underwood establishment. The timid monarch was in search of a safe palace site; he could not have failed to note that the land of the "millionaire missionary" was surrounded on three sides by the protected American legation.

Underwood, seldom meek, rejected the emperor's offer. Thereupon His Majesty called Allen and asked the minister to order Underwood to sell. Allen refused, on the ground that he had no power to coerce Americans. Well, pursued the monarch, he could cable the United States and have the State Department issue the command. No, was the envoy's quick response, America did not possess that type of government. Even the authorities in Washington could not force citizens to give up property they wished to keep. Having thus defended principle, Allen made his peace with Chosen. Underwood had the *right* to refuse to sell. If that was admitted, he might give way, through a voluntary act of friend-

[13] Allen to the Secretary of State, January 5, 1901, Dispatches, State Department Archives.
[14] Quoted in Bishop, *Korea*, 2:269.

ship. That seemed reasonable, and the diplomat managed to persuade his missionary friend to yield.[15]

More telling attacks were made by the Japanese and the Russians. Emphasis was placed on the political meddling of the Americans, on their anti-Russian, anti-Japanese positions. Protests centered around Minister Sill's circular of 1897. "Heedless of the repeated admonitions of their government at home," screamed the *Japan Mail*, "and in lamentable disregard of the duty they owe to a higher authority, they have debased themselves by meddling in the political intrigues of the peninsular kingdom." Of course there were "unusual temptations," but "that is no justification for ministers of God to mingle with servants of the Devil."[16]

When confronted with such statements, Allen defended his countrymen. "Our missionaries here are a particularly well behaved and gentlemanly set," he cried to Alexis Speyer. "While they are not inclined to interfere in politics, you cannot expect that they will live so long in a country without making friends."

"Friends. Ah yes," shot back the Russian minister, "that is all right but political friends No! Your Govm't has publicly announced that it wants no political influence in Korea and it has instructed your people publicly that they must not try to make a political influence. But they all the time talk to their friends on politics."

No, hotly insisted the American envoy, that was not true. He "had to admit" that some native converts mixed in politics, but "our people have abstained ... and refuse to

[15] Underwood, *Underwood of Korea*, 208–210. See also Allen to the Korean Minister of Foreign Affairs, March 30, 1901, April 14, 1902, Underwood to Dinsmore, July 24, 1888, and Allen to Underwood, January 6, 1905, Seoul Legation Files, State Department Archives; Secretary of State Hay to Allen, July 2, 1904, Assistant Secretary of State Adee to Allen, September 30, 1902, January 14, 1903, Instructions, State Department Archives.

[16] Quoted in *Korean Repository*, 4 (1897):275; see also Allen to Ellinwood, December 17, 1900, in the Allen MSS.

take up cases of official persecution among their converts."
Speyer, though unconvinced, may have been impressed by
Allen's spirited defense. In any case, the Tsarist envoy soon
met and talked to missionaries at the American legation. He
had turned his back on them before.[17]

The problem of the interior was likewise a perplexing one.
By treaty foreigners were restricted to the open ports, but
missionaries had ignored restrictions such as these and had
travelled everywhere in Chosen. After some reconnaissance,
they had acquired property in the name of native helpers
and had founded mission stations. Then, established, they
had counted on the legation to protect them from all harm.
As Allen put it, "I have had some flagrant and open violations
of treaty stipulations by American missionaries who expect
me to protect them in these things."[18]

Personally, Allen was opposed to mission residence beyond
the treaty ports. So long as the staffs were still small, he felt,
there were ample opportunities in the open areas. Work
elsewhere stirred up anti-Christian feeling; to Allen's mind
the Boxer rebellion in China was due exclusively to "unwise
missionary effort" in the interior. Even when this sort of
trouble was avoided, there were other difficulties. The State
Department disapproved of treaty violations. The mission
property, being listed in the name of natives, was not recorded
at the legation. Squeezing and persecution of Korean
Christians by provincial governors caused sympathetic
women missionaries to break down. Finally, there was the
matter of mission morals. Allen cited Chinese experience:

[17] Allen Diary, October 14, 1897; Allen to Ellinwood, January 7, 1898,
June 7, 1900, in the Allen MSS; Allen to the Secretary of State, October
16, 1897, March 19, 1898, Dispatches, State Department Archives; Allen
to the Korean Minister of Foreign Affairs, December 8, 12, 1898, and to
Nam Chyung Kin, August 22, 1904 ("very decidedly . . . they are not
here to engage in any kind of political movement."), Seoul Legation
Files, State Department Archives; *Commercial Relations of the United
States*, 1900, 1:1071–1072, note 30.
[18] Allen to his sons, July 21, 1900, in the Allen MSS.

"It was easy to prejudice the people against the Christians, for they were generally believed to be immoral, not without cause, for every one knows how the missionaries themselves travel about in the most indiscriminate manner. A man and several women, or foreign women with native helpers, will go for long trips in the country, cooped up in a little boat. How can the Chinese be persuaded that this is proper[?] It would be the same as though a company of unrelated Chinese men and women should come to America to teach the philosophy of Confucius and then occupy ... and sleep in the same rooms."[19]

But it was clear that the interior of Chosen would be occupied. Knowing this, Allen tried to point the work in what he thought to be the right direction. Missionaries should respect native custom ("try not to court insult"), should give native Christians charge of outlying stations. Itinerating American males could do the rest. The minister did not secure just what he wanted, but extended his protection anyway. Missionaries might be scolded for bad judgment or excess of zeal, but they could not be deserted. That would hurt the cause.

Sometimes Allen failed to pull evangelists out of their difficulties. More frequently he gained specific points or won on principle. An important victory was obtained in 1899, a grant of religious liberty for Whang-hai, the province that contains Pyeng Yang. Lesser triumphs had been achieved before with reference to this important region, notably when Allen was legation secretary. But after 1899 all obstructions were removed. The result was little short of miraculous.

[19] Allen to Frank J. Carpenter, August 23, 1900, to E. V. Morgan, October 5, 1902, and Allen to his sons, in the Allen MSS; Allen to the Secretary of State, September, 1900, Dispatches, State Department Archives; Assistant Secretary of State Hill to Allen, July 24, 1901, Consular Instructions (Department "shares your view that it is inexpedient to encourage American citizens to reside in the remote interior"), Secretary Hay to Allen, January 23, 1905, Instructions, State Department Archives; Allen to Rockhill, July 29, 1900, in the Rockhill MSS.

Work went on with "greater success . . . than in any other mission field in the world." Pyeng Yang eventually outstripped even Seoul.[20]

By 1900, the Boxer year in China, anti-Christian feeling was developing all through the Orient. In Chosen it was expressed in anti-missionary placards, in anonymous notes sent to Allen and other diplomats, and in a general restlessness among the people. Watching closely, Allen decided that repression was absolutely necessary. Ordinarily he favored milder methods; experience had taught him that the Koreans disliked seeing the missionaries too closely associated with the legations. He felt "immense gratification" when the United States sent troops to China in the Boxer crisis. Indeed, he had only scorn for a naval captain who had "refused to fight after his ship had been fired on by the Chinese." That the officer was following instructions merely proved him "one of those weaklings who hesitate to take responsibility." Had Allen been shot at, he would have reinterpreted his orders to permit response.

He did that in Seoul, took what the State Department would have thought a "too active part" in native politics. Hearing of disturbances in the northwest, he persuaded the emperor to use force there. "I know my duty," was his comment to his two sons. If left unchecked, the demonstrations might have engendered an anti-missionary movement. And if the McKinley administration disapproved of Allen's activity,

[20] E. V. Morgan to the Secretary of State, June 28, 1902, November 12, 1905, Allen to the Secretary of State, February 27, 1899, September, 1900, June 7, July 22, October 14, 1901, May 22, August 19, November 19, December 9, 1902, March 20, 1905, Dispatches, State Department Archives; Allen to the Korean Minister of Foreign Affairs, February 13, 1899, Seoul Legation Files, State Department Archives; Secretary of State Hay to Allen, January 25, April 18, 1901, January 13, 1903 (asking "vigorous representations" on behalf of Pyeng Yang missionaries), February 10, 1904 (leaving protection "to your discretion"), Instructions, State Department Archives; Allen to Ellinwood, March 22, 1899, in the Allen MSS; Brown, "Reading Journey through Korea," *Chautauquan*, 41 (1905):542–543; Hulbert, *History of Korea*, 2:325–326.

The City of Seoul, Capital of Korea, in Allen's Day

Some who came to Seoul thought it beautiful, with its stark hills frowning down upon a sprawling, typically Oriental town. Others found it ugly, dreary, dirty, intolerably dull. But on one more significant fact all observers were agreed: that Seoul was the key to the kingdom of Korea and a focal point in the grim imperial conflict for mastery of eastern Asia.

they could replace him with "some one who is more timid."[21]

There was another scare at the end of the year. The Underwoods, who were travelling in the interior, heard of a great anti-Christian plot. Rumor had it that the governor of Seoul had ordered district gatherings of all Confucianists, which was to be followed by a general massacre of the missionaries and other foreigners. The day set was only a fortnight off.

Hurrying to the Haiju telegraph office, Underwood sent the story on to Seoul. To conceal the contents of his message, he put it in Latin; to avoid the appearance of an appeal to the legation, he sent the wire to a Presbyterian colleague rather than to Allen.

The envoy was skeptical when he received a translation of the message. But as he checked up he found some basis for the rumor. Whereupon he demonstrated his characteristic ability to act quickly in a crisis. He issued a confidential circular to the missionaries advising them to use the utmost caution when outside the treaty ports. He exerted pressure on the Korean government, calling in the Russians and the Japanese to help him. And the day set for murder passed without a single death. Three months later one Kim Yung Chan was executed after admitting under torture that he had participated in a movement against the missionaries, Allen and the Russian minister, and the emperor and other native officials.[22]

The next big fight grew out of strife between the Catholics and the Protestants. Surface cordiality did not hide ill feeling in the Christian ranks. The Catholics envied Protestant success at court and in turn were themselves envied for the enormous number of their converts. Catholics talked of the "true Christian faith," and Protestants retorted by classifying missionaries as "Christians" and "Romanists."

[21] Allen to his sons, July 1, 15, 1900, and to Horace Allen, July 10, 1900, in the Allen MSS.

[22] Underwood, *Underwood of Korea*, 199–201; Brown, *Mastery of the Far East*, 58–59; Allen to the Secretary of State, November 20, 22, 1900,

Disagreements reached a peak while Allen served as minister. Protestant appeals for funds to be used in Chosen often centered around the "beat the Papists" cry. Nor did the Protestants grieve too long over the death of three hundred native Catholics on Korea's Quelpart Island. Rather they criticized the Catholic technique of setting up the monks as local magistrates and of demanding extra-territoriality for all their converts. Allen, who was less anti-Catholic than the average Protestant in Seoul, mentioned that the Catholics had been accused of squeezing tactics. Earlier he had taken pride in telling superiors that American Protestants did not bother local officers as the French Catholics did.[23]

Somewhat later, news came in of strange occurrences in Whang-hai province. Native Catholics, apparently, were persecuting native Protestants. In a typical case, six Catholics asked four Protestants for contributions to a church building fund. Met with refusal, they beat the Protestants severely. Acts of this kind were likely to go unpunished, for the Korean Catholics were bidding the law defiance. Their leader, Father Wilhelm, Allen described as a "regular terror," a man who "has been imprisoning and beating official policemen and doing other things as though he were a governor."

Naturally the American envoy was interested in the Whang-hai cases. This time, though, he was beaten to action by the American mission colony. Homer Hulbert's *Korea Review*, a Methodist monthly, blared forth denunciations of the Catholics. Atrocities were described in detail and Father Wilhelm was attacked in bitter words. A Presbyterian missionary was quoted as saying that "many of these French priests connive at such things and are guilty of the grossest acts of injustice." It was implied that the French diplomats were implicated.

Dispatches, State Department Archives; Allen to Townsend, March 23, 1901, in the Allen MSS.

[23] Allen to the Secretary of State, September 15, 1900, July 3, 1901, Dispatches, State Department Archives; Allen, *Things Korean*, 182; Paik, *Protestant Missions in Korea*, 246, showing hostility.

All this made Allen fighting mad, not at the Catholics, but at "that miserable Hulbert." Though "very nasty," the Whang-hai affair could have been settled easily. As French Minister Plancy later said, Father Wilhelm had lost his balance under the strain of a solitary life. Hulbert, in creating a sensation, had forced a fight between the Catholics and the Protestants, had made Plancy feel he must back up Father Wilhelm. This could lead only to tragedy, and to loss of prestige for every Christian body in Chosen. The Japanese were quite elated, and Allen believed that he had seen the "worst blow to missions that we have ever had here."

Things were not as bad as they at first appeared. Allen advised the Protestants to negotiate directly with Wilhelm. ("I will not burden the legation with that kind of work.") When the priest refused to discuss the question, the American minister joined forces with Plancy. Working together, the envoys arranged to have the issue settled at a public trial in the Whang-hai capital. Protestant and Catholic observers were sent out from Seoul, Allen choosing as his representatives two Presbyterian missionaries, Underwood and Moffett. The trial went smoothly. Father Wilhelm took full blame for what had happened, hoping thus to save his charges from conviction. But the court decided that eleven should be whipped and five sent to the chain gang. The Protestants could thus rejoice at having won on principle; and the Catholics could be pleased that the penalties were light. To Allen and to Plancy the important thing was that the controversy was concluded.[24]

When worn out working for the missionaries, Allen tended to be critical of proselyting work. He complained that the Christian agents caused him all his troubles, that they were

---

[24] Allen to E. V. Morgan, February 19, March 6, 1903, and to Ellinwood, April 8, 1903, in the Allen MSS; Allen to the Secretary of State, April 7, 23, 1903, Heard to the Secretary of State, February 10, 1893, Dispatches, State Department Archives; *Korea Review*, 3 (1903):22–29, 73, 77–78, 115–121, 167–175, 499; Underwood, *Underwood of Korea*, 215–216.

"inclined to telegraph me if the eggs spoil overnight." The life of the evangelists seemed "remarkably soft," and the intelligence of many remarkably limited. "The missionary is very human," he said on one occasion in reviewing the difficulties, "and perhaps two thirds of them are inferior men who couldn't make near so good a living at home, and who should never have been sent over here to be as a torch in a dark place."[25]

Those were the words of exhaustion or annoyance. When refreshed and at peace with the world, the American envoy sang a different tune. He talked to proselyters about "our religious work." He spoke of the "exceptionally fine set of young women" in the Seoul missions and wrote enthusiastically about the prospects for conversion of a whole Korean village. He glowed with pleasure to think that "American missionaries are all through Korea by the score and . . . find it the best field for mission work ever known." And he boasted that it was "readily apparent how large a part missionaries have had in opening up the country" to Western enterprise.

He might criticize. Others might not. He objected when the *Japan Mail* called the missionaries "evil forces for hastening the downfall of Korea." Nor did he like to have the native converts called "rice Christians," persons who consented to be baptized in order to get jobs. He knew the saying, "Bread may be bought by profession of faith." He was familiar with the dangers of mass baptism and recognized that there was continual backsliding. But with it all he was convinced that "the people make most consistent and abiding Christians." If they were not, how could they have endured the persecution that often came their way? How

[25] Allen to Ellinwood, July 10, 1898, January 5, 1899, to his brother, March 23, 1903, and to Everett, July 25, 1900, in the Allen MSS. Plancy felt that "if he turns down Wilhelm now the whole population will rise against the Catholics and he must protect the man, while he has admitted to me his regret at some of Wilhelm's doings." Allen to E. V. Morgan, March 6, 1903, in the Allen MSS.

could they have produced poems like the one by James S. Gale's Korean teacher?

> *It was a sign of wondrous grace,*
> *When Jesus shared the sinner's place,*
> *That he might purchase righteousness,*
> *For those in sin and dark distress.*

Surely, as one missionary said in speaking of the leading converts, there was "no namby-pamby, half-frozen, mercenary mainstay for an invertibrate mass of jelly fish Christians; but a self-sacrificing, self-reliant, self-respecting Korean pastorate over a self-respecting, self-giving, self-propagating Korean church."[26]

The picture was particularly pleasant when one looked back. Allen had stood alone among the Protestants that first year of 1884. Twenty-one years later, when he left Chosen, his old Presbyterian mission boasted more than eighty workers, and the other sects brought the Protestant total to double that number. These missionaries led some fifteen thousand baptized native Protestants (half Presbyterians) and seven times as many adherents. This from nothing in 1884.

Having been a missionary physician, Allen was particularly interested in medical missions. Here Chosen had seen a shift in emphasis. Many had thought of medical activity as an opening wedge to be discarded when preaching was once under way. "I came to Korea to use my medical skill as a key to unlock the door for the Gospel," said Allen's old associate Scranton, "but I soon found that I was fumbling at the lock of a door which was already wide open, so I left the medical work and became an evangelist." Others agreed and called the building of hospitals an unwise extension of "institutionalism." The Presbyterian group in Seoul decided that

[26] Allen to Ellinwood, July 10, 1898, in the Allen MSS; Allen to the Secretary of State, September, 1900, Dispatches, State Department Archives; Paik, *Protestant Missions in Korea,* especially pp. 202, 211–213, 243, 250–251; Hamilton, *Korea,* 265; Allen, *Korea: Fact and Fancy,* 142; Sands, *Undiplomatic Memories,* 93.

ten thousand dollars was enough to spend on a new hospital and that there should be but a single doctor on the staff.

Still, medical work had gone on. Not ten thousand but a hundred and fifty thousand was eventually put into the Louis H. Severance Union Medical College and Hospital at Seoul. This was the Presbyterian successor to Allen's old royal hospital. Quite properly, Allen was invited to lay the cornerstone. As he did so, as he wielded the silver trowel and heard a native Presbyterian say a prayer, he must have felt that his work had been well done.[27]

Allen left Korea in the summer of 1905 and thus missed two great movements in Korean mission history. Had he remained a few months longer he would have seen the union of Protestant churches in Korea, with an end of competition and a fair division of the field. Still a little longer and he would have seen the Million movement, the drive for a million converts. He might not have liked this, for it was charged with an emotion that he might have regarded as hysterical. But union would have pleased him. His old chief Sill had backed it, had made at least one "ringing address on the need for church union especially in the mission field." Allen had done the same, had backed mission unity in every way. In his missionary days he had been willing to aid any Protestant work and to take non-Presbyterian doctors into his hospital. As minister he had acted first as a Christian, secondly as a Protestant, and only incidentally as a Presbyterian.[28]

[27] For Korean medical missions, see Paik, *Protestant Missions in Korea,* 318, 321–325; Allen to Ellinwood, July 9, 1901, in the Allen MSS; Allen to the Korean Minister of Foreign Affairs, April 22, 1902, February 16, 1905 (asking Korean aid for Severance Hospital), Seoul Legation Files, State Department Archives; Allen to the Secretary of State, November 28, 1902, Dispatches, State Department Archives; Underwood, *Underwood of Korea,* 210–212; O. R. Avison, "The Severance Hospital," *Korea Review,* 4 (1904):286–294; *Korea Review,* 2 (1902):510–511; Brown, *One Hundred Years,* 440–444.

[28] Victor H. Paltsits to Mrs. Horace N. Allen, November 13, 1932, in

When he left Chosen, in 1905, Allen had been seventeen years a diplomat and only five a missionary. But as he looked back he thought as often of religion as of diplomacy. He liked to recall that he had been a missionary pioneer. He liked to believe that his efforts at the Korean court had won for the Protestants "all sorts of special privileges," had helped make Chosen the "best field for mission work ever known." He was greatly pleased by the praise of missionary officers like Arthur J. Brown, who called the doctor "one of the ablest and wisest American diplomats in the Far East." And after he was re-established in America he wrote to his old missionary colleague Underwood that politics was "dirty work and I never intended to get into it. You are in the best work after all, for when a man can feel that everything he does is for the good of someone, he can have a satisfaction that is rare."[29]

the Allen MSS; Paik, *Protestant Missions in Korea*, 265–274; Launay, *La Corée et les missionaires français*, 365; *Korean Repository*, 2 (1895): 80; Brown, *One Hundred Years*, 328–465, giving a general statement of developments during the remainder of Allen's lifetime.

[29] Allen to Underwood, December 8, 1905, and an article written by Allen in the fall of 1905, in the Allen MSS. For missionary praise of Allen, see A. J. Brown to Allen, October 12, 1904, January 9, 1906; Presbyterian resolutions, September 21, 1904, in the Allen MSS; Secretary of State Hay to Allen, November 30, 1900, Instructions, State Department Archives. For light on Allen's attitude toward Japan and missions, see his letters to Japanese Minister Hayashi, March 22, 1904 (quoting H. G. Underwood to Allen, same date), August 17, October 31, 1904, May 27, 1905, to Moffett, March 5, 1904, to Welbon, March 11, 1904, to G. Lee, May 26, 1904, to clergymen Morse, Reynolds, Scranton, and Underwood, December 26 1904, and memorandum, December 26, 1904, Seoul Legation Files, State Department Archives.

Part III. For Mammon

Too many concessions have been granted through backstairs influence exercised by necromancers, eunuchs and dancing girls and foreign representatives, even those who should know better than to employ such aid.—Edwin V. Morgan

If the State Dep't knew what I have just done they would dismiss me, but I am not here for my health or $1500 a year and take the risk.—Horace N. Allen

8

Selling Chosen's Charms

"THE Administration," wrote Horace Allen in 1904, "is very susceptible to two great influences, the money influence and the Church. When one has both of them at his back as I seem to have, it makes a pretty strong combination."[1]

In those few words the sharp-faced doctor from Ohio summed up much of the Oriental diplomacy of the United States and much of his own career. For, wherever he was situated, Allen was two things—a Christian envoy and a dollar diplomat. He had much to do with making Chosen the "best and most satisfactory missionary station" in the world and with giving Americans their "undeniable predominance" in the Korean investment field.

The religious effort, of course, was instinctive with a man who had started as a missionary. But no less natural was the economic interest. As a mission-minded person, Allen knew that any increase in American influence would help the proselyting people. As a patriot, he wished to strengthen his nation throughout the world. As an individual, he learned that working with business men paid out in cash and jobs.

[1] Allen to Everett, September 3, 1904, in the Allen MSS. On the general subject of concession diplomacy in Korea, see Sands, *Undiplomatic Memories*, 197–211.

For Mammon

There is reason to believe that this latter factor was decisive. The Allens did not care for penny-pinching, and that they had to practice when they were missionaries. Even before the end of 1884 the doctor felt that he must supplement his meager mission salary. To do so, he penned a number of articles and devised inventions which he tried to market (chiefly railroad equipment). But that did not suffice; he had to turn to the business field.

Chosen being virgin territory, there were many possibilities. Trade openings beckoned; as President Chester A. Arthur said, Korea "needs the implements and products which the United States are ready to supply." The field of finance was promising, for Chosen wished to borrow money. And the franchise prospects seemed even better, particularly in the fields of transportation, communication, and mineral exploitation.

In time Horace Allen was to interest himself in all these matters. During his missionary years he concentrated on concessions. Trade apparently did not attract him. He did see a rich future there, if American exporters recognized their opportunity; Korea was "begging" the United States "to come in and take their trade." But personally the doctor did not care to be a trading missionary. He did not want to compete with his friend Townsend, who ran the only American trading house in Chosen. And he reasoned that in any case trade expansion would wait on the development of other interests. Until those came, American exports to Korea were likely to be limited largely to kerosene.[2]

Nor did the doctor do much with loans in his missionary period. Here he was limited by impecuniosity. He might have attached himself to a Wall Street firm, but that would not

[2] Allen Diary, November 10, 1887; article by Allen, April, 1886, in the Allen MSS; Allen, *Things Korean*, 217; letters to the Secretary of State from Foote, June 30, July 17, 25, October 18, 1883, April 29, June 9, July 31, October 7, 1884, and from Foulk, May 25, 1885, Dispatches, State Department Archives; Tyler Dennett, *Americans in Eastern Asia* (New York, 1922), 582, note.

have guaranteed success. For in the eighties there was little surplus capital in the United States, and New York financiers, having openings at home, risked foreign ventures only when the chance for gain appeared extraordinary. Chosen looked unattractive. The government was irresponsible financially. No one in Seoul knew who owed what to whom. The king, the queen, and other officers had borrowed heavily without consulting one another. Most of the money had been supplied by China, directly (a telegraph loan) and indirectly (through the China Merchant Steamship Company). But there were other creditors as well. Japanese and German merchants had loaned substantial sums at interest running up to ten per cent. Townsend's American concern had given credit, and there were many unpaid bills of every kind. The customs brought in annually a quarter of a million dollars, but Korea was plunging further into debt every day.[3]

Politics made matters worse. China knew that her suzerain claims would be strengthened if she could keep Korea financially dependent. One Chinese official wanted his country to lend Chosen money interest free to show his country's generosity and, presumably, to keep the Western nations out. Others, less open-handed, tried to scare off Occidentals by diplomatic warnings and publicity on Korean instability.

Seeing the difficulties here, Allen devoted his attention to the franchise field. But he soon found that he could not separate loans from concessions. Korea wanted money in return for grants; and China used her control of Seoul finance to fight would-be concessionaires.

Years afterward a writer was to call Korea the "happy hunting ground of the concessionists."[4] The record will support his epithet. Americans, Chinese, Japanese, and Germans had been active even before the Allens reached Seoul. In 1884 Americans obtained coastwise navigation privileges. The

---

[3] Tsiang, "Sino-Japanese Relations," *Chinese Social and Political Science Review,* 17 (1933):102–104; Philip Jaisohn, "Korean Finances," *Korean Repository,* 3 (1896):166–168.

[4] H. J. Whigham, *Manchuria and Korea* (London, 1904), 186.

For Mammon

American Trading Company won the right to cut timber on Dagelet Island, and Thomas Edison secured a contract to install electric lights in the royal household. Meantime the Japanese were gaining strength in Fusan, and adviser Moellendorff was bringing in Germans to organize a Chinese-dominated mint, glass manufactory, silk industry, and match factory.[5]

In the customary manner of diplomacy, the business men were aided by their legations. The American representatives had instructions to "seek no monopoly . . . and no advantage over other nations" ("as a general rule it is undesirable that a legation should appear to advocate concessions or exclusive privileges of trade or business in favor of its citizens"). But that did not restrain the diplomats in Seoul. They aided every countryman in sight and even gave assistance to Joseph Rosenbaum, a Moellendorff man who had taken out first papers in the United States. Often there was something more than diplomatic interest in the work. Minister Foote, for instance, seems to have thought of Foote as well as his country. For in 1885, after his retirement as minister, the general obtained a pearl-fishing grant (in the name of one of his associates) and was working for a railroad franchise. Foulk, as chargé, closed the pearl-fishing agreement and also helped the American Trading Company land a group of contracts: for a coastwise vessel, for a palace electric-lighting plant, for a water-power powder mill. Rockhill, who followed Foulk, was equally willing to cooperate with business interests. When trader Townsend was threatened with eviction from his residence he called for a naval vessel. "This measure I conceive

[5] Moellendorff, *Moellendorff;* article by Allen, March or April, 1886, in the Allen MSS; Foulk to Townsend, June 24, 1885, and to the President of the Korean Foreign Office, June 12, 1885, in the Foulk MSS; letters to the Secretary of State from Foote, July 26, 31, September 4, 8, 1884, and from Foulk, August 4, 6, 1885, Dispatches, State Department Archives. Korea's need for capital is indicated in the *Korea Review,* 1 (1901):554, which notes the formation of a Korean drainage company with two hundred dollars capital.

to be within the attributions of this legation," Rockhill wrote, and necessary because of the Koreans' "utter ignorance" of the proper way to handle business.[6]

Allen, as the king's confidant, could not avoid getting mixed up in these matters. As early as the fall of 1885 the Koreans asked him if he wanted an arsenal and powder-mill franchise. This of course did not quite appeal to the doctor as a religious man. But there were other things to come, mines and railroads. Allen heard much of them when he arrived in Seoul. Minister Foote was railroad-conscious and might have had a Seoul-Chemulpo franchise had he not left after the émeute of 1884. And every one talked of the fabulous wealth in the Chosen mines. Even when fable was reduced to fact by Japanese, German, and American investigators there remained a good promise of profit. There was gold, no doubt of that, and coal and copper, iron and silver. Religious and political restrictions and ignorance of Western methods had restricted exploitation by the natives, but even so, there were several thousand Koreans working in mineral industries, and gold exports amounted to more than three hundred thousand dollars a year.

Fascinated by the possibilities of the gold areas, Allen gathered all the information he could. Some he culled from published reports of the investigations of Foulk, John B. Bernadou, and a Japanese engineer. More he wormed from his Korean friends and from trader Townsend, who had visited the native mines. Townsend, who had technical training, estimated that the Koreans realized a hundred and fifty dollars a ton, although their methods were the crudest im-

[6] Acting Secretary of State James D. Porter to Foulk, January 8, 1886, Instructions, State Department Archives; letters to the Secretary of State from Foulk, August 27, November 17, 25, 1885, February 20, November 1, 1886, from Rockhill, February 10, 1887, from Heard, July 15, 1890, with notation by Alvey A. Adee, and from Allen, November 28, 1893, Dispatches, State Department Archives; Foulk to Rockhill, January 25, 1887, in the Rockhill MSS; Allen to Ellinwood, December 22, 1885, December 29, 1886, in the Allen MSS. See, however, Secretary of State

aginable. They had no pumps, no engines, no powder, no mercury; they used soft iron pikes and hammered out the ore on stones. Yet their yield was high. Think what could be done with modern methods![7]

By 1887 Allen was prepared to make his bid. His chance came when the king asked how Chosen could "interest the U.S. Governm't and people in Korea, and secure our help in keeping off China."

"Give the gold mining to an American company," the doctor answered quickly. Or, more specifically, to Allen, who proposed that the king grant him a monopoly in Phyong-an-do, the province reputed to have the best ore.[8]

His Majesty, it seemed, was "perfectly willing" to do as his missionary friend desired. But though Chosen was an absolutist state, the monarch's perfect willingness did not suffice. China had to be considered. The Chinese had applied for the mining rights two years before and claimed priority. Furthermore, an edict of 1885 required that all foreign contracts carry the seal of the Korean foreign office, which was dominated by the Manchus.

There were many other problems, too. Allen, in his amateur enthusiasm, had told the king that Americans would run the mines for a third of the returns. The more typical Chinese

Frelinghuysen to Foote, March 17, 1883, November 6, 1884, Instructions, State Department Archives.

[7] Allen to Everett, July 2, 1887, to Dinsmore, September 22, 1888, to O. N. Denny, August 9, 1888, and articles by Allen, in the Allen MSS; letters to the Secretary of State from Foulk, March 20, May 7, 1886, and from Heard, February 22, 1892, Dispatches, State Department Archives; Curzon, *Problems of the Far East*, 189–190; notes in the Foulk MSS, condensed from a report of a Japanese engineer; *Korean Repository*, 5 (1898):148–149; J. B. Bernadou, "Korea and the Koreans," *National Geographic*, 2 (1890):232–242, especially p. 241 and the map opposite p. 242. Allen's interest in gold is indicated by his purchase of New Mexican mine stock.

[8] Allen to Everett, July 2, 1887, and to Ellinwood, July 11, 1887, in the Allen MSS. See Dinsmore to the Assistant Secretary of State, March 5, 1888, Consular Dispatches, State Department Archives.

bid had specified four fifths as the foreign share.[9] Few foreign capitalists would consider joining any enterprise that called for less.[10]

The doctor discovered that when he began to look for backers. He also learned that money was not easy to obtain on any terms. He had few American connections and could do little even when he worked through Clayton Everett, the Toledo business man who had married Allen's sister Jennie. He had better luck in tying up with men already interested in Chosen. Townsend, to begin with. The trader had a little money of his own. More important, he was associated with James R. Morse, head of the American Trading Company, which had good financial connections in both New York and Yokohama. By another channel Townsend was connected with Commodore Robert F. Shufeldt, who had negotiated the Korean treaty with the United States and who now claimed the backing of the Union Iron Works of San Francisco. Both Morse and Shufeldt knew Chosen and were deeply interested in the opportunities there. Both liked Horace Allen and were eager to associate with a man so powerful at the Seoul court. But neither was a major operator who could raise huge sums at will.

Thus failure followed failure, and Allen's pocketbook remained empty. It might have been endurable had the mission work proceeded smoothly. But with quarrels on the religious side, the doctor decided not to stand it any longer. In 1887 he resigned his Presbyterian appointment and went to America as foreign secretary to Korea's new Washington legation. This more than doubled his income and gave him a chance to play for even larger stakes. If he established

[9] Foulk to the Secretary of State, August 31, 1885, Dispatches, State Department Archives. See Allen to W. B. King, March 13, 1888, in the Allen MSS, for Allen's later difficulties because of his first estimate.
[10] Shufeldt to Rockhill, February 28, 1887, in the Rockhill MSS; Allen to Foulk, July 25, 1887, in the Foulk MSS; Allen Diary, September 11, 1887; Allen to King, March 13, 1888, in the Allen MSS. These references

contact with the American financiers, he would be well fixed indeed. They might give him a berth in one of their concerns. They might help to get him appointed American minister to Chosen. Or, failing that, success might mean recall to Seoul as a well-paid king's adviser.

One thing was certain: Allen's acceptance of a diplomatic post involved him permanently in the economic affairs of Chosen. Had he remained a missionary, his influence in economic matters would almost certainly have been small. But as Korean and American diplomat, he was able to interest America in Chosen, to make his country and his friends predominant in Seoul's investment circles.

Naturally this was not accomplished at one stroke; it was a decade and more before Allen could say that "in Korea everything seemed to be American and our influence to predominate." But in the years 1887–89, when the doctor represented Chosen in America, he laid the groundwork for the edifice that was to be constructed in the future. He launched a basic promotional drive. He made contacts with financiers, won the confidence of a few outstanding capitalists. He outlined programs that were carried into effect later on.

The former missionary found promotion easiest. He lacked the suavity that is advantageous in personal relations, but he had the ingenuity to outline an effective advertising campaign and the force necessary to see it through. Even in his missionary days he had broadcast word of the economic opportunities in Chosen. The articles he wrote for the *New York Tribune,* the *Chicago Interocean,* the *Cincinnati Enquirer,* and the *San Francisco Chronicle* are full of the subject; religion is seldom mentioned. Allen commented on the popularity of products from the United States, of markets for American kerosene and clocks, beer and sheetings, stoves and needles, lights and Gatling guns. Again and again he

indicate that Allen saw Townsend and that the American Trading Company seemed likely to get the contract.

pointed out the opportunities for mineral exploitation and transportation franchises. He attacked the competitors of the United States: Moellendorff's match factory for turning out matches without heads, his silk expert for drawing a salary while living far away in Shanghai. Americans were denounced, too, for neglecting the coastwise shipping franchise they had obtained, for letting China and Japan, England and Germany, get in ahead on Oriental business.[11]

As Korean representative in the United States, Allen continued along these lines. He cultivated press relations, wrote articles, and talked to journalists. He praised the "broad minded intelligent" king of Chosen. He spoke highly of the Korean people, whom he insisted were superior to other Orientals. He bombarded financiers with glowing accounts of Korea's wealth. This was the "Treasure Land," he sang, a kingdom boasting gold and silver, iron and copper, coal and timber. With pumps and engines, with mercury and powder, with good implements and proper supervision, foreigners could get $750 a ton from Korean gold ores. Labor was available at five to ten cents a day in American money, so profits would be enormous. And certain, too, for Russia and Japan would take care of any Chinese move toward annexation. It was all so good that the Germans, French, and English were anxious to get in. The king, though, wanted the Americans; he could "trust a people so lacking in foreign aggressiveness."[12]

While spreading propaganda of this sort, Allen did not neglect the government at Washington. He kindled interest in Senator John P. Jones of Nevada and one of the New England representatives. He approached the Grover Cleveland administration, though he knew the president did not approve of great activity in the Orient. Results were better

[11] Articles in the Allen MSS.
[12] Allen to King, March 13, 1888, to Robert H. Davis, Korean consul in Philadelphia, October 8, 1899, and to Everett Frazar, Korean consul in New York, October 10, 1889, and reply to articles by O. N. Denny and Rockhill, in the Allen MSS.

than he hoped for. After "talking the matter over in a general way" with Secretary of State Thomas F. Bayard, the doctor was able to tell financiers that "Govm't cooperation and protection can be arranged." The secretary of state "expressed himself as desirous of seeing our people improve the golden opportunities offered by Korea in this [mining and lending project] as well as commercial matters. And he further said that while he could not offer gun-boats for the enforcement of Korean or other contracts, he would use his best influence and power in seeing the contracts were adhered to."[13]

This looked promising, but Allen was still unsatisfied. Rock-ribbed Ohio Republican that he was, he found it hard to trust the Democrats. Cleveland's Korean policy, he thought, had "been one of culpable negligence of the most pernicious description." And he thought Bayard's gunboat declaration weak. "Best influence" was not enough in the field of economic imperialism, there must be threat of shot and shell. For a policy that would reassure the bankers "a more active State Department" was required.[14]

As so often in the Allen story, the wish came true. The 1888 campaign brought defeat for Cleveland. His successor, Benjamin Harrison, put the imperialist James G. Blaine at the head of the State Department, and the pair adopted an aggressive foreign policy. Main emphasis was on the countries to the south, but Allen felt he could get Chosen included. He considered himself a persuasive talker, he was

[13] Allen to King, March 13, 1888, to Ellinwood, July 11, 1887, indicating that the king wanted Allen to get senators interested, to James H. Wilson, May 31, 1888, and to Dinsmore, June 21, 1888, in the Allen MSS. See Bayard's memoranda of interviews of February 1, 10, 1888, quoted in Tansill, *Foreign Policy of Bayard,* 446: "this Gov't did not undertake to stand sponsor for every enterprise in which its citizens engage abroad, although just protection would be given them, and there must be no idea of gunboats in the rear of every contract." "I told them it would be worth while to make application to some of the men here from the Pacific Coast. I mentioned Senator Stanford."

[14] Allen Diary, August 23, 1888; Narrative of Facts, in the Allen MSS.

"personally acquainted in the family of the new President," and he considered Blaine "my friend."[15]

A friend Blaine proved to be or at any rate, to quote the doctor, "a broad minded man who will make a strong and well directed effort towards furthering American interests in Korea and other countries." The Plumed Knight lost no time in formulating his Korean policy, in accordance with suggestions made by Commodore Shufeldt, who agreed in general with Allen. Chosen must stop her "double dealing," the new secretary told the former missionary, must demonstrate her independence, preferably by resisting Chinese pressure to replace the Korean minister in Washington by a mere chargé. If Korea failed to seize her opportunity, the Harrison administration might reduce the rank of the American representative in Seoul. But if the Oriental kingdom rose to the occasion, Blaine was "willing to pursue an active policy in Korea and (private) perhaps ask for a U.S. coaling station at Port Hamilton thus giving the Koreans genuine backing" against the Chinese and the Russians. Wall Street would fare even better, for the secretary was pleased to learn that Americans might get railroad franchises and was "greatly in favor" of American development of the Chosen mines. He asked Allen to inform him in advance of any contracts made between United States citizens and Korea. The Washington government would then "guarantee the parties—if of good standing—to take measures looking to the success of their work."[16]

Allen lost no time in adding the Blaine statements to his propaganda file. But even then he labored under difficulties, for China worked against him. The Chinese had opposed establishment of the legation to which the doctor was at-

[15] Allen to Min Yong Ik, December 10, 1888, in the Allen MSS.
[16] Allen to William M. Dye, May 11, 1889, to Frazar, September 12, 1889, to Dinsmore, May 18, 1889, to F. D. Darlington, March 8, 1889, and to Min Yong Ik, July 25, 1889, in the Allen MSS. Chaillé-Long (*My Life*, 397) speaks of Long's efforts to win Blaine away from the Shufeldt point of view.

tached. Having failed to kill the project in Seoul, they had carried the fight to the State Department and the New York press. The American government was assured that Korea was a financially unstable Chinese tributary state with no authority to contract international economic obligations. Newspaper articles said the same, and said it very well. Chinese sympathizers in the United States lent their assistance; W. W. Rockhill, the well-known journalist James Russell Young, and others turned out pieces highly uncomplimentary to Chosen.[17]

Even more effective were the news stories; after reading them few financiers were impressed by what Allen had to say. One story concerned the smuggling activities of Allen's superior, Pak Chung Yang, the Korean minister to the United States. This Oriental gentleman had used his diplomatic privileges to import cigars without paying a customs duty and then had sold the cigars in America. But that was nothing as compared with the baby riots of 1888. These were actually instigated by China, but were used against Korea. Agents of Yuan Shih Kai, Manchu resident in Seoul, spread foolish rumors through the capital. Some were invented locally, some were imported from the Dragon Empire. It was claimed that white men kidnapped Korean babies, using their eyes for camera lenses and boiling the rest for medicine. They pointed out that Westerners had milk, although they owned no cows. Obviously this "condensed milk" was obtained by cutting breasts off native women. The stories soon gained credence, and there followed a series of demonstrations against the foreigners. There was little violence, and excitement soon died down; but Wall Street financiers who

[17] Allen to Darlington, September 4, 1888, to Dinsmore, August 9, 1888, and to Denny, August 9, 1888, in the Allen MSS; Allen Diary, August 23, 1888; *New York Herald*, August 4, 6, 1888; Chaillé-Long, *My Life*, 397; Tsiang, "Sino-Japanese Relations," *Chinese Social and Political Science Review*, 17 (1933):102–104; Heard to the Secretary of State, October 21, 1890, Dispatches, State Department Archives, quoting the New York *Sun*, August 21, 1890.

heard of the episode concluded that Korea must be a completely unenlightened land.[18]

All that was bad enough. To top it off, Allen was restricted in his powers. He was primarily interested in franchise grants, as were most Americans who operated in the Oriental field. But Chosen wanted money first, a two-million-dollar loan for current expenditures, for the king's reform program, and to free the treasury from China's financial grip. To get the cash, Korea's king was prepared to pledge the rich gold mines in north Chosen. He was willing, too, to talk of railroad and waterworks concessions, of gas and lighting franchises, *if* the loan went through. But it was money first.[19]

Allen did the best he could. He began by exerting pressure on his frinds Morse and Shufeldt. Both responded favorably. Morse offered to take over the whole two-million-dollar loan, but he soon beat a retreat when he discovered how difficult it was to raise the money. The Union Iron Works vetoed Shufeldt's plans.[20]

In the United States, Allen had nibbles aplenty. A congressman from Maine was interested in steamship possibilities. New York and Arizona gas companies applied for gas and lighting franchises, and the New York company was willing to discuss waterworks and railroads, too. Senator Jones of Nevada was attracted by the gold mine prospects, as were W. B. King and Alfred James, California capitalists whom Allen visited in April, 1888.

But everywhere the story was the same. All wanted concessions, all were reluctant to consider loans. Many were

[18] Hulbert, *History of Korea*, 2:245; Gilmore, *Korea*, 83–85; Allen to Ellinwood, August 29, 1888, April 24, 1890, and to Darlington, September 1, 1888, in the Allen MSS. Allen said that this was no worse than lynching, but claims to have arranged to send a warship to Korea. See also the statement on famine made by Ye Ha Yong, Korean chargé in Washington, to Secretary of State Blaine, April 16, 1889 (in Allen's handwriting), Notes from Korean Legation, State Department Archives.

[19] Allen to Frazar, September 25, 1889; see, however, Allen to Dinsmore, February 7, 1888, in the Allen MSS.

[20] Allen Diary, November 10, 29, December 7, 1887.

entrepreneurs operating on a shoestring who would have had
difficulty in swinging a franchise, let alone a two-million-
dollar bond issue. And most offered none too generous terms.
The Californians were typical. They were so anxious to get
gold mines that they offered Allen a private commission for
his aid. But they demanded a fifteen- to twenty-year concession with only ten (or at most twenty) per cent royalty to
Chosen's king. And there would be no loan.[21]

Ever responsive to the tides of fortune, Allen was in deep
despair. He protested when his sister Jennie called him
lucky. Quite the contrary, he cried. Were he lucky, he could
make his countrymen see beneath the surface obstacles to
investment in Korea. "It is unfortunate," he wrote in similar
vein, "that our people cannot be more farsighted. They have
lost Japanese and China trade and now when Korea is begging them to come in and take their trade, they hold back
and will eventually lose this very good chance." And again,
"the present great desire is to get America in. It is like a
young lady (with charms) declining numerous offers in hopes
that some more bashful or hesitating suitor will propose. She
may either tire out waiting or be compelled to accept
another."[22]

Good fortune followed bad; eventually Allen reached the
leading financiers. He was aided by the gas people, who knew
they could not expect a franchise until Korea placed her loan.
Still more assistance was rendered by General James H. Wilson of Wilmington, Delaware, whom Allen met early in 1888,
by means of a letter of introduction from Richard B. Hubbard, the American minister to Japan.[23]

[21] Allen to James H. Wilson, May 31, 1888, to Darlington, August 30,
September 1, 1888, to Dinsmore, June 21, 1888, to King, March 13, 1888,
and to Frazar, September 25, 1890, in the Allen MSS; Allen Diary,
August 23, 1888.
[22] Allen to Darlington, August 24, 1888, in the Allen MSS; Allen
Diary, November 17, 1887.
[23] Allen Diary, December 27, 1887; Allen to Frazar, September 25,
1889, noting Wilson's connection with Grant and Company. Until this
time Wilson had concentrated on China and had been willing to give

Little remembered now, Wilson was a famous figure in his day. He was a well-known soldier, a Civil War veteran who was to lead in Cuba and help command the American part of the Boxer expedition. He mixed in politics, coming to know the great men of the land. And he had financial interests, important ones, in the Caribbean and the Orient.

Quick to help a "worthy cause," the general took Allen to New York and introduced him to the leading figures on Wall Street. At the start, these men showed no enthusiasm, but by the summer of 1888 were hearing the former missionary out. Then came what the doctor rightly termed "marvellous success." "One of Wall St's largest firms [*probably Morton Bliss and Company*] signified their intention of taking it up." Soon five or six others were interested and plans were laid for a syndicate, to include "some of America's best and richest capitalists." Besides Morton Bliss, the group was to include Dodge Phelps and Company and others "just as good."[24]

Everything looked well to Allen, especially after Harrison's November victory. That brought in Blaine, who wanted "something of the sort," and Vice President Levi P. Morton, who had been head of the key firm in the syndicate. Plans moved along. Wall Street put up ten thousand dollars for investigation of the Korean gold mines. If the veins were as rich as Allen claimed, the financiers planned to stake out a concession area. They would sink a full half million in machinery and pay Chosen handsomely for mining privileges. The king would get a third of all they made and if all went smoothly, would have his loan as well.[25]

This, Allen thought, was an "astonishingly fair offer." But

Korea to the Manchus to cultivate the good will of the Chinese. Tansill, *Foreign Policy of Bayard*, 422–424, 434.

[24] Allen to Dinsmore, August 9, September 22, 1888, to Darlington, September 1, 1888, and to Min Yong Ik, January 19, 1889, in the Allen MSS; Allen Diary, August 23, 1888.

[25] Charles W. LeGendre, an American adviser to Korea, claimed that Morton was offered much more and was headed off by European opposition. Sands, *Undiplomatic Memories*, 202–203.

it was never to be executed. The plans fell through in 1888 when news of the smuggling and rioting reached New York City. Although lines were eventually re-formed, the financiers were far from confident that Chosen could be trusted. Events lent weight to their fears. Their mining expert encountered obstacles when trying to conduct investigations in Korea. Allen's messages presenting the syndicate's terms were left unanswered by the king or answered in evasive terms, and, finally, His Korean Majesty decided to abandon the whole venture and develop the mines himself.[26]

Again the doctor was disheartened, seeing his future clouded by uncertainty. It was the more distressing in that he and Fannie were once more feeling pinched for funds. To a missionary three thousand dollars had seemed a fancy figure; to a diplomat it was just a bagatelle. Allen made some money speculating, but he still found it difficult to get along. When monthly payments came in late, there was a squeeze indeed. Once the family was down to twenty-eight cents and would have been tempted to give up had they not had "unlimited faith" in the doctor's "powers as a wriggler."[27]

But there were ways out, even when the loan negotiations had collapsed. Allen could stay with the Koreans. Not in Washington—there was little more that could be done in the United States—but in Korea, as a king's adviser. Indeed, His Majesty appears to have offered the doctor the job of modernizing and managing the royal mines. Allen had made the same proposal earlier, when King and James, the California capitalists, had submitted their exorbitant terms. Now, in 1888, he refused the offer, but did help to launch the enterprise. Acting on instructions, he engaged a mining engineer, Wil-

[26] Allen to Frazar, September 25, 1889, to Dinsmore, August 9, 1888, to Darlington, September 1, 1888, to Dye, August 29, 1888, to Everett, October 8, 1888, and notes written in 1924. See also Allen to Dinsmore, February 6, 1888, on the collapse of the water, railroad, and gas proposition. All these documents are in the Allen MSS.

[27] Allen to Jennie Everett, June 3, 1889, to Dye, August 29, 1888, to Dinsmore, November 21, 1888, February 6, 1889, and to Frazar, September 25, 1889, in the Allen MSS.

lard Ide Pierce, and purchased mine equipment. The whole venture failed eventually, but through no fault of Allen's. His sole mistake was one for which he could not be blamed. A royal cable asking for "one machinist foreman" came through "one machinist four men"; and the doctor sent on five. Otherwise he performed his task quite well.[28]

Allen declined the mine position because he had in mind another post—in the American diplomatic service. The urge, of course, was nothing new. From 1885 to 1887 he had sought appointment as American secretary of legation in Seoul. Foulk, Rockhill, and Dinsmore had tried to have the post created for him, only to run foul of appropriation shortages and Democratic disinclination to expand the foreign service in the Orient. But by 1889 the prospect had improved. This was the year of the billion-dollar Congress, and money now flowed freely in the halls of government. Moreover, Republicans were in power, Ohio Republicans like Horace Allen. And the doctor now had strong supporters in the business world. Why could he not have the secretaryship? Or even the ministerial appointment?

Like every office-seeker, Allen scurried to get supporters. He did not forget his old religious friends, who were glad to back a former missionary. And he used all politicians whom he could approach, among them Joseph B. Foraker, Senator John Sherman, and ex-President Rutherford B. Hayes, who was Fannie's cousin. Then, to seal the testimonial, he threw in his business acquaintances. They were glad to support a man whom they already considered one of their kind, a man who might well get them rich concessions. Allen himself, evaluating this aid, believed he had the "greatest support" of any for the post of minister.[29]

Knowing that his Korean connection was a liability when

[28] Allen to Frazar, September 25, 1889, to the Union Mine Works, September 16, 1889, April 19, 1896, to Ellinwood, October 8, 1888, to Kim Ka Chin, June 5, 1889, contract with Pierce, signed November 1, 1888, in the Allen MSS; Allen Diary, August 23, 1888.

[29] Allen to William Dulles, October 10, 1889, to Frazar, September 12, 1889, to Ellinwood, March 9, September 24, 1889, to Everett, February

he applied for an American position, the doctor turned in his resignation. Then he reassociated himself with the Presbyterians, to get a salary while awaiting appointment to the diplomatic service. He was in Korea when the news came through that he had been appointed to the second post, secretary of the American legation in Seoul.[30]

The doctor came to his new position as a known friend of missions and as a known ally of American financiers. The mission link was so apparent that few commented on it. But some did call attention to his business ties, to his acquaintance with leading capitalists and to the way Wall Street had pushed him for the job. "You have heard the startling intelligence of Dr. H. N. Allen's return to the political arena," observed Major John G. Lee in the *Hong Kong Telegraph,* "he having shut his pill and paste pot shop in Chemulpo and seated himself in the long vacant chair of Secretary of United States legation." Why had it happened? Lee claimed the business-minded Blaine had picked the doctor. "Vice President Morton and other New York capitalists together with a 'ring' at the State Department in Washington stirred into action by Sevelon Brown, now Foreign Secretary of the Korean legation in the States, who, by the way was dismissed from the service of the State Department owing to the fact that he was, while in Government employ, Levi P. Morton's real estate agent in Washington, have been interested in Allen's appointment."[31]

23, 1889, to John Sherman, September 14, 1889, to Min Yong Ik, June 20, 1889, containing the curious statement that Allen might not accept an appointment, to Jennie Everett, June 3, 1889, to Darlington, March 8, 1889, promising assistance to business if he received the appointment, to C. A. Welch, April 16, 1889, in the Allen MSS. The ministerial post was offered to William D. Bradley, who declined (April, 1889); then went to Augustine Heard.

[30] Allen to Ellinwood, September 24, 1889, in the Allen MSS; Heard to the Secretary of State, May 20, July 28, August 5, 1890, Dispatches, State Department Archives. Note the statement of Adee on Heard's dispatch of May 20.

[31] Clipping in the Allen MSS. Lee was a strange person, if one can

Allen considered the stronger parts of this statement as "too absurd to need comment." But it was true, of course, that his appointment had pleased Morton Bliss and Company. And Allen had been in touch with Sevelon Brown. So too had he been responsible for Brown's appointment as his successor in the Korean service.[32] Nor was it a secret that the doctor hoped to obtain concessions for Americans in Chosen. Allen had told the Presbyterians that as a diplomat he would maintain his "missionary character" and continue to work in "full sympathy" with his religious brethren. He might also have told his financial acquaintances that as secretary of the legation and later as minister he would maintain his character as dollar diplomat and would work "in full sympathy" with the American business man.

judge from Chaillé-Long (364–365) and from various letters of Allen's and others. See Allen to Dinsmore, September 22, 1888, to Dye, September 22, 1888, and to William C. Cooper, October 2, 1890, in the Allen MSS; Lee to Dinsmore, September 21, 1889, Allen to Dinsmore, February 8, 1889, Lee to Allen, May 29, 1889, Seoul Legation Files, State Department Archives; Secretary of State Blaine to Chaillé-Long, March 29, 1889, and Assistant Secretary Adee to Heard, October 27, 1890, Instructions, State Department Archives. See also Dye's complaints against Lee ("the duty of every American loyal to the common welfare, to aid in purging our good name of the offensive smell that will otherwise continue to be wafted from these shores by every adverse breeze. The atmosphere that taints each and all of us"), in Heard to the Secretary of State, October 1, 1890, Dispatches, State Department Archives. A letter of Dinsmore's to the Secretary of State, March 24, 1890, Dispatches, State Department Archives, contains another clipping from the *Hong Kong Telegraph,* one in which Lee refers to Allen as being in Chemulpo as a missionary, "regretting his past indiscretions, and practising silence; quite ready to succeed Judge Denny, should the king call upon him for that purpose ... The chances are, however, that like Admiral Shufeldt, his luck has passed out and he may have to wait a long while for an entirely new deal before he can again reappear upon the Korean horizon." Lee's attitude toward Allen was due in part to Allen's attacks on Lee. Allen to Lee, April 15, 1889, Lee to Allen, May 29, 1889, January 2, 1890, Seoul Legation Files, State Department Archives.

[32] Allen to Heard, September 5, 1890, and to Dye, September 20, 1890, in the Allen MSS; Heard to the Secretary of State, in Allen's handwriting, September 6, 1890, Dispatches, State Department Archives.

9

A Cripple Creek All of Our Own

KOREA has the richest gold mines on the continent of Asia, in the Un-san district of north Peng Yang. In four decades these mines have yielded nine million tons of ore having a gross assay value of fifty-six million dollars and bringing a net profit of about fifteen million. And they have yielded this, not to Korean miners, not to Japanese overlords, but to American financiers. The story is that of one of the outstanding Oriental holdings of Americans and one of Horace Allen's smartest bits of imperial diplomacy.

The high point of the story came in July, 1895, when His Majesty the king of Chosen granted the concession. But back of the decree lay five years of hard effort on the part of Dr. Allen. More, if one considered Allen's activities as missionary and as a Korean diplomat; but five at least, to begin with his service as American secretary of legation in Seoul.

The outlook for the concession seemed at least fair when the doctor took office in 1890. Many grants had been made in the past half dozen years. There had been telegraph franchises for China, fishing rights for the Japanese, electric, pearl, and timber contracts for Allen's countrymen. The insistence on a loan, which had plagued Allen while in the service of Chosen, had faded from the picture, and the king was ready to grant concessions to Americans on more liberal terms. In fact, His Majesty's attitude in 1890 was much the same as it had been before the émeute of 1884. Then the king had said "that proposals by American Companies to construct Railways and Telegraph lines would be favorably considered . . . that, if companies could be organized in the United States to construct Railways and Telegraph lines within his territory, he would be willing to give liberal franchises for that purpose."[1] By 1890 the Chinese had provided telegraph facilities, but there was not a single modern railroad nor a single modern mine.

Re-established in Seoul, Allen set out to get these things for nationals of the United States. He was assured the aid of his superior, Augustine Heard, for as an old China trader the minister understood and approved Occidental imperialism in its economic aspect. Heard, though, was little more than a figurehead. It was his secretary who had direct contacts with the Korean government. As a decorated nobleman, Allen had the right to appear at court at any time. Indeed, he was welcome there; the royal family had relied on him since 1885, the king had asked President Harrison for his appointment as legation secretary. And the local politicians flocked to him. The court boasted a powerful "American party," which recognized Allen as its leader.

All was well, save for China and Japan. But there lay trouble. From 1890 to 1894 the Manchus were making a last-ditch stand to hold Chosen in their sphere of influence. It could be done, they thought, only by keeping the Korean king in "Chinese harness," by insistence on suzerain rights, and by political and economic exclusion of foreign powers. Naturally the Chinese feared Japan and Russia most, but they were not without suspicion of the United States. The Americans had shown no urge to annex Asiatic territory, but they did favor Korea's independence of China. Thus a

[1] Foote to the Secretary of State, September 8, 1884, Dispatches, State Department Archives.

concession to citizens of the United States meant a strengthening of anti-Chinese forces in Seoul, which the Manchus viewed with alarm.[2]

By 1894 the scene had shifted violently. Gone was the Chinese suzerain claim, gone was the arrogant Chinese Resident Yuan Shih Kai, gone were the Chinese merchants who had been so strong in Chosen. China had matched swords with Japan and was in full and permanent retreat.

But as one heel was lifted, Korea felt another pressing down. Far from claiming suzerainty, Japan insisted that Chosen was as free as any nation in the world. That was on the surface; underneath could be detected Japanese desire to rule the kingdom from which she had driven China. That meant not only political influence but a monopoly of economic enterprises. Only by combining diplomatic pressure did Western nations prevent Japan from obtaining sweeping grants in 1894; even so, she still overshadowed others in the Korean field. She built a paper factory in 1894, a glass works, a rice-cleaning mill, a mint, and a weights and measures building, and made preliminary surveys for a railroad from Seoul to Chemulpo.[3]

When he meditated on this opposition, Horace Allen often moaned despairingly. He had no way of fighting openly against the dominating powers. His country's Korean policy was one of caution. Even Harrison was not prepared to fight for influence in Oriental capitals; and in 1893 the conservative Cleveland was back for a second term. All this meant that Allen had very little support from Washington, and had to rely almost exclusively on Korean court intrigue.[4]

[2] Besides the general sources, see Allen to Morse, October 13, 1891, in the Allen MSS.

[3] Allen to Eben Brener, January 23, 1895, in the Allen MSS: "I fancy the Japanese will keep all these things in their own hands. They are very short of money however and may decide to give the Americans a chance."

[4] Allen to the Secretary of State, April 9, 1894, Dispatches, State Department Archives, stating that Americans "receive less consideration

Fortunately he was an expert in that field. He knew how to get information and how to use what he had. He knew which men Americans could trust and which should be deceived. He knew court etiquette and could match maneuvers with natives who had "imbibed intrigue with their mother's milk."

Allen's technique seldom varied. He matured his plans, then lay low until a crisis developed. In normal times he could accomplish little, for Korea's overlords headed off each move he made. During crisis, however, it was different. Attention was distracted and it was sometimes possible to operate without detection; or, failing that, to play off foes against each other. Opportunities were limited in scope and time, but Allen knew how to work the court machinery and missed few chances.

While marking time in franchise work, the doctor performed many tasks. He advertised Korea by sending information to business men in the United States and gathering scientific material for the Smithsonian Institution. He supervised the planning of Chosen's exhibit at the 1893 Chicago fair and used a leave of absence to help the Korean delegation get established there.[5]

Interesting as such work was, Allen never let it interfere with his major job of seeking franchise openings. He planned for these even when there seemed to be no prospect of immediate success. And as he planned, he discriminated in favor of and against certain financiers.

As a missionary Allen had considered Christian workers

than any other power represented here," that Koreans "seem to think we are long suffering and not to be feared."

[5] Allen to W. S. Evans, December 20, 1890, to Peter Henderson, August 20, 1894, to J. R. Johnson, April 13, 1895, and to W. G. Percival, September 23, 1891, in the Allen MSS. On the fair, see Allen to Walker Fearn, February 18, November 26, December 6, 1892, January 14, 1893, in the Allen MSS, and John A. Cockerill, article in the *New York Herald*, December 22, 1895: the king "hastily knocked together a rather inexpensive collection of Corean junk and shipped it off to Chicago."

the most quarrelsome men on earth. Now he found that business men could be precisely as annoying. Might he himself have been to blame, with his hasty judgments and impatient ways? Had he been right in saying that he "could not get along with people?" Perhaps; but he thought not. As he grew older, Horace Allen came to have fewer doubts of the excellence of his own disposition. What he believed seemed reasonable to him and to ever-faithful Fannie. By logic, then, those who dissented were either dupes or scoundrels. Those who went along with Allen, on the other hand, were temporarily all right.

The case of Everett Frazar illustrates this trait. Frazar, a China trader, had shown an interest in Korea as early as 1883. By courting Korean diplomats and rendering good service as Edison representative, he had obtained appointment as Korean consul in New York. He and Allen had been useful to each other. The doctor had assisted Frazar to obtain the Korean decorations which the merchant had coveted. Frazar in return had helped Allen during the latter's service as Korean representative in the United States. He had shown interest in loan and franchise work, had helped the doctor establish Wall Street connections, and had backed Allen for appointment to the American diplomatic service.

That was fine. Frazar approved of the doctor, Allen liked the merchant's ways, thought him "one of the handsomest and most imposing men I ever saw." But when the Allens returned to Seoul, things were different. Frazar was connected with Judge O. N. Denny, American adviser to the king; and Denny did not get along with Allen. Both were strong men, each was envious of the other's power. Denny thought the doctor was scheming to obtain his job, and in truth the king would have approved the change. And Allen said that the judge's wife had abused him in a letter to the Presbyterian mission board. It was all most complicated. On resuming residence in Seoul, Allen had promised Frazar that he would try to improve his relations with Denny. No improvement came. Distressed, the doctor blamed Frazar as well as Denny. Things became even worse when a Frazar agent passing through Korea failed to pay a social call on Mrs. Allen. That settled it. The American legation secretary called Frazar the "biggest bag of wind I ever saw," and the fight was on.

For Allen the dispute was psychologically depressing; cantankerous though he was, he never relished quarrels. But Frazar suffered more. He lost his consular appointment, which he might have kept had he remained the doctor's friend. He lost as well the influence of the American legation in Seoul. Allen took pains to show him what this meant. "I was in a position to help you more than could any one in Korea," he wrote. But now, after the disagreement, aid was at an end. Although other business men would be assisted, Frazar's bids for assistance would be denied. "I am not allowed to solicit such favors from the Govmt to which I am accredited," were the words employed, "or to urge private interests upon this Govmt."[6]

Somewhat less violent was Allen's dispute with his old friend Townsend. The Chemulpo trader appears to have offended him by failing to express his gratitude for the favors Allen had won for him at the court. To pay him back, Allen withheld assistance when Townsend sought concessions and tried to get the same grants for other individuals. But his antagonism was not unrestrained; he did back the trader when American prestige appeared to be at stake. When native officers challenged Townsend's treaty rights, in 1893, the doctor (then chargé) spoke privately to the king and "got results." Three years later, when the Germans were about to land some major business, Allen managed to switch the orders to the Townsend firm. "Townsend has no gratitude,"

[6] Allen to Frazar, September 12, 25, 1889, January 20, 1892, to Ellinwood, December 29, 1886, January 5, 1891, to Morse, October 13, 1891, and to a friend, August 5, 1897, in the Allen MSS; letter to the Secretary of State from Foulk, November 19, 1883, in the Foulk MSS, from Foote, January 17, 1884, and from Chaillé-Long, February 4, 1889, Dispatches, State Department Archives. An editorial statement in the *For-*

was the doctor's comment, "but I had to do this or let it go to the Germans."[7]

As others fell in favor, Allen became ever more attached to Townsend's former partner, James R. Morse, president of the American Trading Company of New York and Yokohama. Morse and his charming wife had entertained Fannie and the doctor royally in 1887 when they felt so abused because of missionary criticism. Thereafter their friendship grew, though both men had quick tempers. Fruitful conference and a friendly correspondence soon made Morse sure that Allen was the man to manage his Seoul lobbying. The doctor was as certain that Morse was the man to Westernize Korea. Morse stated flatly that Allen would have his reward —the ministerial appointment or a lucrative position with the Morse Korean enterprises. And Allen, captivated, came to use the first person plural when he talked of the hoped-for Morse concessions. "I say *we* in all this," he explained on one occasion, "but I am of course careful to do nothing that will interfere with my present calling." Obviously, for the doctor knew that he could render Morse "more service all around right where I am" than he could if he did not have a diplomatic post.[8]

The first sign of an opening came in 1891, the year that Frazar lost his consular appointment. Allen was pleased when Morse obtained the vacant post, with the title of commercial agent in New York. The same year saw some stillborn franchise hopes. The king had Allen write to the United States

eign Missionary, 44 (1885):284, covers a few of the problems involved in the Allen-Frazar-Denny relationship.

[7] Allen to Morse, June 24, 1895, January 25, 1896, in the Allen MSS; Allen to the Secretary of State, November 28, 1893, Dispatches, State Department Archives. See, however, Heard to the Secretary of State, September 29, 1892, Instructions, State Department Archives, praising Townsend.

[8] Allen to Morse, October 13, 1891, to Everett, November 29, 1897, to Jennie Everett, November 5, 1895, and notes, in the Allen MSS; Allen Diary, November 29, 1887.

for city electric estimates. He had in mind a lighting plant that would also supply the power for a trolley line. Allen sent the letters. That was all. Yuan Shih Kai stepped in and the project died a speedy death.[9]

Allen saw a better chance the next year. China was in diplomatic trouble—too busy, the doctor thought, to notice all that happened in Seoul. It was a splendid time to press the claims of Morse. So expertly did he do this that His Korean Majesty improved his already good opinion of the American Trading Company's chief executive. Allen was not exaggerating when he told his friend that the king had "more confidence in you than in any other business man living."

Goaded by the American legation secretary, the monarch finally took action. He cabled Morse through the Korean legation in Washington that he had "full intention" of granting the American Trading Company extensive mine and railroad concessions. To seal the bargain, Morse should come to Seoul for the signing of the contract.

Morse made the long journey. He came with confidence and modesty. He would not insist on everything, on all the mines and railroads of Chosen. One grant would be enough —the right to build a railroad from Seoul to Chemulpo. It was wise to start with caution.

Six thousand miles the business man had travelled when he reached Allen's residence in the Korean capital. And all in vain, for in the meantime Chinese influence had been brought to bear in Seoul. Morse found no general contract awaiting him, no mine nor railroad grant of any kind. He sputtered with indignation, growled to Allen, snapped at native officials, gathered up his bags and left in rage. It did no good. The Koreans would not yield and even denied that they had asked Morse to come to Seoul. The foreign office

[9] Allen to the Thompson Huston Electric Company, Boston, October 23, 1891, and to the Brush Electric Company, Cleveland, October 23, 1891, in the Allen MSS.

promised to consider the American Trading Company when
grants were made ... but that might not be for years to come.[10]

If Morse suffered, so did Allen. Minister Heard "sat all
over" him for violating instructions by mixing in the matter.
Heard, listening to the natives, was sure that Allen, not the
Koreans, had summoned Morse to Seoul. The envoy "finally
got out of his funk ... but he was not 'nice' when he was
in it."[11] His subordinate had reason to worry for the future
of his diplomatic career.

The doctor was even more concerned over the reaction of
his friend Morse. For, after all, the legation secretaryship
paid only fifteen hundred dollars. Dismissal would not bring
great loss, for a physician need not starve. A break with Morse,
by contrast, meant the end of Allen's chances to be United
States minister or a well-paid business man. So Allen tried
his best to repair the damage. He told his friend that the
American Trading Company had been the "victim of one
of the numerous feuds" in a court which was a "very hot bed
of intrigue." The "recent strange action" of His Majesty
implied no lack of love for Morse. On the contrary, when
the Chinese relaxed their hold, the king would welcome
Morse with open arms.[12]

So Allen reasoned; but it was three years before another
good opportunity presented itself. Meanwhile Cleveland had
become the president of the United States and had shifted
ministers in Seoul. This had not affected Allen, who, on
Heard's endorsement, had been retained as secretary and
continued to run the legation "practically without interference" from the new envoy Sill. Changes had been more vital
in Korea, with Japan's rise after her triumph in the Sino-
Japanese war. The speed of the Japanese victory prevented

[10] "Narrative of Facts," Allen to Morse, May 9, 1892, to Townsend,
May 20, 1892, and to Heard, May 18, 1892, in the Allen MSS.

[11] Allen to Morse, July 6, 1892, and to Townsend, May 20, 1892, in
the Allen MSS.

[12] "Narrative of Facts," Allen to Morse, May 9, 1892, in the Allen
MSS.

Allen from getting a concession in the confusion of conflict, but in 1895 the situation looked more promising. Diplomatic reversals had impaired the prestige of the Japanese and given the Korean king a bit of courage. His queen had set herself against the Japanese and was anxious to have her husband grant franchises that would bring in Americans as allies of the crown. At the same time Japanese Count Inouye, feeling the weakness of coercive methods, had just announced a new and milder Korean policy, which made room for grants to Occidentals.

Here was the moment that Allen had awaited, the chance to snatch his first concession. He was prepared for the opportunity, had won the whole good will of the royal family by "great service to the King and to Korea during the past year." The Japanese, too, he expected to be more cooperative than the Chinese had been, for he had helped them in several ways and believed they would "feel grateful."

Negotiations started when Allen was summoned to the palace one night.[13] He found the king most friendly, anxious to express his gratitude for the political advice Allen had been supplying since 1885. It was regrettable, pursued His Majesty, that the doctor had received no pay for all this work, had remained poor while less useful persons had grown rich. He would like to rectify that situation by the gift of a gold mine. This would square accounts and help Chosen besides —for surely the United States would take an interest in a land in which one of her citizens possessed a rich and vital economic stake.[14]

Now at last success seemed within reach. Allen hastened to surmount the obstacles that still remained. One was his diplomatic status. As an employee of the Cleveland administration, he was forbidden to accept presents or to enter into

[13] Notes and Allen to Morse, June 24, with postscript of July 16, 1895, in the Allen MSS, cover these negotiations in detail.

[14] Allen, in a letter to Arthur J. Brown, April 30, 1905, in the Allen MSS, states that the first suggestion came from the queen.

any intrigue to get grants for others. But there were ways of evading prohibitions such as these. The concession could be issued in the name of Morse, and Allen could get his percentage off the record. Even a Morse grant might be disapproved by Washington, but this was not so likely if the State Department had no news till all was over. To manage this, the doctor approached Minister Sill. "I told him early of what I was doing," runs the doctor's own account, "and that I expected to do a good thing by myself in it. And that if it makes any trouble to the Legation I am willing to resign. I can be of more service to the Morse enterprises right where I am, but $1,500 a year is not inducement enough to keep one very anxious for the service." That did the job, kept Sill from sending any word until a month after the closing of the deal.

Allen straightway turned to his next job, reorganizing the Korean government. The old government was impossible, being packed with Japanese partisans who would have taken pleasure in blocking the gold mine grant. Intrigue solved the problem; the men whom Allen thought obnoxious were disgraced, transferred, or kicked upstairs. To replace them the American legation secretary "soon succeeded in getting all my friends appointed to high office." Ye Cha Yun, a leading member of the American party, was made minister of the royal household. Another confidant, Ye Wan Yong, received a post of equal rank, and Pak Chung Yang, who "was never thought of as Prime Minister till I suggested it," headed up the cabinet. Pak's appointment was inspired. It pleased the Japanese, who thought the old man was innocuous; and it fixed affairs for Morse and Allen. Pak was the doctor's "Korean father," and had come to respect Allen while serving as titular head of the Washington legation which the doctor served as foreign secretary.[15]

[15] Allen's opinion of Pak's ability is indicated in his letter to Dinsmore, November 21, 1888, in the Allen MSS: "had the governmt scoured the

A Cripple Creek All of Our Own

With this array of backers and with Japanese envoy Inouye absent on leave, Allen was ready for the final push. He let the Koreans take the lead. They did so by inquiring what prospect there was for an American loan. Immediately the doctor switched the conversation over to mine matters. "I saw the opportunity," he reported to Morse, "and informed them that, with no American interests here such a thing was impossible, the best way to proceed would be to interest Americans in the development of Koreas resources and then such aid might be obtained." The Seoul-Chemulpo railroad franchise would be best, but since the Japanese were after that, Allen asked them to "grant a mining franchise to reliable Americans as a just and immediate step. They seemed to regard it favorably and not wishing to put myself too much in evidence, I wrote off a contract after the style of your former ones . . . making over the Uhn San [Un-san] mine (which is the best in Korea) to you."

When squabbles over terms were settled, Allen had the approval of the leading ministers. Only one man posed a major problem—Kim Ka Chin, head of the public works department which controlled the Korean mines. Kim was a true chameleon, who shifted his position weekly. Both Allen and the Japanese could claim him as a friend, but neither could trust him for a moment. Fearing that he would be betrayed if Kim became involved, the American legation secretary adopted a "clever ruse," based on his knowledge that all Koreans coveted the approval of the king. He dropped the hint that Kim would gain in royal favor if he transferred certain mines to the royal household, where (as in Japan) they would be under His Majesty's direct control. Kim snapped up this suggestion and made over the Un-san district. But, contrary to Allen's hopes and expectations, the transfer did not give control to the doctor's ally, Household Minister Ye Cha

whole peninsula they could not have found a man more unfit for the place [*post of minister in Washington*]."

Yun. Kim, hating Ye, specified that the mines be handled by a lesser household bureau, one headed by the pro-Japanese Chung Pyung Ha. And Allen, of course, could not object without revealing his ulterior motive.

For a while everything seemed black. Kim and Chung, if advised of the mine maneuvers, would doubtless advertise them. This would bring in Japan and some Americans whom Allen wished to leave outside—notably Townsend and adviser Clarence R. Greathouse. Other perils loomed. An important native nobleman, Pak Yong Hyo, was using his influence to stalemate Allen. And the king, far from being pleased over the gift of the mine, was angered because only part of the mines had been so transferred.

Then, suddenly, all turned out well. Allen did not even need to get Kim transferred to Washington and Chung to a country post, as had been his plan. The queen made that unnecessary by stepping in and ordering the franchise granted. Had her timid husband remained in charge, Allen might have failed completely. With Her Majesty interested, the contract was soon signed, delivered, and, on July 15, 1895, deposited in the American legation safe.

Minister Sill called the terms "as broad as possible." Certainly they were broad and very favorable to the grantee, a newly created Korean Development Company. The concession was to run for twenty-five years and was to take in all the Un-san district of Peng Yang. The company could choose its mines and have exclusive right of exploitation, even as against Koreans on the ground. Chosen engaged to help by handling the natives, by providing rights of way, by protecting the company's foreign employees; and in addition the concessionaires were to have immunity from every sort of tax and duty. The favored party gave very little in return. It presented the king with twenty-five thousand dollars (one quarter) of the company's stock. It agreed to use native labor whenever possible and to teach Koreans Western methods;

and it promised to refrain from opening or removing graves without consent. Obviously, Allen said, "the advantage to the Koreans in this matter was chiefly to be the greater interest America would take in the country."[16]

Morse, the concessionaire, knew nothing of the negotiations until the franchise had been granted. Allen had managed everything and had done it without creating any obligations, save that of Morse to him. There were not even any bribes to pay. The doctor suggested that Morse would do well to cultivate Ye Wan Yong[17] and Ye Cha Yun, who had been of much assistance. But no one expected "to be given any shares or money for services rendered" to the cause. "Except," the doctor hastened to add, "such as you deem my getting up and putting thr'o the whole thing may entitle me to."

This broad hint, this virtual request for remuneration, symbolizes one of the strangest aspects of the Un-san case. Horace Allen was a diplomat, a paid employee of the United States. As such, he was expected to refrain from accepting money on the side. Allen knew this and more than once insisted that his record was spotless. "I am not and never have been interested in electric or other contracts, franchises or interests in Korea," he was to write in 1904. "I am not and never have been interested partly, wholly or indirectly in any real estate in Korea aside from a summer place I have long owned, outside of Chemulpo. I am not directly or indirectly interested in any financial enterprises in Korea nor in the stocks, bonds or securities of such concerns nor have I any promises of any such future interest. I have not undertaken the promo-

[16] There is a copy of the contract in the Allen MSS. The location was named by Allen, who had information as to the wealth of the Peng Yang mines. Allen, *Things Korean*, 232. See also Allen's memorandum of May 16, 1900, in the Allen MSS. Sill to the Assistant Secretary of State, August 15, 1895, in Allen's handwriting, Consular Dispatches, State Department Archives states that it was the "first real grant of this kind; it will have a good effect upon the development of Korea."

[17] Ye Wan Yong had also helped in the 1892 negotiations. See Allen to Morse, May 9, 1892, in the Allen MSS.

tion, protection or furtherance of any financial enterprises here for the purpose of financial gain."[18]

The last of these strong statements rings false in view of Allen's stated motives in the mine negotiations. The others must be set beside the developments that followed. Morse did not give the doctor stock in the Korean Development Company or its successor, the Korean Mining and Development Company, incorporated in New Jersey. Allen did, however, accept a sizeable present from Morse in 1898 or 1899. He also accepted gifts from Leigh S. J. Hunt and J. Sloat Fassett, who bought Morse's mine in 1897. "When their interests were settled and the property was running smoothly," Allen put it, "they gave me a present of money on two occasions." The Morse and Hunt-Fassett contributions, plus Allen's savings (increased by Morse's market tips) were invested in two business blocks in Toledo.[19]

How did Allen justify these actions? For one thing he said that they related to services rendered before his appointment as minister. Thus he implied that the code of diplomatic ethics was not binding on ill-paid legation secretaries. But even there the dividing line was far from clear. Although the services had been supplied in the secretary period, some of the cash appears to have changed hands while Allen was minister. And after eight years in that post the doctor could write that he certainly hoped that Henry Collbran, another concessionaire, "would make me some sort of compensation" for aid given.[20]

Furthermore, Allen said, the money came unsolicited and

[18] Allen to the Secretary of State, June 13, 1904, Dispatches, State Department Archives. A colleague of Allen's has said that "Allen was a superlatively honest man," adding, however, that "during that period . . . our consular officers were not as strict about personal financial gains while in office as they are today." Sands to the author, May 28, 30, 1939.

[19] Allen to Morse, April 26, 1905, to Arthur J. Brown, April 30, 1905, to Everett, March 6, 1898, and to Jennie Everett, November 5, 1895, noting Allen's expenditures in the mine affair, in the Allen MSS.

[20] Allen to Morse, April 26, 1905, in the Allen MSS. Heard told the Secretary of State (letter of July 28, 1890, Dispatches, State Department

after the event, hence could not have affected his diplomatic activities. "What I received from you and Hunt," he told Morse, "could not be called graft. You did not have to pay it. Your business would have been attended to just the same." Again, the gift from Hunt and Fassett "was entirely voluntary on their part. I accepted it without any compunction."

Besides, Allen read justification in the attitude of others. Brother-in-law Clayton Everett, who had helped invest the money in Toledo, saw nothing wrong in Allen's actions. Neither had Minister Sill; and Gordon Paddock, legation secretary from 1900 to 1905, had cried, "Why Dr. you have positively leaned over backwards in your desire to be straight."[21]

Finally, brushing aside principle, Allen said that the gifts were "small . . . considering what I have done." He had received a few thousand dollars for launching an enterprise that was to net twelve millions in his lifetime. Surely, he maintained, it was ridiculous to censure him for that.

And in any case it must be granted that the doctor was efficient. However badly he may have betrayed his diplomatic trust, he did not fail the operators of the Un-san mines. Without him there would have been no charter; and no less vital was his work in the first ten years of exploitation.

One of his tasks was to urge his friends on. Morse was cool on the mining proposition, especially after landing a railroad franchise in the spring of 1896. But Allen would not let his friend forget a grant which bid "fair to be one of the

Archives) that the general impression was that Allen's salary was inadequate. Allen, in a letter to Rockhill, January 30, 1898, in the Rockhill MSS, does the same; commenting on Sands' appointment as secretary of legation, Allen said, "I hate to see a young man like him take a position of this kind . . . the pay is so poor that he will be sure to be dissatisfied." One of Allen's plans to supplement his income is outlined in Allen to Everett, August 15, 1896, in the Allen MSS. Allen refused gifts from Collbran and Bostwick after his promotion to minister. Allen to A. J. Brown, April 30, 1905, in the Allen MSS.

[21] Allen to Morse, April 26, 30, 1905, and to Brown, April 30, 1905, in the Allen MSS.

noted gold mining properties of the world." "Don't let the grass grow on this," he wrote to Morse. "While the R.R. proposition is a big thing I feel confident that our big money will come from our mines . . . We have a 'Cripple Creek' there all of our own."[22]

Though Morse remained unconvinced, Allen did not fail. He won the ear of a powerful associate of Morse's—Leigh S. J. Hunt, a Seattle capitalist with political connections. Hunt was in China in 1896 seeking business openings. Visiting Chosen to examine the Morse concessions, he became as enthusiastic as Allen himself over the Peng Yang mines. After that nothing would discourage Hunt, not even an expert's report which used the term "good *little* mine." Obviously, he growled, this was an understatement calculated to make Morse sell out to the expert's friend, Henry Collbran. At the moment these tactics seemed improper, but Hunt soon took them over himself. In 1897 he and J. Sloat Fassett, a political and business friend from New York state, sought out Morse in Yokohama. As Morse reported the interview, the pair was willing to buy the Un-san franchise if the price was right. "They made out a very bad case [for the mines] but said they were willing to take some chances, and that it was a huge gamble at best." As this coincided with Morse's own interpretation, the American Trading Company's president believed it and sold out a concession worth several millions for thirty thousand dollars.[23]

[22] Allen to Morse, March 30, 1896, and to Stevens of the American Trading Company, February 10, 1900, in the Allen MSS; Bayard memorandum of February 10, 1888, in Tansill, *Foreign Policy of Bayard,* 447, note. Temporary discouragement is indicated in Allen's letter to Morse, on or about September 1, 1898, in the Allen MSS.

[23] "Narrative of Facts," Allen to Morse, April 15, on or about December 15, 1896, and Morse's wail to Allen, April 15, 1904, in the Allen MSS. Hunt's summary of his own career reads: "first an educational career ending in the presidency of the State Industrial College of Iowa, which position he resigned to enter upon a business career that has made him a familiar character the world over." *Who's Who in America,* 1910–11.

A Cripple Creek All of Our Own

Once in control, Hunt and Fassett set out to work the mines in earnest. They formed a five-million-dollar organization, the Oriental Consolidated Mining Company, incorporated in West Virginia on September 29, 1897, and financed in part from English sources. Hunt was vice president, Fassett a director. The president was Henry C. Perkins, and among the other officers were Ogden Mills, William L. Bull, and William P. Palmer. The company sank huge sums in equipment and built up a large staff. By 1903 there were seventy Occidentals working at the mines, almost as many Japanese, nearly seven hundred Chinese, and more than two thousand natives. These employees were operating eight mines—three cyanide plants, five mills, two hundred stamps —and in 1903 they handled two hundred thousand tons of ore. This brought an operating profit of three quarters of a million and resulted in the first dividend, twelve and a half per cent.[24]

Being a clever man, Hunt handled his Seoul business through Secretary Allen. There had been certain difficulties in establishing this tie, for Allen was a friend of Morse, who felt he had been cheated in the 1897 deal. But Hunt took care of that. He and Fassett made Allen grateful by helping him obtain promotion to the rank of minister in 1897. Gifts of money were added and Allen wrote with real enthusiasm: "Hunt has a pious look but does his best to make up for appearances. He can tell you more of the inside of things Asiatic than any American I know, and he is doing more for the advancement of American interests out here than all the *talking* promoters that swarm over the land."[25]

The practical assistance which Allen gave to Hunt can

[24] Financial and other statements and Allen to Hunt, July 25, 1902, in the Allen MSS; Allen's reports in *Commercial Relations*, 1896–1901; Allen to the Secretary of State, June 1, 1904, February 16, 1905, Dispatches, State Department Archives. Allen's letter to Henry S. Kerr, January 28, 1907, in the Allen MSS, indicates the strong English interest in the Oriental.

[25] Allen to Rockhill, October 23, 1899, in the Rockhill MSS.

hardly be overstated. He saved the original Morse grant in
1896 by securing a new concession extending the one-year
limit for the opening of mine operations. In doing so he
strengthened the franchise by getting the minister of foreign
affairs to witness the signing of the contract. Three years
later the doctor pushed through an agreement by which
Hunt's company bought the king's fourth share for what
Allen called "a mess of pottage"—a hundred thousand dollars
and a yearly income of twelve thousand.[26] The new document
extended the company's rights to 1924, four years beyond the
date set in the first concession.[27]

In 1900, "after six weeks of the worst worry I ever had in
Korea," the doctor managed to obtain still more. For the
very small consideration of $12,500 cash, he secured a fifteen-
year extension with an option for fifteen more. This extended
the franchise to March 27, 1954. More important, the new
concession eventually came through signed by the foreign
minister as well as by the household secretary. This, as Allen
said, "secures our position." For by edict of 1885 all foreign
contracts required the seal of the foreign office. The early
Un-san grants, having only the approval of the household
ministry, had been defective in a key particular.[28]

While improving the basic grant, Allen helped in other
matters. He secured interior passports for mine employees
and free passage for supplies. He arranged for dynamite ship-
ments, a special problem created by treaty clauses. He per-

[26] Less later, as these figures were expressed in Yen.

[27] Allen to Fassett, May 20, 1900, to Hunt, March 22, 1900, and to
Morse, April 18, 1896, and notes by Allen, especially a memorandum
dated May 16, 1900, in the Allen MSS; Allen to the Secretary of State,
March 27, 1899, June 6, 1900, Dispatches, State Department Archives.

[28] Allen to Hunt, April 16, 21, 1900, and memorandum dated April
28, 1900, in the Allen MSS; Allen to the Secretary of State, April 5,
1900, Dispatches, State Department Archives. On the 1885 precedent,
see Foulk to the President of the Korean Foreign Office, June 12, 29,
August 21, 1885, with confidential reply of September 3, Korean Legation Files, State Department Archives. Sands, *Undiplomatic Memories,*
200–201, and Allen to the Secretary of State, June 6, 1901, Dispatches,
State Department Archives, show the importance of form.

James R. Morse, American Investor

His was the vision but not the reward. A pioneer in Oriental commerce, Morse early saw the investment opportunities in Korea. With Allen's aid he won the first mine and railroad grants; but numerous difficulties forced him to yield his mines to other Americans, his railroads to the Japanese.

suaded the king to keep Peng Yang officials from squeezing the American investors. And he took care of the labor problem.[29]

This was a serious one. The Un-san grant covered an area already "honeycombed by native miners." In the winter of 1896 these men were ordered to stop work to make way for a foreign company. And soon they saw the new monopolist taking what they had regarded as theirs. Naturally some raised a protest. Sixteen of the more prosperous miners wrote to United States Minister Sill:

We are gold miners [who] have been engaged in opening quartz mines in the Li Tap Mountains . . . , but in the 7'th moon last year, American miners took away from us by force all the mines without a single payment, under the pretence that they had purchased the same while we were working them.

Also . . . big and little fir trees which we planted and cared for for several hundred years in the neighborhood of our homes and our fathers graves were cut down leaving only the bare hills, by the American miners without any compensatio[n]. . . .

Is it in accordance with international law that any one can take away by force the property of another without payment? . . .

We trust you will immediately let us have 6,600,000 cash or more for the price of the mines, crushers and trees, and do not let us be ruined to our destruction.

Also, coolies from Seoul and Peng Yang who are employed in the gold mines are looting the native people and committing wicked acts under the pretence of mining work, therefore every native of said district will become a beggar, as they give up their farming work because of the hindrance of said coolies. If they are coerced by their officials great disturbance and collisions will occur between the coolies and the natives.

[29] Allen to Morse, October 4, 1896, June 28, 1897, and to Morgan, October 5, 1902, in the Allen MSS; Allen to the Secretary of State, December 13, 1900, November 20, 1902, January 14, February 4, 1903, Dispatches, State Department Archives; Allen to the Reverend C. D. Morris, August 25, 1904, and to the Korean Minister of Foreign Affairs, March 18, June 27, October 10, 1898, November 5, December 15, 1900, February 1, May 29, 1901, October 6, 23, 1902, February 13, 1903, Korean Legation Files, State Department Archives.

We trust you will instruct the overseer (manager) of mines in our district to expel these evil coolies of Seoul and Peng Yang and give the work to the native people.[30]

As a missionary Allen had labored for Koreans such as these who now petitioned his legation. But as a dollar diplomat he could see no justice in the natives' claims. "The Koreans can never see what is for their own best good," was his reaction, "and seem to take more delight in a piece of intrigue that will give them a few present dollars, than in promoting a thing that is manifestly for the great good of the majority." Having become minister soon after the petition was received, he considered the problems raised from the viewpoint of the concessionaires. He settled the timber question by arranging to pay the government—not the people— for lumber taken. As to the natives, he declared that they would all be taken care of by employment as company laborers.[31]

Even there the minister's attitude showed the employer's slant. He boasted of low labor costs—three thousand workers for a hundred-thousand-dollar yearly outlay. He had liquor barred from the mining districts to keep the natives peaceful. And when he heard of thefts of gold and dynamite, he cried out in rage against the workers. He told the manager of the Un-san mines that he was "certainly in favor of the judicious whipping of Koreans, who understand it and would not understand its absence."[32]

[30] "A Petition Written by 16 Citizens of the Uhn San District in Northern Peng Yang Province, to the Minister of the United States, May, 1897," in the Allen MSS. See also Allen to Hunt, November 17, 1896, May 1, 1897, in the Allen MSS; the second of these quotes the natives: "it is no use, we will die anyway, so we may as well kill off these Americans as we cant be more than killed anyway."

[31] Allen to Hunt, November 15, 1896, August 10, 1897, in the Allen MSS.

[32] Allen to Meserve, November 1, 1900, in the Allen MSS; Secretary of State Hay to Allen, January 25, 1901, Dispatches, State Department Archives; Allen to the Assistant Secretary of State, November 3, 1897 (comparing Koreans favorably with Indians and Negroes), Consular Dispatches, State Department Archives.

A Cripple Creek All of Our Own

Instead of trying to increase the share of labor, Allen spent his time attempting to get more for the American investors. By 1898 he was urging that Hunt be given the management of all Korean mines in return for a loan of two and a half million dollars. He did effective work in advancing the proposition at the Seoul court, while Hunt spent forty thousand chasing prospects. Eventually, though, plans failed, even for a second, ten-mine proposition. Hunt appears to have received an offer from the household department, staffed by members of the American party, only to meet with objections from the foreign office, which was controlled by Russia. Russia had a prior claim, it was said, and Tsarist minister Pavloff added that "the placing of such a large amount of money in the hands of the Koreans would simply hasten their downfall . . . the Company would be the practical owners of Korea." Japan and England echoed Russian disapproval, and Allen could make no headway, even when he applied directly to the Russian diplomats and said that Hunt was willing to use Russian capital. The maneuver merely served to persuade the Russians that their claims were valuable. When Hunt and the Russian agent, Baron Gunzburg, did get together on a joint mine enterprise, in 1903, it was too late to stand against Japan. It was still possible for Gunzburg to obtain from Ye Yong Ik, Treasurer of the Imperial Household (November 27, 1903), a twenty-five-year grant which covered rights of way, lumber privileges, and "iron, coal, silver, gold and all other mineral products" in a district to be selected in northern Korea. A company was formed, in which Hunt had a quarter interest; and Meserve, Hunt's mine manager, was appointed to select a site. Outbreak of the Russo-Japanese war interfered with plans, but Gunzburg, hoping that the franchise would carry over, asked Allen to take care of the matter for the duration of hostilities. Japanese victory, however, ended opportunities along this line.[33]

[33] Allen to David Deshler, February 21, 1900; to Hunt, November 25,

But despite other disappointments the Un-san project remained successful. Other nations obtained mine franchises, but no such money-maker. As late as 1904 an Englishman remarked that the Americans had the "only mine in Korea which pays."[34] Even when other mines were developed successfully, the properties that Allen had obtained still paid the best.

Nor did politics affect the profits. Japan made Chosen a protectorate in 1905 and five years later annexed the region. But the Oriental Consolidated Mining Company held on. Allen's work had been well done, the Japanese could find no flaw in the legality of the mine grants. On went the work, on went the dividends, averaging twelve per cent a year from 1903 to 1917. There was a downward dip after the first World War, cutting the average return in half during the nineteen twenties. But profits were up again in the depression years to make the average annual dividend for the period 1903–38 more than nine per cent, the total well over fourteen millions.[35]

December 8, 1899, April 21, July 29, 1900, to Stevens of the American Trading Company, February 10, 1900, to Everett, February 11, 1900, and to Morse, December 29, 1899, December 4, 1900, in the Allen MSS; Allen to the Secretary of State, November 18, 1899, February 23, 1901, Dispatches, State Department Archives; Allen to Rockhill, July 29, 1900, in the Rockhill MSS; Vonliarliarsky, "Why Russia Went to War with Japan," *Fortnightly Review*, 93 (1900):1034–1035; Pierre Marc, *Quelques années de politique internationale* (Leipzig, 1914), 171–174; Friedrich von Steinmann, *Russlands Politik im Fernen Osten und der Staatssekretär Bezobrazov* (Leipzig, 1931), 43–50. Conflict among American capitalists also held Hunt and Allen back. Memorandum dated March 11, 1901, and Allen to Fassett, November 3, 1900, in the Allen MSS; Allen Diary, August 25, 1903.

The Russian claim grew out of the unsuccessful efforts of Russians with high official connections in St. Petersburg to secure a general mine concession in 1896. The Hunt-Gunzburg agreement is seen in Gunzburg to Allen, March 30, 1904, with concession and supplementary agreement of December 2, 1904; Gunzburg to Meserve, December 10, 1903, and Allen to Gunzburg, January 23, 1906, in the Allen MSS.

[34] Hamilton, *Korea*, 151; Whigham, *Manchuria and Korea*, 187; article by Allen, dated October 1, 1905, in the Allen MSS.

[35] The situation is summarized in *Moody's Manual of Investments:*

A Cripple Creek All of Our Own

With that, the Oriental came to the road's end. Japan was getting firm by 1939. No longer could the Oriental send gold abroad. The company was required to sell it to the Japanese government, and to take payment in depreciated currency. Besides, bad Japanese-American relations made confiscation not improbable. Wisely the owners of the Oriental salvaged what was possible, sold their rights to a Japanese concern for eight million dollars.[36] And so concluded an imperial adventure started more than four decades before by Horace Allen.

Industrial Securities, 1939, p. 1276, and *Poor's Industrial Volume,* 1939, pp. 3106–3107.

[36] "Chosen Gold," *Time,* 34 (1939):78. Payments on the balance due stopped in 1941.

10

One for Japan

I DON'T think the Japanese will do other than ask for similar favors," Allen had written when he secured the Un-san mine franchise in July, 1895. His guess was right, for Japan did not attempt to void the new concession. But she did consider future policy. Inouye thought the Allen coup showed need for a gentler touch in Seoul—had not Japanese harshness driven Chosen into another's arms? Japanese extremists, on the other hand, saw the solution in more force.[1]

Inouye had won at first and, working through Allen, had even made peace with the queen. By fall, though, his opponents had forged ahead. Jingoistic Viscount Miura, new Japanese envoy in Seoul, inaugurated terroristic methods. He and his native allies—the friends of the Tai Wen Kun—killed the queen on October 8, 1895, and made a prisoner of the king. There followed a period of Japanese dictatorship, which lasted until February 11, 1896, when his Korean Majesty escaped and took refuge in the legation of imperial Russia.

While the conciliatory Inouye was on top, Allen had hopes of getting something for Americans—and, indirectly, for him-

[1] Allen to Morse, postscript of July 16 to letter dated June 24, 1895, in the Allen MSS; letters to the Secretary of State from Allen, September 18, 1895, and from Sill, July 27, September 4, 1895, Dispatches, State Department Archives.

self. His prospects faded with Miura's rise, but returned when the king obtained asylum from the Russians. For the Russian minister, Allen's good friend Waeber, approved of franchise grants for the United States. Wishing to curb Japan, the Tsarist envoy thought it advisable to strengthen all Occidental nations on the ground.

What Allen wanted most was a railroad grant for Morse, a franchise for a line from Chemulpo to Seoul. The whole subject of rail transportation fascinated the doctor, as is indicated by his repeated efforts to design railroad equipment. More important, Morse desired the franchise, considered it more valuable than the Un-san mines. If he obtained a grant, Allen was almost sure of another reward.

The doctor had thought of railroad possibilities ever since his first unpleasant journey to Seoul. Two years later he had laughed at the Japanese for contemplating a steamship service to the coast. In his opinion a railroad was much to be preferred. The route was short, twenty-six miles, less than half the water distance. The rails could be laid cheaply, save for the crossing of the Han River south of Seoul. And it was clear that all costs would be met by freight and passenger receipts.[2]

Though China had checked the doctor's bid of 1891, the Japanese supplied most of the competition. This could be met in 1892 and 1893, for Allen's native agents stood on even terms with Chung Hyung Ha, the Japanese front man. But later Japanese victory in the war with China put the Americans in second place.

Undismayed, the American legation secretary worked out new tactics based on recognition of Japanese superiority. "Let the Japanese build the R.R. if they would," he explained to Morse, "if they would not then [have Korea] sign your former contract." It would be useless to buck Korea's overlord. But a shortage of capital might keep Japan from railroad building. Even if she started she might fail. Her Seoul paper

[2] Allen to Ellinwood, April 11, 1886, in the Allen MSS.

factory produced no paper, her rice-cleaning mill did not clean rice. If her railroad ventures fared no better, Morse might then step in and prosper.[3]

Working along this line, Allen teased out of Japanese Minister Saito the statement that if his own government decided against the railroad, he was sure Inouye would help get it for Morse. Korean officials were equally agreeable. Some wavered when a Korean-American, Dr. Philip Jaisohn, tried to cut Morse out, but Allen soon took care of that. He informed the court that Morse had priority among Americans and persuaded Jaisohn to give way.

That done, Allen could only wait for the Japanese to fail. Restless by disposition, he found that difficult, for Japan was often near to victory. In 1894 the doctor was fretting over a survey the Japanese had made, and thereafter his worries multiplied. He feared that a formal grant would be announced, putting an end to his hopes. And January, 1896, did see at the point of signature a Japanese-Korean contract which provided for a Japanese loan of some two million dollars to Chosen. This sum would be turned to construction, with the Japanese in firm control.[4]

Fearing that the game was up, Allen advised Morse to associate with the Japanese. Apparently the islanders were going to construct the railroad, but Morse might at least sell them rails and rolling stock. Indications were that England might be favored, so Allen too set out to court Japan. On February 7, 1896, he wrote Inouye pretending pleasure that the Japanese were making headway with their railroad plans. This of course was sheer hypocrisy, for simultaneously the legation secretary prepared to complain to Washington about the monopoly methods of Japan in Chosen.[5]

[3] Address to the Naval War College and Allen to Morse, June 24, 1895, in the Allen MSS.

[4] Allen to Morse, January 30, 1896, to Inouye, February 7, 1896, and address to the Naval War College, in the Allen MSS; Sill to the Assistant Secretary of State, January 17, April 6, 1895, Consular Dispatches, State Department Archives.

[5] Allen to Inouye, February 7, 1896, to Morse, January 30, February

Pretense became unnecessary four days later, when Japan lost out in Seoul. When that happened Allen dropped the idea of conciliation instantly. Gone was his willingness to let Japan have the first try. Now, by the grace of the Tsar, America had a chance for the leading position. On the very day that Russia gave the Korean king asylum, Allen wrote Morse that Chosen's new overlord would be glad to have him get the franchise.[6]

For six full years the doctor had been working for this concession; now he clinched the deal in six weeks time. And the grant of March 29, 1896, gave Morse all that a concessionaire could wish. He had a full year to start operations and three in which to complete the work. Labor provisions favored the employer and the railroad was exempted from taxes of every kind.[7]

In closing his negotiations Allen had studied every angle. He had taken care of his own government. He had handled Japan and Russia, Britain, France, and Germany; and he had managed Chosen, too. All was in splendid order.

But his own government gave Allen much concern. He and Minister Sill had just been censured for taking a too active interest in Korean politics, and both had been told to mend their ways. If Secretary of State Richard Olney heard that Allen was maneuvering for a concession, dismissal would almost surely follow. And news might leak out in a dozen ways. Sill might inadvertently let slip a damning scrap of information—he had done that before. Or the Japanese, as sharp competitors, might "make it warm" for the doctor by letting out some secrets.[8] Altogether it was a risky busi-

1, 11, 1896, and to Edward Dun, February 7, 1896, in the Allen MSS. In the last letter, written to the pro-Japanese American minister in Tokyo, Allen said, "we have endeavored to assist Japan over here."

[8] Allen to Morse, February 11, 1896, and to Morse and Hunt, June 29, 1896, in the Allen MSS. Russia approved, Allen thought, because "it gives a fine appearance to Korean independence on the outside."

[7] Copies of suggested contracts and the final agreement are in the Allen MSS.

[8] Allen to Morse, April 6, 1896, in the Allen MSS.

ness, worth trying only because the prospect for personal gain was so good.

As it happened, all went well. The Japanese kept quiet and Sill made no misstep. Indeed, as in the mining matters, he "had not the faintest thing to do" with the greater part of the negotiations. Allen obtained the franchise and wrote the news to Washington, Sill merely dignifying the dispatch with his ministerial signature.[9] The dispatch, of course, contained no hint of Allen's backstairs work; it was so tame that the State Department gave it to the press.

Japan could not be handled quite so easily. Still, Allen thought it best to try to win her favor—it would save trouble if she came back to power. So he had her sounded out on the railroad project, asked if she minded seeing the Americans secure control. Two answers were obtained. Komura, Japanese envoy in Seoul, withheld approval when Allen had Sill ask for it. Morse, working in Tokyo through American Minister Edwin Dun, got a pleasanter reaction. Hara, chief of the commercial bureau of the Japanese foreign office, intimated that since Japan could not obtain the line, it was well to have Americans in charge. That was enough for Allen. He could forget Komura and take the Hara statement at its face value.[10]

But it was Russia, not Japan, that counted most in 1896. Knowing that, Allen gave great attention to negotiations with his old friend Waeber. His heart sank in dismay in mid-February, when the Russian minister seemed cool. Then up his spirits came as Waeber resumed his old-time cordiality, perhaps because of orders from St. Petersburg.[11]

[9] Allen to Morse, April 6, May 8, 1896, in the Allen MSS; Sill to the Secretary of State, April 16, 1896, Dispatches, State Department Archives.

[10] Allen to Morse, February 18, March 29, May 8, 1896, in the Allen MSS; Sill to the Secretary of State, July 13, 1897, Dispatches, State Department Archives.

[11] Allen's letter to Morse on May 21, 1896, in the Allen MSS, suggests, on the basis of information obtained through Morse, that Waeber was opposed to the grant, but received instructions to pacify the United States and Great Britain.

" I spoke to Waeber to know if Russia would object to seeing America get that road," runs Allen's version. "Waeber is under some obligations to me and we went together last fall during the troubles [*murder of the queen*]. He shrugged his shoulders and said that as for himself it would be all right but he could not answer for his Govm't. I gave him two weeks to find out what his Govm't thought and then went at him again ... He gave his full assent ... I wrote up a contract ... and made a few corrections at the request of my friends. Then it went to Mr. Waeber and he had it over two weeks. I was sick and confined to my bed most of the time but when not under morphine he would come and we worked it out little by little."[12]

There was no doubt that the Russian envoy showed "very much interest in the project." In reviewing Allen's contract he labored over every article and suggested many changes. His alterations ran along three lines. First, he wanted Morse to have broad powers, setting precedents for grants to Russia later. At the same time he asked for a few privileges for Chosen, that he might pose as the king's friend. Lastly, he insisted on excluding specific mention of the Russians from the treaty lest the cry of influence be raised.

Allen agreed to everything that Waeber asked and offered to toss in a clause granting Russian troops free transportation on the new railroad. That Waeber did not want. Instead he asked that Morse's American Trading Company surrender its Dagelet Island timber-cutting privileges to Russia (though, of course, this was not to be mentioned in the treaty). Allen saw that this was done. Anything to please the Russians—and besides, there was little lumber left, and the concession had apparently expired.[13]

---

[12] Allen to Morse, March 29, 1896, in the Allen MSS. This letter contains the best account of the negotiations.

[13] On the Dagelet lumber contracts, see letters to the Secretary of State from Foulk, August 4, 6, 1885, and from Allen, April 24, 1903, Dispatches, State Department Archives; Foulk to Townsend, August 24, 1885, in the Foulk MSS; and Allen's address to the Naval War College,

Having given Waeber satisfaction, Allen thought his own work nearly done. There was a little trouble with the French and Germans, who were also bidding for the franchise. "But," as the doctor said, he and Waeber "were too much for them." France had to be content with a Seoul-Wiju grant, certain to be a money-loser; and Germany obtained nothing.[14]

This left only the Koreans, whom Allen always handled well. And here the circumstances were most favorable in 1896. Having escaped from the Japanese and located. at Russia's legation, His Korean Majesty had chosen a new cabinet, drawing ministers from the ranks of Allen's friends. The advantage was increased by reason of the fact that the Koreans in question had lately been refugees in the American legation. Naturally they were expected to "defer to Russian opinion in matters of consequence"; but when they could they also worked for Allen.

It was "clear sailing" but for one man, Chyo Pyung Chik, the minister of public works. Chyo, whom Allen dubbed "an ignorant old fossil," objected to a clause that gave Korea the right to buy the railroad after fifteen years, or twenty-five, or thirty-five, and so on. Chyo insisted that the road should be presented free to Chosen after fifteen years. Japan, he said, had made a proposition similar to that.

Allen had "very strong suspicions" that Dr. Philip Jaisohn was behind Chyo's stand. This man, born So Jay Pil, had been involved in the émeute of 1884. When it had failed,

in the Allen MSS. The following shed light on Russian concession interests: Steinmann, *Russlands Politik im Fernen Osten*, 35–61; Marc, *Quelques années de politique internationale*, 170–200; Vonliarliarsky, "Why Russia Went to War," *Fortnightly Review*, 93 (1900):816–831, 1030–1044; and J. J. Capanovich, "Sino-Russian Relations in Manchuria, 1892–1896," *Chinese Social and Political Science Review*, 17 (1933):283–306, 457–479, an abstract and review of a study by B. A. Romanov.

[14] Allen to Morse, March 30, April 3, 18, May 21, 1896, to Hunt, April 16, August 27, 1896, and to Morse and Hunt, June 29, July 17, 1896, in the Allen MSS; Sill to the Secretary of State, July 17, 1896, Dispatches, State Department Archives.

he had migrated to America, where he had acquired a new name, American citizenship, and a Johns Hopkins medical degree. Upon returning to Chosen in 1895, he had become a government adviser, attached in 1896 to Chyo's public works department. "Presumably to be on hand for mines and railroads," stated Allen, who had had trouble with the adviser in the fall of 1895.

It was the king who settled the difficulty between Chyo and Allen. Allen did his best, only to decide that Chyo was "so ignorant . . . and stubborn that it was almost impossible to move him." The more gentle Waeber likewise failed to change the old man's views, whereupon His Majesty was requested to break the deadlock.[15]

With victory won, Allen totaled up the obligations. Natives had assisted greatly. The doctor had worked through two veterans of the mine negotiations, Ye Wan Yong, now foreign minister, and Ye Cha Yun, Chyo's vice-minister. These men had volunteered their services, so there was "no one to 'fix' in this matter. It is all clean & square and nothing underhanded." But while it was "not compulsory," Allen thought that Morse should give these men some stock, "say $15,000 to Ye Wan & $10,000 to Ye Cha." Jaisohn might also be worth cultivation, for he could be "a useful or a troublesome cuss. Dont give him an interest that he could realize on but if you can use him in connection with mines and railroads, take him on at a salary, say $3000 per annum."[16]

The Korean contribution to the enterprise was overshadowed by the Russian. Waeber had "really done us yeoman service" and had topped it off by letting Allen use a

[15] Allen to Morse, March 29, 30, 1896, and to Hunt, April 16, 1896, in the Allen MSS. Jaisohn expressed pleasure at Allen's final success (Seoul *Independent*, April 6, 1896): "on the whole this is the most satisfactory contract of a similar character the government ever made with a foreign firm."

[16] Allen to Morse, March 29, 30, April 18, 1896, in the Allen MSS. The last states that Allen had promised something to Ye Wan and Ye Cha.

For Mammon

Russian cruiser to send Morse the contract in Japan. Repayment would be difficult, but at least a gesture might be made. Morse, for example, might write a letter offering to transport Russian soldiers free when the railroad was completed. The desire to hide the Russian hand had kept that sort of clause out of the franchise, but Waeber would accept the favor gladly if it came through private channels.[17]

Ye Wan Yong, Ye Cha Yun, Minister Waeber, each had helped enormously, but Allen put himself ahead of them all: no one but he could have obtained the railroad grant and the mine franchise, which he regarded as the "best diplomatic successes of our service during the last year." And there had been enormous risk; he knew that if the State Department should learn of what he had done, they would dismiss him; but he confessed, "I am not here for my health or $1500 a year and take the risk."[18]

In short, reward was due. In the mine affair the goal had been a business job and cash. Now it was promotion, to be obtained through Morse and his associate Leigh Hunt. "If McKinley comes in next time I shall try for this mission," Allen wrote to Morse, "and if Mr. Hunts syndicate has the backing you say it has, they should help me in their own interests. A N.Y. syndicate secured Denbys appointment [*as minister to China*] against the wishes of Vice-Prest Hendricks, why cant they help me."[19] And aid they did, to help produce the coveted appointment in August, 1897.

In his last months as legation secretary and in his first as minister, Allen engaged in follow-up work on the new Morse grant. For obstacles appeared—new opposition from Japan

[17] Allen to Morse, March 30, 1896, in the Allen MSS.
[18] Allen to George K. Nash, September 14, 1896, and to Morse, March 30, 1896, in the Allen MSS.
[19] Allen to Morse, March 30, 1896, Hunt to Allen, July 24, 1897, John B. McCullough to Allen, April 29, 1897, Thomas W. Power to President McKinley, January 23, 1897, and Allen to Jennie Everett, November 5, 1895, in the Allen MSS. Allen told Mrs. Everett that "Morse declares I must be the next Minister."

176

and Germany, Hunt's lack of interest in the line, Morse's difficulty in obtaining capital. These might spell failure, which would be a heavy blow to Allen and to American prestige all through the Orient.[20]

To avert calamity the doctor labored mightily to push the railroad through. He showered Morse with letters of advice. He tried to get financial aid from his Ohio friends. And he smoothed the way for Morse by handling nasty native problems. Thus during labor troubles he pointed out a strike-breaking clause he had inserted in the concession, giving Morse the right to import Chinese coolies.[21]

Things looked a little brighter during 1897. Even though he lacked the aid of Hunt, Morse won support from Senator Calvin S. Brice and let a contract for construction. Work was begun one week inside the stipulated period, Allen being present at the inauguration ceremonies and claiming that success was almost certain now that "one of Mr. Hanna's great friends is in the deal." Morse was "going to realize handsomely on his little investment."[22]

Joy was short-lived. Morse's backers soon shied off, leaving Allen's friend in sore financial straits. His own resources and contacts were limited, and American investors were suspicious of enterprises in countries as turbulent as Chosen. Wherefore Morse was forced to mortgage his concession at Japan's Specie Bank and in 1898 to sell out to the Japanese.[23]

Allen was frantic when he heard of Morse's movements. Russia had allowed, Chosen had granted him his franchise for the very purpose of heading off Japan. ("One of the ad-

[20] "Narrative of Facts," and Allen to Morse, August 18, 27, 1896, in the Allen MSS.
[21] Allen to Rockhill, June 14, 1897, and to Morse, June 28, 1897, in the Allen MSS. See also the *Korea Review*, 1 (1901):414.
[22] Allen to Jennie Everett, February 25, 1897, in the Allen MSS; *Korean Repository*, 4 (1897):113, 313–314; Sill to the Secretary of State, April 12, 1897, Dispatches, State Department Archives. Brice was interested in Chinese railways.
[23] Allen to the Secretary of State, May 23, 1898, Dispatches, State Department Archives.

vantages of the present [American] arrangement is that the road will be in the hands of people belonging to a power which under no conceivable circumstances could be suspected of ulterior motives of a political nature," was the Korean view when the grant was made.) The Russian-inspired law against the narrow gage, the Korean resistance to the Japanese clamor for a Seoul-Fusan grant all tied in with the drive against Japan. Knowing this, Allen pounded hard at Morse as early as 1896. Russia "would regard it as dishonorable if you should let the Japanese in," Koreans would consider it "a low down and unprincipled thing," and even Japan would "think Morse was not square with the Koreans."[24]

Morse may have been impressed by these strong words. In any case he did refuse a Japanese offer in 1897.[25] And later, when he felt called upon to sell, he did not insist on dealing with Japan. Russia would have pleased him just as well. Allen, of course, preferred the Russians—they had been his friends. But at this juncture Russia was withdrawing from Seoul and did not wish to increase her responsibilities. Vainly did Waeber's successor Speyer urge the matter on his home government; St. Petersburg refused to move.

Failing there, Speyer and Allen talked of other possibilities. Speyer thought a private Russian company might be tried. It could quietly advance the money for the mortgage at the Specie Bank of Tokyo, then take the railroad over when construction had been completed. Allen was more impressed by another possibility—obtaining funds through the Russian ally France. A hurry call went out for French envoy Grille, and the case was put before him. Grille was impressed, as was the Paris syndicate with which he communicated; but unfortunately the French bankers held out for a Russian guarantee which could not be obtained.[26]

[24] Allen to Morse, September 20, October 2, 8, 1896, January 23, 1897, January 23, March 30, 1898, and to Morse and Hunt, June 24, 1898, in the Allen MSS; Seoul *Independent*, April 16, 1896.

[25] Allen to Rockhill, June 14, 1897, in the Allen MSS.

[26] Allen to Morse, April 29, May 28, 1898, January 23, 1899, and to

One for Japan

Sadly Allen yielded to the inevitable, a victory for the Japanese. It came in March of 1898 and was announced by Morse's telegram: "S.C.R.R. has been sold to Japanese syndicate I have connected with as member." "Very disagreeable," wired back the doctor. "American control was desired." It was worse to learn that the syndicate had "a close connection with the Japanese government." "This," Allen felt, "is the hardest thing I have had to handle." It was "regarded as an act of bad faith" in Seoul and hurt every concessionaire there. The doctor's own influence waned; on one occasion he saw the king avoid him to consult the British minister. And when Hunt requested a new mine, Allen had to answer, "I couldn't get another gold mining concession now to save me."[27]

As if that were not enough, more humiliation followed. Allen turned and gave assistance to the Japanese, his former foes—and received no thanks at all. He began to feel that "this R.R. business has become a veritable stinking nuisance over here."[28]

It was Morse who induced Allen to assist Japan. In selling his franchise the doctor's business friend had become connected with the Tokyo purchasers. Thus his interests were linked with theirs. He stood to gain if they obtained new

Collbran, February 12, 1898, in the Allen MSS; Allen to the Secretary of State, March 30, 1898, Dispatches, State Department Archives; "The Seoul-Chemulpo Railroad," *Korean Repository,* 5 (1898):272. The Russians seem to have feared that Russian activity would cause trouble with Japan or would lead the Japanese to demand a Seoul-Fusan franchise. Allen told Morse (April 29, 1898) that Speyer got "severe raps" from his government for his part in the negotiations.

[27] Allen to Hunt, August 11, 1898, to Morse, March 29, 30, 1898, and to Woolsey, September 11, 1898, in the Allen MSS; Allen to the Secretary of State, January 11, December 1, 1899, Dispatches, State Department Archives; Allen to Korean Minister of Foreign Affairs, January 2, 1899, Seoul Legation Files, State Department Archives; Sands, *Undiplomatic Memories,* 204; "The Seoul-Chemulpo Railroad," *Korean Repository,* 5 (1898):272–273. Secretary of State Sherman wrote Allen on February 23, 1899 (Instructions, State Department Archives): "You appear to have handled a delicate matter with tact and discretion."

[28] Allen to Morse, August 12, 1898, in the Allen MSS.

railroad grants in Chosen. At the very least he could expect to handle purchases of equipment in the United States; that much had been promised him by the new premier, Count Okuma.

Asked to help in Seoul, Allen "hesitated very much." The State Department had told him to "avoid entanglements with other nations." He had often violated those instructions, risking "serious trouble" with superiors. But departure from the rules had always been for friends. Why should he do it for Japan? Japan had not befriended him; her representatives had fought him tooth and nail since 1894.

Morse could tell him why he should aid Japan. The doctor was in Seoul "to promote, protect and look out generally for American interests." As the Japanese were gaining, it became Allen's "duty" to play along with them in order "to secure for American Manufacturers," through Morse, "the sale of a large amount of equipment."[29] Besides, the American minister was bound to Morse by money ties. Would it not be best from the point of view of personal finances to go along with the president of the American Trading Company?

Persuaded in July of 1898, Allen agreed to help the Japanese. Seeking Kato, Japanese minister in Seoul, the doctor asked him point-blank whether he wanted aid in his efforts to obtain the Seoul-Fusan railroad grant. Since American interests would be affected, he felt justified in discussing matters; hence he informed Kato that he "was being consulted about the matter [by His Majesty] and it was in such shape that I felt confident I could, if I desired, get the concession entirely away from them and to ourselves; I would not do such a thing however, and I simply wished now to know from him if he desired my assistance. If he did not, I would simply refuse to give any advice at all and let the matter drag its own course, which did not seem to be a very rapid or satisfactory one."

"I would wish very much for your assistance," Kato an-

[29] Allen to Morse, July 24, 25, 28, 1898, in the Allen MSS.

swered. Naturally: for Allen had great influence with the monarch of Chosen, and Morse had'an old claim to the concession.

What would Japan do in return?

"If you will help me," Kato promised, "I will do my best to see that things manufactured in America are purchased and American interests are promoted through Mr. Morse."[30]

That seemed fair enough, so Allen pledged and gave his aid. Without it Japan would have had great difficulty, for Chosen, fearing Russian ire, did not wish to deal directly with the Japanese.[31] Negotiations long bogged down were resumed as soon as Allen became the go-between, and in the fall of 1898 the franchise was obtained.

Japan was thus indebted to both Morse and Allen. But the debt was not repaid. Morse found the Tokyo bankers hard to deal with, decided to sever his connection with the Seoul-Chemulpo syndicate. In doing so he realized a handsome profit on the sale of his concession, but did not get a penny for his assistance in the Fusan matter. Nor did equipment purchases work out as Kato and Okuma had predicted.[32]

Allen likewise found the islanders a bit ungracious. They announced the Seoul-Chemulpo transfer when he wanted it soft-pedaled for a while. Kato refused to let the doctor look at the Fusan grant which he had helped to land. Americans building a Seoul trolley line encountered bitter opposition from the Japanese legation, and Allen did not receive a pass

[30] Allen to Morse, April 17, and, in particular, July 28, 1898, in the Allen MSS.

[31] That the Japanese needed outside aid is indicated by Allen's letters to Morse of August 13, September 1, October 12, 1896, March 30, July 24, 25, 1898, and to Woolsey, September 11, 1898, in the Allen MSS, and by the *Korean Repository*, 3 (1896):334.

[32] Address to the Naval War College, Allen to Woolsey, September 10, 1898, and to Morse, September 19, 1898, in the Allen MSS. Allen advised Morse to get out. For mention of later purchases of American rails and bridge materials see Paddock to the Assistant Secretary of State, November 4, 1904, Consular Dispatches, State Department Archives.

for the Seoul-Chemulpo railroad, which he rightly regarded as his creation.[33]

So ran the path of an economic imperialist who lacked the backing of his government and his home country's financiers. Allen moaned that he had gone too far for Morse, "even going further than I was warranted in going,—in justice to my Gov'mt." He could not figure out the situation, he could not "understand the Japanese at all." Only one thing was apparent; he had "unintentionally played into the hands of the Japanese all along."[34] Starting with a concession won with the aid of Japan's foes, the Russians, he had ended by contributing to Japanese glory.

Yet in defeat much had been saved. As a dollar diplomat, Allen could rejoice that Morse had made a profit in the deal.[35] So had Collbran and Bostwick, the American contractors who built the Seoul-Chemulpo. And Allen, too, for Morse did not forget his diplomatic friend.

In the process, prestige had been sacrificed. But Chosen still desired to deal with Allen and the United States. By 1897 the doctor-diplomat could boast of having made possible the first Korean railroad and the country's first well-operated mine. Eight years later he could point as well to Chosen's first trolley line, first city lighting plant, first public water supply, first telephone system, first modern office building. Each and every item bore the stamp of Allen's influence, and all were projects started and completed by his countrymen.[36]

[33] Allen to Morse, July 24, 1898, December 29, 1899, to Collbran, July 24, 1898, to a friend, October 14, 1899, in the Allen MSS.
[34] Allen to Wilson, December 16, 1902, to Morse, August 9, 1898, to Woolsey, September 10, 1898, in the Allen MSS.
[35] A million dollars, according to German Consul Krien. Allen to Morse, May 28, 1898, in the Allen MSS.
[36] There is a tone of optimism in Allen to Morse, January 5, 1899, in the Allen MSS.

11

In the Light of the Rising Sun

WITH the Spanish-American War of 1898 the United States launched her imperial course. But even after annexation of the Philippines, America still lacked an aggressive interest in the Orient. Allen never received the forceful backing other diplomats had, could never get the State Department interested in concession-chasing in Seoul.

Indeed, the tendency was the reverse. Washington was so desirous of sidestepping trouble that Allen was told "to not show any interest in things, and especially not to give any advice." When he tried to get a gigantic sugar beet concession for George P. Morgan, Assistant Secretary of State Adee objected on the ground that "monopolies always give rise to disputes." When he tried to open two Korean ports to foreign trade, Rockhill spoke of "a 'bull in a china shop'" and thought "something should be sent him restraining his too great show of energy." Another official condemned Allen's whole franchise drive, saying "too many Korean concessions have been granted through backstairs influence exercised by necromancers, eunuchs and dancing girls and foreign representatives, even some of those who should know better than to employ such aid."[1]

[1] Allen to Morse, January 23, 1898, in the Allen MSS; notes of Adee,

Only occasionally was the doctor encouraged to be active in economic matters. In the sugar case, Adee was answered by another State Department official, F. Van Dyne. He agreed that monopoly was bad but supposed that "in such countries as Korea and China" the department would not "draw the line closely in cases where the good offices of our Legation are sought to obtain for an American a concession which would otherwise go to a foreigner."

But it was not Van Dyne who made it possible for Allen to remain a dollar diplomat. It was indifference. Officials in Washington paid little heed to what went on in Seoul, let Allen do as he saw fit. "All they seem to want is to be let alone," the doctor said, "and that I shall run Korean matters smoothly with no trouble to them. They do not read my dispatches even, unless the jacket shows that the matter is of unusual importance."[2]

Perhaps that was an overstatement. There is evidence that State Department officers knew that Chosen was "in a somewhat abnormal position, internally, and much has been left to the discretion of our legation there."[3] In any case Allen was able to intervene in Seoul politics in spite of State Department attitudes. Methods, of course, were not reported to headquarters. Instead the doctor terminated each manipula-

Rockhill, and F. Van Dyne on Allen to the Secretary of State, December 6, 1903, March 17, May 12, 1905, Dispatches, State Department Archives; E. V. Morgan to Rockhill, June 4, 1904, in the Rockhill MSS. See also Secretary of State Bayard to Foulk, May 28, 1885, Instructions, State Department Archives.

The rise of Japanese influence ended the sugar beet project. Had he been able to secure a monopoly grant, Morgan would have launched a five- to ten-million-dollar company with Allen as president at ten thousand a year. Morgan to Allen, March 30, May 8, 1905, July 14, 1906, Allen to Morgan, March 18, 23, 1905, and proposed concession, February 9, 1905, with statement by Morgan, in the Allen MSS.

[2] Allen Diary, October 1, 1903; Allen to Rockhill, October 23, 1899, in the Rockhill MSS.

[3] W. L. Phillips, note on Paddock to the Secretary of State, June 30, 1903, Dispatches, State Department Archives. The interest of the State Department in Korea may have been indicated by its elevation of Allen

tion by announcing, "I have done nothing in furthering this matter that the Department could possibly object to."[4]

Under these conditions Washington officials seldom checked Horace Allen's operations. In truth, the cautious attitude of the United States was a major asset in Seoul. For Korea liked the mildness of America and, with the aggressive nations balancing each other, found it possible to slip some favors through to Allen.

The first, of course, were the Un-san mines and the Seoul-Chemulpo railroad. But that was just the start, the prelude to "other good business." Before the ink was dry on the railroad contract, Allen's native friends were talking of steamship lines, of water and electric systems, of coal mines and the ginseng monopoly.[5]

News of these new possibilities prompted Allen to ask if Morse was interested.[6] But Morse was not, he had enough to do with what he had. Besides, His Korean Majesty was beginning to suspect the American Trading Company's financial limitations and its president's willingness to deal with the enemies of Chosen. There was need of some one else to do the honors for America.

When it came to gold, there was no problem. Allen could and did rely on Leigh S. J. Hunt, the man who had bought the Un-san mines from Morse. Hunt's backers had put five millions into this development and had as much more for

from minister resident and consul general to envoy extraordinary and minister plenipotentiary in 1901. In this connection note the letter from Edward H. House to John Hay, February 15, 1897, in the Rockhill MSS: "the outlook at Seoul gives me more apprehension than I feel with respect to either Tokio or Peking, for a blunder in these big capitals may be promptly detected and remedied; whereas in that little boxed up kingdom, no end of mischief may be done before the searchlight can be turned on."

[4] Allen to the Secretary of State, February 15, 1898, in the Allen MSS.

[5] Allen to Morse, April 3, May 1, 1896, January 23, 1898, and to Morse and Hunt, May 31, 1896, in the Allen MSS.

[6] Allen to Morse, January 5, 1899, in the Allen MSS. Allen described Morse as "one of the truest men that ever befriended me." Letter to D. W. Stevens, April 8, 1906.

For Mammon

other "worthy" projects. "Worthy" meant gold; the Hunt group was not interested in other considerations.

Among the other operators were Walter D. Townsend and David W. Deshler. Townsend, already an established merchant, gained strength when he became an official distributor for Standard Oil. He worked in harmony with Deshler, who, like Foulk and Townsend, took a Japanese girl for his bride. A native of Ohio, Deshler became a close friend of the Allens, helped them get promotion and was helped in turn. His interests were broad, but in due time he concentrated on steam and navigation and on shipping Korean laborers to the Hawaiian sugar fields. His work was applauded and approved by Horace Allen.[7]

The major gap remaining was closed by Henry Collbran and Harry Bostwick. Collbran was a naturalized American who was to spend his last days repatriated in Great Britain. In 1881 he had migrated to America and had chosen transportation as his field. In seven years, when he was only thirty-five, he became general manager of the Colorado Midland Railway. Thereafter he constructed the Cripple Creek line and served as president of the Midland Terminal Railway of Colorado. In 1896 he was called to Korea, where he took the construction contract for the Seoul-Chemulpo in association with

[7] For Townsend, see John A. Cockerill, article in the *New York Herald,* December 1, 1895; Hamilton, *Korea,* especially p. 149; Allen to Morse, September 30, December 26, 1904, in the Allen MSS.

Deshler's activities are covered in the *Korea Review,* 3 (1903):30, 265–266, 529–533; 5 (1905):151, 411–413; Allen to Hunt, June 6, 1896, to Fassett, May 17, 1903, to Morse, September 10, 1896, and to E. V. Morgan, May 21, 1902, in the Allen MSS; Allen to the Secretary of State, May 19, October 29, 1903, Dispatches, State Department Archives.

Among those who seem to have shown a passing interest in Korea were E. H. Harriman, Paul Morton, David F. Francis, George P. Morgan, and Jacob Schiff. Letters from Allen to Everett, September 3, 1904, to George P. Morgan, February 13, 1905, to Harry Bostwick, March 24, 1905, to Lloyd Griscom, April 7, 1905, to Allen's sons, May 21, 1905, and to Wilson, September 10, 1897, in the Allen MSS; Allen to the Secretary of State, March 17, 1905, Dispatches, State Department Archives.

one Mr. James of Chattanooga. James soon faded from the picture, to be replaced by Bostwick, a young San Franciscan protégé of Collbran's.[8]

Allen never cared much for this business pair, never liked them as he did Morse and Hunt. In explanation he mentioned their "grasping ways" and Collbran's willingness to "do anything to accomplish his financial ends."[9] But whether he liked them or not, Allen found the partners useful. They were Americans, their gains reflected credit on the doctor's diplomatic record. Then, too, Collbran and Bostwick were ideal working colleagues. Instead of throwing all the burdens of negotiation onto Allen's shoulders, they did their part in the court maneuvers, whether the negotiations were with the governor of Seoul or the central government. And when they closed a contract, they carried out the terms religiously, leaving no unpleasant aftermath.[10]

Their first franchise was for a street-car and lighting system for Seoul. The offer came direct from Chosen late in 1896, unannounced and unexpected even by the well-posted American legation. A year of negotiations ensued, ending with the signing of a contract early in 1898—just before Morse sold his railroad to Japan.

Reporting home, Allen denied that he was involved in this matter, Actually he was in neck-deep. Collbran and Bostwick

[8] *Who's Who in America*, 1910–11. For James's resentment on the railroad deal, see Morse to Allen, March 20, 1905, in the Allen MSS.

[9] Allen to E. V. Morgan, November 21, 1902, March 2, 1904, in the Allen MSS.

[10] "Narrative of Facts," Allen to Hunt, April 18, 1900, in the Allen MSS; Allen to the Secretary of State, February 15, 1898, Dispatches, State Department Archives. But see E. V. Morgan to Rockhill, June 4, 1904, in the Rockhill MSS, and Allen's memorandum dated March 11, 1901, in the Allen MSS, for an arraignment of the methods of the partners. Collbran and Bostwick gave a loan to Allen on his Chemulpo summer home, and appear to have offered him an interest in the business. This Allen refused. Allen to A. J. Brown, April 30, 1905, in the Allen MSS. For their methods, see also Louis Graves, "Willard Straight at the Legation in Korea," *Asia*, 20 (1920): 1081, mentioning their gifts to the emperor.

had received the initial proposition while in Allen's home and had immediately requested his advice and aid. From that time on the doctor was in on every step in the negotiations, so much so that he described the closing of the contract as the "finest little piece of work I have done."[11]

Fine it surely was, for Collbran and Bostwick were all but guaranteed against a loss. That was Allen's doing. From the very start he had told them to demand a cash consideration. Working through friends like Ye Cha Yun, he had obtained just that, to the amount of fifty thousand dollars. More was promised, the theory being that Collbran and Bostwick were contractors working for a Korean corporation, the Seoul Electric Company. That, though, was theory only, for the Americans were to control both the construction and the operation. And if the payments were not made as specified, Collbran and Bostwick would own the trolley and the lighting properties outright.

Rushing construction, the pleased concessionaires had the lights and street cars running by May, 1899. Speed meant more jobs for Collbran and Bostwick: a contract to extend the trolley to the royal tombs; a concession for a waterworks which Allen had been urging ever since the cholera epidemic of 1886; employment as "confidential banker" to the king, keeping money safe from the court grafters; a telephone franchise, a nickel coin contract, an office building project, and finally gold mines.

Allen did not favor all these schemes. The extension of the street-car line he thought pure nonsense, "anything to spend money you know." He approved the telephones, the bank, the office buildings, but felt that Hunt should get the mines. Yet that did not prevent him from assisting Collbran and Bostwick. He gave his aid even for the projects which he disapproved, commenting merely, "Funny business, isn't it?

[11] Allen to Everett, March 6, 1898, to Morse, January 23, 1898, and to Henry S. Kerr, November 13, 1906, in the Allen MSS.

This is about the queerest place in the world for some things."[12]

In general, prosperity attended the new ventures. Seoul's foreign colony was glad to pay for each new service offered. The tradition-bound Koreans were a bit reluctant, but eventually did come around. To the street cars, for example. Collbran and Bostwick hastened the process by hiring rope-walkers to perform at one end of the line. They planned a merry-go-round as well, and did install a moving picture theater (admission charge, three cents).[13]

But even this salesmanship did not entirely overcome the prejudice of the natives. Many of them blamed the drought of 1899 on the new electric wires. The trolley met with even greater opposition, led by jinricksha men who of course had a basic economic motive for opposing any improved means of transportation. Employment of the hated Japanese as motormen gave the objectors one good talking point. Accidents supplied another as decapitation followed the Korean practice of using the street-car rails for pillows. The result was violence, unchecked by native soldiers standing by. Mobs crying "death to the foreigners" smashed and burned cars, wrecked depots, and injured trolley employees. After which came boycotts, and rough handling of Koreans who dared to patronize the line.

Politicians and the press joined the attack. The street-car line was violently denounced by Ye Yong Ik, an anti-Ameri-

[12] Allen to Rockhill, July 29, 1900, February 28, 1901, in the Rockhill MSS; Allen to the Secretary of State, October 10, 1901, November 24, December 24, 1902, March 8, 1904, Dispatches, State Department Archives; Allen to the Korean Minister of Foreign Affairs, November 19, 1902, Seoul Legation Files, State Department Archives; Allen to his sons, September 30, 1902, in the Allen MSS. Explaining his support in his letter to the Secretary of State, March 8, 1904, Dispatches, State Department Archives, Allen said, "every such company constitutes a centre for the importation of American products." The Allen MSS contain detailed statements of the Collbran-Bostwick operations.

[13] Allen to his sons, April 6, 1901, and to a friend, March 25, 1900, in the Allen MSS; *Korea Review*, 3 (1903): 268.

can Korean who obtained ascendancy at court in 1903. With Financial Adviser Brown ("the real head of the British Legation"), Ye was responsible for the witholding of money due Collbran and Bostwick. On his own initiative he organized anti-trolley mobs and had the American business men denounced as typical representatives of "countries that eat the flesh of the weak."[14]

Here was work for the legation, for Allen had told Collbran that "once the company is authorized I think I can manage the rest in protecting American interests." He and his secretary (William F. Sands, chargé in May, 1899, when the first disturbances occurred) lost not a moment in giving full support to the street-car line. Sands helped to arrange the importation of Americans as motormen. With Allen, he kept after the authorities until the jinricksha men were rounded up. Later, to deal with the refractory Ye Yong Ik, Allen called up several score marines. There could be no doubt as to his purposes, for most of the men were quartered on street-car property.[15]

Allen went further. He planned to press for damages, basing claims on the inactivity of the Korean soldiery. Further, he called for force, the force his country had not desired to use. It was necessary now, the doctor claimed in 1902 and 1903; the United States should seize a naval base in payment

[14] Letters from Allen to his sons, May 20, July 15, 1900, January 15, 1904, to E. V. Morgan, August 11, 1901, May 20, 1902, May 29, November 28, 1903, to Morse, June 21, 1902, September 30, 1904, to E. E. Rittenhouse, January 20, 1903, January 24, 1904, to Hunt, May 16, 1903, and the "Narrative of Facts," in the Allen MSS; Allen to the Secretary of State, November 21, 1902, November 28, 1903, January 22, 1904, Sands to the Secretary of State, June 5, 1899, Dispatches, State Department Archives; Allen, *Things Korean*, 236; Ladd, *In Korea*, 360–361.

[15] Allen to Collbran, December 13, 15, 1897, in the Allen MSS; Allen to the Secretary of State, January 14, February 18, May 10, 1904, Dispatches, State Department Archives; Korean Minister of Foreign Affairs to Allen, July 13, 1904, and Allen to the minister, July 19, 1904, Seoul Legation Files, State Department Archives; Sands, *Undiplomatic Memories*, 204–206.

of the sum due Collbran and Bostwick.[16] Down to 1902 nego-tiations had sufficed; now "no one here seems able to accom-plish anything, except with a club." Allen's secretaries echoed these pronouncements. In 1900, when Ye Yong Ik refused to pay for nickels ordered through Collbran, Gordon Paddock (who had Sands's old job as American legation secretary) cried that the United States "can do nothing without pressure." The year before Sands had exclaimed, "It is useless to argue with an Oriental. One can never reach an issue with him, and finally must conclude, after much loss of time, that the only thing is to act without further consideration of his feelings. This is particularly true of Korea."[17]

Dispatches such as these did not impress the State Depart-ment. Allen could have marines and peaceful ("useless") naval demonstrations. That was all. Washington saw no will-ful malice in the trolley riots, only Oriental prejudice against new things. Consequently Allen should not press for repara-tion. As to intervention or any sort of strong-arm tactics, Roosevelt's adviser Rockhill thought that "wholly unjustifi-able and dangerous as establishing a precedent which may be used to destroy what little semblance there still remains of Korean independence." Nor was it useless to argue with an Oriental; and probably Allen was at fault in quartering marines on private concession property. American diplomats

[16] Allen to John Hay, November 21, 1902, and to E. V. Morgan, October 5, 1902, in the Allen MSS; Allen to the Secretary of State, November 21, 28, December 2, 1902, Dispatches, State Department Archives. Secretary of State Hay wrote Chargé Paddock that "the Gen-eral Board of the Navy Department, to which the matter was referred, does not recommend the acquisition of Sylvia Bay or any other site in Korea." Letter of June 23, 1903, Instructions, State Department Ar-chives. Allen wrote General Wilson on December 14, 1905, that an admiral and other officers of the navy favored a naval base in Korea; Wilson replied the next day: "regret exceedingly . . . that you ever rec-ommended . . . it is bad business for the United States . . . [and] discredits your judgment." The letter is in the Allen MSS.

[17] Allen to E. V. Morgan, March 6, 1903, in the Allen MSS; letter to the Secretary of State from Paddock, February 8, 1902, and from Sands, August 10, 1899, Dispatches, State Department Archives; Assistant Sec-

were advised to act in "a considerate and conciliatory manner even when the circumstances might seem to justify the assumption of a high and imperious tone."[18]

Thus soundly rebuked, Allen resumed his court intrigue. In good time he helped to pull Collbran and Bostwick out. Part of his work consisted in declaring the trolley and lighting plant forfeited to the concessionaires. Later, when the Russo-Japanese war made Korea anxious for the friendship of America, back payments were made in full. More than that. To Allen's "amazement," and to the "surprise" of Collbran and Bostwick, the emperor paid three hundred and seventy-five thousand dollars for a half share in the trolley and lighting enterprise, asking only that it remain American. At the same time the monarch surrendered to the Americans all rights in the expensive waterworks and "in consideration of the really abominable treatment he had allowed them to receive" threw in a mine concession.[19]

From 1902 to 1904 few could have predicted this satisfactory outcome. For in those years the position of Collbran and Bostwick was "certainly most distressing." There were native foes, headed by the mighty Ye Yong Ik. And there were the Japanese and Russians, the English, French, and Germans, the Belgians and Italians, all working against the Americans and trying to land grants for their own countrymen.

At first this opposition had not disturbed Allen. He was

retary of State Pierce to Allen, February 11, 1902, Consular Instructions, State Department Archives. Commenting on Sands's statement, Rockhill said, "I cannot agree." Memorandum of December 18, 1899, with Dispatches, State Department Archives. Marc tends to support the view of Allen, Paddock, and Sands. See his *Quelques années de politique internationale*, 39.

[18] E. V. Morgan to Rockhill, June 4, 1904, in the Rockhill MSS; Allen Diary, September 30, October 1, 1903; Rockhill memorandum on Allen to the Secretary of State, November 7, 1899 (dated December 18, 1899), Dispatches, State Department Archives; Secretary of State Hay to Allen, February 27, 1904, Assistant Secretary Pierce to Allen, January 25, 1902, Assistant Secretary Loomis to Paddock, July 3, 1903, Instructions, State Department Archives.
[19] "Narrative of Facts," and Allen to his sons, August 9, 1902, in the

sure the efforts of the leading powers would cancel out, leaving him to snatch the spoils. As he phrased it, "I am on such good terms with the Russians, Japanese and English, as well as Koreans, that I think we will get some more of the chestnuts while the others are burning their toes." It had been so in the trolley matter. "Russia thought she had everything but while she was squabbling with the others I got the 'bone'. I did it in such a manner too that the Russian Minister had to entirely approve of it, while the Jap. and British Representatives, were tickled to see it go from Russia."[20]

Gradually, however, the situation changed. Russia, which had favored the United States, became less powerful in Seoul and also far less sympathetic to America. There was good reason for the latter change—the sale of Morse's railroad to Japan and Allen's effort to get concessions Russia did not want him to have.

As the Russians lost in strength, others bid for favor. Russia's ally France was eager to obtain concessions, as were the Germans and the English. And finally Japan, regaining power lost in 1896, sought the very grants Americans desired.

With all these nations on the ground, Allen felt that "concession hunters" were "getting as thick as fleas in a Korean blanket here now."[21] And each provided competition for America. Russia's " 'dog in the manger' manner" spoiled Hunt's plans to broaden American gold-mine operations until the Hunt-Gunzberg arrangements of the fall of 1903. One well-backed Englishman, Chance, nearly took the waterworks away from Collbran; and another, Pritchard Morgan, did obtain a fair gold mine. The French, besides obtaining mine and railroad grants, beat Allen to a customs loan. The Germans, who obtained two inferior mines, competed so fiercely for concessions that Allen and the German consul

Allen MSS; Allen to the Secretary of State, February 16, March 8, 1904, Dispatches, State Department Archives; *Korea Review*, 2 (1902):364.

[20] Allen to Rockhill, January 30, February 29?, 1898, in the Rockhill MSS; Allen to Everett, March 6, 1898, in the Allen MSS.

[21] Allen to Hunt, November 21, 1899, in the Allen MSS.

ceased to speak. Even Italian and Belgian capitalists were involved; the latter offered two hundred thousand dollars for a first-rate mine.[22]

One could call this most annoying. Stronger words were needed for Japan. As early as 1900 Allen was noting the "amazing increase of Japanese influence,"[23] the beginning of the drive that was to swallow all Korea and snuff out hopes of making Chosen an economic satellite of the United States.

Russia and lack of capital retarded Japan, but bit by bit she intensified her economic warfare. To clear the field she told the emperor that Americans "would surely rob him," that "the Japanese would do the same work better and cheaper." Then her nationals snapped up the ginseng monop-

[22] On the general subject, see Kanichi Asakawa, *The Russo-Japanese Conflict* (New York, 1904), *passim;* Sands, *Undiplomatic Memories,* 197–211; Hamilton, *Korea, passim; Korean Repository,* 1896–98; "Remarks 1903, in the Allen MSS; letter to the Secretary of State from Sill, April in Regard to Opposition Experienced in Connexion with Mining Concession Dated Feb. 15th, 1904," in the Allen MSS; Allen to the Secretary of State, August 31, 1900, February 25, 1901, Dispatches, State Department Archives; and Allen to Hunt, July 29, 1900, in the Allen MSS. For Russia, see Allen to the Secretary of State, February 15, March 30, 1900, Dispatches, State Department Archives; for Belgium, Allen to Hunt, April 11, 1903, in the Allen MSS; for Germany, Allen Diary, July 22, 1898, "Previous Mine Concessions"; Allen to Hunt, June 21, 1898, to J. A. Duff, August 16, 1898, and to James H. Wilson, May 31, 1898, in the Allen MSS; for France, Allen to the Secretary of State, August 31, 1900, April 24, 26, 29, May 6, 21, 1901, Dispatches, State Department Archives; Allen memorandum, April or May, 1901, in the Allen MSS; for England, Allen to the Secretary of State, November 18, 1899, March 17, June 6, 1900, Dispatches, State Department Archives; "Narrative of Facts"; "Previous Mine Concessions"; Allen to Hunt, November 22, 25, December 2, 1899, and to Morse, December 29, 1899, in the Allen MSS. Allen fought all the English promoters and also mixed in British quarrels, favoring Pritchard Morgan over Chance. In his "Narrative of Facts," Allen says Great Britain "seemed to think it was simply impudence on the part of the Americans to get such rights in Asia where they themselves had been supreme so long." For Italy, see Allen's letter to Henry S. Kerr of November 13, 1906, in the Allen MSS, in which he claims that an Italian syndicate paid part of the expenses of the Italian legation in Seoul.
[23] Allen to Fassett, May 20, 1900, in the Allen MSS.

oly which Allen had desired for an American. They took the steamer business that he had earmarked for Hunt and Morse, even selling Chosen a one-ship navy at a fancy figure. In this they rivalled Edward Lake, an American who years before had sold Korea a boat for nine thousand dollars, repurchased it for an eighth that figure, and then complained about the deal.[24]

Not content with beating Allen's bids, the Japanese attacked American enterprises already under way, in the hope of driving out these chief competitors. Their commercial drive was featured by imitation of American trademarks: Standard Oil kerosene, Richmond Gem cigarettes, Eagle Brand milk, Armour meat, Californian wine and fruit. Chosen forbid these practices on penalty of death when Allen asked her to, but in true Korean fashion the prohibitions were unenforced.[25]

Collbran and Bostwick suffered similarly. To embarrass them the Japanese attempted to obtain a competing electric franchise in Seoul. And by 1900 they were interfering with the trolley system. Claiming exclusive rights under Morse's

[24] Address to the Naval War College, and Allen to a brother, March 23, 1903, in the Allen MSS; letter to the Secretary of State from Sill, April 7, 1895, and from Allen, August 31, 1900, Dispatches, State Department Archives; Secretary of State Olney to Sill, March 6, August 20, 1896, Instructions, State Department Archives; Assistant Secretary of State Rives to Dinsmore, December 7, 1887, Consular Instructions, State Department Archives; Lake to Dinsmore, July 1, 1887, and to Rockhill, January 8, 1887, Dinsmore to the President of the Korean Foreign Office, July 16, August 1, 1887, Seoul Legation Files; Dinsmore to the Assistant Secretary of State, October 10, 1887, Consular Dispatches, State Department Archives. The last summarized the Lake matter best (Lake "sold the ship for an enormous price," then "bought her at a forced sale at far less than her value." "The Koreans are sore naturally."). By this time Japan had 21,000 nationals in Korea, the United States 241. Paddock to the Assistant Secretary of State, November 4, 1904, Consular Dispatches, State Department Archives.

[25] Hamilton, *Korea*, 165–166; Allen, *Things Korean*, 217–218; Allen to the Secretary of State, September 10, 1904, with notes by Van Dyne and Adee, Dispatches, State Department Archives; Secretary of State Hay to Allen, October 19, 1904, Instructions, State Department Archives.

liberal Seoul-Chemulpo charter, they announced that they would treat the street-car line "like any other obstacle" and would refuse to let the trolley route cut through the Seoul-Chemulpo right of way. They demanded removal of the street-car tracks from a busy suburban avenue to the unpopulated hills beyond. Removal would be easy to accomplish, Minister G. Hayashi told the governor of Seoul, for the Americans "amounted to nothing."[26]

With prestige and profits in the balance, the American legation hurried into action. The electric proposition was quashed by Allen's native friends, and in the doctor's absence Secretaries Sands and Paddock spoke out on trolley matters. Upon his return, Allen finished off the matter. Hayashi when cornered denied any wish to have the tracks removed; and Allen could announce with pride that "prompt and firm action alone prevented grave annoyance and loss to the American firm who held the Seoul Electric Railway, as well as an unfortunate blow to the prestige of Americans in Korea by the Japanese, who do not seem to take kindly to the fact that the Americans are so influential here in commercial matters."[27]

Allen seemed to have triumphed, but he knew that the days of victory were numbered. He was justified in boasting that "all the considerable financial undertakings in Korea are our own." He could point out that travellers "always commented ... that in this country they find the only Asiatic community of foreigners, where American influence predominates." He

[26] Allen to the Secretary of State, November 18, 1899, April 14, 18, July 29, September 5, 1900, June 19, 1901, August 29, November 28, 1902, January 22, 1903, May 27, October 20, 1904, January 5, March 31, May 30, 1905, Dispatches, States Department Archives; Allen to Japanese Minister Hayashi, October 7, 1904, Seoul Legation Files, State Department Archives; Allen to Morse, December 29, 1899, December 3, 1902, April 2, 1903, and to Wilson, December 16, 1902, in the Allen MSS.

[27] Allen to the Secretary of State, April 18, 1900, Dispatches, State Department Archives. To Allen's regret (Allen to E. V. Morgan, April 6, 1902, in the Allen MSS), this controversy was aired in *Foreign Relations*, 1900, pp. 771–777.

could even say that "American influence is as great as it could be unbacked by any show of force. It is probably as great as we have any desire it should be." But the future plainly rested with the Land of the Rising Sun.[28]

Allen realized this at the century's turn; in the summer of 1900 he wrote, "Japan will undoubtedly get this country soon." Even that might not mark the end, for it was "just as probable that Russia will take it way from her in due course of events."[29]

This meant that American concessionaires "must trim sails for every breeze." And he would lead them. Time after time he said that he was getting ready for the crash. "I am trying to have American affairs in shape for the inevitable what ever way things go," he wrote in 1900, and again in the same year, "I am working to perfect some American interests before Korea goes under Japanese control."[30]

Even that was difficult with Japan closing in. In 1902 Allen was moaning that he could not sell Korea "gold dollars for silver yen."[31] Only crisis gave him opportunity, for the king would turn to the Americans whenever trouble loomed.

Crisis came, in 1904, with the Russo-Japanese war that was to give Korea to Japan. Immediately the emperor evinced a

[28] Allen to the Secretary of State, September 17, 1897, April 9, 1904, Dispatches, State Department Archives; Allen to C. E. Fiske (British and American Tobacco Company), September 8, 10, 1904, Seoul Legation Files, State Department Archives; Allen to Rockhill, January 30, 1898, in the Rockhill MSS; Allen to A. E. Buck, June 4, 1898, in the Allen MSS; Hamilton, *Korea,* 143, 150. Hamilton called American interest "composite in its character, carefully considered, protected by the influence of the Minister, supported by the energies of the American missionaries, and controlled by two firms, whose knowledge of the wants of Korea is just forty-eight hours ahead of the realisation of that want by the Korean."

[29] Allen to Hunt, July 24, 29, 1900, and to E. V. Morgan, March 6, 1903, in the Allen MSS.

[30] Allen to Hunt, July 24, 1900, to Everett, September 18, 1900, and to Rockhill, July 29, 1900 in the Allen MSS; Allen to the Secretary of State, November 21, 1902, Dispatches, State Department Archives.

[31] Allen to Fassett, November 30, 1902, in the Allen MSS.

"violent desire" to count "in his extremity upon his old friendship with America." This friendship had been built around the personality of Horace Allen, but ties had loosened with the rise of the Japanese. Now His Korean Majesty would have them tightened once again, in the hope that America would aid him in keeping Chosen independent.[32]

Thus again, and for the last time, opportunity presented itself to Allen and his business friends. The chance was not lost by the firm of Collbran and Bostwick, which "never fails to profit in a legitimate business manner from any excitement or threats of disturbance." The company settled back accounts, made a good deal on the electric enterprise, and grabbed a mining grant as well. This last they won on February 15, 1904, eight days before Japan established a virtual protectorate.[33]

In these negotiations Allen played little part. For he knew why the grants were offered—they were a bid for American assistance which he could not supply. If Collbran and Bostwick did their own contracting, he would not be bound. Indeed, he put himself above suspicion when he "came near seeming to oppose [the Collbran and Bostwick settlements] by cautioning the Koreans lest they get too great an idea of what the U. S. will do for them in way of assistance in consequence."[34] That put him in the clear without wrecking the Collbran and Bostwick deal.

[32] Allen to Morse, March 7, 1904, in the Allen MSS.
[33] Allen to the Secretary of State, June 6, 1900, February 16, March 8, October 10, 1904, Dispatches, State Department Archives; "Narrative of Facts," "Remarks in Regard to Opposition Experienced in Connexion with Mining Concession Dated Feb. 15th, 1904" and other notes, and letters from Allen to Morse, March 7, 1904, to Rockhill, May 6, 1904, and to Rittenhouse, May 15, 1904, in the Allen MSS. Under these arrangements the American Korean Electric Company was incorporated in Connecticut in July, 1904, with a capital of a million dollars. An American Korean Mining Company was incorporated in the same state, which later gave way to the Seoul Mining Company, incorporated in Connecticut in 1908 with a capital of a half million.
[34] Allen to Morse, March 7, 1904, and to E. V. Morgan, March 11, 1904, in the Allen MSS.

It was after all was over that the doctor was drawn in. For the mining grant reopened an old quarrel between Collbran and Hunt. Long before, in 1896, Collbran had offended Hunt by commenting adversely on the Un-san project. Disagreement had developed into hate and a conflict that plagued Allen more than once. Then Collbran, with his gold franchise, entered a field which Hunt claimed as his own. Moreover, Collbran's was a last-minute grant, which Japan might set aside and use as a precedent for seizing Hunt's Un-san properties.

Seeking to end the controversy and get much-needed capital, Collbran offered Hunt an interest in his new venture. Hunt refused politely, then turned his guns on his old enemy. He flayed Collbran in letters to Denison, American adviser to Japan; and he had his ally Fassett say the same to the American State Department.

Allen, to whom the quarrel was soon referred, took sides with Collbran. Not that he liked the latter; quite the contrary. But he and Hunt had drifted far apart by 1904. The sharp-dispositioned Hunt had resented the doctor's failure to get him more mines. Allen, equally quick-tempered, came to feel that Hunt was peddling gossip that was harmful to his reputation.[35]

Such quarrels, of course, were but the froth of the concession struggle. Collbran and Hunt might fight and cause distress to Allen. But it mattered little what they did, for they were both back numbers now. By 1904 the Japanese had begun to take over; in 1905 they had economic matters well in hand.

Expecting this, Horace Allen had made sure that all American agreements were properly binding. Hunt's mines were his until 1954, and the Collbran-Bostwick enterprises were simi-

[35] Allen Diary, August 25, 1903; Allen memorandum, March 11, 1901, Allen to Fassett, November 3, 1900, to Morse, April 26, 1905, and to A. J. Brown, April 30, 1905, Morse to Allen, March 20, 1905, in the Allen MSS.

larly protected. The Japanese might fume and fuss, but they were bound by Chosen's actions.[36]

Yet, in the end, Japan was to win. She need give nothing more to America, need only wait till the grants ran out. Indeed, not that long; she could exert a little pressure. She could handle commerce as she saw fit, even without trade manipulation. And, as Allen knew, she could make concessionaires "feel the screws of Japanese oppression . . . until American enterprises are practically crowded out of Korea." This was to be easy after 1905, when Roosevelt withdrew the United States legation from Seoul.[37]

By 1905 Morse was already gone. His American Trading Company operated in many lands but not in the one which he had thought most promising. Collbran and Bostwick, holding on, abandoned their independent status and accepted partnership with Japanese and British financiers. Hunt's Oriental Consolidated Mining Corporation was to hold on for a generation and a half, then go the way of the others, fifteen years before its franchise had expired. That left the traders—notably Standard Oil—to fight as best they could alone.[38] By then, of

---

[36] "Narrative of Facts" and notes in the Allen MSS. Homer B. Hulbert, in an article entitled "Korea, the Bone of Contention," *Century*, 68 (1904):153–154, observed optimistically that "not one plank in her [*Japan's*] platform suggests a policy that would be inimical to American enterprise in any of its major forms."

[37] Article by Allen, 1905, and Allen to E. B. Townsend, May 15, 1904, in the Allen MSS; Allen to the Secretary of State, March 27, 1904, May 31, 1905, Dispatches, State Department Archives. Allen believed America's withdrawal of legation unwise on commercial grounds. Allen to Yun Chi Ho, November 30, 1905, in the Allen MSS.

[38] The tendencies are noted in "Remarks in Regard to Opposition Experienced in Connexion with Mining Concession Dated Feb. 15th, 1904"; in Allen to Hunt, November 22, 25, 1899, to Morse, December 26, 1904, March 11, 1905, to Griscom, February 15, 1905, and to Henry S. Kerr, January 28, 1907, and Bostwick to Allen, October 8, 1907, in the Allen MSS; and in letters to the Secretary of State from Allen, February 14, March 30, April 5, 1905, and from E. V. Morgan, November 4, 6, 1905, Dispatches, State Department Archives. For the bitter quarrel between D. W. Stevens, American adviser to Japan, and the partners

course, America had long abandoned Chosen to her fate, and Horace Allen had passed on to his grave. But the end was to be what the doctor had expected and had written in 1907 as an epitaph upon his record as a dollar diplomat.

"Formerly American visitors were usually struck with the unique situation in Korea," he explained, "where their own people were seen to be in the lead. To those who made the trip by way of the Suez Canal and had visited that wonderful belt of commercial colonies under British rule . . . this condition of affairs in Korea was particularly impressive. Whereas the American element and American interests were something of a negligible quantity in the bustling marts that mark Britain's progress from Egypt through the Indian Ocean to the China seas, in Korea everything seemed to be American and our influence to predominate, quite reversing the situation as compared with the other foreign settlements of the Far East.

"This agreeable sensation will not now be experienced by Americans who may visit Korea . . . American vested interests will have to be respected, but these will gradually drift into Japanese hands, until conditions will correspond with those pertaining in Japan. It is and will be—Korea for the Japanese."[39]

Collbran and Bostwick, see Allen to Henry S. Kerr, November 13, 1906; Stephen L. Selden, attorney for the company, to Bostwick, November 22, 1905, describing Stevens as "a stench in the nostrils of every white man in the country"; and Bostwick to Allen, October 8, 1907, indicating that Stevens "honestly thought that we were scoundrels, adventurers of the very worst type." These letters are in the Allen MSS.

Mitsui and Company later withdrew from the Japanese-American-British syndicate formed to handle the Collbran-Bostwick mines. Collbran and Bostwick then proceeded alone, organizing the Seoul Mining Company, which proved financially successful for a few years and cleared over a third of a million dollars in 1912. Reports in the Allen MSS.

[39] Allen, *Things Korean*, 255. Allen, in a letter to the Secretary of State, March 27, 1904, Dispatches, State Department Archives, stated that it "will be increasingly difficult to properly protect and advance American interests."

Part IV. And the Japanese

We have unintentionally played into the hands of the Japanese all along.—Horace N. Allen

To us who know the Japanese as they really are in Corea, it is strange that Japan should for so long have deluded European nations and Governments into believing that she is a civilised Power, or desirous of becoming one.—Bishop Charles John Corfe

12

The Biggest Man in Town

T HE gospel and the dollar are the keys to Horace Allen's
life and to American diplomacy in Chosen. Yet as religion was pushed and openings were sought for capital, the
problems of world politics crept in. True to isolation precedents, the State Department said that these world problems
should be ignored. But there they were, and residents of Seoul
could not dodge them. Even as a missionary Allen was plagued
by them, and never did he evade them so long as he remained
in Korea.

Allen heard some talk of missions when he reached Chosen
and more of money-making schemes, but overshadowing both
was talk of international diplomacy. In every house, at every
table, there was speculation over the role of Korea in world
affairs. Would she remain a Chinese vassal state? Would Russia or Japan drive China out? Would Chosen by some chance
emerge as independent? Every foreigner wanted to know, all
tried to gather whatever information they could.

As mission lobbyist and friend of Chargé Foulk, Allen
picked up more than most. And it was well that this was so.
For in August, 1886, that year of crisis, the doctor from Ohio
was plunged into the boiling cauldron of Asiatic imperialism.
While still a missionary and without the slightest warning, he

became *de facto* head of his country's diplomatic establishment in Seoul.

It happened when George Foulk was away on a vacation in Japan. Minister Parker was drunk, as drunk as any mortal man can be. He had swilled in public till his knees had buckled under him and then had carried on in the privacy of his own room. There were days when the envoy could not pull his rum-soaked frame from bed, and when he did stagger to his feet it was only to drink some more. Wherefore Allen, as legation doctor, became the only responsible official at the United States legation.

Few had suspected Parker's weakness when the envoy's sedan chair had been brought into Seoul. A "nice old gentleman," Allen thought, pious, dignified, friendly, competent. Surely his record was impressive. "General" Foote's title had been won in the courtroom; Captain Parker's had been earned as a fighting Southern naval officer. He had been graduated first in his class at Annapolis. He had helped to capture Vera Cruz in the war with Mexico and had made his power felt for the Confederacy in the war between the states. The Confederate naval academy was largely his creation, and he and his cadets had taken care of the archives and the treasury on the flight south after Richmond had capitulated. Moreover, the captain's pen was as mighty as his sword. He had produced six volumes when Grover Cleveland gave him the appointment to Korea.[1]

Author, fighting man—and dipsomaniac. Parker's secretary and naval escort had tales to tell of the envoy's alcoholic past. Of sprees and illness on the passage over, of a body weakened and a mind gone dull.

Could diplomatic duties be entrusted to such a man? Apparently, for the president of the United States had made the captain minister resident and consul general for Chosen. It would have been less tragic had the new appointee been able

[1] Allen to Evans, June 17, 1886, in the Allen MSS; *Dictionary of American Biography*.

to lean on the veteran Foulk. But Foulk, as Allen testified, was "in such a condition of body and mind that it will be hazardous for him to remain in Korea during the rainy season." The ensign might have taken the risk had he been entreated to do so, but Parker would not urge him to remain. On the contrary, he insulted his subordinate by treating him with disrespect if not disdain.[2]

Parker was sober on June 8, the day he reached Seoul, and sober on the thirteenth, when he presented his credentials to the king. But thenceforth the bottle beckoned, and beckoned more each day. Within a fortnight the captain was too drunk to read or think or recognize his callers. Allen did his medical best, worked hard on the inebriated representative. All to no effect—Parker would not take the cure. Sometimes he paused a day or two, then he was off again, drinking heavily and calling huskily for more. All evidence agrees. The Americans felt "greatly disgraced by our minister," who was "intoxicated during a considerable part of his residence." Parker was "drunk all the time," was in a "maudlin drunken state," in a "besotted stupor," in a "condition I may not describe." "Good enough when sober," Allen wrote in July, "but he is not sober long enough to attend to business." And, later, "he tried to force a Japanese woman to sleep with him and I was called on to quiet him. He has done no business for two weeks and when sober is very dazed."[3]

In July, 1886, the captain's conduct did not matter much—Seoul was far too worried over an epidemic of cholera. But in August there was a Chinese effort to seize control of Chosen, one that called for action from the United States legation. It

[2] Allen to Evans, June 17, 1886, and certificate dated June 28, 1886, in the Allen MSS; Foulk to the Secretary of State, June 27, 1886, Dispatches, State Department Archives.

[3] Allen Diary, June 24, 1886; Allen to Ellinwood, July 9, August 20, 1886, in the Allen MSS; letters to the Secretary of State from Parker, June 10, 1886, and from Foulk, June 27, September 7, 1886, Dispatches, State Department Archives; Tansill, *Foreign Policy of Bayard*, 433, note, quoting material from the Bayard MSS. Parker wrote a friend on July 5, 1886, that he used "no liquor, beer, or wine of any description."

was in that exciting month that Allen said, "as Capt Parker was drunk all of the time ... I had to figure largely in the work of the Legation."[4]

Manchu fears brought on the crisis of 1886. For years the Chinese rulers had lived in dread that foreigners would snatch Korea, key to the Celestial Empire's eastern provinces. Japan, of course, was to do just that in time. In 1886, however, she was temporarily eliminated as a menace. Her Korean agents had suffered a double failure in the émeutes of 1882 and 1884. That made her military men anxious to fight at once, before the Chinese had a chance to arm. "Sheer madness," said Ito and the other civilians in control; and on they went to compromise in the Li-Ito agreement. This was a play for time; as Li Hung Chang, viceroy of China, correctly guessed, the Japanese were to be ready for a contest in ten years.

Meantime the islanders centered their attention on commercial matters. They did protest the English seizure of Port Hamilton and were "very angry" to hear that China planned to get that area. Takahira told Foulk that Japanese "interference ... would seem to be imperatively necessary" if China became too active in Seoul, and Allen wrote Dye that "little Japan backed by Russia and the United States ... is playing her cards with a view of coming in for a slice of the cake." But generally Nippon seemed satisfied with a back seat, and China could concentrate on other competitors.[5]

On the United States, for just a moment; America was thinking of a Korean naval base. Then on Britain, who seized Chosen's strategically located Port Hamilton in 1885. This

[4] Allen Diary, September 5, 1886.

[5] Japan's lack of aggressiveness is emphasized in Foulk to the Secretary of State, June 18, 1885, Dispatches, State Department Archives; Allen to Ellinwood, June 15, 1887, in the Allen MSS, stating that Japan's low tariff held her back; Kengi Hamada, *Prince Ito* (London, 1937), 68; Treat, "China and Korea," *Political Science Quarterly*, 49 (1933):514–543; Tsiang, "Sino-Japanese Relations," *Chinese Social and Political Science Review*, 17 (1933):85–107; Hishida, *International Relations of Japan as a Great Power*; Ariga, "Diplomacy," in Stead, *Japan by the Japanese*; *Korean Repository*, 3 (1896):341; Treat, *Diplomatic*

move could be termed "defensive," the British reaction to the strained condition of Anglo-Russian relations. Finding the location of limited utility, Britain soon withdrew. Still, the seizure had occurred, a precedent had been established; and Korea worried, fearing more to come.[6]

Although she snatched no territory, Russia seemed a greater foe than Britain.[7] Chinese officials shuddered in 1885 when the Romanoffs inaugurated diplomatic intercourse with Korea. They listened with distress to the reports of Russian interest in Port Lazareff and the commercial possibilities of north Korea. They were panic-stricken by the news than Moellen-

Relations between the United States and Japan, 2:219; Langer, *Diplomacy of Imperialism,* 170–171; Foulk to the Secretary of State, October 14, 1886, Rockhill to the Secretary of State, March 5, 1887, Dispatches, State Department Archives; Allen to Ellinwood, November 17, 1887, and to Dye, May 11, 1889, in the Allen MSS.

[6] Foulk to the Secretary of State, May 19, 20, 21, June 16, 18, 26, 1885, Dispatches. State Department Archives; Foulk to Kim Yun Sik, President of the Korean Foreign Office, May 20, 1885, in the Foulk MSS; Allen Diary, May 29, June 19, 1885; Allen to Ellinwood, May 7, 1885, and to James H. Wilson, May 31, 1888, in the Allen MSS; Moellendorff, *Moellendorff,* especially p. 82; Cordier, *Relations de la Chine avec les puissances occidentales,* 3:3–4; Langer, *Diplomacy of Imperialism,* 169.

The president of the Korean foreign office wrote Foulk on May 19, 1885 (Seoul Legation Files, State Department Archives) that he was "anxious" over Port Hamilton, "a place of weighty importance." If England left, "we shall see her true, good friendly heart, but if she does not do so, what shall our country do?" The British commander at Port Hamilton told Korean officials that he acted "by the order of the Naval Commander-in-Chief. Our country, thinking that Russia might seize this island, the friendly relations of England and Russia being broken, has in advance occupied the island as a precaution." Foulk accepted this view in his reply of May 20, but Allen was betrayed into saying that England was acting with Russia against China and Japan. Allen to Ellinwood, June 22, 1885, in the Allen MSS. The United States Navy had expressed a desire for Port Hamilton, and after the crisis Rockhill suggested that Korea "lease it to a power at once friendly and entirely disinterested." *Report of the Secretary of the Navy,* 1884, p. 41; Rockhill to the Secretary of State, January 13, 1887, Dispatches, State Department Archives.

[7] Allen, in a memorandum dated November 17, 1890, now in the Allen MSS, quoted Kim Ka Chin, president of the Korean foreign

dorff had called in Russian military advisers. Although Moellendorff had some support from the king of Chosen, that move was headed off. But the Chinese remembered that it had been proposed and that a Russian agent, Alexis Speyer, had threatened "punishment" if the Korean king refused to back up Moellendorff.[8]

To ward off Russia, to guard against Japan and other

office: "the great fear at present, he said, is that Russia's necessity for a terminus for her great railway might induce her to consent to a division of Korea or in case of war between Russia and China Korea would be utterly used up." In 1887 Allen mentioned Russia's desire for an ice-free port to a reporter from the *San Francisco Examiner,* adding that "Korea's geographical position is such that Russia is bound to maintain its independence for should China gain control it would mean that Great Britain was the almost controlling power, and that would be antagonistic to Russian interests. England would be glad to get that controlling power." Note and article by Allen, dated December 20, 1886, in the Allen MSS; Hosea B. Morse, *The International Relations of the Chinese Empire* (3 vols., London, 1918), 3:8, note; Tsiang, "Sino-Japanese Relations," *Chinese Social and Political Science Review,* 17 (1933):88; Heard to the Secretary of State, October 21, 1890, Dispatches, State Department Archives; Langer, *Diplomacy of Imperialism,* 170. Anglo-Russian rivalry doubtless stimulated British writers to play up the Russian menace, as Archibald R. Colquhoun did in his *English Policy in the Far East* (London, 1885), 24–26.

[8] Letters to the Secretary of State from Foulk, June 18, 23, 24, July 3, 5, 1885, January 18, 1886, and from Parker, August 3, 1886, Dispatches, State Department Archives; Foulk to the President of the Korean Foreign Office, May 20, 1885, in the Foulk MSS; Allen Diary, May 29, June 3, 19, October 22, November 4, 1885, and Allen to Ellinwood, June 22, 1885, in the Allen MSS; Tsiang, "Sino-Japanese Relations," *Chinese Social and Political Science Review,* 17 (1933):90–91; Cordier, *Relations de la Chine avec les puissances occidentales,* 3:222–223; Langer, *Diplomacy of Imperialism,* 169; Moellendorff, *Moellendorff,* 81–111 *passim.* Moellendorff and Allen (see his diary entry of November 4, 1885) believed that English influence caused Moellendorff's fall. On June 21, 1885, Allen wrote in his diary that "the King sent to Mr. Foulk for help concerning the demands made by the Russians. He [*Foulk*] said he could do nothing as he had heard that one of the Koreans had said that the Americans were not wanted. The King was wroth and ordered the man spied out and executed. It was found that Mullendorff was the man. His connection with the Foreign Office was severed and the King asked Foulk if he had the right to kill him. F[oulk] told him to deport him."

Yuan Shih Kai, Manchu Agent in Korea

His cleverness and vigor, his ambition and lack of scruple, later made Yuan
president of China. In the eighties he was in Seoul, bullying the Koreans
and fighting foreigners, using Chosen as a buffer to protect the Manchus
against Russia and Japan.

enemies, China tried to persuade Korea to "shrink voluntarily Chinawards, to become but a jealously guarded outlying province of that country."[9] The Chinese could not use troops to gain their ends—that was forbidden by the Li-Ito agreement—but "various surreptitious ways" were open. The Manchus profited by constructing and controlling the telegraph facilities of Chosen. Henry F. Merrill, Moellendorff's successor as Korean customs chief, was an American employee of Sir Robert Hart's Chinese customs service, and acted under orders to "keep steadily in view the possibility of union between Korean and Chinese customs." Another American, Judge O. N. Denny, replaced Moellendorff as foreign adviser; and he, too, was a Manchu man, having been selected by Li Hung Chang. Denny proved less pro-Chinese than Merrill, but when the judge moved independently, he found himself hedged in by the Chinese Resident Yuan Shih Kai and Yuan's numerous Korean partisans.[10]

But even this did not create a monopoly for China. Korea's king resented Manchu interference, disliked the superior airs and bullying tactics of Resident Yuan. Too timid to act alone, His Majesty sought foreign aid for his "free Korea" program. After Japan had failed him, in the 1884 émeute, he turned to the United States. He gave the hospital to Allen; he hired Americans to run a royal school; he bought electric lights and tableware from the United States; he favored the introduction of American agricultural methods. All that, he hoped, would make the republic across the sea "protect" Korea and send advisers who could make the kingdom's army strong enough to check the Chinese annexation movement.

Americans, then, had a "wonderful opportunity." Allen

[9] Letters to the Secretary of State from Foulk, December 29, 1885, November 1, 1886, from Dinsmore, May 27, 1887, and from Rockhill, January 22, 1887, Dispatches, State Department Archives; Charles Denby to Rockhill, January 26, 1887, in the Rockhill MSS; Allen Diary, August 10, 1887.

[10] Hart to Merrill, November 30, 1885, May 29, 1888, in Morse, *International Relations of the Chinese Empire*, 3:13–15; Foulk to the Secre-

was sure Korea would be "saved" if the advisers came; moreover, grateful Chosen would make sure that Americans "had everything their own way." Foote had been as positive. "The influence of Foreigners holding confidential positions in these Oriental Countries," was his observation, "seems to add largely to the influence of their respective Governments." And Foulk had said the same.

But America did not respond. When asked for aid, the government in Washington reduced the rank of its Seoul legation and failed to carry out an early promise to appoint the military supervisors. Foulk pleaded that "American influence and reputation for good faith are at stake," but few read and none responded to his words. Indeed, there was talk of getting out entirely, and handling Chosen's problems through Peking. Thomas F. Bayard, secretary of state for anti-imperialist President Cleveland, called Korea a "centre of conflicting and almost hostile intrigues involving the interests of China, Japan, Russia and England, and . . . it is clearly the interest of the United States to hold aloof from all this and do nothing nor be drawn into anything which would look like taking sides with any of the contestants or entering the lists of intrigue for our own benefit."[11]

Korea's king still clung hopefully to America with a "firm-

tary of State, August 16, 1885, April 2, 23, June 2, 1886, Dispatches, State Department Archives; O. N. Denny, "China and Corea," in *Congressional Record*, 50 Congress, 1 session (1888), 8135–8140.

[11] Secretary of State Bayard to Foulk, August 19, 1885, Instructions, State Department Archives. See, however, Bayard to Rockhill, December 18, 1886, Instructions, State Department Archives. The bid for American assistance is covered in the Allen Diary, June 3, 19, December 20, 1885, January 17, 1886; Allen to Ellinwood, May 7, 1885, and to Dye, May 11, 1889, articles by Allen written in April, 1886, and Allen's memorandum of November 17, 1890, in the Allen MSS; letters to the Secretary of State from Foote, October 19, December 18, 1883, April 3, June 9, July 3, September 10, 17, 1884, from Foulk, March 9, December 1, 1885, October 3, 1886, and from Dinsmore, August 12, October 24, 1887, Dispatches, State Department Archives; Rockhill to Foulk, January 24, February 10, 1887, and Foulk to the President of the Korean Foreign Office, June 19,

ness" that Foulk thought "very remarkable" and "highly com-plemintary." But it was inevitable that the king should tire of waiting and paying for cablegrams that brought no return. And as he despaired of the United States, His Korean Majesty naturally turned to Russia. Surely *that* country would be eager to supply instructors and to back an anti-Manchu king.

The first overtures were made in 1886. Korea's foreign minister dispatched a note to Waeber, the genial Russian representative at Seoul. Chosen desired to free herself from suzerain claims, the foreign secretary stated. Russia could make this possible by supporting a royal declaration of Korean independence.[12]

Getting wind of what was happening, the Chinese saw the new development as both threat and opportunity. Russian intervention, if it came, would be a dire calamity. The United States was bad enough, with its anti-Chinese predilections and developing desire for naval bases. But Russia! The Russians faced the Chinese-English combination from Persia to the Pacific. If strong at Seoul, the Romanoffs might get the neutral zone they wanted in the Tumen River area and then push into Korean territory. Ice-free Port Lazareff would then attract them, with a right of way through all north Chosen. And by then Korea's army would be Russianized. . . .

But there were other possibilities. Lack of funds, lack of preparations, fear of Britain, China, and Japan might thwart the Russians. If so, the overtures indulged in by Korea's king could be used as an excuse for a Chinese movement into Chosen. "China *will not only* fight anybody rather than give up

1885, in the Foulk MSS; Russian documents in *Chinese Social and Political Science Review*, 18 (1934):244, noting uncertainty of Russian officials as to American policy; and Tansill, *Foreign Policy of Bayard*, 422–425. Sands, in a letter to the author, May 28, 1939, accurately describes the position of the Korean king: "all that he wanted was the shadow of the protection of the United States."

[12] Tsiang, "Sino-Japanese Relations," *Chinese Social and Political Science Review*, 17 (1933):90. See also Foulk to the Secretary of State, June 24, July 3, 5, 1885, Dispatches, State Department Archives.

her suzerainty," announced Sir Robert Hart, *"but will* be forced to absorb Korea if troublesome scheming goes on there."[13]

Leading the absorption school was Yuan Shih Kai. As a young man on the make, the Resident was anxious to succeed in his Seoul job. And success seemed certain if the Dragon swallowed Chosen. That step would eliminate the foreign agents, check the anti-Chinese king, and teach a lesson to the Mins, cool since China had befriended the Tai Wen Kun.

Yuan's efforts for annexation began before the king's appeal to Russia. In 1885 he created an artificial crisis by insisting that Kim Ok Kiun was planning to invade Korea from Japan. But Nippon stopped that, cut the excitement short by demonstrating that there was no danger; and Yuan was forced to seek another pretext for Chinese intervention.

This he found in the "Russian threat." In June, 1886, he began to telegraph excited messages to Li Hung Chang. A Chinese expedition must be sent to Seoul, to ward the Russians off. Tsarist influence was driving pro-Chinese officials out of office. There was a treaty establishing a Romanoff protectorate. The English consul general said a Russian fleet four warships strong was concentrating at Port Lazareff.

Investigating, the cautious Li found that many of his agent's claims were exaggerated. The fleet of Russian warships at Port Lazareff proved to be a single surveying vessel, and the pact of protection did not appear at all. Whereupon the viceroy censured Yuan, and Peking ordered him removed.

But before the ouster was effected, the situation changed abruptly. Allen's old patient Min Yong Ik suddenly reappeared in Seoul, apparently as a Chinese agent. Using his palace connections, he soon learned of the note to Waeber, and passed his information on to Yuan.

Armed with a convincing story of real danger, the Resident secured support from China in August, 1886. Li instructed

[13] Hart to Merrill, May 29, 1888, in Morse, *International Relations of the Chinese Empire,* 3:15.

the Chinese minister in St. Petersburg to inquire into the Russian aspects of the matter. Simultaneously, the viceroy ordered the Manchu fleet to Chemulpo and directed a military force prepared for embarkation. Foreigners at Tientsin began to feel that "something serious was going to happen."

It was a propitious moment to strike in Seoul. The capital was cut off from the outside world in mid-August, 1886. For a full fortnight there was to be no mail connection with Japan, and the Chinese telegraph conveniently ceased operating. The Manchus, as Allen said, "had things all their own way."

On August 10 Allen and the other foreigners in Seoul heard that four Korean officers had been arrested and sentenced to decapitation. There was no novelty in that—but the character of those involved made the act significant. All were foes of Yuan Shih Kai, all royal favorites opposed to Chinese influence in Chosen. Then, having bullied the king into arresting them, the Resident was out for the scalps of twenty more.

Nor did it stop with that. Yuan plainly aimed at the dethronement of His Korean Majesty. He rounded up his partisans and shouted that the monarch had betrayed Chosen, had signed a Russian protectorate agreement which he, Yuan, had seen with his own eyes. He lied, of course, in the hope that he could precipitate a show of force when the Chinese fleet came in. After that the king could be dethroned and exiled with his wife and son, and Yuan's good friend the Tai Wen Kun could step in as front man for a Manchu government.[14]

This would mean trouble for the foreigners. There might

[14] The émeute of 1886 can be followed in Tsiang, "Sino-Japanese Relations," *Chinese Social and Political Science Review,* 17 (1933):96–97; Treat, "China and Korea," *Political Science Quarterly,* 69 (1933):528–533; Morse, *International Relations of the Chinese Empire,* 3:16, including note; Denny, "China and Corea," *Congressional Record,* 50 Congress, 1 session, 8135–8140; Denny, as quoted in the *New York Herald,* August 4, 1888; Allen Diary, December 20, 1885, September 5, 1886; Allen to Ellinwood, January 20, October 28, 1886, January 17, 1887, and to Commander McGlensy, August, 1886, in the Allen MSS;

be civil war in Chosen or an international conflict involving China with Japan or Russia. There would be mobs again, as in 1882 and 1884; indeed, the population of Seoul stirred as soon as the decapitation edict was issued.

The situation called for action—but who could act? The Japanese representative in Seoul was committed to a watching policy. The British agent favored China. Yuan would consider as provocative any move made by the Russian minister. And the American envoy lay in a drunken stupor.

Besides these, there was the German consul general. Kempermann lost no time in throwing his official weight against the decapitation penalty announced for Yuan's four enemies. Perhaps he caught the Chinese Resident off guard. In any case, the king changed the sentence, first to banishment and finally to mere dismissal. Yuan's will was not yet law.

Kempermann's intervention coincided with that of three Americans—Judge Denny, the king's adviser; Merrill, the customs chief; and Horace Allen. Denny had done his best to head Yuan off, had attacked the Resident in messages to Li Hung Chang. That failing, the judge called Yuan a liar to his face and openly accused him of precipitating a needless crisis. He also duplicated Kempermann's appeal for the condemned Koreans, one of whom had been a Denny agent. And, with Merrill, he appealed to the drunken Parker for an American warship and American marines.

Active as he was, Denny could make little headway. The king's Koreans distrusted him as a Li appointee, the Chinese regarded him as a traitor.[15] So the judge remained at home and worked through Horace Allen.

letters to the Secretary of State from Parker, August 25, 1886, and from Foulk, September 7, 8, October 14, 1886, Dispatches, State Department Archives, Commander McGlensy to Parker, August 5, 9, 24, 1886, Seoul Legation Files, State Department Archives. Allen, in a letter to Ellinwood, January 17, 1887, in the Allen MSS, stated that England urged China on.

[15] On this interesting case, see Allen Diary, September 5, 1887; Allen to Ellinwood, December 29, 1886, January 17, 1887, in the Allen MSS.

Allen's role was many-sided and exciting in that hot summer month in Seoul. He carried messages from Denny. He toiled with Parker. He talked with his old patient Min Yong Ik, who appears to have been acting as a double spy. He tended and talked to Their Majesties, who were prostrated by heat, disease, and fear.

It all meant more prestige, so much that rumor marked the missionary for assassination.[16] It also meant responsibility, for with Parker lost to the world, Allen felt called upon to do the work of the legation. He must see to it that the outside world heard what the Chinese were doing at Seoul; and he must protect the missionaries by having a warship summoned to Korea.

With Allen decision meant action. The telegraph was closed to all but Chinese messages, and no mail was to leave for a week or more. But the Japanese had boats at Chemulpo, and Nippon had every reason to desire Yuan's schemes exposed. Denny thought of a plan, Allen carried it through. He wrote a note to the commander of the U.S.S. *Ossipee* and asked the Japanese representative to have it forwarded by a Japanese gunboat to Chefoo.

Then followed the dreadful days of uncertainty. Allen, worried himself, saw terror in the eyes of others. The king was near collapse, and Min Yong Ik was so distressed that he could not control his bladder. All sorts of rumors were circulated, yet no one was certain of the plans of Yuan Shih Kai. All knew that the Resident had threatened the king of Chosen and, as he himself confessed, had nearly struck His Majesty. All knew that the Tai Wen Kun was gaining power at the palace. But what came next? What would happen when the Chinese warships steamed into Chemulpo?

So flared the crisis of August, 1886. As it reached its height, it suddenly died away. The Chinese telegraph system resumed its general operations. Yuan's threats slid by without a Chi-

[16] With Min Yong Ik. Allen to Ellinwood, August 20, 1886, in the Allen MSS.

nese attack on Chosen, without the dethronement of the Korean king.

China, it seemed, had secured diplomatic satisfaction. Russia had denied that there had been a bid for protection, and Korea had withdrawn the offending note to Waeber. That was enough for Li Hung Chang, who knew that further sword-rattling might bring in the Japanese. Yuan Shih Kai, despite his ambitions, had reason to acquiesce, for his revolutionary plans had miscarried miserably. The Resident's precautions had not kept the Japanese, the Germans, and the Americans from sending out news of his maneuvers. Min Yong Ik had proved a feeble ally. And the Chinese fleet that Yuan had counted on had been delayed by a fight with the citizens of Nagasaki.[17]

Not knowing all the facts, Horace Allen felt that he and his friends had turned the tide. The "energy of a few of us" had brought the *Ossipee* to Chemulpo on August 24, thus counteracting the impression made by the arrival of seven Chinese vessels the same day. Commander McGlensy and twenty marines reached Seoul two days later, producing a "good effect." "The Chinese cooled down" after that, and the Americans had "saved Korea."[18]

Erroneous though it was, this view affected Allen's future. It gave him confidence, convinced him he could handle politics as well as he had handled mission-lobbying. It made him willing to become political adviser to the king, and to add to his religious work a devotion to what he called "larger affairs."[19]

By 1887 these "larger affairs" were absorbing a good deal of the doctor's time. "I have been in daily conversation with His Majesty," he wrote his brother-in-law, "and have had much to do in the way of advising." His inside knowledge of

[17] The Chinese were sent there, Allen thought, "to menace the Japs by their presence." Allen Diary, September 5, 1886.

[18] Allen Diary, September 5, 1886; Allen to Ellinwood, October 28, 1886, in the Allen MSS.

[19] Allen to Ellinwood, June 15, 1887, in the Allen MSS.

court intrigue improved each day, and by the summer of 1887 he could truthfully say that as a result of his reports the Presbyterian Board of Foreign Missions was "as a fact, better informed [on Korean diplomatic developments] than our State Dept. even."[20]

His advising covered many fields. There was Parker's case, for instance. The king asked Allen whether Korea could request the minister's recall and Foulk's appointment to the post. No, answered Allen, that would be undiplomatic and might antagonize the government in Washington. It was better to let the Americans ease the booze-drenched envoy out. Allen could and did draw up a medical certificate stating that Parker's longer residence in Seoul "would surely result disastrously to him, both physically and mentally." And Foulk, called back from Japan, hustled the minister off with little ceremony.[21]

More frequently the royal questions dealt with military matters. The king was much distressed by the poor equipment, the lack of training, the total ineffectiveness of his fighting forces. The United States had failed to send the long-promised army aides. Foulk had been unable to get leave to act as adviser. What could Allen do?

Perhaps the doctor should not have answered such a question—after all, he was in Seoul to preach peace, not war. But Allen was one of those who believe preparedness to be a way to peace. So he did all he could to make Korea capable of military deeds. When His Majesty discussed the possibility of new advisers, the missionary said a pleasant word for Shufeldt, a man well trained in the art of war. His Majesty responded favorably, and Allen cabled for the commodore,

[20] Allen to Everett, July 2, 1887, and to Ellinwood, July 11, 1887, in the Allen MSS.
[21] Health certificate, August 28, 1886, in the Allen MSS; letter to the Secretary of State from Parker, August 29, 1886, and from Foulk, September 7, 1886, Dispatches, State Department Archives; letter to the President of the Korean Foreign Office from Foulk, September 2, 1886, and from Parker, September 2, 1886, in Foulk's handwriting, in the Foulk MSS.

summoning him to Seoul for a conference. Noticing a sketch of a Maxim gun in the *Scientific American,* Allen showed the magazine to Min Yong Ik. The noble passed the picture on to the king, who told Allen that Korea wanted five such weapons. Seeing no reason why a missionary should steer clear of the munitions market, the doctor cabled Shufeldt to approach the manufacturers.[22]

A few days earlier Allen had done an even stranger thing; he had asked his church to enter the recruiting business. The king had moaned about the non-appearance of the military advisers from America till Allen felt that American prestige and honor were involved. So, to save his country's reputation, he composed, witnessed, and approved a petition from the Korean home office to Frank F. Ellinwood, secretary of the Presbyterian Board of Foreign Missions in New York. Religion was not mentioned in the document; the Presbyterian officer was asked to "secure for and send to us three able men of proper and sufficient education for the instruction of soldiers in the methods of modern drill and warfare. The same to serve as instructors to the Korean forces."[23]

Allen's view was not endorsed by Ellinwood. Nor did the doctor's other views meet with unanimous approval. Yuan Shih Kai fought them all for their anti-Chinese character. Even Foulk did not applaud on all occasions. He was visibly annoyed by Allen's endorsement of Shufeldt, whom he regarded as a rival. Then, too, he thought that Allen and his friends had made a "grave error" during the crisis of 1886. They had done right to call the *U.S.S. Ossipee* and ask for a detachment of marines. But when the Chinese-dominated foreign office of Korea had protested, the Americans had said that the guard was only an "escort" for McGlensy on that commander's visit to Seoul. That set a vicious precedent,

[22] Allen to Ellinwood, October 28, 1886, July 11, 1887, and to Shufeldt, July 11, 1887, in the Allen MSS; Allen to Foulk, July 25, 1887, in the Foulk MSS.

[23] Petition of the Home Office, June, 1887, witnessed by Allen, and Allen to Ellinwood, July 4, 1887, in the Allen MSS.

thought Foulk. Using it, the Chinese might evade the Li-Ito agreement and conquer Chosen with an "escort."[24]

Such criticism did not trouble the ever-confident Dr. Allen. Neither did it check his growing influence at court, and when Foulk left Seoul in 1887 the missionary could truthfully say that he had succeeded the ensign as the most respected, the most consulted, the most influential white man in Korea.[25]

There was a story in Foulk's departure, one of great importance to the foreigners. For Foulk did not leave voluntarily; he was forced out by Yuan Shih Kai, who felt the time had come to eliminate all Occidental influence from Chosen.[26]

Always powerful, the Resident had gained in strength with the Chinese diplomatic victory of 1886. The initial triumph, the breakup of the plan for a Russian protectorate, had been followed by other victories. The Russians had given a non-aggression pledge, Britain had left Port Hamilton. As Japan remained inactive, China now had little competition in Korea; Yuan could move on with confidence.

After a preliminary (and unsuccessful) attempt to force all foreign traders to leave Seoul, the Chinese agent centered his efforts on driving out George Foulk. If he succeeded he would deal a body blow to the influence of the anti-Chinese Americans. He would also humiliate the king of Korea, who loved and trusted Foulk and wanted him to stay. Victory in a test case of such importance might leave Yuan the undisputed master of Chosen.

As usual, the Resident acted through his active allies. Not

[24] Foulk to the Secretary of State, September 7, 8, 1886, Dispatches, State Department Archives.
[25] Allen Diary, September 11, 1887, and Allen to Ellinwood, July 11, 1887, in the Allen MSS.
[26] The Foulk removal is described in the following: Dennett, "Early American Policy in Korea," *Political Science Quarterly*, 38 (1923):99–102; Harold J. Noble, "United States and Sino-Korean Relations," *Pacific Historical Quarterly*, 2 (1933):300–304; Tansill, *Foreign Policy of Bayard*, 437–442; Allen Diary, June 15, 1887; Allen to Ellinwood, May 9, 21, June 15, July 31, 1887, in the Allen MSS; Secretary of State

Yuan but the Korean foreign office asked for Foulk's recall. The charge was that the naval officer "grossly calumniates Korea," that his published dispatch on the 1884 émeute showed him to be the kingdom's enemy. The report contained a slighting reference to Chosen's heir-apparent. More, it stated clearly that Foulk "sat quietly by" at the time of the émeute "and saw our nobles butchered, our king imposed upon, our people thrown into consternation[,] our government well nigh overturned and though he knew it was coming opposed not this movement and is thus as bad and the same as the rebels themselves."

This charge had force in that it touched one weak point in Foulk's Korean record, his association with the "traitorous" progressives. In other respects Yuan's claims were weak. They were based on a bad translation of a statement Foulk had every right to make, a confidential report to his own government. And the derogatory remarks therein about the crown prince did not disturb the young man's father.

Foulk was in no state to help himself. He had been ill when he relieved the drunken Parker and had soon been forced to cable for relief from his chargé duties. For once, the State Department did what was requested and sent Rockhill as chargé, then Dinsmore with a ministerial appointment. But lightening the burden was not enough. Dysentery and malaria still plagued the naval attaché. He fretted over the king's requests that he become an official adviser to Korea and worried over his friends' advice that he refuse these offers. Apparently the sole escape from woe

Bayard to Rockhill, March 3, 1887, and to Dinsmore, May 11, June 17, 23, July 12, 27, 1887, Instructions, State Department Archives; letters to the Secretary of State from Rockhill, January 3, 24, March 3, 1887, and from Dinsmore, May 3, 9, 24, 30, June 20, 21, 25, 1887, Dispatches, State Department Archives; Kim Yong Sik, President of the Korean Foreign Office, to Rockhill, March 28, 1887, in the Rockhill MSS; Foulk to Rockhill, January 2, 1887, Rockhill to Foulk, January 24, 1887, Foulk to the Secretary of the Navy, May 6, 1887, and to Dinsmore, June 8, 1887, Dinsmore to Foulk, June 25, July 31, 1887, in the Foulk MSS.

was in getting "pretty well corned" or in leaving the Seoul "hurly-burly."[27]

It was Rockhill who parried the first thrust made by Yuan's foreign office partisans. It came early in 1887, while Foulk was on vacation in Japan. "Incredible," was Rockhill's answer to the charge. Foulk, he told the king, was "sincerely devoted" to the "true interests" of Korea. The foreign office should apologize.

Yuan lost that round, and the complaints were dropped. But not for long. In May the Resident attacked again, from many flanks. He packed and threatened to leave Seoul if Foulk remained in the United States legation. He had the Chinese envoy in Washington throw all his weight against the naval officer. He had Chinese officials talk to Denby, American minister in Peking. And his Korean foreign office friends came out flat-footed for recall, bringing crisis to Seoul once more.

Allen, a crisis veteran, was troubled by what he saw. Obviously Yuan was out to demonstrate and to increase his power; and the Resident, as Foulk had said, was capable of "childishly rash" acts when he became excited.[28] The affair might end with Foulk's assassination or with a coup to force the abdication of the king. The possibilities alone sufficed to throw Seoul into excitement, and the doctor sensed a general uneasiness at a "foreign" banquet given by the Japanese.

As in other times of trouble, Allen was more than a mere

[27] Foulk to the Secretary of the Navy, February 6, 1885, Foulk to the Secretary of the Navy, July 4, 1886, and reply from J. G. Walker, Acting Secretary of the Navy, August 18, 1886, Foulk to Rockhill, December 23, 1886, February 28, 1887, Rockhill to Foulk, February 10, 12, 1887, Bernadou to Foulk, March 6, 1887, in the Foulk MSS; Secretary of State Bayard to Foulk, March 31, 1886, Instructions, State Department Archives.

[28] Foulk to the Secretary of State, September 8, 1886, Dispatches, State Department Archives. Yuan's renewal of activity may have been connected with an effort to start another insurrection; Foulk, aided by other foreigners, headed off such an attempt at this time. Allen to Everett, July 2, 1887, in the Allen MSS; Dinsmore to Bayard, August 23, 1887, Dispatches, State Department Archives.

observer. Striking at Foulk, Yuan struck also at Allen, presenting a memorial against the Presbyterian hospital.[29] And His Korean Majesty, pressed by the Chinese, turned to his missionary friend for aid. The foreign office had acted without his knowledge or consent, the monarch insisted through a trusted messenger; he had heard of the recall negotiations only indirectly. Allen must help, he said, must see that Dinsmore and the other Americans supported Foulk. Why not petition the United States, saying that all Americans would leave Seoul if the ensign was recalled? Allen could draw the document and get his fellow countrymen to sign.

The petition plan fell through, but the message did have some effect. By showing that the king supported Foulk it strengthened Dinsmore's opposition to the demands for recall. Did not the king outrank his foreign secretary?

The message came on May 2; the Foulk affair dragged on for six weeks more. The diplomatic colony was much concerned; only the Japanese remained neutral. The anti-Chinese representatives of France and Russia gave Dinsmore much support; the English and the Germans stood with Yuan Shih Kai. Gradually the latter gained ascendency until Chinese word seemed law at the Korean court. Before the end of May Allen felt that Yuan would win. Dinsmore sounded a still more pessimistic note; Chinese gains, he felt, made "the prospect for Korean independence . . . gloomy."

Despite discouragement, Allen and Dinsmore labored on. The minister spoke sharply to Yuan's Korean friends and presented Foulk's case in Washington. Allen kept in touch with the king, seeing His Majesty three times one week. This meant much to the monarch, who was surrounded by pro-Manchu courtiers. It gave him news from the outside, it gave him Allen's counsel, and it was an opportunity to send out

---

[29] Allen felt that Yuan was trying to buy him out, but persisted in his support of Foulk, partly because he felt the ensign's recall would harm the mission cause. Allen to Ellinwood, February 26, 1886, June 15, 1887, in the Allen MSS.

vital messages. Allen, in turn, heard much of value and passed it on to Dinsmore. Once at least the minister kept all Americans indoors because the doctor warned of trouble. These efforts resulted in defeat; the United States transferred Foulk from his Korean post. Perhaps the government in Washington decided that Chosen was not worth a diplomatic quarrel with China at a time when American business men were seeking railroad opportunities in the Manchu empire. Perhaps, as was claimed, Secretary of State Bayard felt that he could not inquire into the merits of the question, but was bound to respect the formal request of the Korean foreign office. In any case the order came directing Foulk to report to the *U.S.S. Marion.* Hearing the sad news, the king had Allen routed from his bed at three in the morning, and asked him to delay the naval officer's departure. But Foulk left, aching in body and mind, convinced that his own country had betrayed him.

Allen, remaining behind, inherited his friend's influence at court, power "above that of all other foreigners." The king called him in every day, consulted him on everything, and "always" took his advice. Proudly the doctor wrote of his position, told friends he could "arrange" things even when it came to getting gold-mine franchises. On "most matters of importance" he "managed to consult our minister Mr. Dinsmore."[30] That, however, was little more than form; Minister Dinsmore's opinions were based on advice and information received from Allen.

Even so, the doctor did not gain control of Chosen's des-

[30] Allen to Everett, July 2, 1887, to Evans, June 16, 1886, to Ellinwood, May 31, 1886, June 5, 1887, to Foulk, July 25, 1887, and to Mason, October 19, 1887, in the Allen MSS; Allen Diary, September 5, 1886, September 11, 1887; Dinsmore to Foulk, July 12, 1887, in the Foulk MSS; R. B. Hubbard to Bayard, December 6, 1887, quoted in Tansill, *Foreign Policy of Bayard,* 446, note. Allen's memorandum of November 17, 1890, in the Allen MSS, casts light on Allen's advising technique: "mindful of Foulks experience I dont propose to put my head under the stones by exposing it." This refers to a refusal to endorse an assassination project.

tinies. After the Foulk affair Korean officials felt free to disregard the royal wishes and heed instead the word of Yuan Shih Kai. Yuan "provides, dictates and directs all," wrote Dinsmore sadly, "under a system of intimidation mixed with an affectation of disinterested kindness." The Resident's women insulted palace females with impunity, and the king yielded "with sickly acquiescence" to the Resident's demands for ceremonial precedence.[31] There was a new move to replace His Majesty with a friend of China, and natives as prominent as Min Yong Ik feared that Chosen's days of independence were now numbered.

Still, there was hope. Russia and Japan would probably prevent the outright annexation of Korea to the Manchu empire; and while a spark of independence lasted, Yuan's power could not be complete. Indeed, the king, if well directed, might resist the Resident. And resist he did, with Allen's aid. He dismissed and banished the foreign office president who had asked for Foulk's recall. He intensified the effort to get advisers unconnected with Li Hung Chang. And he decided to establish permanent legations in Europe and America. This would show that Chosen was independent; and it would provide recruiting points for advisers and for foreign capital.

The legation action, like the others, was largely Allen's doing. The king asked why America was so indifferent to Chosen's fate. Why were there no advisers, why no capital, why had Foulk been forced to leave? Easily answered, said Allen; Korea had no permanent legation in Washington. Noting this fact, Americans accepted the Chinese claim that the Land of Morning Calm was a Manchu subject state.

Then, cried the king, a legation must be organized; "everything depends on ... interesting America in this country." Allen must prepare a statement of expenses and then go as the legation's foreign secretary. He was the "only available

[31] Dinsmore to the Secretary of State, May 27, 1887, Dispatches, State Department Archives.

person," a man the king would trust to pick advisers and do the real work of floating a two-million-dollar loan.[32]

Missionary wrangles and money matters put Allen in a mood to accept the offer. And there were other reasons, too. It was a chance to visit home and relatives. His health might profit—three summers in Seoul had turned the doctor "seedy," and the last had brought his younger son near death. Finally, with Yuan in Seoul, the missionary thought the city "too me[n]acing for a young man."[33]

[32] Allen to Ellinwood, July 11, August 2, 1887, to Foulk, July 25, 1887, and address to the Naval War College, in the Allen MSS.

[33] Allen to Ellinwood, December 29, 1886, June 15, July 31, 1887, in the Allen MSS; Allen to Foulk, July 25, 1887, in the Foulk MSS.

13

A Circus for a Fact

"THE minister is a weak imbecile of a fellow," wrote Allen while he and his Korean colleagues were en route to the United States, "the regular interpreter is an idiot and cannot speak English." Another member of the party was a "snoop," and all were "filthy beyond endurance." More specifically, "they persist in standing upon the closet seats which they keep dirtied all the time and have severely marked with their hob nailed shoes. They smell of dung continually, persist in smoking in their rooms which smell horribly of unwashed bodies, dung, stale wine, Korean food, smoke, etc. The ships people are very kind but will be exceedingly grateful to be rid of them, as I will myself. I go regularly every morning to see the minister and get him up on deck. I can't stop long in their rooms as I have had to point out lice to them on their clothes, which with the bad smells seem to make no difference to them."[1]

These statements indicate an intolerant Occidental's reaction to unfamiliar standards. They also reveal Horace Allen's growing impatience with the hardest job he had yet undertaken—the job of herding ten Koreans and directing their diplomatic debut in the United States.

[1] Allen Diary, December 26, 1887.

A Circus for a Fact

Trouble began even before the party left Chosen. Manchu politicians who saw the mission as a slap at Chinese suzerainty set out to kill or cripple the whole enterprise. They had not objected to the appointment of a Korean minister to Japan in August, 1887, for they felt it necessary to conciliate the jealous islanders. No such requirement applied to the distant United States. The Foulk affair had shown that America had little interest in Chosen. Like as not she would do nothing to check Chinese intrigue against the Korean mission to Washington, even if that intrigue struck at American influence in Seoul.

The Manchus started quietly. They made no protest when Korea announced the mission and the appointment of Pak Chung Yang as envoy extraordinary and minister plenipotentiary to the United States. They let it be assumed that Pak and Allen would leave as scheduled; indeed, they seemed so indifferent that American Minister Dinsmore felt free to leave Korea for a vacation in Japan. Then, with Dinsmore gone, they sprang to action.[2]

To begin with, the Chinese threatened Pak through their native ally, the Tai Wen Kun. Resident Yuan Shih Kai then began another of his strange campaigns. He burned the wires to Tientsin with excited messages. He called attention to himself by playing sick and not calling Allen, though the doctor was the Resident's physician. He told Koreans they should call their new mission off and dropped sharp hints of punishment if they refused.[3]

The Korean king knew what this meant. If the mission

[2] Allen Diary, September 23, 1887; Dinsmore to the Secretary of State, August 20, 23, September 30, 1887, Dispatches, State Department Archives. Good summaries of this affair are available in Treat, "China and Korea," *Political Science Quarterly*, 49 (1933):535–538; Tsiang, "Sino-Japanese Relations," *Chinese Social and Political Science Review*, 17 (1933):100–101; Hsü, *China and Her Political Entity*, 133–140; Tansill, *Foreign Policy of Bayard*, 443–446.

[3] Allen to Welch, September 21, 1887, and to Mason, October 19, 1887, in the Allen MSS; Dinsmore to the Secretary of State, October 5, 9, November 11, 1887, Dispatches, State Department Archives.

left despite the threats, His Majesty would have demonstrated his "independence" to the powers. If the mission was recalled, it would give the Chinese a greater advantage over him than they had ever had. Consequently the monarch refused to see Resident Yuan, "was steadfast and insisted that the minister [to Washington] should go at every hazard." "Was steadfast"—and shook with fright. "Insisted"—and trembled at the thought of what might come. And called for Allen.

Something must be done, the worried monarch told the doctor, and America must do it. Pak, who was in peril, needed immediate asylum at the United States legation. And Yuan might wreck the whole enterprise unless an American warship provided the threatened mission with protection and safe passage to Japan.

But what to do? For all his willingness to assume authority, Allen did not feel that he could use the legation for asylum while Dinsmore was away. Neither could be guarantee a man-of-war. But he could try for that. He helped persuade Judge Denny to write to Captain Jewell of the *U.S.S. Essex,* riding at anchor off Chemulpo; and when the adviser decided not to send his letter, the doctor dispatched two of his own. In one he asked the American Trading Company's agent in Chemulpo to harbor the Korean diplomats and call on the navy in case of trouble. In the other he applied direct to Captain Jewell.[4]

Meanwhile Minister Dinsmore was enjoying his leave in Nagasaki, ignorant of the developments in Seoul. On September 18, the day that Allen penned his two appeals, the minister said he was "encouraged with the present outlook for Korea." Disabused of his optimism by a wired report, he dashed back to his post; but Allen, who met him in

[4] Allen to Commander of American Warship off Chemulpo, probably September 21, 1887, and to Welch, September 21, 1887, in the Allen MSS; Dinsmore to the Secretary of State, September 30, 1887, Dispatches, State Department Archives.

Chemulpo, thought he had come "too late."[5] Nor had the doctor's letter reached Captain Jewell in time. Yuan Shih Kai had triumphed, Pak Chung Yang had been recalled.

It had happened suddenly. Allen, packed to go, had had his farewell audience on the twenty-second. Arrangements had been made for the mission to start from Seoul the next morning. The Allens were to meet Minister Pak outside the city gates, and there the Americans had waited, but Pak had not appeared. Without Allen or Dinsmore to back him up, and without the aid of the United States Navy, the king had given way to China.

This was sad for Chosen, and sad for the Horace Allens. Under Korean diplomatic rules, the missionary couple could not go back to Seoul. They would not have wanted to in any case. They had said good-bye to all their friends and enemies, had completed their mission obligations and disposed of their household goods. So on they went to Chemulpo, to live in crowded quarters with their friends the Hutchinsons. There they waited wearily for a whole month.

For Fannie the month was without any break at all. Allen was a bit more fortunate, for he made at least two trips to Seoul. He had been commanded to do so. The king desired the doctor's counsel and wanted him to negotiate with members of the diplomatic corps.

Dinsmore, Allen found, was determined that the United States should not become a "catspaw to rake out the Korean chestnuts for the Chinese." To prevent it, he fought the Manchus fiercely and offered the Korean diplomats passage to Japan on an American man-of-war. Japanese Minister Kondo gave Dinsmore strong support, saying Japan "could not regard China's conduct with indifference." The Russian envoy Waeber was also helpful, though he advised delay until instructions came from Washington and St. Petersburg.

At first Allen inclined to Waeber's policy of delay. He

[5] Dinsmore to Foulk, September 18, 1887, in the Foulk MSS; Allen Diary, September 23, 1887.

changed his mind, however, when he heard that the Chinese telegraphers were garbling diplomatic messages by mixing the ciphers. Thereafter he urged action. He carried to the king and Dinsmore a suggestion from the captain of the *U.S.S. Omaha*—that this war vessel carry the Korean diplomats all the way to the United States. And he told His Majesty that the mission must be sent at once if Chosen valued her good name.[6]

Soon after that the royal backbone seemed to stiffen. The king announced that the proposed mission would depart. If Minister Pak remained in Seoul—his son was ill—a new appointment would be made. If other difficulties were encountered, Allen would go ahead alone, carry messages, hire advisers, show samples of Korean gold and raise a two-million-dollar loan. As it proved, however, Pak found it possible to make the trip, and joined the Allens in Japan.[7] Pondering the sudden change of trend, the mission's foreign secretary was sure the Chinese had been humiliated. Perhaps the advice of Allen, Kondo, Dinsmore, and Waeber had made Korea's coward king courageous. Or was it the news that the long-expected military men would soon come from America?

Allen had still another explanation. His story featured a Manchu fleet, sent to intercept Pak and his aides. In the nick of time the *Omaha* had taken the Korean diplomats on board. The chagrined Chinese had been forced to substitute salute for seizure. Even that had terrified the agents from Chosen, but the United States flag had seen them through.[8] Allen's explanation was dramatic but totally inaccurate. What really counted were the Korean conversations with China.

[6] Allen Diary, September 23, 30, October 1, 15, 1887; Dinsmore to the Secretary of State, September 30, October 2, 15, 1887, Dispatches, State Department Archives; Secretary of State Bayard to Dinsmore, October 7, 1887, Instructions, State Department Archives. As it turned out, the *Omaha* took the Koreans only as far as Japan.

[7] Allen Diary, October 1, 6, 7, 8, 10, 18, 21, 29, 1887; Allen to Ellinwood, October 25, 1887, in the Allen MSS.

[8] Notes by Allen, address to the Naval War College, and Allen to

Chinese opposition to the mission obviously rested on the Manchu suzerain claim. Chosen could send a minister to Washington, no harm in that. All that the Dragon Empire demanded was that Korea ask permission first and observe rules laid down by the overlord. And that Chosen agreed to do when Yuan and Li turned on the pressure. The king of Korea had hoped to send off a mission free from all encumbrances. On September 23 he saw that this was impossible. Yuan had a telegram from Li Hung Chang, citing an imperial decree and quoting the Chinese foreign office: "Before sending representatives to western countries," it read, "Korea must necessarily ask first our instructions, and only after our consent has been given can these representatives leave. In this manner they will observe the laws applicable to dependent countries."

What could a feeble, timid monarch do but yield? The Korean king addressed the Chinese emperor in humble phrases. He had received the Manchu message "on his knees," was "moved by it and terrified more than he could say." He could only whisper words of veneration and meekly request the heavenly Chinese ruler "to authorize by an exceptional Celestial favor" the appointment of the missions to America and Europe.[9]

Here was an outright recognition of suzerainty, a denial that the missions represented anti-Chinese sentiments. Having this to publish, Viceroy Li had little ground to fear a decline of Manchu might in Seoul. Still, he thought it best to drive his points home by telegraphing three conditions:

First, After arriving at his post the Corean representative has to call at the Chinese legation to ask the assistance of the min-

Ellinwood, April 24, 1890, in the Allen MSS; Allen, *Things Korean*, 163–164.

[9] Cordier, *Relations de la Chine avec les puissances occidentales*, 3:223–225; Secretary of State Bayard to Dinsmore, March 20, 1888, enclosing a letter from Denby to the Secretary of State, January 20, 1888, Instructions, State Department Archives. In this connection see also Allen to Mason, October 19, 1887, in the Allen MSS.

ister and to go with the Corean representative to the foreign office to introduce him, after which he may call where he likes.

Second, If there happen to be festivities at the court, or an official gathering, or any dinner, or the health of some one is drunk, or in meeting together, the Corean representative has always to take a lower place than the Chinese representative.

Third, If there happen to be any important or serious question to discuss, the Corean representative has first to consult secretly with the Chinese minister, and both have to talk over the matter and think together. This rule is compulsory, arising from the dependent relations, but as this does not concern other governments, they will not be able to inquire into the matter.[10]

The Korean king seems to have accepted every point. In addition he appears to have agreed to withdraw Pak after the minister presented his credentials, thus leaving the Washington legation in the hands of a low-ranking chargé d'affaires.

The Chinese victory was virtually complete. Not quite, for the king of Chosen kept his surrender to himself. America was deeply concerned, yet His Majesty said nothing to Minister Dinsmore. Nor was Horace Allen told of the pledge to China. Pak assured him that the mission had full powers. That was serious, for the misinformed physician was to dominate the mission to America.

In theory and in ceremony, the doctor ranked below Pak Chung Yang. The minister was directed to run the legation, using Allen as adviser and loan negotiator. In practice, old Pak was just a figurehead, dominated in matters large and small by his strong-minded assistant. ("Allen . . . while nominally only Secretary of Legation, is really, more than any other, the *confidential Agent* of Corea in matters of vital interest to that Kingdom and its future prosperity," explained Richard B. Hubbard, American minister in Tokyo. "I all but ordered the meals for these people," added Allen.)

[10] Quoted in Denny, "China and Corea," *Congressional Record,* 50 Congress, 1 session, 8138; Dinsmore to the Secretary of State, November 11, 17, 1887, with enclosures, Dispatches, State Department Archives.

Before leaving the Orient the doctor fought for and won authority to draw direct on Korean funds. After that he took full charge of travel plans and made it obvious that he intended to mold legation policy. Pak's objections were resolved by flattery. Ordinarily the overblunt Allen was none too good at this, but here he turned the trick by "playfully" adopting Pak as his "father," to the "infinite delight" of the aging plenipotentiary.[11]

Allen's power was tested as he and Pak were passing through Japan. Lieutenant Mason A. Shufeldt, son of the famous commodore, asked to join the mission as naval attaché. The king of Korea, ever obliging with friendly foreigners, gave him the appointment. Pak Chung Yang was willing to accept the situation, Allen was not. The doctor knew and liked the Shufeldts. But there was danger that a Shufeldt could outshine an Allen. Feeling that this would never do, the doctor took matters in his own two hands. Young Shufeldt wired for the mission to await his coming; Allen answered brusquely and hurried his associates out of Japan. Shufeldt then tried to catch the party at San Francisco, but failed and so faded from the picture.[12]

But greater trouble was in store for Allen. On reaching Washington he found that the Chinese minister expected to control Pak Chung Yang and that the Korean envoy was satisfied to have it so. The doctor might have guessed the truth, that the Korean king had sold the mission out. He preferred to believe that Pak was timid and that the Chinese were bent on recouping earlier losses. And reasoning thus, he saw his duty clear. He must check the Chinese and assert the independence of Chosen.

It was well that Allen was a fighter, for he had walked

[11] Note by Allen, 1924, and Allen to Dye, April 15, 1889, in the Allen MSS; Allen, *Things Korean*, 164–165.

[12] Allen Diary, December 9, 26, 1887; Chaillé-Long to the Secretary of State, December 8, 1887, Dispatches, State Department Archives; President of the Korean Foreign Office to Mason Shufeldt, December 7, 1887, Seoul Legation Files, State Department Archives.

into a bitter quarrel. He was facing China, the China that had whipped George Foulk. And he had to fight without allies. The Koreans could not aid him; their king had accepted the Manchu domination that Allen now opposed. Nor would America assist. Dinsmore might be sympathetic, but Cleveland's Secretary of State Bayard was determined not to intervene.

The first round came on the question of diplomatic calls. Pak planned to follow Li Hung Chang's instructions, to call on the Chinese minister before he presented his credentials. But that, said Allen, was against all diplomatic etiquette. To prove it, he sounded Sevelon Brown of the State Department. Brown agreed; protocol forbade ministers to pay calls before they had presented their credentials at the State Department.

All that was well, said Pak, but he must call. The Chinese expected it, as they had shown by sending a secretary of legation to the Koreans. Allen might say that the United States would feel insulted. He might insist that a call would "defeat our purpose in establishing Korea's independence." But Pak would go.

Despairing of success, Allen tried threats. He would resign, he cried, if Pak called on the Chinese representative or sent his card before he saw the American officials. And as a parting shot the doctor warned the envoy that "the King would surely decapitate him. I mean cut off his physical head."[13] This left poor Pak in a miserable position. He feared the Manchus, and he needed Allen. Which the more? The latter, he decided. Great as was his dread of China, it was surpassed by his need for counsel. His was no great mind; Allen felt that the Koreans could have "scoured the whole peninsula" without finding "a man more unfit" for high diplomatic post.[14]

[13] Allen Diary, January 13, 1888; notes by Allen, Allen to Pak Chung Yang, February 18, 1888, and to Dye, May 11, 1889, in the Allen MSS.
[14] Allen to Dinsmore, November 21, 1888, in the Allen MSS. Yet Allen had Pak made prime minister of Korea in 1895.

And what little wit the envoy had possessed had deserted him when he left his native soil. The strange new sights bewildered him; he needed Allen.

This show of independence distressed and angered the Chinese minister. He had planned to introduce the Koreans to Bayard and to Cleveland. Indeed he had told the secretary of state that he would do just that, and that he wished to have "outsiders" (like Allen) excluded from the audience. Encountering Allen's opposition, the Manchu diplomat satisfied himself with a conversation with Secretary of State Bayard, in which he tried "to connect the Chinese government with the Corean . . . to suggest a certain supervision . . . as if the thing had been done with the consent of the Chinese government."

That was on the twelfth of January, the day before the presentation of the Korean envoys. Allen did the honors at that ceremony. Fearing that the Manchus might try to head him off, the doctor had his Koreans routed from bed early that morning. Although it was raining, Allen would not delay departure to the State Department. Arriving there, he found that all was well; no Chinese was waiting to assert his country's rights.[15]

The Cleveland presentation went as smoothly, and Allen felt the mission to be a "success." By instituting a permanent legation "against the opposition of the Chinese government," the Koreans had been able to "establish their independence." Self-congratulation naturally followed, for the doctor regarded the outcome as "owing entirely to my efforts and thus giving me the unique advantage of having been chiefly if

[15] Allen Diary, January 13, 1888; Secretary of State Bayard to Dinsmore, January 26, 1888, Instructions, State Department Archives; Tansill, *Foreign Policy of Bayard*, 445–446, with memoranda of conversations between Bayard and the Chinese minister; *Foreign Relations,* 1888, pp. 380–381, 453, quoting correspondence with Chinese and Korean ministers; Korean Minister Pak Chung Yang to Secretary of State Bayard, January 10, 1888 (in Allen's handwriting), and notes from the Korean Legation, State Department Archives.

not wholly responsible for securing for the country the independence she had long striven for."[16]

Allen died convinced that those brave words were true. But, after all, Korea had asked celestial permission. And in defying China, Pak had violated his instructions. Summoned home in accordance with the Chinese plan to limit Chosen to a chargé, the minister did not dare enter Korea until Allen gave him a document assuming full responsibility for what had taken place in Washington. Even then Pak suffered for his insults to the suzerain power. He was kept out of Seoul, his promotion was blocked, his "persecution" became one of the most "strenuous activities" of Yuan Shih Kai.[17]

Allen escaped these punishments, but encountered other difficulties. He found that America was disinclined to take his charges seriously. The Koreans in their Oriental garb excited amusement rather than respect. Some Americans might guess that these strange individuals were diplomats. The rest reacted like the vaudeville troup manager who asked Allen where he was showing next.

Certainly Pak and his aides were out of place in the United States, unprepared for the wonders of industrial civilization. They had seen electric lights in Seoul and other trappings of machine-age culture in Japan and Hong Kong. But that was nothing. Arriving at the Palace Hotel in San Francisco, they were crowded into a tiny room. Small, they thought, for

[16] Notes by Allen, 1924, Allen to Dinsmore, November 21, 1888, to Jennie Everett, June 3, 1889, and "Narrative of Facts," in the Allen MSS; letter to the Secretary of State from Sill, January 9, 1895, and from Allen, April 9, 1904, Dispatches, State Department Archives. But see Secretary of State Hay to Allen, November 17, 1904, March 11, 1905, in the Allen MSS: "I cannot imagine why Korea keeps a Legation here. It is positively of no use to them."

[17] Tsiang, "Sino-Japanese Relations," *Chinese Social and Political Science Review,* 17 (1933):101; letters from Allen to Pak Chung Yang, February, 1888, to Dinsmore, February 6, 1888, to Min Yong Ik, January 19, 1889, and to Dye, May 11, 1889, and address to the Naval War College, in the Allen MSS; Allen, *Things Korean,* 164. Chaillé-Long's *My Life,* 348–349, contains the entirely false statement that Pak was punished for introducing dancing girls to Washington society.

so considerable a party; and then, to their amazement and horror, the room began to move. They trembled and cried that it was an earthquake, come to plague them in a foreign land. Allen explained how elevators worked; but after that the Koreans used the stairs.

The first audience at the White House was equally distressing. Pak expected to prostrate himself before the "great American king in uniform." But Cleveland came in democratic unpretentiousness, dressed so soberly that Pak did not identify him as the president. To this embarrassment was added a second—denial of permission to give the bows due royalty. Completely confused, the envoy from Chosen lost his voice, muffed his lines, and threw his entire speech off key.

Pleasanter, though just as disconcerting, were Washington's receptions. "Gesang," Pak called when he saw the women at Mrs. Secretary Whitney's—"dancing girls." No, Allen said, these were the wives and daughters of leading citizens. Could it be, the minister wondered, did Americans allow their women to appear unclad in public? Décolleté, was it? Anyway, said one of the Koreans, that scantily dressed lady who was shivering would feel more comfortable if she wrapped her train around some of the uncovered parts of her anatomy.

Pak, recovering from his initial shock, asked if he might talk with the women. Told that he might, he had a splendid time conversing with those who approached him. Several of the ladies seemed most interested in announcing their husbands' ranks. One fat matron called attention to her pearls, which, she insisted, were genuine. Finally a Southern girl told Pak he should travel South to see the lovely ladies there. The envoy, who had faltered when he faced the president, made no error here. With Oriental grace he said that he could well believe the South was full of beauties, for he saw one right before his eyes.[18]

Allen found such episodes diverting, even when he had to

[18] Allen, *Things Korean*, 152–161, 241–242; Allen Diary, January 25, 28, 1888. A highly entertaining description of a Korean's reactions to

interpret for the Korean interpreter. Other incidents were less humorous. There were the escapades of Pak's one-eyed valet, a "great frequenter of bawdy houses." There were the difficulties of the abler Ye Wan Yong, legation secretary who was threatened with a breach-of-promise suit. There was landlord trouble brought about by the dirty cook and the rough and filthy legation staff.[19] Worst of all, there was the smuggling episode, which the distraught Allen called "a circus for a fact."

Having handled the travel arrangements, the doctor knew that his associates had more luggage than was necessary. He assumed, however, that the trunks contained Korean articles desired by natives when abroad. He said as much to the San Francisco customs officers, swore the mission had no goods to sell. Then, six months later, the *New York Herald* came out with a smuggling story.

It was dismally true. Pak confessed his depravity to Allen "in the most abject grovelling misery." Yes, he had used his diplomatic immunity to bring in duty-free three cases of Manila cigars. Ye Kay Pil, a Korean student at Lincoln University, had disposed of them, selling them secretly in Philadelphia.

By preference, Horace Allen was an honest man; but now he lied. It would not do to implicate the minister, a servant must assume the blame. So Pak's attendant swore that he had done the job, and Allen straightened matters out with the customs men. It was a necessary trick, though it made the former missionary feel "cussed mean"; "I hate to see people," he groaned.

And well he might, for Pak, despite his tears of penance, could not be trusted. Three more cases were prepared in the legation, packed by night and shipped away. Old clothes, said Pak, sent to Korea to be washed. But negro servants

America may be found in "A Korean Abroad," *Korean Repository*, 4 (1897): 104–107, 180–183, 241–244.
[19] Allen to Dinsmore, September 22, November 21, 1888, February 6, 1889, in the Allen MSS.

said that all the clothes in the legation would fit into a single crate. Allen wrote in righteous anger: "I have talked and written, addressed meetings and stuffed reporters, till I have worked up a favorable spirit toward the Koreans and silenced the grunts of the Chinese. This I gladly do but to have to perjure myself to cover the contemptible dishonesty of the Kings representative, who has so little regard for his country as to jeopardize her interests just when peace is obtained is too mean."[20]

Here Allen represented high-minded rectitude at war with petty thievery. Odd, therefore, that later on he helped make Pak prime minister of Chosen. Still stranger was an episode in 1893. The doctor, back in Seoul as American secretary of legation, sent a shipment of jade to ex-Minister Augustine Heard, then in New York. Heard, who was poor, intended to sell the jade for gain. Knowing this, Allen asked a Korean diplomat to carry the shipment through the customs lines. Diplomatic immunity would take care of the duty, with jade as with cigars, and Heard would have a handsome profit.[21]

But all that was still in the future. In 1888 the doctor could storm to his heart's content, could blame cigars for Chosen's failure to obtain prestige in Washington or to get a loan on Wall Street. The mission's better points, by contrast, could be attributed to Allen's able diplomatic management. Else why did the Koreans moan when he resigned in 1889?[22]

Perhaps the doctor was not far from right. But one thing he neglected to observe. It was that he was working for Japan. In linking Chosen to the diplomatic corps in Washington, Allen dealt a blow to Chinese suzerain claims. Time was to show that Korea would not profit by destruction of the suzerain pattern, that the gain would go to the Empire of the Rising Sun.

[20] Allen to Dinsmore, June 21, 1888, in the Allen MSS; Allen Diary, November 21, 29, December 9, 1888.
[21] Allen to Heard, December 29, 1895, in the Allen MSS.
[22] Allen to Gillespie, October 7, 1889, in the Allen MSS.

241

14

Exit the Dragon

IT WAS an Oriental War of Roses, Inouye said, "a story of conspiracy, plot, assassinations, poisonings, treachery, fratricide, and common murder unequalled in the world's annals."[1] The illustrious count was accurately describing the domestic politics of Chosen in the generation down to 1895. He need not have stopped there. His words would have applied with equal force to the diplomatic struggle in Seoul in those last years of Chinese suzerainty.

Such was the atmosphere to which Horace Allen had become accustomed from 1884 to 1887. He found things little different when he returned in 1890 as secretary of the American legation. The Mins still held the offices, although their hold was miserably, calamitously weak. So weak as to encourage native opposition, creating strife that was to rob the kingdom of what little strength she had. So weak as to enable China to rule Korea as she wished and hence bring on an Oriental war, to be fought on Korean soil.

The climax came in 1894, with Japan victorious, China in retreat, and the proud Mins humbled by the Tai Wen Kun. Allen was to witness all that from the inside, for while lega-

[1] Interview by John A. Cockerill in the summer of 1895, *New York Herald*, October 17, 1895.

tion secretary he resumed the court advising which had marked his missionary years.

Allen's advice ran along familiar lines. Korea must be independent, he insisted, as he had while a Korean agent. Korea must be free of suzerain ties, he declared, as had Foote and Foulk before him. She must assist herself, must learn to stand alone. So long as she remained a vassal state, she would make no headway. Alone she could advance at will, develop her resources with the aid of Western capital and establish profit-making trade with all the world.

What held her back? China, Allen cried, China and the suzerain claim. Unprogressive China and Yuan Shih Kai, the "bully" who represented her in Seoul; plus the British, who cooperated with the Dragon Empire. After three years' absence, Allen found the Manchus "more openly arrogant than formerly"; Yuan's dictation "knew no bounds." As before, the foreign office of Chosen was virtually a branch of Yuan's legation. The Chinese agent wielded extraterritorial rights with vigor; Allen witnessed a Chinese street decapitation. And jurisdiction was extended to natives who displeased Yuan; his men beat up Korean officers and interfered with the American advisers. Finally, the Manchu representative haughtily refused to be considered as a diplomat or to be bound by diplomatic rules. He scolded Allen's chief, Minister Heard, for calling up marines without consulting him. When foreigners were in danger, he announced, he, Yuan Shih Kai, would provide the required protection.

China's attitude was easily explained: fearing Russia, dreading Japan, she was tightening control of "the wall which protects our three eastern provinces." That was clear. But how could Korea's attitude of acquiescence be explained? In Allen's view, even "utter weakness" did not justify acceptance of dictation from Tientsin. Yet he found Chosen "gradually succumbing to the dragon" when he took office as legation secretary. China ruled "with a rod of iron," and the Koreans "kiss the hand that smites them." Even, or especially, the king. In 1890, for instance, when the Chinese envoys sent to lament the death of Queen Dowager Cho failed to wait on His Korean Majesty, he went outside Seoul to pay homage at the Chinese tributary arch and to welcome the suzerain's men to Chosen. No humble gates for these envoys; they came into the capital by a special bridge over the walls. They were then assigned a separate palace, where they received the king once more.[2]

As a friend of Chosen, as an American seeking opportunities for his own countrymen, Allen was irked by all these actions. And whenever he could, he struck a blow against the Manchus. He reasoned with the king, he instructed his American superiors. He claimed that Chinese protection was unnecessary, that Korea could solve her problems without the suzerain's aid. As chargé in the winter of 1892–93 he opposed a Chinese-inspired embargo on rice exports and took a fighting stand against Yuan's supra-diplomatic status.

The last involved a point of ceremony, a symbol of the Manchu overlordship. Yuan rode while Japanese and Occidental diplomats walked in the palace grounds. That would not do, said Allen, it must be all or none. Rounding up the other diplomats in town (except the Japanese), the chargé served an ultimatum on the king. Yuan rode, he said, so should the others. Else they would refuse to grace the king's New Year reception. For why should they trudge through the slush while Chinese went by in style?

No victory: one could not hope for that while Yuan remained in Seoul. ("This ceremonial rule is one of great difficulty to change," wrote the Korean foreign minister.

[2] Allen Diary, December 22, 1885; Allen to Ellinwood, April 24, 1890, memorandum by Allen, November 9–11, 1890, and address to the Naval War College, in the Allen MSS; letters to the Secretary of State from Dinsmore, May 27, 1887, February 1, 1890, from Heard, June 8, 11, October 15, 21, November 17, 18, 1890, January 22, 24, 1891, and from Allen, November 23, December 20, 1893, Dispatches, State Department Archives; Allen, "Acquaintance with Yuan Shi Kai," *North American Review*, 196 (1912):113.

It is inconvenient for me to state the matter [to] His Majesty.") But there was compromise, with enough of triumph to keep the mud and snow off diplomatic feet. Yuan still had his sedan chair, but the others were presented with a decent walking area—a long and handsome gallery connecting the gate with the palace.[3]

So, too, did Allen fight for the American advisers. He struggled to obtain appointments ("keeping the American element up to full strength"); he labored to get checks for those already on the payroll. Some of the men brought in were lazy or incompetent, but even these were to be preferred to Chinese agents. And the work went on in spite of scoldings from the State Department, which felt that Allen "should not have used his good offices to secure teachers or other employees for the Korean Government. This was not a part of his official duties."[4]

Did that help, did any of the Allen moves assist Korea toward independence? Hardly, for they checked China not at all. And even if they had forced back the Dragon, Chosen would still not have been freed. For, as a Japanese spokesman said later, Korea was "lacking in some of the elements which are essential to responsible independence." Indeed, the very sound of "independence" was strange to the Korean ear;

[3] Letter to the Secretary of State from Dinsmore, May 27, 1887, from Allen, October 6, 1893, and from Sill, August 24, 1894, Dispatches, State Department Archives; joint note of P. A. Demetrevsky, Allen, H. Frandin, and W. H. Wilkerson to the President of the Korean Foreign Office, November 1, 1893, with reply of November 2, Seoul Legation Files, State Department Archives; address to the Naval War College, in the Allen MSS. Japanese Minister Kotori wrote Allen on November 1, 1893 (Seoul Legation Files, State Department Archives) that he agreed "in principle" with the Occidental diplomats on the chair question, but thought it "preferable to arrange the question verbally." On the final grant see President of the Korean Foreign Office to Sill, August 23, 1894, Seoul Legation Files; Secretary of State Gresham to Allen, November 21, 1893, and Assistant Secretary Uhl to Sill, October 3, 1894, Instructions, State Department Archives.

[4] Some of the problems are suggested in the Allen Diary, January 28, 1888; Allen to Dye, August 29, September 22, 1888, February 8, 1898, to Dinsmore, September 22, 1888, to Rear Admiral Daniel Ammen,

most citizens of Chosen neither understood its meaning nor craved its blessings.

Nor was there any foreign interest in the subject. Allen cared and so did his immediate superiors, Ministers Heard and Sill. But who in Washington? Blaine, for a fleeting moment, though even he became disgusted with Korean lack of backbone. And Blaine was gone by 1892. In the crisis years of 1893–95 Cleveland was in office in America—Cleveland, whose secretaries of state were mild as milktoast in the Orient. Vainly did Korea plead for the aid of the United States, vainly did her monarch say that "he had always looked on America as a disinterested friend on whom he could rely in times of emergency." There was no response save that of Secretary of State Walter Q. Gresham: "with few exceptions the record of our diplomatic history shows no departure from the wise policy of avoiding foreign alliances and embarrassing participation in guaranteeing the independence of distant states." Alvey A. Adee translated these generalities into specific instructions for Horace Allen: "The Department infers . . . and approves, a disposition on your part not to permit the legation to favor, even in appearance, the unfortunate intrigues which are engendered at Seoul by rival interests, and take no part in remonstrance against proposed economic

April 16, 1889, to Heard, July 12, 1892, to Brener, January 23, 1895, and to Legendre, February 24, 1896, in the Allen MSS; letters to the Secretary of State from Dinsmore, February 7, April 3, May 11, 1888, September 25, 1889, January 27, March 24, April 15, 1890, from Heard, September 9, 13, 22, October 1, 6, 1890, January 19, August 31, December 17, 1891, and from Allen, May 28, 1891, February 13, 1894, March 7, 1898, Dispatches, State Department Archives; President of the Korean Foreign Office to Heard, June 28, 1890, Seoul Legation Files, State Department Archives. Allen disobeyed orders in mixing in questions involving advisers, as he himself admitted: "dont mention to any one," he said on one occasion, "that I am instrumental in this as it is against our regulations." Allen to Frank J. Carpenter, April 4, 1895, and to Pak Yeng Kim, Korean minister to the United States, April 4, 1895, in the Allen MSS. See Assistant Secretary of State Uhl to Sill, May 31, 1894, Instructions, State Department Archives: "Americans are, of course, aware of what they expose themselves to in entering the Korean service."

Exit the Dragon

measures except so far as may be needful for the express protection of any legitimate American interest thereby injured." And, as to advisers, "it is not deemed expedient to exhibit solicitude for the appointment of Americans to official position."[5]

Other countries had like policies. England found it convenient to help China. Neither France nor Germany saw any reason to give assistance to Korea. Japan talked independence but actually desired self-aggrandizement, the eventual annexation of the kingdom. Some Russians had like views with ice-free ports in mind. Others (including Minister Waeber in Seoul) thought a strong and independent Chosen would be a useful buffer. But even these did little to advance the cause of Korean freedom. For they were under no illusions as to the kingdom's capacity for betterment. And besides, their government had adopted and announced a hands-off-Korea policy in 1886.

With no one pushing hard for independence, there was no chance for Allen to obtain it for Korea, which meant that all his efforts were misplaced. When he fought China in Seoul, he did not pave the way for Chosen's freedom. He merely helped to drive out one competitor and make way for another.

That other was Japan. After backing out in 1885, the islanders had affected "complete indifference" as to the fate of Korea. No longer did they fight the Manchu suzerain claims. Instead they pushed them to keep Russia back. And, by so doing, to save Chosen for Japan when the time was propitious for driving the Chinese out.[6]

[5] Gresham, quoted in Robert T. Pollard, "American Relations with Korea, 1882–1895," *Chinese Social and Political Science Review,* 16 (1932):465; Allen to the Secretary of State, December 20, 1893, with note by Adee, Heard to the Secretary of State, June 28, 1893, Dispatches, State Department Archives; Secretary of State Gresham to Allen, February 5, 1894, Instructions, incorporating Adee's statement, State Department Archives; Allen to Eben Brener, January 23, 1895, in the Allen MSS.

[6] Langer, *Diplomacy of Imperialism,* 168–171; Treat, "China and

And the Japanese

Evidence of Japan's purpose came soon after Allen entered the diplomatic service of America. The island empire's fishermen became extremely active in the Quelpart area of Korea. Japanese residents in Chosen became more aggressive. Japanese diplomats took a stronger stand than they had for a decade. Hot-headed young Oishi was outstanding. After coming to Seoul in 1893, he used bulldozing tactics to collect one of his country's claims. Pleased, the Japanese community in Chosen petitioned for the removal of Oishi's more moderate successor.[7]

Allen did not welcome signs like these. He thought Oishi's conduct was outrageous, drew up a catalogue of Japanese sins. She had cheated Chosen, he maintained, she had palmed off bad ships and worse machinery, all sorts of worthless goods on

Korea," *Political Science Quarterly*, 49 (1933):514–543; Tsiang, "Sino-Japanese Relations," *Chinese Social and Political Science Review*, 17 (1933):90–106; Hsü, *China and Her Political Entity*, 122–125; Vagts, "Der Chinesische-Japanische Krieg," *Europäische Gespräche*, 9 (1931): 285–302.

At this time Heard reported a rumor that Korea had refused a Russian offer of three million dollars for a northeastern province. The Tsarist envoy in Seoul, however, assured Heard that "we have not the slightest intention to seize any part of Korea. We are perfectly satisfied as we are." "Yes, no doubt you are at present," answered the American, "but there is what we call 'manifest destiny.'" "Oh no!" came back Demetrevsky, "if we wanted to do that we should not have spent and be spending thousands of dollars in making Vladivostock a first class fortified port, and we have an ice-breaking steamer to keep it open all winter." To which Heard said, "Bah!" In the same interview Demetrevsky said, "the Chinese do not like the Japanese you know, and they have lost all fear of us." Heard to the Secretary of State, February 10, 1893, Dispatches, State Department Archives.

While Heard and Allen were on vacation, Joseph R. Herod of the American legation in Japan assumed charge at Seoul. His comments are most revealing. In a dispatch to the Secretary of State, August 21, 1893 (State Department Archives), he said that a Sino-Japanese conflict was inevitable, adding that Japan might temporarily have "agreed to a combination of the two great Asiatic powers to prevent, together with the growth of American and European influence in Korea, the further advance of Russia southward."

[7] Treat, *Diplomatic Relations between the United States and Japan*, 2:412–417; Hulbert, *History of Korea*, 2:247; Heard to the Secretary of

the incautious Korean government. And in consequence she was detested "by every Korean from the Northern Boundary to the Southern Sea."

Should such a nation rule Korea? Allen thought not. His was the view expressed by Heard: "If Korea falls into the hands of Japan, God help her!" And by the English Bishop Corfe: "To us who know the Japanese as they really are in Corea, it is strange that Japan should for so long have deluded European nations and Governments into believing that she is a civilized Power, or desirous of becoming one."[8]

So Allen thought; and yet, to whip the Manchus, he gave aid to the Japanese. In the fall of 1893, for instance, when Yuan Shih Kai had Korea announce an embargo on rice exports, Japan, the leading purchaser, protested this; and Allen, then chargé, joined her in a memorial to the Seoul government. The doctor approved of the embargo, thought it was needed to stave off Korean famine. But nonetheless he set himself against it, partly because American trader Townsend had large rice interests, and partly to show sharp opposition to Manchu control of Chosen's government.[9]

Thus Allen acted in the final Chinese year, as partner of the next Korean overlord. To the doctor's mild surprise, war

State, October 8, 1891, March 27, April 6, May 6, 1893, Dispatches, State Department Archives, the last of which mentions a Franco-Russian request that the United States join in a demonstration for Korea; letter by Allen, January 14, 1893, in the Allen MSS; Allen to the Secretary of State, November 20, 1893, Dispatches, State Department Archives.

[8] Augustine Heard, "China and Japan in Korea," *North American Review*, 159 (1894):304–308; Allen to the Secretary of State, November 20, 1893, Dispatches, State Department Archives, marked "interesting" by Adee; Corfe's statement, quoted by R. S. Gundry, in "Corea, China and Japan," *Fortnightly Review*, 62 (1894):620.

[9] Allen to the Secretary of State, December 20, 1893, Dispatches, State Department Archives, stating that Korea was "very slow in discharging its obligations to Americans, and they might as well see that these controversies should be reciprocal." President of the Korean Foreign Office to Allen, December 17, 1893, Seoul Legation Files, State Department Archives.

was to come in 1894. To his complete amazement China was to lose.

"The relations of China and Japan had become petro-leum," wrote a national of the latter country, "and the Tong Hak was the match." The Tong Hak were anti-foreign Koreans who rebelled against the government. To whip them Chosen called for Chinese troops. China sent them, serving notice on Japan. But the Japanese objected to the suzerain claims incorporated in the note. Accordingly she sent troops too, and war began.

For all of this the American legation secretary blamed Japan. Plainly China did not want the conflict; just as plainly Nippon did. For years Japan had resented her lack of influence in Chosen, for years she had prepared to rectify the situation. ("By making a judicious use of the present unique opportunity," Count Okuma said, "it will be possible for the Japanese Government to retrieve all past errors.") What was more, there was domestic crisis in Japan in 1894, and a diversion was not unwelcome. "Our situation at home is critical," stated one island diplomat, "and war with China would improve it."[10]

Perhaps Japan went further to create the crisis of 1894. The Tong Hak rebellion reached its peak at a time con-venient for Nippon, and that was not quite accidental, for the Japanese appear to have poured funds into the move-ment. So did the Tai Wen Kun, who in his wisdom had for-saken China for Japan. Among the others interested was Kim Ok Kiun, Korean rebel of 1884, who lived in Japan and was controlled by the Japanese.[11]

Step One, the Tong Hak rising, was thus tied up with Tokyo. So was Step Two, the calling of the troops from China.

[10] Morse, *International Relations of the Chinese Empire,* 3:29; Langer, *Diplomacy of Imperialism,* 172–173; and, especially, Gresham's memo-randum of conversation with Tateno, in Vagts, "Die Chinesische-Japanische Krieg," *Europäische Gespräche,* 9 (1931):297–298.

[11] Sill to the Secretary of State, June 18, 1894, *Foreign Relations,* 1894, Appendix 1, p. 16; *The Secret Memoirs of Count Tadasu Hayashi,* edited

Allen was acquainted with the background there. He knew that Sugimura, Japanese legation secretary in Seoul, had urged the measure on Yuan Shih Kai. Allen and the other Occidental diplomats made light of the Tong Hak, asserting that it represented purely local troubles. The Japanese by contrast magnified the danger, insisted that Chosen could not handle the insurgents. Wherefore, said Sugimura, China should accept suzerain responsibility.[12]

So it was to be. Yuan Shih Kai, always apprehensive, wrote panicky letters to Tientsin. Superiors were prompt to send aid—ammunition for Korea, a promise to transport Korean troops on Chinese men-of-war. Later, when Yuan had wrung a petition out of the King of Chosen, Manchu troops were sent as well.[13] And this brought on Step Three, the intervention of Japan.

One, two, three—a clearcut program for the coming masters of Chosen. But seldom does the record show monopoly of blame. If the Japanese were splashed with war guilt, so was China. For, urged or not, Yuan Shih Kai did call for Chinese troops; and Viceroy Li Hung Chang dispatched them. More than that. The Manchus had given cause for all to hate them in Seoul. They had allowed Korea to be opened to the world, then had denied the opportunities which foreigners desired.

by A. M. Pooley (New York and London, 1915), 37–39; Heard, "China and Japan in Korea," *North American Review,* 159 (1894):303–304; Ariga, "Diplomacy," in Stead, *Japan by the Japanese,* 201–202; Hitrovo, Russian minister to Japan, to Waeber, February 21, 1894, and Hitrovo to the Russian Minister of Foreign Affairs, June 8, 1894, *Chinese Social and Political Science Review,* 17 (1933):480–481, 485–490.

[12] Address to the Naval War College, in the Allen MSS; Hsü, *China and Her Political Entity,* 124–125; Waeber to the Russian Minister of Foreign Affairs, July 4, 1894, *Chinese Social and Political Science Review,* 17 (1933):508; Heard, "China and Japan in Korea," *North American Review,* 159 (1894):303; Vagts, "Der Chinesische-Japanische Krieg," *Europäische Gespräche,* 9 (1931):285–302.

[13] Letters to the Russian Minister of Foreign Affairs from Cassini, Russian minister to China, March 10, July 1, 1894, and from Waeber, July 4, 1894, *Chinese Social and Political Science Review,* 17 (1933):483, 501, 508.

And the Japanese

After talking of reform and progress, Yuan had smilingly acquiesced in the worst political abuses. Japan had suffered more than most by this "dry-rot of Chinese conservatism." Her merchants had wielded little influence at court, her nationals had been in danger of attack, her food supply had been threatened by the Yuan-Korean export prohibitions. One can comprehend the cry of Ito—"China's insolence has become increasingly intolerable."[14] One can understand, if not approve, the Japanese desire for war.

Nor was Korea guiltless. The utter impotence, the hideous corruption of her government robbed natives of their patriotism, made it certain that Chosen would not resist attack, and constituted a standing invitation to foreign states to intervene.

Allen did not despair of the Korean kingdom, believed efficiency and patriotism could be developed there. Yet even he admitted that things were getting worse instead of better. He found the Koreans "so oppressed officially that they dont care who rules them as they think their condition could be no worse." He heard of women hitched to plows to pay for the debauches of the tax-enriched aristocracy. He met men who would not work bcause they knew the magistrates would take all that they earned. And he knew the squeeze was getting worse. To increase the sale of offices, the king had cut the term of country governors. Which meant that they robbed faster to be assured a good return on their investment.[15]

[14] Hamada, *Ito,* 111; D. W. Stevens, "China and Japan in Korea," *North American Review,* 159 (1894):313; Treat, "China and Korea," *Political Science Quarterly,* 49 (1933):506–543. Population figures are worth noting (see Heard to the Assistant Secretary of State, December 31, 1892, Consular Dispatches, State Department Archives): Japanese in Korea, 9132 (5060 in Fusan, 2615 in Chemulpo, 334 in Seoul, 723 in Wonsan); Chinese, 1249 (47 in Fusan, 409 in Chemulpo, 748 in Seoul, 45 in Wonsan): Americans, 78 (3 in Fusan, 4 in Chemulpo, 69 in Seoul, 2 in Wonsan); British, 51; French, 28; Germans, 25; Russians, 13; Danes, 4; Italians, 3; Norwegians, 3; Portuguese, 2; Spanish, 1.
[15] Address to the Naval War College, Allen to Ellinwood, April 24,

"As the drips of the candle on the banquet table fell, did the tears of the people," runs an Oriental proverb, "and as music swelled in merry-making, the outcry of the discontented masses became loud."[16] And in 1893 it swelled to a chorus in Korea, as the Tong Hak offered leadership.

The Tong Hak, "Eastern Learning," dated back a generation and a half to an obscure South Korean scholar, Choi Chei Woo. Fascinated by every manner of religion, Choi was suddenly inspired to blend them all into a new, Korean faith. Whereupon he was beheaded by the regent Tai Wen Kun for practising Catholicism (So Hak, "Western Learning"). But Choi's cult lived on, surviving persecution and emerging in the eighteen nineties as a mighty movement.

As it grew, the Tong Hak shifted stress from theology to politics. Theirs was a powerful appeal. "Incompetency marks the men in Seoul," runs one of their memorials, "and ability to extort money, those in the country. Great discontent prevails among the people, property is insecure and life itself is becoming a burden and undesirable ... Our country's condition now is worse than it has ever been before ... Can we endure these things much longer? Are the people to be ground under and destroyed? Is there no help for us? We are despised, we are forsaken ... We, the people of the whole realm, have determined to resist unto death the corruption and oppression of the officials ... Let not the cry of 'traitor' and 'war' disturb you, attend to your business and be prepared to respond to this appeal when the time comes."[17]

1890, in the Allen MSS; Hippisley to Rockhill, August 20, 1894, in the Rockhill MSS; A. Henry Savage-Landor, "A Visit to Corea," *Fortnightly*, 62 (1894):184.

[16] Paik, *Protestant Missions in Korea*, 161. Allen predicted an uprising in a letter to Ellinwood, January 5, 1893, in the Allen MSS, but did not guess the character.

[17] "A Retrospect, 1894," *Korean Repository*, 2 (1895):30–31. On the Tong Haks, see Hippisley to Rockhill, August 20, 1894, in the Rockhill MSS; Heard to the Secretary of State, April 20, May 10, 1893, Allen to the Secretary of State, September 28, 1893, Sill to the Secretary of State, June 1, 1894, Dispatches, State Department Archives; Ariga, "Di-

And the Japanese

Allen and the other residents of Seoul saw the Tong Hak leaders in the spring of 1893. They came in all humility to ask their king to grant toleration for their sect. Denied, they withdrew quietly to launch their fight against the government and the hated foreigners. The capital soon heard of raids, of attacks on magistrates, of Tong Hak power to end sickness and crop failure and to turn opponents' bullets into water. Before the close of 1893 the rebels had been whipped by royal troops, but back they came in the next year and this time they won battles, bringing in both China and Japan.

Tong Hak leaders seem to have hastened intervention by accepting aid from Japan and pro-Japanese Koreans. Fatal error, for intervention spelled disaster for the Tong Hak cause. Their legions melted at the news that China's troops were on the way. The Japanese victory brought no help, no end to taxes, no end to squeezing magistrates and blood-sucking noblemen. Indeed, after China had been beaten the Japanese turned savagely on the Tong Hak. Never after 1893 did Allen cast eyes on a living Tong Hak chieftain; but when the Japanese took hold he saw a number dead, their severed heads exposed on poles, their bodies tossed out to the dogs of Seoul.

By 1895 the Tong Hak was forgotten. Indeed, it slipped from public notice even while its raids were going on. With international conflict clouding the Oriental sky, it was difficult to concentrate on native insurrections or the suffering of the Korean masses.

Allen felt the atmosphere of crisis in the spring of 1894, months before the declaration of hostilities. It was then that

plomacy," in Stead, *Japan by the Japanese*, 202; Gale, *Korean Sketches*, 197; Heard, "China and Japan in Korea," *North American Review*, 159 (1894):302–304; "Confessions of a Tong Hak Chief," *Korean Repository*, 5 (1898):234–236; William L. Junkin, "The Tong Haks," *ibid.*, 2 (1895):56–60; "Among the Tong Haks," *ibid.*, 2(1895):201–208; Robert E. Speer, *Missions and Modern History* (2 vols., New York, 1904), 2:359–392. See also the claims of the President of the Korean Foreign Office to Allen, June 8, 18, 1894, Seoul Legation Files, State Department Archives: "their power is getting decrease."

Kim Ok Kiun was killed, assassinated by a false friend who had lured him to the Anglo-American settlement in Shanghai. Japan resented this, resented losing so able a politician; and it was hardly mollifying to learn that the assassin acted under orders of the Chinese-dominated king of Korea. Worse still, the culprit escaped chastisement. China turned him over to Chosen for trial and public laurels. Kim's body was delivered at the same time, on a Chinese gunboat, with the words "arch rebel and heretic" splashed across his coffin. Koreans treated the corpse of the Japanese protégé with even more indignity, slicing it to bits for display in the several provinces.

Allen played a curious role in the Kim Ok Kiun affair. He was chargé when the murder was committed, and heard that Korea wished the corpse in order to mutilate it, but was concerned to hear that it was in an area controlled by Britain and America. Would Allen help to solve that problem?

Yes, Allen would. Sitting down, the doctor penned a letter to the American consul in Shanghai. It was a bad mistake. Kim was obtained without his aid, and he received two sharp rebukes for his participation in the affair. One came from the consul in Shanghai; he would have none of the ghoulish business. The other came from a State Department that disapproved of all types of intervention.[18]

On the heels of the Kim affair came the Manchu intervention in the Tong Hak troubles. News of this reached Seoul during one of Yuan Shih Kai's banquets. The dining ceased forthwith, and all present seemed to realize what was in prospect. War for China and Japan, war to be fought and won on the neutral soil of Chosen.

Allen and most of the others present thought that the

---

[18] Allen to the Secretary of State, April 6, 17, 1894, Dispatches, State Department Archives; Acting Secretary of State to Allen, May 31, 1894, Instructions, State Department Archives; Treat, *Diplomatic Relations between the United States and Japan*, 2:445–447; address to the Naval War College, in the Allen MSS; Ariga, "Diplomacy," in Stead, *Japan by the Japanese*, 201–202; Cordier, *Relations de la Chine avec les puissances occidentales*, 3:228–231.

Chinese would win, would teach the Japanese a lesson. They would have done better to accept what was written on the faces of the banqueters. For the Chinese were cast down in gloom as though they knew that this would be their final banquet in Seoul. In contrast the Mikado's men were beaming with pleasure at the thought of triumph soon to come.[19]

And soon it came. China sent troops and ships to Chosen; so did Japan and with more speed. The Chinese encamped as though to fight the Tong Hak rebels. The Japanese ignored the insurrectionists and concentrated on the Chinese. With lightning speed they took Chemulpo, took the approaches to the capital, secured control of Seoul itself. That done, Japan had struck and won. She separated Chosen from the suzerain. She wiped the Manchus from the seas, she drove their armies back to China. And in the spring of 1895 she dictated the peace.

The conflict gave Allen and his Western diplomatic colleagues much to do. One job was to prevent or end the war. Korea asked that this be done, asked that the Western nations intervene. So did China. But no intervention came. In June, a month before the guns went off, the American, Russian, French, and British representatives in Seoul asked Japan and China to withdraw from Korea simultaneously. That failed, as did other efforts sponsored chiefly by the English. Allen and American Minister Sill wanted to help Korea, but received no great encouragement. True, Secretary of State Gresham instructed his Seoul agents to use "every possible effort" in the cause of peace, talked good offices, asked Japan to move with moderation. But "in no event could we jointly intervene with other powers." However unfortunate, a Sino-Japanese war "endangers no policy of the United States in Asia."[20]

[19] Allen, *Things Korean*, 244–246; Allen, "Acquaintance with Yuan Shi Kai," *North American Review*, 196 (1912):115. See also Hitrovo to the Russian Minister of Foreign Affairs, June 19, 1894, *Chinese Social and Political Science Review*, 17 (1933):502–503.

[20] On the peace efforts, see Payson J. Treat, "The Good Offices of the

Exit the Dragon

Peace or not, Sill and his aide kept busy. Protecting the Americans, for one thing, calling in the missionaries and getting up a guard. This was far harder than it sounded. For many missionaries tended to defy the safety regulations of the diplomats; and naval officers were most reluctant to detach details. Americans needed no protection, snorted one, if they would "attend to their own affairs and avoid politics." Another steamed off in midst of crisis, taking all his sailors and marines with him.

Bad enough at best, this situation was complicated by the turn of Seoul politics. For with the Japanese ascendant, many Korean enemies of Japan sought refuge in the American legation. How could one protect these quaking politicians with a terror-stricken native guard? And how could Sill fulfill a promise he had made when the Japanese had landed troops? "I had promised the King asylum, in case of emergency," the minister moaned in one dispatch; "Admiral's departure places me in a humiliating and most perilous position."[21]

United States during the Sino-Japanese War," *Political Science Quarterly*, 47 (1932):547–555; Max von Brandt, *Drei Jahre ostasiatischer Politik, 1894–1897* (Stuttgart, 1897), 137–142; Treat, *Diplomatic Relations between the United States and Japan*, 2:443–544; Langer, *Diplomacy of Imperialism*, 173–175. Otto Francke, *Die Grossmächte in Ostasien von 1894 bis 1914* (Hamburg, 1913), 31–85, is useful, and "Vladimir" [Z. Volpicelli], *The China-Japan War* (New York, 1896) is still the best account of the conflict. Attention may be called to the pathetic notes which Chyo Pyung Chik, president of the Korean foreign office, addressed to Sill on July 6, 20, and 23, 1893 (Seoul Legation Files, State Department Archives), noting China's willingness to withdraw and describing Japanese actions as "not in accordance with the law of nations," "a dangerous precedent . . . and a menace to the peace and integrity of His Majesty's Realm." See also Secretary of State Gresham to Sill, May 20, July 9, August 30, 1893, and Assistant Secretary Uhl to Sill, June 22, 1893, Instructions, State Department Archives.

[21] Sill to the Secretary of State, July 2, 8, 21, 1894, Dispatches, State Department Archives; Assistant Secretary of State Adee to Sill, July 8, 1895, Instructions, State Department Archives; Admiral J. S. Skerett to Sill, May 17, June 9, 20, 22, 24, 27, 28, July 2, 1894, and B. F. Day to Sill, July 20, August 3, 1894, Seoul Legation Files, State Department

And the Japanese

That was worked out in time, as the navy grudgingly assigned the necessary guards. But other problems were less easily resolved. Allen and his compatriots found the Japanese "exceedingly insolent" in their newly won power. Their soldiers beat the English consul and attacked some missionaries from America. Not even the legations were immune. On one occasion ladies gathered in the Allen home were startled by the entrance of a Japanese postman, who began to thrash one of Allen's servants.[22]

Nor was recourse to be found anywhere in Seoul. Japan controlled the government, controlled it with a firmer hand than Yuan Shih Kai had ever exercised. On July 23, 1894, Japanese troops had stormed into the palace grounds and made the king their prisoner. Next the Tai Wen Kun had been called to rule in line with Tokyo's orders. Out went the Mins, the queen's pro-Chinese relatives. In came others, men whose master was Japan, men who pushed through "Japanese reforms" in un-Korean haste.

These new enactments fell into a single category. All were laws designed to end the age-old influence of China in Korea and to replace them with the institutions of Japan. Thus strangulation by the Japanese replaced decapitation by the Chinese. Wide hat brims, long shirt sleeves, class distinctions, the arrest of criminals' relatives, limitation of petition rights— all were prohibited in order that Chosen might forget the past which linked her to the Manchus. Chinese rights of residence in Chosen were curtailed; the Chinese privilege of riding in the palace grounds was extended to all diplomats. For Korean government was reorganized in the interests of efficiency, so that Japan could rule with greater ease. Im-

Archives. Skerett expressed his view thus: "Disturbances are constantly arising among the people in Korea but it has generally been found that the Authorities have been able to afford the necessary protection and I trust such may also be the case in this instance." Again he suggested that Americans rely on Japan for protection.

[22] Sill to the Secretary of State, July 17, 1893, February 12, 1895, Dispatches, State Department Archives; admission to Inouye in interview, *New York Herald*, October 17, 1895.

The American Legation in Seoul

This sorry little Korean house was the despair of every American diplomat assigned to Seoul. Uncomfortable and unpretentious, it inevitably suggested to the Koreans that the United States could with impunity be ignored.

Entrance to Royal Palace in Seoul

Of the several palaces in Seoul, this was the most important in Allen's day. The royal residences were handsome, but, being spread out, lacked grandeur.

prisoned foes of China were released from jail, and the government pulled down the Chinese tribute arch. Korea declared all suzerain ties destroyed, which left her free before the world. Free but obligated to Nippon. She lost no time in signing a treaty of alliance. She issued mine, post-office, quarantine, and army regulations which the Japanese desired. She was apparently prepared to grant to Tokyo virtual monopoly of Korea's economic wealth. For Japan asked fifty years of exclusive railroad privileges, twenty-five for telegraphs, and five for posts.

In the early days of 1895 it seemed as if Japan would obtain all she desired, would establish permanent control of Chosen. The opposition was in hiding, the Western diplomats had reason to be discouraged, the king had given up all thought of offering resistance. To prove it, he took an ancestral temple oath in January, 1895, promising to uphold the Japanese reforms and to keep down the power of the Mins.[23]

Then, suddenly, there was a change. Japan encountered diplomatic obstacles. Her peace treaty with the Chinese was revised by Russia, France, and Germany. Meantime Sill combined with others to head off plans for Japanese monopolies in Chosen. Even what was left (a Japanese loan to Korea) was cut by lack of capital in the Japanese empire.[24]

Koreans were not notable for bravery in 1895—it was said that they were wounded only in the back. But when they saw the Japanese slow up, they ventured to express their own opinions. Even in 1894 the Koreans were "evidently not enthusiastic" about the alliance with Japan. In February, 1895, the American legation reported that the Japanese were "so cordially hated—almost unanimously—that their ultimate success, if possible at all, is plainly a matter of the distant future." And one month later, apropos of the monopoly

[23] Hulbert, *History of Korea*, 2:266-278; Langer, *Diplomacy of Imperialism*, 397; Brandt, *Drei Jahre ostasiatischer Politik*, 143–161.
[24] Langer, *Diplomacy of Imperialism*, 174–190, covers these developments. See also Sill to the Secretary of State, May 11, 1895, Dispatches, State Department Archives.

requests: "The Koreans unexpectedly developed a quite stubborn determination not to swear away all these rights and priviledges."[25]

Behind all this resistance was the queen. Japan had tried to drive her out of politics. Her family had been proscribed, her bitter foe the Tai Wen Kun had been elevated to power. Even the king had been used against her; in the ancestral oath His Majesty had sworn that his wife would no longer figure in the political life of Korea. But that had not restrained Queen Min, who immediately resumed her operations.

Cleverest of Her Majesty's maneuvers was the one involving Pak Yong Hyo. Pak, veteran of the 1884 émeute, came home in 1895 to serve with the Tai Wen Kun as puppet ruler for Japan. Exercising all her talents, the queen separated the newcomer from her father-in-law, then caused Pak to break with the Japanese. Whereafter Pak did as the queen directed until he was driven out of Seoul in June, 1895. He engineered an indirect attack on the Tai Wen Kun, having the old man's favorite protégé arrested as a traitor. And he resisted manfully all Japanese demands, even after Japanese envoy Inouye called him to task severely.[26]

Allen, of course, approved of Queen Min's actions. They were consistent with his desire for an independent Chosen, tended to ward off Japanese monopoly, which might put an end to opportunities for the United States. So he advised the king to take Pak Yong Hyo as his prime minister. His timid Majesty would not do that, but did let Allen argue him into

[25] Sill to the Secretary of State, October 12, 1894, February 12, April 17, May 25, 1895, Dispatches, State Department Archives. Secretary of State Olney, in a letter of June 21, 1895 (Instructions, State Department Archives), scolds Sill for joining other diplomats in objecting to monopolies; it was, he said, "utterly at variance with your enjoined attitude of strict neutrality."

[26] Hulbert, *History of Korea*, 2:280–285; letters to the Secretary of State from Sill, March 1, April 29, July 9, 1895, and from Allen, September 18, 1895, Dispatches, State Department Archives; *Korean Repository*, 2 (1895):199; Brandt, *Drei Jahre ostasiatischer Politik*, 162–165.

selecting Pak Chung Yang, a relative of the man rejected. Milder and less competent than Pak Yong Hyo, the new appointee was nonetheless distinctly anti-Japanese. This was reflected in the continued difficulties Nippon had in Seoul and the July, 1895, grant of the Un-san mine to an American concessionaire.[27] Observing how the wind was blowing, Japan tried compromise. Her Seoul envoy, Count Inouye, decided to abandon strong-arm measures and to conciliate the queen. For it was plain to see that repression had not worked; all the king's ancestral temple oaths would not eliminate Queen Min from politics. Conciliation, then; but would Her Majesty pay heed? Inouye did his best to get an audience, only to meet with refusal. In all her life the queen had received just a handful of male foreigners.[28] Why should she make a special exception to please a diplomat whom she had long known as a foe?

Despairing, the Japanese minister turned to Horace Allen. The American legation secretary knew Her Majesty, he was among the foreign males who had been admitted to her presence. Could he get her to listen to Inouye? When Inouye asked, the doctor was in no position to refuse. He had just obtained the Un-san franchise, and did not want Japan to challenge its legality. Besides, he was glad to help Japan back down, if that was what she wished to do; and as a mere legation secretary he was flattered to be noticed by the great Inouye.

He would help, he promised that. And he did so. With Allen as his sponsor, Inouye was admitted to the presence of Her Majesty and had a most important audience. He wished to cooperate, said the Japanese representative. He knew the queen's talents, he knew the love her people bore her; together she and Inouye could do great things.

[27] Allen to Morse, June 24, 1895, in the Allen MSS; Brandt, *Drei Jahre ostasiatischer Politik*, 162–164.
[28] See, however, Moellendorff, *Moellendorff*, 77.

Yes, put in Her Majesty, they could work well in partnership. Inouye's respect for her was matched by her own admiration of Japan. But the Japanese had treated her most shabbily. Her family had been persecuted, she had been told to quit the field of politics. And her arch-enemy, the Tai Wen Kun, had been taken from a well-deserved retirement to be petted and rewarded by Japan. Could she trust the island empire after that, could she feel safe while Nippon held the reins of power?

Oh, she was safe, Inouye could give assurances of that. While Japan had a bit of influence in Seoul, the royal family need fear no harm. Just friendship, loving friendship, and desire to work with the Korean queen. "In the event of ... treason against the Royal House," Inouye "gave the assurance that the Japanese Government would not fail to protect the Royal House even by force of arms."[29]

Was Inouye lying, asked the queen of Allen later. No, replied the doctor, Her Majesty could now forget her fears. There was no danger of bodily attack upon the members of the royal family. The Japanese had come to the conclusion that bullying did not pay.

For Inouye, that interpretation might have been correct. But the count was not Japan, nor was his compromising spirit universally accepted in his mother country. There were signs that the extremists would have much to say about Korea. In July of 1895 Seoul heard of a plot to kill the queen. August saw the prime ministry entrusted to Kim Hong Gip, one of the queen's opponents and a friend of the Tai Wen Kun.[30] And on September 1 Inouye was replaced as Japanese envoy by the harsh Viscount Miura.

Miura was no career diplomatist, but a rough fighting

[29] Sill to the Secretary of State, July 27, 1895, Dispatches, State Department Archives; address to the Naval War College and "Narrative of Facts," in the Allen MSS; *Korean Repository*, 3 (1896):131–132; Hulbert, *History of Korea*, 2:286–288.

[30] Sill to the Secretary of State, July 9, August 25, 1895, Dispatches, State Department Archives.

man. His appointment suggests that Allen was altogether mistaken in accepting Inouye's words, and that Japan, far from easing up, was planning to lay a heavy hand on the Korean government. Surely the Viscount Miura thought so. "By profession a soldier," he announced on the eve of his departure for Seoul, "I have had no experience in diplomacy." Careerists "took pity" on him and offered their advice; but, as Miura said, "I declined all their well meant offers, being content to rely on my own resources." In other words, on the resources of a soldier. "I have a diplomacy all my own, which I propose to try in Korea," was the Viscount's statement. "I believe that it is a fit place to try my own theory of diplomatic methods."[31]

Upon reaching his post the new appointee immediately proceeded to "insult" Korean royalty. He appeared in ordinary dress at a formal banquet held in celebration of the queen's escape during the 1882 émeute. Simultaneously he backed Korean politicians who were hated at the palace and entered into close relations with the queen's old enemy, the Tai Wen Kun.

Still, Allen felt there was no danger. He believed that there would be "great disorders" during the winter. But by that he meant Tong Hak insurrections in the provinces and brawls between the army and Seoul's police. The king and queen, being covered by Inouye's pledge, were likely to be safe from harm.[32]

Such was the situation on October 7, 1895. On that day Korea sent a prince as royal representative to thank Japan for liberating Chosen from the yoke of China. Less than twenty-four hours later the Japanese were to strike a deadly blow in Seoul.

[31] *Japan Daily Mail*, September 5, 1895, quoted by Allen in a letter to the Secretary of State, September 18, 1895, Dispatches, State Department Archives.
[32] Allen to the Secretary of State, October 7, 1895, Dispatches, State Department Archives.

15

The Peace of Asia

THE queen was a striking figure, and even at fifty-four was pretty in a way. She could be positively beautiful when her dark eyes flashed and a smile appeared on her pale thin face. But smiles belonged to bygone, happier days; in 1895 Her Majesty's eyes were sad.[1]

A thousand unsolved problems tortured Queen Min's mind in her last months on earth, a thousand woes weighed down her aching heart. Her years upon the throne had not been years of glory; all she loved had been profaned. Two decades before, her beloved family had been proud in power and respect. Then Min fortunes had declined. Civil strife cut down the family's best and made weak the wills of many more. Mins had been reduced to puppet stature by the Manchus, and with the downfall of China sank still lower in the scale. Japan, having taken up with the queen's father-in-law, the Tai Wen Kun, purged the queen's relatives from the government of Chosen and appeared determined to destroy them entirely.

That was tragedy enough for any queen. But Her Korean

[1] Bishop, *Korea*, 2:37–39; Underwood, *Fifteen Years among the Top-Knots*, 24, 89–90; Annie Ellers Bunker, "My First Visit to Her Majesty the Queen," *Korean Repository*, 2 (1895):373–375.

Majesty had greater troubles. One involved the future of her only child, the heir apparent to his father's throne. The boy was handsome, sweet and gentle, as loving as could be. But his mind was dull, incapable of concentrating upon the simplest things. That naturally distressed his mother. It was all right so long as she was there; she was strong and could support the lad. But afterward? Might not the politicians push aside the little boy and choose another for king? Perhaps the favorite grandson of the Tai Wen Kun, or the legitimitized bastard the king had had by a royal concubine? Any one could see that the rival candidates were brighter than the queen's son; and men as keen as Secretary Allen thought it possible that Her Majesty's offspring would be passed by.

Thus there was grief for the Mins and for the crown prince too. And linked with both was grief for the kingdom of Chosen. What was to happen to the queen's unhappy land? "Poor Korea, poor Korea!" a native had exclaimed on learning of the culture of the Western world. Her Majesty agreed. "Oh, that Korea was as happy, as free and as powerful as America!" she murmured to a woman missionary on Christmas eve in 1894. Whereupon the visitor told of a better land, beyond all earthly ills. The queen listened quietly, sadly, thoughtfully. "Oh! how good it would be," she mused, "if the king, the prince and myself might all go there!"

But, however discouraged, Queen Min had not abandoned her position. She fought back when the Japanese attempted to eliminate her influence. She stiffened the jellyfish backbone of her royal spouse. And in the summer of 1895 success seemed possible. First, Pak Yong Hyo was helpful. Then Count Inouye said Japan wanted to cooperate with the queen. That was encouraging; it might even mean a comeback for the Mins. It was comforting, too, to hear the trusted Dr. Allen say that the queen and her son need not fear violence so long as Japan held the reins.[2]

[2] Inouye gives an excellent characterization of Her Majesty in an

And the Japanese

Then, on the twentieth day of the eighth moon, in the five hundred and fourth year of the Yi dynasty—on October 8, 1895—disaster came. The palace was invaded, and Queen Min brutally murdered. As her royal body fell before the blows of the assassins, the last hope of the Mins died, the hopes of the crown prince, and many of the hopes of all Korea.[3]

Had she not felt immune from danger, Her Majesty might have fled to safety, as she had done in 1882. At least so thought the American legation secretary, who believed that his own words had given the queen a false sense of security. He and Inouye had helped to lead an able woman to her doom.[4]

Allen had arisen at dawn on that fateful day; the sound of firing had awakened him. He was greatly concerned, for Minister Sill was on vacation, and he himself, as chargé, was responsible for the protection of Americans. And, having said that there was no danger, he felt morally responsible for the safety of the king and queen.

Soon came news. Ye Pum Chin, minister of public works, dashed in with a communication from the king. His Majesty begged Allen to hurry to the palace. Naturally another mes-

interview printed in the *New York Herald* on October 17, 1895. For a violent denunciation, see Ladd, *In Korea*, 284–286; and see also Graves, "Willard Straight at the Legation in Korea," *Asia*, 20 (1920):1081–1082, based on statements of McLeavy Brown. Brandt (*Dreiunddreissig Jahre in Ost-Asien*, 3:253) says that she was the "only man in the family." Gilmore, in his *Korea*, 106–107, cites an example to prove the same.

[3] The story of the queen's murder can best be traced in Allen's letters to the Secretary of State, October 10, 11, 13, 14, 1895, with enclosures, Dispatches, State Department Archives; *Korean Repository*, 2 (1895): 386–392, and 3 (1896):118–141 (report of an official Korean investigation), 216–220; and Bishop, *Korea*, 2:60–76. For comment on the latter, see "General Dye on 'Korea and her Neighbors,'" *Korean Repository*, 5 (1898):439–442; McKenzie, *Tragedy of Korea*, 58–75, 263–267; Homer B. Hulbert, *The Passing of Korea* (New York, 1906), 129–147; Treat, *Diplomatic Relations between the United States and Japan*, 3:4–11; *New York Herald*, October 14, 17, 1895; and Brandt, *Drei Jahre ostasiatischer Politik*, 163–168.

[4] Address to the Naval War College and Allen to the Secretary of State, August 31, 1900, in the Allen MSS.

senger had been sent to the Japanese legation—the Japanese envoy could never be ignored. But, as Allen knew, "His Majesty in his great distress looks with absolute confidence only to this [*the American*] legation."[5]

Mindful of the advantage of numbers, the American chargé hastened to his friend Waeber, the Russian representative; and together the two sought Miura. Finding that the Japanese envoy had gone on ahead, they followed rapidly, pushing their way through the gathering crowds of natives. Soon they gained an idea of what had happened. As they entered the royal grounds and approached the palace, they saw "30 very evil looking Japanese with disordered clothes, long swords and sword canes, coming away." These men were Japanese civilian residents of Seoul, *soshi* who sometimes did the dirty work for the Japanese legation.

The presence of the soshi suggested many things. Anxious to know the truth, Allen and Waeber immediately began to investigate. Their task was anything but easy, for the Japanese had no desire to talk and the Korean civilians who remained in the vicinity were cowed and much confused. Gradually, however, the representatives accumulated scraps of evidence and worked the pieces into a logical and bloody pattern.

As Allen saw it, the "chief devil in the trouble" was the king's father, the Tai Wen Kun. By 1895 the years had told on the old conspirator. His once strong frame was weak and bent, and he used a cane as he edged along. But inside the old fires still burned, so brightly that the aged man decided on one last drive against his old Min enemies. Thus was started the last campaign in Chosen's War of Roses.

In 1895 the royal parent had been out of power for some twenty years. His coup of 1882 had ended in defeat and exile, and his shift to the Chinese cause had profited him little. He was close to Yuan Shih Kai from 1886 to 1888, but after that the Manchus preferred to work through the ex-

[5] Sill to the Secretary of State, May 14, 1895, Dispatches, State Department Archives.

regent's hated foes, the Mins. When the Japanese came in, the Mins lost out, and the Tai Wen Kun was temporarily on top. But later Japan, too, chose to work through others, through the Korean progressives, rather than the royal parent's forces. Again the Tai Wen Kun's prestige declined, even with the commoners who had worshipped him.

But presently a new opportunity presented itself. Many of the progressives proved to be anti-Japanese. Even the rebels of 1884, whom Japan had sheltered for a decade, showed a disposition to bite the hand that fed them. Whereupon the Tai Wen Kun stepped in, offering Japan his aid. Cooperation was informal at the start, involving only a few offices. Then Miura came. The Tai Wen Kun was close to the new envoy "from the start," and soon there was firm union on the basis of a drive against the Mins. The queen would be assassinated, other Mins would be purged from the government, leaving Japan and the Tai Wen Kun in power.[6]

When he was approached by the Tai Wen Kun, Miura was already certain that "things in Korea were tending in a wrong direction," and, being a "blunt soldier man," he "felt it to be of urgent importance to apply an effective remedy." So, hearing the wishes of the king's father, he prepared to act.

For details Miura consulted Sugimura, who had been Japanese legation secretary for seven years, and Okamoto, Japanese adviser to the Korean war and household ministries. The three agreed "that this opportunity should be availed of for taking the life of the Queen, who exercised overwhelming influence in the Court." The Tai Wen Kun was recognized as a useful but very slippery ally; to hold him tight, the Japanese insisted that he sign a statement promis-

---

[6] Light is thrown on the Tai Wen Kun's activities by Allen's letter to Ellinwood, April 24, 1890, in the Allen MSS; Sill to the Secretary of State, May 25, 1895, and Allen to the Secretary of State, October 10, 1895, Dispatches, State Department Archives; *Korean Repository,* 2 (1895):199, 437; Heard, "China and Japan in Korea," *North American Review,* 159 (1894):303–304.

ing the Japanese special privileges if he secured control. This the old man did, as did also one son and grandson (brother and nephew of the king). The Japanese then threw their weight into the venture. "At the instigation of Miura" Japanese civilians prepared to enter the palace and to "dispatch the Queen." The *kunrentai,* Japanese-trained soldiers of the Korean army, fell into line because of their dissatisfaction with the treatment accorded them by the court. Finally, success was to be assured "by causing the Japanese troops stationed in Seoul to offer their support to the enterprise."[7]

A threatened disbandonment of the kunrentai furnished an excellent opportunity to strike. Seizing it, the Japanese moved on the palace in the early morning hours of October 8. Japanese troops escorted the Tai Wen Kun in from his country residence. Simultaneously the kunrentai, the soshi, and the Japanese soldiers advanced on their prey. Miura stayed at his legation to avoid the appearance of participation, but the messenger who carried him the king's alarm found the Viscount fully dressed and ready to enter his waiting sedan chair.

Those inside the palace grounds had ample warning of catastrophe. For two days excitement had been high; the Japanese had been engaged in unusual maneuvers, and the kunrentai collided with the capital police. But the royal family did not flee. Allen and Inouye had assured them that all was well, as did a leading native—Chung Pyung Ha, who had sold out to the Japanese.

At two in the morning the Korean commander of the palace guard heard that soldiers were moving into the barracks outside the palace walls. Japanese troops had occupied these barracks since 1894, but the reinforcement after midnight suggested something more than occupation.

Worried, the guard commander hurried a detachment forward to defend the front gate. It was at best a feeble gesture.

[7] Statements of the Japanese court which investigated this affair, quoted in McKenzie, *Tragedy of Korea,* 263–267.

And the Japanese

As American adviser William M. Dye said, the palace guard was "by no means perfect."[8] Half the five hundred guardsmen were unarmed; the rest had inferior equipment. The Japanese had seen to that when they were on the top in 1894. They had carted off the palace ammunition and had confiscated all good weapons, replacing them with rusty guns that lacked locks, cocks, and bayonets. General Dye had struggled manfully to repair the damage done, had assembled a few good rifles, and had fished up ammunition that had been thrown into a royal lake. But even these heroic measures were undone. The American officer's special weapons were stolen from his quarters and just before October 8, 1895, the guard had been reduced in size.

Thus if there had been a battle, the palace defenders would have crumbled before the more numerous and better trained attackers. But there was no fight. The nervous guardsmen fired some random shots, then broke and fled at the mere sight of the Tai Wen Kun and the oncoming kunrentai and Japanese. After that there was not even a pretense of defending the palace. The members of the guard cast off their uniforms and the invaders streamed in unimpeded.

The object of the attacking force could not be mistaken. For, once inside the walls, the soshi sought the queen. Rushing to the family house of Their Korean Majesties, they seized all the natives they met and addressed to each one question, "Where is the queen?" Force was used to get an answer. Officials pleading ignorance were handled roughly, palace women were hauled around by the hair. Even the king and the crown prince were pushed and yanked about with utter disregard for the rank of royalty.

Finally the queen was found, guarded only by a cabinet official and some ladies of the palace. It was easy to identify Her Majesty; the household minister gave everything away by standing as a shield before the royal lady. His loyalty cost this man his life, and the soshi sprang at the queen. Her

[8] Letter in *Korean Repository*, 3 (1896):216–220.

Majesty cried out that she was just a visitor and tried to escape. But the conspirators were upon her. They struck her down, jumped upon her breast, hacked her with their swords. With one last effort, the queen called for her son; and as she called she died.

Even then the murderers were not content. They wanted to remove every sign of the murdered woman. So they threw some cloth around the corpse and carried it to a little park inside the palace grounds. There, in a spot made beautiful by nature, they soaked the royal winding sheet with kerosene and set it on fire. Soon the flames were consuming all that remained of Her Majesty.

The deed was done before Allen reached the palace. The queen, the household minister, the guard commander, and three palace ladies were dead. And, as might have been expected, the fruits of victory were already in the grasp of the Japanese. Minister Miura and the Tai Wen Kun had served an ultimatum on the king, demanding partial reorganization of the government—to include the appointment of His Majesty's elder brother as minister of the royal household. Trembling with fright, the monarch had yielded. After that, the Japanese left in safety, surrendering control to their allies, the king's father and brother and the troops of the kunrentai.

This meant, of course, that the king was once again a prisoner in his own palace. Allen and Waeber knew that even before they were sure that the queen had been assassinated. When they requested an audience, they were put off a full two hours on the shabbiest of pretexts. And when they marched unannounced into His Majesty's apartments, their suspicions were confirmed. They saw Viscount Miura and the Tai Wen Kun hovering near the monarch of Chosen; and they saw the king twitching with terror and misery. His Majesty still hoped his queen had managed to escape, but his quivering frame and frightened eyes showed that he feared the worst, feared that he was left alone to face his kingdom's foes.

Alone? Or would the diplomats assist him? Could he not count upon his dear friends from America and Russia? With his father near, with Miura standing by, the king dared make no plea for aid. But Allen and Waeber could see all in the poor man's eyes, could see a weak, forlorn, and helpless creature crying out for pity and assistance.

Self-interest joined with sympathy to dictate action. Waeber's empire would suffer if the Japanese took hold in Seoul. Allen felt that America, too, had good reason to check the Japanese. He was sure that a great crisis was at hand. The queen's loss, soon to be confirmed, was "irreparable." She had been a "strong character and one of the great personages of Asia." Her death meant that "the surest support to progressive ideas" had been removed,[9] that opportunities for American penetration might soon disappear. Only a strong stand, quickly taken, could prevent this unfortunate development.

A cautious man would have taken stock of the obstacles. Allen's rank being limited, important decisions should have been reserved for Minister Sill. Moreover, the State Department prohibited interference in the domestic politics of Seoul. Diplomatic instructions made this point specifically, as did a dozen other messages on file in the legation.

But Allen was not by nature cautious. He felt he "had to protect American interests" as he conceived them. Feeling thus, he threw his entire weight again the Japanese. Openly he accused them of having caused the trouble. He refused to deal with the Tai Wen Kun's pro-Japanese Korean government. He gave aid and comfort to the king when the Japanese attempted to make a mere puppet ruler of him. He assisted natives who remained loyal to His Majesty and plotted counter-revolution.

Publicity was the first task. The doctor felt he could check

[9] Allen to the Secretary of State, October 10, 1895, December 23, 1898, in the Allen MSS; article by Allen, 1905, in the Allen MSS.

the Japanese advance if he exposed Miura. If the Viscount had a chance to consolidate his power before the facts were known, he might hold on indefinitely; if all the world knew of his actions, Japan might be forced to disavow them.

Losing no time, Allen sent a flood of telegrams and letters on to Washington. He minced no words. "The leaders were the Japanese," he said; the "murderers were Japanese in civilian dress." The legation was involved, "no doubt" of that; evidence of Miura's participation was "overwhelming."

Allen's statements did not go unchallenged. Miura denied them flatly on October 8, in a meeting of the diplomatic corps. Waeber, who spoke "with full consent" of the Occidental diplomats "and with an occasional suggestion," outlined what he and Allen felt to be the facts, The Japanese representative replied that he and his staff, his soldiers, and his superiors were as innocent as newborn babes. What of the eyewitness testimony which pointed to another conclusion? It was a tissue of falsehood; Miura "had it on the truth of Japanese officers and soldiers that no outrage of the kind alleged ever occurred and their word was certainly more worthy of credence than that of Koreans who were notoriously addicted to spreading absurd rumors." Japanese participation had begun when Miura was roused from bed by a palace messenger. Even the soshi were innocent; though perhaps evil had been done by Koreans "dressed as Japanese in European clothes."[10]

Miura's statements had considerable support. The new pro-Japanese foreign minister said that "not a single Japanese was present." Officials in Japan "most positively" asserted that their government had "nothing whatever to do with it." Their words were echoed by Dun, America's pro-Japanese minister in Tokyo. Dun, through whose offices the Allen cables passed, could not believe the statements of his Seoul

[10] Allen to the Secretary of State, October 10, 11, 13, 14, 1895, Dispatches, State Department Archives.

colleague and advised the State Department that Allen's information differed from his own.[11]

In time, however, Chargé Allen was upheld. As early as October 9 Japan's consul in Seoul admitted that a few soshi had gone along "to see the fight." Soon Japanese newspapers spoke of harboring "strong suspicion" and "little doubt" that the soshi had been involved. Officials in Tokyo said that Miura, though guiltless, "could have frustrated" the conspirators. And within a fortnight men as prominent as Inouye's son announced that "Viscount Miura was undoubtedly cognizant of the conspiracy and was himself one of the conspirators."[12]

This change in front is attributable to many factors. Some of the Japanese party saw no reason to conceal activities of which they were proud. Others, differing, desired publicity so that the blame would be placed on Miura, not Japan. Still others may have seen that secrecy, however desirable, was impossible in the face of the dispatches of Allen. Waeber, and their friends. Allen, always disposed to magnify his own importance, accepted the latter interpretation. As he saw it, it was his prompt reporting that exposed Miura to Japan and to the world.

The doctor did more than write dispatches. Without consulting his superiors in Washington, he took an open stand against the new, pro-Japanese Korean government. That government was issuing royal decrees designed to crush what was left of the anti-Japanese supporters of the queen. One, the edict of October 11, attacked and degraded Her Majesty

[11] Treat, *Diplomatic Relations between the United States and Japan,* 3:4–7; Korean Minister of Foreign Affairs to Allen, October 8, 1895, Seoul Legation Files, State Department Archives; Sill to the Secretary of State, November 20, 1895, Dispatches, State Department Archives, enclosing statements of the Korean Minister of Foreign Affairs; *Korean Repository,* 3 (1896):129.

[12] Treat, *Diplomatic Relations between the United States and Japan,* 3:9–11; Allen to the Secretary of State, October 17, 19, 1895, Dispatches, State Department Archives; Japanese press as quoted in *Korean Repository,* 2 (1895):432–434.

for her "extreme wickedness" in helping her relatives dull the king's senses "by their evil counsel." Interesting in itself, this decree threatened to open the way for dynastic rearrangements. With the queen degraded, rules of mourning and succession could be set aside, to the advantage of the Japanese.[13]

Allen acknowledged receipt of a copy of this document in most undiplomatic language. He censured the government for speaking as though the queen were still alive. He demanded an investigation of the events of October 8, and, setting aside standard rules of diplomatic etiquette, flatly refused to "recognize this decree as coming from His Majesty."

The doctor also violated his own country's instructions concerning neutrality and separate action in international controversies. He consulted with Waeber and with the English, French, and German representatives in diplomatic meetings from which Miura was excluded. He played a major part in organizing a united front against the Japanese. And all adopted Allen's method of denying recognition to the new government's decrees.[14]

While fighting the group in power, the doctor gave much assistance to the opposition. He steadied the nerves of the jittery king. Every day he, Waeber, and the English consul (and sometimes the German too) called on His Majesty. The diplomats sympathized with the imprisoned monarch, made sure he was not abused, and gathered such information as the king dared whisper in their ears. Generally the whispered words were pleas for aid. These the diplomats answered by summoning marines to Seoul. Allen called up fifteen from the *U.S.S. Yorktown.*

But even this was not enough. Allen was sure that the

[13] Allen to the Secretary of State, October 11, 1895, Dispatches, State Department Archives; Korean Minister of Foreign Affairs to Allen, October 11, 1895, with decrees, Seoul Legation Files, State Department Archives; *Korean Repository,* 3 (1896):133.

[14] Allen to the Secretary of State, October 12, 13, 17, 1895, Dispatches, State Department Archives, the dispatch of October 13 enclosing Allen's note to the Korean Minister of Foreign Affairs; *Korean Repository,* 3 (1896):135.

king's own life was in peril, and was determined to protect him. He asked the missionaries to cooperate. The men would take turns staying in the palace, thus cheering the king and reducing the danger of a secret assassination. The women, meantime, assisted Mrs. Allen and the European legation ladies in preparing food for the monarch of Chosen. Poisoning was an old Korean custom, so time-honored that with the change of government His Majesty became reluctant to taste the palace fare. For a period the monarch would touch nothing but boiled eggs and condensed milk, items that were opened in his presence. Then the Occidentals came to his rescue. From their own kitchens they brought him food in a tin box carefully guarded by the missionaries. The Tai Wen Kun complained: "Why do you take all that good food in to him? He doesn't need it. I am old, my teeth are gone, I need it far more than he." But the practice was continued, and the king of Chosen began to feel that he might live.[15]

Still greater help was given the lesser figures in the anti-Japanese bloc. Half a dozen of the most outstanding were granted asylum in the American legation. Allen found them there on October 8 when he returned from the scene of the queen's assassination. They were crowded into the doctor's bedroom and Fannie was caring for their wounds. The chargé knew that his superiors demanded that he exercise caution in accepting refugees; but there they were, old friends in need. "I cannot drive them out to their death now," he said in a dispatch written two days later. It would be cruel, and politically bad to boot.[16] So the men stayed on, and as they stayed formed plots against the government.

Those were days of exaltation for Horace Allen. Action

[15] Underwood, *Underwood of Korea*, 146; Underwood, *Fifteen Years among the Top-Knots*, 154–156; Allen to the Secretary of State, October 11, 13, 1895, Dispatches, State Department Archives; address to the Naval War College, in the Allen MSS.

[16] Allen to the Secretary of State, October 10, 1895, Dispatches, State Department Archives; address to the Naval War College, in the Allen MSS; Allen, *Things Korean*, 233–234.

always sent him soaring to the heights. Besides, he occupied the spot he loved the best—the center of the stage. He could boast that the other Occidental diplomats had accepted the course he had plotted. He could say quite truthfully that the king "literally depends on me like a child on his father" and that the anti-Japanese Koreans looked on him with great devotion.[17]

Even the opposition bid for favor. For one, the Tai Wen Kun, whom Allen described as "begging my intercession for himself." All was not well with the king's old father. The Japanese had used him to get power, then had cast him into the discard. The old man found that it profited him little to have disposed of his enemy the queen. The cabinet he hoped to dominate was controlled by the Japanese, and he was edged outside.[18]

Those in power turned to Allen, too. November 1 saw Inouye in Seoul, as special agent for Japan. He had come to seek the favor of the Occidental diplomats in Chosen, hoping to overcome hostility without yielding any of his country's newly won influence. After surveying the field, he decided to start with Allen. Minister Sill was back in town again, but Allen seemed a more important catch. The doctor had enormous influence, and he could be approached much more informally than Sill.

To break the ice, the count told Allen that Japan did not resent his actions as chargé. It was obvious that the doctor had merely told the truth and done his duty. Then Inouye came to the point. He wished Allen "to do many things, chief of which were to secure the confidence of the King in himself and his intentions, place him on friendly terms with the Russian minister so that they could work together and avert a general war, to draw up a scheme for a new Governm't, and for the punishment of those involved in the

[17] Allen to Jennie Everett, November 5, 1895, in the Allen MSS.
[18] *Ibid.*; Allen to the Secretary of State, October 14, 1895, Dispatches, State Department Archives.

recent troubles, to secure the cooperation of the Diplomatic Corps and to be present at his interviews with the King and to get the latter to express himself fully and frankly" as he would to Allen himself.[19]

Allen, already excited by events, now felt that he had reached the peak of diplomatic power. Heretofore he had centered much of his attention on the domestic situation in Korea; now he saw his horizon broaden. He saw the queen's assassination forcing Russo-Japanese relations to a crisis, pictured himself as the person who must prevent a war between the two great powers. Such a war, in his opinion, "would involve England & France as well and Germany could hardly stay out." Consequently the doctor was convinced that "the peace of Asia possibly of Europe in a great measure depends upon me." Strange, perhaps, but "small men sometimes hold great stakes."

In the process of averting world catastrophe, Allen hoped to straighten out Korean politics. He should have liked to see America in control and was sure that "if our own Governm't would only take a hand I could get them the control of affairs." But "they would not consider it of course." The alternative he preferred was "a joint commission Japanese and Russian to conduct Korean affairs." Neither would allow the other to gain ascendancy, but together they might bring order to Seoul.[20]

While formulating such plans, the American legation secretary set out to do what Inouye had requested. He succeeded after days of work. Waeber and the king, Sill and the other Western diplomats agreed to meet the Japanese ambassador and re-establish friendly intercourse.

And what came of it all? Inouye said he regretted Chosen's

[19] Allen to Jennie Everett, November 5, 1895, in the Allen MSS; Sill to the Secretary of State, October 31, 1895, Dispatches, State Department Archives.

[20] Allen to Jennie Everett, November 5, 1895, in the Allen MSS. Allen expressed the same view in writing to the Secretary of State on August 23, 1900 (Dispatches, State Department Archives) and to Fassett on

October turmoil. He told the diplomatic corps that he "could not but express his strong condemnation of outrages that had been committed, and he failed to find words strong enough to describe his disapprobation of the assassination of the Queen and the indecent and outrageous decrees the 'blackest . . . in Korean history' with reference to her degradation." Moreover, he "had no doubt" that his government would accept the suggestion of Sill and others that Japan assume responsibility for getting rid of the present native government and providing for the safety of the king.[21]

Actually, little was accomplished. The obnoxious degradation decrees were withdrawn, but in other respects conditions remained unchanged. The king was still a prisoner when Inouye left for home, and the pro-Japanese administration in Korea still held on.

Yet Allen was not discouraged. After all, Miura had been repudiated and recalled. And Inouye's conciliatory attitude had helped to allay a crisis. Allen's "firm stand" after October 8 had had "a good effect." Why could not more be done by a continuation of that policy?

But then Allen faced a real setback—the government in Washington repudiated all his work. President Cleveland and Secretary of State Olney might try out jingo trumpets in the Caribbean, but in the Orient they continued to be cautious. As Allen's cables began streaming into Washington, reprimands were shot back to Seoul. It was a "matter of regret" that the chargé had attended a diplomatic conference from which the Japanese representative had been excluded. It was "no part of his duty" to refuse to recognize the dead queen's degradation—diplomatic instruction 64 forbade "intervention in political concerns of Korea." Moreover, Allen's

March 13, 1898 (Allen MSS). In the latter he declared that a Russo-Japanese condominium would be "for the best interests of American enterprises."

[21] Memorandum prepared by Allen and checked by Hillier and Inouye, in Sill to the Secretary of State, November 20, 1895, Dispatches, State Department Archives; Allen to Jennie Everett, November 5, 1895,

cooperation with European diplomats was "open to serious objections on account of our consistent policy ... of abstaining from cooperating with other persons of whatever nature ... our strength lies in our independence and the knowledge all countries possess that we never seek anything beyond what our treaties clearly entitle us to, and only do what disinterested friendship naturally suggests." Allen, acting with others, might unwittingly advance some sinister scheme of a treacherous European government.

Telegram after telegram, letter after letter, all the same. Only here and there was a word of praise to be found. Olney, condemning the doctor's methods, did commend "Mr. Allen's desire to serve the interests of His Majesty the King of Korea, for whose person this Government entertains sincere friendship." Rockhill, writing privately, assured his old friend that there was "absolutely no personal dissatisfaction with you in any way. Your judgment may have been wrong or may not as the case may be but any man can make those kind of mistakes." And again, "do not take it too much to heart"; "we do not propose to 'sit on you.' " But, softened or not, it was apparent that a rebuke was intended.[22]

Allen was stunned and hurt by these communications. "I did my duty to the best of my ability under the rather trying circumstances," he said to Rockhill. And who had called him wrong? Not the naval men; they approved his actions. Not Minister Sill. The old school superintendent may have had some doubts at first, but after reaching Seoul he had adopted all his secretary's policies and cabled, "Allen's conduct of affairs excellent." Cooperation? "Naturally" Sill joined Waeber and Walter C. Hillier (the British representative); but America was "not committed nor are we compromised." Exclusion

in the Allen MSS. See also the item in the *Japan Daily Mail* of October 28, 1895, enclosed in a letter from Sill to the Secretary of State, November 20, 1895, Dispatches, State Department Archives.

[22] Secretary of State Olney to Sill, November 11, 20, 21, December 2, 31, 1895, Instructions, State Department Archives; Rockhill to Allen, November 23, 1895, March 17, 1896, in the Rockhill MSS.

of the Japanese minister? "How could we" associate with a proven "culprit"? And Japan had not minded. Rather Inouye had been "profuse in his thanks" for Allen's aid, had said Nippon "will be under great and lasting obligation to you." Interference in domestic affairs? He had steered clear of counter-revolutionary plots, had refused to consider a royal plea for a palace guard of English, Russian, and American marines. All in all, the doctor said, "I had fancied until the telegrams began to come ... that I might be given some credit for doing well."[23]

That was Allen's reaction to his reprimand. He did not yield, did not state (as Sill was later to do) that he "did err unintentionally." No, he stood by his decisions. He was sorry that his superiors did not see the light, but he was determined not to make their error his.

Such an attitude might well have led to an abrupt dismissal. But Allen had a shield, Minister Sill. As soon as Sill ratified his assistant's action, censure shifted from the secretary to the minister. And there it stayed, though Allen was the guiding spirit of the legation. Sill, carrying on the doctor's refugee policy, received a stinging rebuke in December, 1895. "Refugees cannot be sheltered by you against officers of de facto government charged with apprehending them as violaters of the laws of their country," read the dispatch. "The Department sees with disfavor your disposition to forget that you are not to interfere with local concerns and politics of Korea, but are to limit yourself strictly to the care of American interests." An even sharper reprimand came a month later after Sill had publicly announced his approval of Allen's non-recognition of governmental decrees. This time Olney cabled in angry phrases: "Continued intermeddling with Korean political affairs in violation of repeated instructions noted with astonishment and emphatic disapproval. Cable briefly

[23] Allen to Rockhill, December 29, 1895, and to Jennie Everett, November 5, 1895, in the Allen MSS; Sill to the Secretary of State, October 26, 1895, January 13, 1896, Dispatches, State Department Archives.

any explanation you have to make; also answer whether you intend to comply with instructions given."[24]

Poor old Sill apologized profusely and promised to do better in the future. "Possibly the circumstances by which I am surrounded have influenced me unconsciously," he explained, "for I live in an atmosphere of continual and often arbitrary and violent interference in Korean affairs. Sometimes this interference is directly antagonistic to American interests. Sometimes, in my judgment, it endangers the peace and good order of Korea and, by consequence, the safety of American life and property. In either case, there is some temptation to meet interference with counter-interference."

In apologizing, the minister neglected to mention the most powerful of all the influences operating on him—the will of Secretary Allen. Nor did he include the doctor when he made his promise to obey. And the plain truth was that Sill did not control his aide, was unable to keep Horace Allen from mixing in the domestic affairs of Chosen.[25]

[24] Sill to the Secretary of State, October 26, November 9, December 1, 2 (with Allen's notes), 1895, Dispatches, State Department Archives; Olney to Sill, December 2, 31, 1895, January 10, 11, 1896, Instructions, State Department Archives; Allen to Jennie Everett, November 4, 1895, in the Allen MSS; statement of John A. Cockerill, who was in Seoul, in the *New York Herald*, December 1, 1895.

[25] Sill to the Secretary of State, January 20, 1896, Dispatches, State Department Archives.

16

Russia Takes a Hand

RUSSIA absolutely needs a port free and open throughout the whole year," scribbled Nicholas II in the spring
of 1895. "This port must be located on the mainland (south-
east of Korea) and certainly, connected with our possessions
by a *strip of land.*" Here was one reason for the upsurge of
Russian interest in Korea after 1895. A second was expressed
by the Tsarist envoy in China, who declared, "Japan undoubtedly is an undesirable neighbor for us on the mainland."[1]

To head off Japan and get the port was the job of Waeber,
Russian minister in Seoul. A hopeless task, apparently, in
view of the Japanese control which followed the assassination
of the queen. But four months later a palace guard was care-
less and the situation shifted in a single day. Power slipped
from the hand of Japan's allies in Seoul and passed to
Russia.

Allen, connected with most Korean movements, had his
finger in this one too. By attacking the regicides, by fighting
Japan's puppet cabinet and sheltering that cabinet's foes, he
helped make possible a movement of reaction. And that re-

[1] Note by Nicholas on a dispatch of Lobanoff, Russian minister of
foreign affairs, to the Tsar, April 6, 1895; also Cassini to the Russian

action came, came from the people as well as from the politicians. At the time of the assassination the Korean public seemed apathetic to each and every field of politics, to regard them all as a "quarrel of the aristocracy" which "did not concern the people."[2] But the tale of the queen's demise and the king's imprisonment touched a chord of popular resentment.

Working with this sentiment, anti-Japanese Korean politicians began "getting their forces together ... to kill the traitors of the Government and wash away their infamous crimes." They planned to take the palace on November 28, 1895. Naturally they could not have whipped a guard of Japanese; but Japan, trying to avoid the appearance of intervention, had left the palace defense in charge of the Korean kunrentai. It might be possible to defeat these.

Allen knew of this anti-Japanese plot some time before it broke; he had authoritative information concerning it. Still his was not the master mind behind the effort. Rather he opposed resort to force at just this time, in the hope that the Japanese would withdraw voluntarily. There seemed a possibility of this in late November, 1895; two days before the counterrevolution the Japanese had allowed His Majesty to withdraw the degradation decrees and dismiss two strong pro-Japanese officials.

Hearing that an attack was to be made, Allen concentrated on the safety of the king. With Minister Sill's authority, he asked some missionary friends to stay close to His Majesty and guard against a mishap. This was done. Underwood,

Minister of Foreign Affairs, July 7, 1894, *Chinese Social and Political Science Review,* 17 (1933):511; 18 (1934):263; Langer, *Diplomacy of Imperialism,* 169, 396. See also the minutes of a meeting of the Governor General of Amur and the head of the Asiatic Department of the Russian Ministry of Foreign Affairs, May 8, 1888, *Chinese Social and Political Science Review,* 18 (1934):236–244, and Allen to Morse, February 1, 1896, in the Allen MSS. Allen in writing to the Secretary of State on November 7, 1897 (Dispatches, State Department Archives), quotes Waeber as saying, "after six years, then you will see."

[2] *Korean Repository,* 2 (1895):391, quoting the king.

Avison, and Hulbert (who "did not deny that they had revolvers in their pockets") went to the palace and obtained admission by the use of a card from their legation. Until the shooting started they stayed with American adviser Dye; then they dashed to the royal quarters. Soldiers of the kunrentai made one attempt to stop them. But the missionaries knew that they were wanted—they could hear the king whining, asking "Where are the foreigners? Where are the foreigners?" So on they came, Underwood using his revolver to knock aside a sword waved by a member of the kunrentai. In an instant he and the others were by His Majesty. They spent the balance of the night comforting the frightened monarch, taking turns at holding the royal hand.[3]

Meanwhile, firing had begun in earnest. Allen and Sill, jumping from bed, set out for the palace, joining the English and Russian diplomats along the way. All was over before they reached the royal grounds. Forewarned by information leaks, the kunrentai had appealed to the Japanese legation. That had not worked, for Japan had "good reason for not wishing to put her troops in motion." Even so, the kunrentai came out ahead. They had ample time to get prepared for an assault and repulsed it when it came.

Checked, the insurgents acted in the customary Korean manner: they turned to foreigners for aid. While launching their attack they had asked the Occidental representatives to take care lest the king be killed. When they met with strong resistance, they sent a messenger to the diplomats who were advancing toward the palace. They had gained the outer gate, they said, and would proceed inside the palace, *if the Western diplomats would join them.* That suggestion dumbfounded even Allen and others long familiar with the techniques of

[3] Allen to Frank Carpenter, February 2, 1896, and to Dun, November 28, 1895, in the Allen MSS. This counterrevolution is described in Sill to the Secretary of State, December 3, 1895, Dispatches, State Department Archives; Underwood, *Underwood of Korea*, 149–153; Underwood, *Fifteen Years among the Top-Knots*, 159–165. For Russian activities see also Francke, *Die Grossmächte in Ostasien*, 215–216, 284–287.

intervention. And, as was natural, the Occidentals refused and went back to their homes.

Thus died the counterrevolution; but even in death it still plagued the Americans. Sill, Allen, and the missionaries were openly accused of being party to the trouble. Certainly the circumstantial evidence pointed in that direction. Missionaries were with the king that night, and by request of the legation. Both before and after the attempted coup the legation and mission people gave asylum to opponents of the government. General Yun had formulated plans for the revolution while living in the Underwood establishment, and had returned there when they collapsed. Later Christian workers helped the general and a friend get out of Chosen by disguising them as missionaries. The legation went just as far, asking Washington to authorize use of a warship to carry refugees to safety, "to *get them out of the way*" before the Korean government demanded their surrender.[4]

Such actions inevitably aroused all manner of suspicion. Allen could insist that "the desire of this legation is to stay strictly out of all complications with internal affairs." Sill could say that the missionaries, though "indiscreet in their expressions of sympathy and interest," had no "guilty knowledge" of the coup. But few believed them.[5]

After the failure of the counterrevolution Allen faced the future with anxiety. Actually, however, the turn of events worked out very well for the doctor-diplomat. For the affair

[4] Sill to the Secretary of State, January 20, 1896, Dispatches, State Department Archives, italics added by an official in Washington; Gale, *Korean Sketches*, 206; *Korean Repository*, 3 (1896):35, 44; McKenzie, *Tragedy of Korea*, 77; Underwood, *Underwood of Korea*, 149, 152–153; Brandt, *Drei Jahre ostasiatischer Politik*, 168; Underwood, *Fifteen Years among the Top-Knots*, 159–160, 164–165; Allen to Rockhill, January 25, 1896, in the Allen MSS; Sill to the Secretary of State, February 15, 1896, Dispatches, State Department Archives, enclosing a statement from the *Salt Lake Herald* of December 25, 1895.

[5] Sill to the Secretary of State, December 3, 1895, Dispatches, State Department Archives; Allen to Dun, November 28, 1895, in the Allen MSS.

of November 28 drove all the prominent anti-Japanese Korean politicians under cover, and gave the leadership of their old party to the Russian representatives. This suited Allen in that it strengthened opposition to Japan and gave power to his good friend Waeber, the Russian minister.[6]

Though headed by Russians, the anti-Japanese movement still drew its strength from the Korean masses. Many of the people of Chosen deeply resented the murder of Queen Min. They were enraged by the Japanese court order in the Miura trial, which found Miura and his aides guilty of plotting against the queen, and then freed them on a technicality.[7] But far, far more distressing were the laws passed by Japan's puppet government in Seoul.

In one sense this new legislation was entirely proper. It cut red tape, it eliminated many sinecure positions, it reformed governmental practices and struck at foolish social customs. It was not right, said one decree, "that in this day of communication by ships and vehicles, we should stick to the old customs of the exclusive past." So out went curfews and night bells and in came commerce courts and the Gregorian calendar.

Sensible, indeed; but custom outweighed sense in the Korean mind. This had been demonstrated during the first regency of the Tai Wen Kun, who had attempted to institute some dress reforms. Feeling was still stronger in 1895, because of the Japanese connection with the new decrees.

[6] Sill to the Secretary of State, December 3, 1895, January 13, 1896, Dispatches, State Department Archives; Allen to Morse, February 18, 1896, and note by Allen, 1905, in the Allen MSS. In the last, Allen called the murder of the queen "a diplomatic blunder of such stupendous proportions as to cement the centuries old hatred of the Koreans for the Japanese and to nullify any power for good in Korea that Japan may have possessed. Thereafter everything went over toward Russia as being the most interested power."

[7] McKenzie, *Tragedy of Korea*, 263–267; Treat, *Diplomatic Relations between the United States and Japan*, 3:21–22; Sill to the Secretary of State, February 7, 1896, Dispatches, State Department Archives, enclosing a statement from the *Japan Daily Mail* of January 30, 1896.

And, as before, opposition centered around the changes in costume. One edict outlawed the wearing of the Korean topknot, which was declared to "stand in the way of activity and health." The king was required to set the standard by having his removed, and non-complying citizens were to be brought into line by military force.[8]

Outsiders might regard this as a minor statute; but it spelled defeat for Japan in Korea. Natives prized the topknot as a symbol of Korean manhood. Loss would mean a national humiliation far more real than that brought on by the queen's assassination. The general attitude was well expressed by the father who committed suicide when his two sons accepted the decree. Provincial officials found it wise to ignore the orders of the government. Produce prices jumped in Seoul, for farmers stayed at home lest they be shorn by soldiers at the city gates. Soon revolt was under way. It started in the provinces, as had the Tong Hak troubles. An army sent from Seoul could not beat the rebels, and by February, 1896, it was apparent that the capital was in some danger.[9]

Allen, Waeber, and the king now saw a chance to drive the Japanese to cover. There was an issue everyone could understand. The people were aroused, and all would favor any move against the government. His Majesty need only get away from his palace prison and he could bid defiance to Japan.

Events rushed to a climax. On February 9 the Russian guard was increased by more than 150 soldiers. On the following day the king asked Allen if it would be wise to seek the aid of Russia. This was of course just what the legation secretary wished. He hastened to endorse the king's sugges-

[8] *Korean Repository*, 3 (1896):79.
[9] Allen to Morse, February 11, 1896, and article by Allen, 1905, in the Allen MSS; Sill to the Secretary of State, February 11, 1896, Dispatches, State Department Archives; Bishop, *Korea*, 2:173–180; X.Y.Z., "The Attack on the Top Knot," *Korean Repository*, 3 (1896):263–272; Gale, *Korean Sketches*, 67.

tion and personally assisted in perfecting plans. That night he took the Russian minister to the house of a Korean officer entrusted with the royal plans. There he left the two, conferring; and on the next morning His Korean Majesty fled his palace to take refuge in the Russian legation.[10] The escape had been carefully planned. Palace women had been going in and out for weeks. At first the guards had challenged each of these and searched all chairs. But that grew tiresome. The women seemed quite harmless, and they were friendly, too—they brought hot dishes to the guards on chilly mornings. Such treatment had its effect. The better known females were soon allowed to pass through the gates at will. It happened so in the early morning of February 11, 1896. A palace woman left the grounds, and with her went the king, dressed as a coolie, and the crown prince, clad in woman's clothes.[11]

Once outside the walls, the royal fugitives dashed to the Russian legation; and there they stayed for a full year. This meant that Russia, not Japan, was to give orders for a while.

[10] Allen to Jennie Everett, February 14, 1896, and address to the Naval War College, in the Allen MSS; Assistant Secretary of State Adee to Allen, September 22, 1898, and Secretary Hay to Allen, January 30, 1899, Instructions, State Department Archives. Heard, in a letter to the Secretary of State, December 23, 1891, Dispatches, State Department Archives, refers to an earlier request for Russian aid. The attitude of the State Department was expressed by Secretary of State Sherman in his letter to Allen of November 19, 1897 (Instructions, State Department Archives): "It behooves the United States and their representatives, as absolutely neutral parties, to say, or do nothing that can in any way be construed as taking sides with or against any of the interested powers. Any such partiality would not only be in itself improper, but might have the undesirable and unfortunate effect of leading the Koreans themselves to regard the United States as their natural and only ally for any and all such purposes as Korea's rulers might adopt. This Government is in no sense the counsellor of Korea as to its internal destinies, neither is it bound to Korea by any protective alliance."

[11] On the escape see Gale, *Korean Sketches*, 208–209; Sill to the Secretary of State, February 11, 1896, Dispatches, State Department Archives; Allen to Heard, May 20, 1896, in the Allen MSS; and Brandt, *Drei Jahre in ostasiatischer Politik*, 169–177.

("Russia is on top and Japan is eating crow.") The Japanese, in driving out the Manchus, had found another foe. And the Korean king sent an envoy to St. Petersburg to file request for the formal protection of the Tsar.

Eventually the Russians were to yield their newly won power. As Allen said, "Things here are now quite Russian, but I am pretty well convinced that Russia intends to make her conquest of Manchuria the chief business in this part of the East."[12] Korea was for buffer purposes. There was little urge for Russian annexation, which would certainly mean war with Japan and possibly with Britain too. Consequently the Tsarist government was willing to make deals with the officials in Tokyo, giving way in Seoul in return for Japanese concessions. Two agreements concluded in the spring of 1896 illustrate this point. They provided for a check on the Japanese soshi, limitation of Japanese and Russian troops, and eventual departure of the king from the Romanoff legation. Two years later the Russians were to withdraw almost all their Korean agents and, in the Rosen-Nishi convention, grant that Japan had special interests in Chosen. These moves of 1898 of course tied in with the Russian lease of Chinese Port Arthur, which provided the ice-free railroad terminus which Russia had hitherto been seeking in Korea.[13]

Yet, even though the Russians did withdraw, their day at court was an important one. At the very least it postponed Japanese absorption of Korea and gave an opportunity to Japan's foes. Safe in Waeber's legation, the Korean king

[12] Allen to Heard, May 20, 1896, to Wilson, March 11, 1897, and to Ellinwood, April 26, 1897, in the Allen MSS.

[13] In a letter to Wilson, March 11, 1897, in the Allen MSS, Allen terms the Waeber-Komura agreement of 1896 a "fine piece of Russian diplomacy." The diplomatic moves involved can be followed in Steinmann, *Russlands Politik im Fernen Osten*, 24–32; Langer, *Diplomacy of Imperialism*, 396–397, 404–408, 456–457; Marc, *Quelques années de politique internationale*, 33–39; and Asakawa, *Russo-Japanese Conflict*, 262–270. There is reason to believe that the Russian promises to withdraw were not made in good faith.

struck at all the work of the island empire. He suspended enforcement of the top-knot rule and pardoned men the Japanese had had incarcerated. He did public penance for having associated with the islanders. "Alas!" he cried in a public proclamation, "on account of Our unworthiness and mal-administration the wicked advanced and the wise retired." That made him "blush and sweat for shame," made him call for the heads of those who had misled him. Later he announced his preference for legal methods, but by then the people were employing other means. All the long-accumulating hatred burst forth in a mob hunt of the friends of the Japanese. Few of the old cabinet survived. The prime minister, the home secretary, the war, finance, and public works ministers, all were killed and most were mutilated.[14]

Had Waeber wished, the Russians might have chosen the new government and dictated all its policies. But the Russians preferred a cautious game. They insisted that the king was "perfectly free in the administration of affairs pertaining to this kingdom." The Koreans would be expected to "defer to Russian opinion in matters of consequence," Russia was intent on "keeping . . . the paramount influence in Korean affairs safely in her own hands."[15] Otherwise, the

[14] *Korean Repository*, 3 (1896):81–94; Brandt, *Drei Jahre ostasiatischer Politik*, 169–180; Hulbert, *History of Korea*, 2:303–304; Bishop, *Korea*, 2:181–183; Sill to the Secretary of State, February 11, 1896, Dispatches, State Department Archives; Korean Minister of Foreign Affairs to Sill, February 16, 1896 ("very sorry that traitors were killed in accident without a legal trial"), Seoul Legation Files, State Department Archives. Steinmann's *Russlands Politik im Fernen Osten*, 24, contains an interesting but not entirely correct statement of Allen's activity at this time.

[15] Sill to the Secretary of State, March 6, October 27, 1896, Dispatches, State Department Archives; Allen to Ellinwood, April 26, 1897, in the Allen MSS. On June 29, 1896, Allen wrote Morse and Hunt that it was "doubtful" whether Russia would "care to see other powers interested in this land. She is showing her hand pretty plainly. It seems that while she does not intend to take Korea over and will try to preserve her so-called independence, she Russia fully intends to have the actual control of affairs and see that no one else encroaches upon her own interests. She would probably be glad if America had not these concessions [*Un-*

representatives of St. Petersburg would keep well in the background.[16]

This attitude brought several persons to the fore, men who took up the work which Russia did not choose to do. One was McLeavy Brown, English financial adviser who now became a virtual dictator in his field.[17] Philip Jaisohn was another—Jaisohn, the Korean-American adviser who had clashed with the American legation on franchise affairs. A third was Horace Allen. The king desired his counsel, trusted Allen above all other men. And Waeber quite approved the monarch's choice. The doctor was a friend of his, a man he could address with frankness. The legation secretary demonstrated friendship in helping to arrange for the king's flight. Besides, he came from the United States, which had no major reason for opposing the Asiatic policies of Russia.[18]

Allen's work began immediately after the escape. Sum-

san mine and Seoul-Chemulpo railroad] but as it is they will not injure her interests and it gives a fine appearance to Korean independence on the outside." Allen MSS.

[16] *Korean Repository*, 3 (1896):81; Allen to Morse, August 18, 1896, in the Allen MSS; Sill to the Secretary of State, September 28, October 13, 1896, Dispatches, State Department Archives; Hillier, in Bishop, *Korea*, 1:vii, speaking of the "almost disappointing moderation" of Russia; Mrs. Bishop, quoted in the *Korean Repository*, 4 (1897):231–235, asserting "that the Korean pear, when fully ripe, will drop into her [*Russia's*] mouth, I have little doubt, but I think she will not shake the tree." Allen confessed to Morse (letter of October 2, 1896, in the Allen MSS), that he could not "quite understand" Russian policy. "It seems a sort of *Laissez Faire* adopted to tempt Japan to some overt act that may precipitate a crisis with Russia. At any rate Russia sees to it that Japan gets no foothold here."

[17] Mrs. Bishop, quoted in *Korean Repository*, 4 (1897):233; Hamilton, *Korea*, especially pp. 74–86.

[18] Allen to Morse, February 11, 1896, and to Heard, May 20, 1896, in the Allen MSS; Allen to the Secretary of State, October 5, 1897, Dispatches, State Department Archives, noting that the only competition between Russia and the United States was in kerosene sales. In 1924 Allen wrote that the escape of the king "made American influence predominant in Korea, and gave us that long thereafter enjoyed commercial advantage, thus offsetting the machinations of Japan, Germany, and France, and forcing Russia and England to accede to and approve of American success." Note in the Allen MSS.

moned by the king, he was requested to suggest names for a cabinet; and his entire slate was accepted. The list was of course drawn from among the opponents of Japan. Most of those recommended were refugees whom Sill and Allen had been sheltering since the assassination of the queen.[19]

Naturally Allen rated well with the new ministers. Through them he won the Seoul-Chemulpo railroad grant and an extension of the Un-san mine franchise. He obtained besides a mighty influence in all political decisions made in Seoul. Nor was that all. Allen's native friends, with the aid of Brown and Jaisohn, were creating a better Korea, a reformed Korea that promised to attract the attention and capital of the United States. Native finance, long a study in chaos, was put on a sound, efficient basis. Provincial administration was thoroughly reorganized, and a drive was launched against the squeezing magistrates. The streets of Seoul were cleaned and widened, the police of the capital became a bit less inefficient. An American normal school was started. And mine, railroad, and lumber operations were planned by the Germans, French, and Russians.

So many gains—was not the day of glory soon at hand? Allen thought so for a fleeting moment, agreed with a writer who cried, "There is hope for Korea."[20] But then the dark clouds gathered once again, the weeks of hope gave way to months of gloom. A legation fight, trouble with Washington, difficulties with Jaisohn and the natives, a clash with Russia.

Petty though they were, the legation quarrels often overshadowed other problems, paralyzing all American activity in Seoul. As in his missionary period, Allen found it hard to get along with colleagues. Harder now, for he was a subordinate, possessing "all the influence" and doing "all the work" while another drew the honor and the pay.

Down to 1896 it had been bearable. In spite of disagree-

[19] Allen to Jennie Everett, February 14, 1896, and to Morse, February 18, 1896, in the Allen MSS; Allen, *Things Korean*, 234.

[20] See, for example, Bishop, *Korea*, 2:281–282; Hamilton, *Korea*, 33–34; Allen, *Korea: Fact and Fancy*, 18; *Korean Repository*, 5 (1898):28.

ments, Heard and Allen had parted friends in 1893; and Sill had started out on good terms with his secretary. Then Allen had obtained the mine and railroad grants. This had made the doctor patronizing and his superior jealous. Later there had come a fierce job competition. Sill, a Cleveland Gold Democrat, hoped for reappointment from President McKinley; and Allen likewise craved the post. The brickbats flew. Sill charged that Allen had gone back on his word after promising assistance. It was not so, shrieked Allen, Sill was "small," a liar, "a spoiled old man in his dotage."[21]

Allen, as it proved, had the winning cards. Sill was a Democrat and had not backed McKinley. Allen had, and possessed so many sponsors that he was accused of conducting a "shot gun campaign." There were religious leaders who valued the doctor's missionary background. There were business men who thought Allen "of all men . . . the most important to our interests in Korea." There were politicians, brought in by the others. Judge George K. Nash, leader of the Allen forces and a future governor of Ohio, was connected with the Korean enterprises of David Deshler. Congressman Jacob Fassett was associated with Leigh Hunt, who also accounted for Senator Matthew Quay and the journalist Herman Kohlsaat. General Wilson and W. W. Rockhill were still to be relied on, and Secretary of State John Sherman had not forgotten Allen ("I remember Allen. He has red hair"). Morse and his friends may have reached the great Mark Hanna; and John G. McCullough, president of the Chicago and Erie Railroad, was on Allen's side: To top it off the king of Korea asked that the appointment go to Allen, an "old and thoroughly valued friend to himself and to Korea." What could McKinley do but say the word that made it possible for Allen to take oath of office as United States minister on July 27, 1897?[22]

[21] Allen to Morse, April 15, 18, October 2, November 17, 20, 1896, to Rockhill, December 29, 1896, to Jennie Everett, February 2, 6, 1897, and to Everett, January 30, 1897, all in the Allen MSS.

[22] Allen to Judge George K. Nash, September 14, 1896, January 22, 1897, to William McKinley, September 14, 1896, to H. H. Kohlsaat,

That settled the legation fight and made it possible for Allen to turn to matters of more moment. It did not, however, give the doctor a free hand. He was still answerable to Washington, to a State Department which was cautious even under the Republicans. Indeed, the instructions of McKinley differed little from those of Cleveland; and the rebukes of Sherman resembled those of Olney.

First censure came in Sill's last months in office. The Japanese filed protest at the State Department, objecting to the way the minister and Allen had been helping Russia. Specifically, the pair was (correctly) accused of having asked a Korean cabinet officer, Ye Wan Yong, to withdraw his objections to a Russian plan to supply Chosen with drill instructors. Wasting not a moment, Sherman cabled, "Department instructions positively forbid you to mix in internal affairs of the country. Explicit compliance therewith requested." Sill wiggled out of this, denying the charge and calling Japan "unjustly suspicious."[23] But Allen did take heed. When sworn in as the minister, he promised to obey both the letter and the spirit of his instructions. That is, he pledged himself to be "absolutely neutral ... to say or do

September 16, 1896, to Fassett, September 17, 1896, to Morse, October 2, 1896, to Archibald Lybrand, December 26, 1896, to Everett, December 26, 1896, to Rockhill, December 29, 1896, to Jennie Everett, January 7, February 25, 1897, and to James H. Wilson, March 11, 1897; Frank G. Carpenter to McKinley, December 1, 1896, Nash to Morse, January 16, 1897, Nash to his son, March 4, 1897, and to John L. D. Borthwick, May 19, 1897, Thomas W. Power to Allen, January 23, 1897, John G. McCullough to Allen, April 29, 1897, Carpenter to Allen, April 7, 23, July 21, 1897, Redfield Proctor to McCullough, May 7, 1897, A. Lybrand to Allen, May 27, 1897, Morse to Allen, July 17, 1897, Hunt to Allen, July 24, 1897, all in the Allen MSS; Sill to the Secretary of State, July 29, 1897, Dispatches, State Department Archives; Assistant Secretary of State Adee to Allen, July 26, 1897, Instructions, State Department Archives. A curious angle of the situation is indicated by Sands in his *Undiplomatic Memories* (p. 29), which he develops in a letter to the author, May 28, 1939. Nash later asked Allen for appointment as Korean representative in the United States.
[23] Secretary of State Sherman to Sill, May 8, 1897, Instructions, State Department Archives; Sill to the Secretary of State, May 8, 11, 1897, Dis-

nothing that can in any way be construed as taking sides with or against any of the interested parties."[24]

Doing that—or pretending to—held Allen back considerably. And other obstacles appeared. Adviser Brown, as a loyal Britisher, was none too friendly to Allen's plans to bring in capital from the United States. Neither was Philip Jaisohn, whose Independence Club was opening a "Korea for the Koreans" attack on franchise-granting. The king remained friendly, but with Queen Min gone His Majesty became "so absorbed with vanity and conceit that he will only attend to matters which minister to his personal pleasure or pride,"[25] and gave less and less time to affairs of state. While he caroused his favorites took over, court sycophants who fought the graft-elimination programs which Allen thoroughly approved.

Finally, Allen's Russian tie did not prove adequate. For Waeber was recalled in 1897 to be replaced by an aggressive imperialist, Alexis Speyer. Waeber Allen had called a "very able and courteous representative" who "suits us all right." Speyer he thought "an impudent pup," "a most arrogant and boisterous man," and a bitter enemy of the United States.[26]

The position of Speyer is not hard to understand. He was an ardent expansionist, one who wanted Chosen linked with

patches, State Department Archives; letters from Allen to James H. Wilson, October 11, 1897, to Frank J. Carpenter, May 8, 11, 1897, and to Deshler, May 11, 1897, in the Allen MSS; Treat, *Diplomatic Relations between the United States and Japan*, 3:49. The Sill and Allen dispatches exonerate Allen.

[24] Allen to the Secretary of State, September 13, December 27, 30, 1897, Dispatches, State Department Archives; Allen to Alvey A. Adee, November 16, 1898, in the Allen MSS. Allen had made a similar pledge in 1890. Allen to the Secretary of State, September 2, 1890, Dispatches, State Department Archives, promising to "carefully carry out the spirit and letter of these instructions."

[25] Allen to John Hay, November 21, 1901, and the address to the Naval War College, in the Allen MSS; Allen, *Things Korean*, 152–157; Mrs. Bishop, quoted in *Korean Repository*, 4 (1897):232.

[26] Letters from Allen to James H. Wilson, October 11, 1897, to Morse,

Russia. Plainly the United States stood in the way. Back in 1885 America had fought him, when he and Moellendorff had tried to force Chosen to take some Russian drill instructors. Twelve years had not brought a change. Allen and his countrymen were willing to accept all favors Russia gave them, but showed no gratitude and even opposed some of the Russian schemes.

Allen was the worst offender. Not that he hated Russia. Quite the contrary; he was sure American interests were made "vastly more valuable by having Russia as Korea's overlord." But he could not resist a chance to help Americans. Thus, after taking Waeber's aid in the Seoul-Chemulpo railroad matter, he bid for a concession which the Russian envoy did not wish him to have, commenting, "I expect the Russians will have a fit when they hear of this." Later Ye Wan Yong, one of Allen's best Korean friends, frustrated Waeber's drillmaster schemes. Sill had Allen urge Ye to desist, lest he be fired. This Allen did with great reluctance, and privately he told the king that he did not disapprove of Ye's anti-Russian stand.[27]

Such actions irritated Speyer and made him sure that Allen was the leader of all St. Petersburg's opponents. Notably, the new Russian agent linked the doctor with the violently anti-Russian Independence Club. Was not Jaisohn, the club's founder, an American like Allen? Were not Allen's native allies mixed up in the movement? Did not the missionaries from America approve of Jaisohn's newspaper and let their converts join the Independence Club?[28]

Speyer lost no time in striking at the cause of trouble. He

October 11, November 17, 1896, and to Fassett, March 13, 1898, also bitter comments written in 1924, in the Allen MSS; Allen to the Secretary of State, October 2, 1897, Dispatches, State Department Archives.

[27] Letters from Allen to Morse and Hunt, May 31, June 29, 1896, to Everett, October 12, 1897, and to Frank J. Carpenter, May 8, 1897, and the address to the Naval War College, in the Allen MSS; Sill to the Secretary of State. May 11, August 3, 1897, Allen to the Secretary of State, October 5, 14, 1897, Dispatches, State Department Archives.

[28] Allen to Deshler, May 11, 1897, in the Allen MSS; Allen Diary, Feb-

told His Majesty "very plainly and forcibly, that he must take Russian advice upon all matters and advise only with Russia; that Russia will see that he is not troubled; and that he will have ample funds for his enjoyment." Even more, he would be "smeared with sweetness," allowed to take the imperial title in October, 1897.

In the process Allen and his friends were to lose all their influence. Out went the doctor's native allies, and Speyer announced that "no Korean entertaining friendly sensations for America shall have a place in the Government." American advisers would likewise lose their power, save for Clarence R. Greathouse, an alcoholic Russophile employed by Chosen as a legal expert.[29]

Offended by this treatment, Minister Allen cried that the Russians "have received more sympathy & support from Americans in Korea than you are aware of."

"Oh! Yes! . . . ," shot back the Tsarist envoy, "when the Japanese controlled everything, they were very willing to come to us to get their Korean friends out of trouble, but lately, No!"

"What have they done lately that you find fault with?" insisted Allen.

"Well," answered Speyer, "they went so much against the matter of our military instructors." Including the missionaries, by the way.

How could that be? Sill and Allen had been reprimanded by Washington for asking Ye Wan Yong to withdraw his objections to the drill instructors. And American missionaries in Seoul were "a particularly well behaved and gentlemanly set . . . not inclined to interfere in politics."

ruary 24, 1898; Allen to the Secretary of State, March 19, 1898, Dispatches, State Department Archives.

[29] Allen to the Secretary of State, September 17, October 2, 16, December 1, 1897, Dispatches, State Department Archives; to Morse, August 2, October 15, 1897, to Frank J. Carpenter, May 11, 1897, and to James H. Wilson, October 11, 1897, and address to the Naval War College, in the Allen MSS; Allen Diary, October 1, 2, 14, 16, 1897.

"Ah . . . ," protested Speyer, "they all the time talk to their friends on politics as in the matter of the military instructors." No, no, the opposition came from pro-Russian natives like Allen's good friend Ye Wan Yong. "That man!" yelled Speyer, "He is ze worst I have seen. I have put a cross on his name and he shall never hold any office in Korea while I am here. He is ze head of the pro-American party what is always crying Independence, Independence, you shall see. I shall put that party out of Korea, they shall not exist."

"It seems to me you are taking a great deal upon yourself," barked back Allen, "especially as this idea of independence was born in your Legation and nurtured by your predecessor." "Oh! Mr. Waeber. I do not approve of Mr. Waeber. I like not many things he has done. You will find me a true Russian. Mr. Waeber is not."[30]

So that was that. "All powerful" Russia would no longer serve America in the Land of Morning Calm. With some encouragement the emperor would have broken traces and taken up residence in the American legation. But that was clearly quite impossible. As Allen said, his government "would never consent to play the role which Russia had played and which some other powers would be glad to play."[31]

Allen's strength declined; but Speyer's did not develop in proportion. He had bold plans, embracing domination of Korea's army, timber, mineral, and railroad enterprises, a Russo-Korean bank, a Russian economic tsar to replace McLeavy Brown, and a Russian base on Deer Island off Fusan. The monarch of Chosen hardly dared to fight these schemes; but others did, and prevented their fulfillment.

The British furnished some of the resistance, reinforcing the Russian belief that "incontestably our principal and most

[30] Allen Diary, October 14, 16, 1897; Allen to the Secretary of State, October 16, 1897, Dispatches, State Department Archives; Allen to Everett, October 12, 1897, in the Allen MSS.

[31] Allen to Ellinwood, April 26, 1897, in the Allen MSS.

dangerous adversary in Asia is England." Specifically, Queen Victoria's navy prevented Brown's removal with a gunboat demonstration. Meantime Japan was doing all she could to check the Russians, as was the Korean Independence Club. Allen also did his bit, working for the retention of Brown and opposing the Deer Island lease. The last he did with some effect, claiming that the area involved was pledged for a foreign settlement. Chosen had engaged to give the Occidentals room in Fusan; and Allen with some others had long considered the area desired by Russia as the only suitable location. No definite commitment there, but ample room for argument.[32]

Topping off this opposition was pressure from St. Petersburg. There were imperialists aplenty at the Tsarist court—politicians, speculators, navy men who saw great possibilities in Chosen. In 1898, however, this group was a minority. Most of the court was satisfied with the Port Arthur outlet; few thought Korean ventures worth the great financial risk. So it was that Speyer failed to persuade superiors that they should buy the Seoul-Chemulpo railroad, and saw the line go to Japan. So it was that Russia missed an opportunity to tie up with Leigh Hunt's mining operations or to develop the lumber grants of her own nationals.[33]

Eventual result was the practically complete withdrawal of Russia from Seoul. In Speyer's first weeks in office, it looked as though the Russians would absorb Chosen; Allen, for one, believed "the jig is up for Korea."[34] Thereafter Russian power fell. In January, 1898, Allen stated that Russia was "losing her grip a little"; in March he added that Speyer was

[32] Allen Diary, September 14, October 7, 26, 1897; Allen to the Secretary of State, March 23, April 3, 1901, Dispatches, State Department Archives; Allen to Rockhill, May 6, 1904, in the Rockhill MSS.

[33] Allen to Fassett, May 17, 1898, in the Allen MSS; Langer, *Diplomacy of Imperialism*, 404–408, 690.

[34] Allen to Morse, November 7, 1897, and to Bishop Joyce, January 6, 1898, in the Allen MSS; Allen to the Secretary of State, December 20, 1897, Dispatches, State Department Archives. Allen told Bishop Joyce that all Europe had decided to let Russia have Korea.

"in a bad way. He has played his trump cards all the while and now when he needs them they are gone."[35]

One month more and all was over. The Russian envoy forced the issue by a violent attack on his native enemies, "idlers . . . claiming to be gifted politicians." Concluding this, Speyer asked point-blank if Chosen wanted to receive advice from Russia. Somehow the Korean government found courage to say no. Whereupon, to the great surprise of all, the Russians pulled up stakes. Military and financial advisers left Seoul, the Russo-Korean bank was liquidated, and Speyer was replaced by a somewhat less aggressive man.[36]

Startled, Allen and his colleagues explained the Russian retreat as a temporary and strategic move. "No one here seems to think that Russia has withdrawn permanently . . . ," Allen told a friend, "She will probably come back when the time comes for her inevitable conflict with Japan, and she will then come for good and all." Just one thing could prevent that outcome, thought the doctor; Russia might not dare return "if the reported alliance between Japan and England proves to be a fact, especially will this be the case if our [Spanish-American] war results in anything like an alliance between the U.S. and England."[37]

[35] Allen to Morse, January 31, March 3, 1898, in the Allen MSS; Allen Diary, November 3, 1897; Allen to the Secretary of State, December 21, 1897, January 21, 1898, Dispatches, State Department Archives.
[36] Allen to the Secretary of State, March 17, 1898, Dispatches, State Department Archives; Hayashi, *Secret Memoirs*, 95–96; "The Deer Island Episode," *Korean Repository*, 5 (1898):109–113.
[37] Allen to Robert Speer, June 5, 1898, and to Morse, April 18, 1898, in the Allen MSS; Whigham, *Manchuria and Korea*, 206; *Japan Daily Mail*, May 21, 1898, as quoted in Robert E. Speer, *Missions and Politics in Asia* (New York, 1898), 249, note. Late in 1897 and thereafter Allen believed a Russo-Japanese war at least possible, if not probable. See Allen to the Secretary of State, December 20, 1897, November 18, 1899, March 13, 1901, Dispatches, State Department Archives; to Hunt, May 16, 1901, and to Everett, February 11, September 18, 1900, in the Allen MSS. In the last he stated, "Japan seriously contemplates it." Early in 1897 he had stated that there was no chance of war between Russia and Japan or England. Allen to the Secretary of State, January 23, 1897, Dispatches, State Department Archives.

You Can't Tell Roosevelt a Thing

SEPTEMBER 30, 1903, was a memorable date in the life of Horace Allen. On that day the doctor brought his diplomatic career to a climax by crossing swords with Theodore Roosevelt, president of the United States. The clash, a bitter one, took in the whole field of American Far Eastern policy, revealing a conflict that was fundamental then and continued so in the years to follow.

For a half decade before the interview Allen had been watching the Japanese gain strength in Seoul. In the Russian period he had considered Nippon "powerful enough to put a brake to the wheel." When Russia yielded power, in 1898, he saw "the Japanese . . . obtaining great influence." Soon there was an "amazing increase" in Japan's importance in Chosen, the native politicians being "chiefly controlled" from Tokyo. As early as 1899 Allen had reported, "gradually Japan has become aggressive here until they now seem to regard Korea as their own peculiar sphere of action and all others to be mere interlopers." Shortly thereafter he asserted that with Russia holding back, Japanese control of Chosen appeared to him "inevitable"; and down to 1903 there was no cause to change this view.[1]

[1] Allen to the Secretary of State, July 18, 1898, November 18, 1899,

You Can't Tell Roosevelt a Thing

Japan had not advanced without resistance. Her every gain had been contested bitterly. Koreans had opposed her, Allen and his friends had put hurdles in her way, the Russians had tried to meet her challenge, all to no avail. Japan had come to stay.

Russia provided the severest competition. True, the Tsarists had bowed out in 1898, taking their advisers with them. Envoy Matunin allowed one of Russia's best Korean agents to be executed by the Seoul government; and back at home Count Witte, finance minister, had discouraged business men from showing interest in Korea. ("The participation of the Treasury in the matter of the Corean mining proposition, in whatever shape or form, is to be refused.")

Still, many Russians were unwilling to abandon Chosen. The navy wanted Masampo, midway between Vladivostok and Port Arthur, and key to the Straits of Japan. Speculators had great hopes for the timber concession obtained in 1896, and were on the lookout for other opportunities. Finally, there were political imperialists who thought a Russian destiny was manifest for Chosen. Each group had access to Tsar Nicholas; each had influence in the imperial court. And each was heard at the Seoul legation of the Russian state. Matunin, Speyer's successor, was personally associated with the lumber enterprises, and Pavloff, who followed Matunin, was an out-and-out expansionist with a record of imperialist activity in China.[2]

With the Russian court demanding caution, Matunin and

August 23, 1900 ("evidently the Russians feel they must acquiesce in letting Japan control Korea for the present."), Dispatches, State Department Archives; Allen to Fassett, May 20, 1900, October 9, 1902, and to Morse, May 20, 1900, in the Allen MSS; Bishop, *Korea*, 2:291–292; Hamilton, *Korea*, 157.

[2] Letters to the Secretary of State from Allen, March 19, April 5, 1900, and from Paddock, February 21, 1902, Dispatches, State Department Achives; Isvolski, Russian envoy in Japan, to the Russian Minister of Foreign Affairs, October 16, 1901, and Kuropatkin, Russian Minister of War, to the Russian Minister of Foreign Affairs, November 27, 1901, in *Chinese Social and Political Science Review*, 19 (1935):245–258; Allen

And the Japanese

Pavloff worked by indirection instead of attempting to continue the bluster tactics of their predecessor Speyer. They worked through their country's ally France, interesting Chosen in pro-Russian French advisers and concessionaires. They introduced missionaries of the Orthodox persuasion, hoping for new allies. They used their navy, impressing the Koreans with demonstrations and parades. They cooperated with unofficial agents—with Antoinette Sontag, the charming Alsatian relative of Mrs. Waeber, with the strutting Baron Gunzburg, Seoul representative of Russian lumber interests, and with the pro-Russian natives, headed by the coarse illiterate Ye Yong Ik. A strange man was Ye, strange even for Korea. Of humble birth, he had been sweeping floors when Allen met him, back in 1884. Shrewdness and a total lack of scruple soon put him in another class, made him the king's financial counsellor, a Richelieu "played in miniature," the "most enduring personality" at the ever-changing court in Seoul. Gratitude helped to attach Ye to the Russian cause—the Russians sheltered him when he ran into trouble. Besides, he had more freedom as a Russian agent than the Japanese allowed their partisans.[3]

By making use of all these channels the Russians salvaged something after 1898. French advisers were put into Korea's post office, her legal department, her arsenal, her mining and manufacturing enterprises. Neglect to start construction cost the French their Seoul-Wiju railroad grant of 1896; but Ye Yong Ik revived the project as a native enterprise, with

to E. V. Morgan, August 17, 1902, March 30, 1903, in the Allen MSS. See also Steinmann, *Russlands Politik im Fernen Osten*, 12–35, and Marc, *Quelques années de politique internationale*, 171–172, 199–200.

[3] Allen to the Secretary of State, September 1 (quoting *Japan Daily Mail*), October 1, 1901, Dispatches, State Department Archives; Allen to James H. Wilson, October 11, 1897, to Morse, April 2, 1903, and to Fassett, May 17, 1903, in the Allen MSS; Allen to Rockhill, January 4, 1904, and Rockhill to Allen, February 20, 1904, in the Rockhill MSS; *Korea Review*, 2 (1902):553–555; Hamilton, *Korea*, 54–57; Langer, *Diplomacy of Imperialism*, 456–457, 688–692; and, especially, Asakawa, *Russo-Japanese Conflict*, 263–294.

French technicians and materials. At the same time Russian artisans were coming in, glass-makers, weavers, iron-workers. In 1900 Speyer landed a whaling concession, got special privileges at Masampo, and obtained renewal of the lumber grant of 1896. Later his ally Ye Yong Ik struck direct blows at Japan, securing the imprisonment and execution of Koreans and preventing the Japanese from buying Roze Island off Chemulpo.[4]

Yet, though the Russians took some tricks, Japan had the game in hand. Her commerce far outran that of her rivals, her tonnage accounted for three fourths of all Korea's foreign trade. To balance the Russian artisans and French advisers she had thousands on thousands of colonists in all the major cities of Korea, and was pushing inland. While Russia talked of railroad possibilities, the Japanese had the Seoul-Chemulpo in operation and had started on the line to Fusan. So with the sea; Japan had forty thousand fishermen off the Chosen coast, and, with a later grant, outran the Russians in the whaling business. Fusan was all but ceded to Nippon after Russia had been denied the right to lease near-by Deer Island. Russian diplomats selecting land at Masampo found they had been anticipated, that the Japanese had bought the choicest property from native owners. And Baron Gunzburg's lumbermen, starting far behind their schedule, ran into island men who were ignoring Russian rights and felling Korean trees by arrangement with local dignitaries.

Japan's success may be attributed to many factors. The retreat of 1898 had impaired the prestige of her chief opponent Russia. Meantime Japan had built a natural trade in a normal manner. Politically she had begun to learn the value of the velvet glove. ("The Japanese are obtaining great influence," wrote Horace Allen in the summer of 1898, "but

---

[4] Allen to the Secretary of State, April 3, 1899, June 4, October 20, 24, 1900, May 31, 1902, April 24, 1903, Dispatches, State Department Archives; address to the Naval War College, in the Allen MSS; Tyler Dennett, *Roosevelt and the Russo-Japanese War* (Garden City and New York, 1925), 138–140.

they are careful to do nothing to bring them under censure.")
And when trouble loomed, Tokyo could count on London.[5]

It was 1902 before the Japanese joined Britain in alliance.
But long before, in 1899, there had been cooperation enough
to prompt Allen to speak of "at least a local alliance for
Korea." The Japanese and British envoys worked as partners,
opposing repeated Russian efforts to oust adviser Brown,
heading off a Franco-Russian loan involving a twenty-five
year pledge of Chosen's customs.[6]

And as for Allen and the Americans? Theirs was the fate
of the Koreans who favored neither the Mikado nor the Tsar
—they were ground between two stones, Japan advancing,
Russia in retreat.

Instructive is the history of the Korean Independence Club,
founded in 1896. This organization aimed to make Chosen
a strong free nation, able to stand alone before the world.
That meant eliminating Russia, then Chosen's overlord. A
noble goal, thought the Japanese, for it was obvious that "the
aims and purposes of the Independence party were directly
in line with Japanese interests." Jaisohn of course denied
having foreign connections; and it is clear that he was not
pro-Japanese in 1896–98. Though he regarded Japanese-
Korean trade relations as inevitable, he said, "Japan needs

[5] Asakawa, *Russo-Japanese Conflict,* 1–28; Japanese report, in Brown,
"Reading Journey through Korea," in *Chautauquan,* 68 (1905):561–565;
Dennett, *Roosevelt and the Russo-Japanese War,* 102, and note; *Korea
Review,* 1 (1901):499, 502, 503; Allen to Rockhill, February 28, 1901, in
the Rockhill MSS; to James H. Wilson, December 16, 1902, in the Allen
MSS; and to the Secretary of State, July 18, 1898, November 18, 1899,
November 23, 1900, March 18, May 20, 1903, Dispatches, State Depart-
ment Archives.

[6] Allen to Wilson, October 11, 1897, in the Allen MSS; Allen to the
Secretary of State, October 9, 1897, November 18, 1899, and Paddock to
the Secretary of State, February 21, 1902, Dispatches, State Department
Archives; Sands, *Undiplomatic Memories,* 53, 56–57; Asakawa, *Russo-
Japanese Conflict,* especially p. 278; Langer, *Diplomacy of Imperial-
ism,* 691. For observations on the earlier coolness between England and
Japan see Allen to Morse, February 1, 1896, and to Hunt, June 21, Au-
gust 11, 1898, in the Allen MSS.

Korea more than Korea needs Japan." He referred to the "inborn and inbred antipathy" of Koreans to the Japanese, complained of the "known combativeness," "rude ways," and usurious practices of the Japanese merchants in Seoul. Still, Jaisohn and his friends could count on Japan to aid them in their attacks upon the Russian drillmasters, the Russian economic schemes, the powerful Russophile court favorite Ye Yong Ik.[7]

Then, of a sudden, Japan catapulted into first position. The Independence Club had not changed its sentiments; it still wanted strength and freedom for Korea. But it no longer had Japan's sympathy—what Japan wanted was a Chosen independent of St. Petersburg, but not of Tokyo. Had they retained Japanese support, the Independence politicians could have taken over the Seoul court. Without it they were beaten by Korea's corrupt conservatives. Japan stood calmly by as Jaisohn was dismissed, voiced no protest when the reactionary pedlars' guild beat up the Independence mobs and drove their movement into hiding.

Knowing the Independence party well, Allen realized that it harbored opponents of America and extremists whose ac-

[7] Allen to the Secretary of State, December 23, 1898, Dispatches, State Department Archives. The files of the *Korean Repository* and the Seoul *Independent* for 1896 to 1898 are packed with information about the Independence movement. The Seoul *Independent*, April 7, 1896, contains a statement of program. See also Hulbert, *History of Korea*, 2:318–324; McKenzie, *Korea's Fight for Freedom*, 62–74; Underwood, *Fifteen Years among the Top-Knots*, 205–215; and Allen to the Secretary of State, February 14, March 19, August 4, September 7, October 13, 17, November 14, 28, 1898, Dispatches, State Department Archives. Sir Ernest Satow, English envoy in China, called it a "spontaneous revulsion of Corean feeling against the too active interference of the Russian Charge d'Affaires," Speyer. Satow to the British Minister of Foreign Affairs, March 26, 1898, quoted in G. P. Gooch and Harold Temperley, eds., *British Documents on the Origins of the War, 1898–1914*, 1:26 (London, 1927). The *Korea Review*, 4 (1904):353, said the movement "must have been favored by the Japanese." See also Langer, *Diplomacy of Imperialism*, 688. The Seoul *Independent*, April 18, May 2, 14, 1896, states anti-Japanese views. Note that these statements were made during a period of Russian ascendancy.

And the Japanese

tivities were a menace to the peace of Seoul.[8] Even so, the Club seemed better than Japan or Russia; and Allen threw his weight behind it. In the fall of 1898, when agitation reached its peak, he secured a royal promise that Korea's army would not fire upon the Independence mobs. Perhaps he helped persuade the emperor to dismiss seventeen opponents of the Independence group and to accept demands made by the party. In any case he deplored the monarch's quick departure from those promises and publicized his views so well that the pedlars threatened the United States legation.[9]

Washington, as usual, objected to the doctor's enthusiasm. In reply the minister explained that Korea was "so corrupt, and the country is in such a state of misrule or disrule, that it seems necessary at times to speak of practices which will, if unchecked, become beyond control to the severe detriment of interests purely American." Since that would not altogether satisfy his superiors, Allen threw in a denial that he had intervened. "It would be a most easy thing for me to take a prominent part in Korean affairs," he said, but "I carefully abstain from any such interference or from giving advice. No Foreign Representative in Seoul is more free from any implication of such interference . . . than myself." Then, having denied his customary practices, the doctor immediately resumed them.[10]

When the Independence movement failed, Allen lost some of his power. Many of his native friends went down with the beaten party. Some tied up with Japan or Russia, and later others deserted the United States legation to follow the lead of American adviser Sands, ex-legation secretary who had

[8] Allen to the Secretary of State, August 4, 1898, Dispatches, State Department Archives. In a letter to the author, June 16, 1939, Philip Jaisohn discusses differences between himself and Allen.
[9] Allen to the Secretary of State, November 13, 1897, March 19, April 27, September 17, 27, November 14, 28, 1898, Dispatches, State Department Archives; *Korean Repository*, 5 (1898):352.
[10] Allen to the Secretary of State, December 27, 30, 1897, February 2, 1898, September 19, 1902, Dispatches, State Department Archives; Allen to William H. Stevens, March 18, 1901, in the Allen MSS.

broken with Allen after taking up employment with Chosen's government. Allen observed with sadness, "The Koreans have the idea that we dont count any more. We live in this little disreputable Korean bungallow, and put on no style; make no threats and they think they can neglect us. . . ."[11]

Although weakened, Allen yet retained his original source of influence—friendship with the emperor. True, there was a year of friction over business deals (1902–03), and the monarch's quest for pleasure often pushed diplomacy into the background. But friendly aid was the normal pattern, with Allen gaining such important privileges as the right to sit down in the royal presence. "It makes no difference which one (Russia or Japan) gets the most influence in the Palace," he wrote, "the Emperor always turns to me and the more they scare him the more eager he is to turn everything over to the Americans."[12]

In advising the monarch and in laboring for his own countrymen, Allen ran head on into the clash between Japan and Russia. Time after time he had to choose between the two contestants, take sides in a quarrel not properly his own. Precedent would have allowed him either side. Years back, in the Manchu period, he had been pro-Japanese. Then, with Nippon on top, he had befriended Russia. Speyer had made him shift again, over to Japan; and in 1898 he was not sure just where he wished to go.

[11] Allen to E. V. Morgan, February 3, April 26, 1902, and to Fassett, November 30, 1902, in the Allen MSS; Allen to the Secretary of State, October 27, 1899, November 21, 1902, Dispatches, State Department Archives. The split with Sands can be traced in the following: Allen to Rockhill, October 23, 1899, April 24, 1901, to Hunt, April 18, 22, 26, July 14, 1900, to Fassett, November 13, 1900, to Rockhill, April 24, 1901, and to E. V. Morgan, February 19, 1903, in the Allen MSS; Sands, "Korea and the Korean Emperor," *Century*, 69 (1905):582; Sands, *Undiplomatic Memories*, 221, 224; Sands to the author, May 28, 1939; and Allen to the Secretary of State, October 22, 27, 1899, March 8, 1904, Dispatches, State Department Archives.

[12] Allen to Rockhill, February 28, 1901, in the Rockhill MSS; Allen to the Secretary of State, December 27, 1897, August 31, 1900, Dispatches, State Department Archives; Allen to Hunt, December 2, 1899, and to

And the Japanese

While still wavering, the doctor applied one of his oldest rules of thumb. He fought each move that meant monopoly and consequent loss of opportunity for the United States. Thus he joined forces with the Japanese and English representatives to block a projected Franco-Russian customs loan of 1901; (and perhaps, as one observer said, "his attitude went a long way towards helping the Emperor to make up his mind"). Again, he worked with other diplomats to force the opening of north Korean ports, giving trade to the Americans and helping to prevent the Russians from taking over there.[13] Here, twice, the doctor had cooperated with the Japanese. As he also helped Japan in railroad matters, some came to feel that he favored the cause of Japan. Or, as one London journalist would have it, Allen "had no doubts whatsoever as to which side he should take in the long struggle between Russia on the one hand and Great Britain and Japan on the other."[14]

This, though, was not the case. Allen had helped the islanders in what he thought to be the interests of America. He had no love for Japan, thought the Japanese had been "cruel and unwise" in their treatment of Koreans, "dont act well at

E. V. Morgan, April 26, 1902, in the Allen MSS; Sands, *Undiplomatic Memories*, 48.

[13] Allen to the Secretary of State, April 21, 24, 26, 29, May 6, 11, 21, 25, June 6, October 11, 1901, April 14, 1904, Dispatches, State Department Archives; address to the Naval War College, in the Allen MSS; Allen to Rockhill, May 6, 1904, in the Rockhill MSS; Whigham, *Manchuria and Korea*, 176–204 *passim*. Compare Secretary of State Hay's letter of June 6, 1901, to Allen (Instructions, State Department Archives), allowing unofficial opposition to a French loan because of the interest of Collbran and Bostwick, with Assistant Secretary of State Hill's statement to Allen (July 5, 1901, Consular Instructions, State Department Archives) that "interference, even though non official, in the affairs of other nations in their relations with Korea involves a departure from our traditional methods of diplomacy and from our present policy."

[14] Whigham, *Manchuria and Korea*, 203; Rockhill to Allen, June 30, 1904, in the Rockhill MSS; Allen to E. V. Morgan, April 6, September 2, 1902, in the Allen MSS. In his first letter to Morgan, Allen said the Japanese were claiming that the United States was in the Anglo-Japanese alliance; in his second he states that after talking to Rockhill he told Baron Komura, Japanese minister of foreign affairs, that Japan should

all over here." And when he thought of the future of American enterprise if Tokyo took hold, he shared "the continual nervous terror of the Japanese, which seems to haunt every Korean . . . and particularly affects the King."[15]

Often and in many ways did Allen fight Japan. He defied the Nipponese envoys in Seoul, refusing to concede Japanese "predominating interests." He headed off Japanese attempts to get franchises, snatched grants that officials in Tokyo desired. He attacked pro-Japanese natives, built up hostile sentiment in the minds of those Koreans he could reach. And, finally, he favored Russia, took the side of Japan's leading foe.[16]

Allen hesitated long before he took this stand. It was wise, he thought, to curb Japan; but it was far from easy to cooperate with the "treacherous" Russian agents in Seoul. Gunzburg and Matunin seemed reluctant to admit Americans like Hunt to their north Korean exploitation schemes. Pavloff's personality annoyed Allen (it was like the doctor's own) and Mrs. Pavloff, still in her teens, was far too gay a person for the straightlaced envoy from the United States. Worst of all was Ye Yong Ik, who positively refused to work with the Americans. "He has the idea that whatever is done to the Americans will not be resented," commented Allen bitterly, "and his advice always opposes us so that even the most trivial matters of routine cannot be put through."[17] But, be

cooperate with the United States. See also the memorandum of T. B. Hohler, Second Secretary in the British Legation in Japan, October 13, 1904, in *British Documents on Origins of the War*, 4:65, and De Margerie, French chargé in Washington, to the French Minister of Foreign Affairs, July 27, 1902, in *Documents diplomatiques français, 1871–1914*, Second Series, 2:414–415.

[15] Allen to Rockhill, October 23, 1899, in the Rockhill MSS; Sands to the Secretary of State, August 10, 1899, Dispatches, State Department Archives; Allen to James H. Wilson, December 16, 1902, in the Allen MSS, noting clash between British and American interests; Sands to the author, May 28, 1939.

[16] Jaisohn, in a letter to the author, June 16, 1939, discusses this policy of Allen's in an interesting fashion.

[17] Allen to Hunt, June 24, 1898, to E. V. Morgan, June 25, September 2, 1902, May 29, 1903, to John Hay, November 21, 1902, and to his sons,

And the Japanese

that as it might, it was advisable to throw a barrier in Japan's way. It was just possible that Korea might be saved; if not, there might at least be some hope for the Manchurian area beyond.[18]

By 1903 the doctor was convinced that there was. And, being sure, he was prepared to do missionary work on his superiors, to preach his diplomatic gospel in true proselyting style. Not with dispatches, which headed straight for pigeon-hole obscurity. It must be done in person, while the Allens were on leave.

Yes, it must be done in person; but could the time be spared in 1903? Allen had said, "if I thought it was imminent I would not leave" Seoul. And war did seem to be quite close, what with Russia failing to evacuate Manchuria and frightening Japan by starting lumber operations on the Yalu. In May Allen said it looked "a little like a fuss between Japan and Russia." But as the days passed without bringing a crisis, the doctor decided to go to America; the war would wait till his return. There was to be "trouble on the Yalu & possible bloodshed" when the Russians confiscated lumber cut under local agreements of the Japanese; but it was to end in compromise. The "inevitable war" was to be postponed at least until the date set for the final evacuation of Manchuria.[19]

On the trip to Washington Allen's pro-Russian views were put to the test. For he and Fannie made the trip by way of Russia, travelling over the newly opened trans-Siberian railway. And they found much wrong with Russia. Siberian

November 30, 1902, in the Allen MSS; Allen to the Secretary of State, April 5, 1900, February 13, 1902, Dispatches, State Department Archives.

[18] Allen to Fassett, August 6, 1900, and to Morse, February 27, 1904, and memorandum by Allen, February 26, 1904, in the Allen MSS; Allen to the Secretary of State, August 31, 1900, Dispatches, State Department Archives.

[19] Allen to the Secretary of State, January 23, December 20, 27, 1897, November 18, 1899, March 13, 1901, April 24, May 26, April 1, 19, 1903, Dispatches, State Department Archives; Allen to Everett, February 11, 1900, to Hunt, May 16, 1901, May 29, 1903, and to Maurice Allen, May 14, 1903, in the Allen MSS.

houses were "not nearly so good as the Korean peasant huts." The condition of the people was hopeless. They counted for nothing, were kept ignorant while the aristocracy was shamefully extravagant. There was inefficiency on every side, so many officials that none took any initiative; "the power house has a tile floor but the lights went out while we were at dinner." "Russia will have a severe awakening when she comes to a clash with Japan," was the traveller's first impression, "unless the red tape forms of the latter serve to counterbalance Russian tom foolery."

All true, but there was another aspect, which was to linger longest in the doctor's mind. This was the vastness of the Russian state, which seemed to guarantee a noble future. Moving along hour after hour one could not help feeling that this was a *"wonderful country*... an enormous country ... It could almost accommodate the world. One cannot help feeling angry at the stupid blunder of England and Germany in preventing this vast country from getting an outlet on the Mediterranean. It simply bottled her up and made her phiz until she blew a vent hole for herself on the China sea, just as she will surely blow another on the Persian Gulf if she is kept in ... on that side. There must be a great future for all this country."[20]

Reaching the United States, Allen lost no time in expressing his views. He talked with Henry White the diplomat and the lawyer Joseph Choate, both of whom seemed to be impressed. Then he "went to Dep't and started things." On his way to Roosevelt he talked with his old friend, that "splendid fellow" W. W. Rockhill.[21]

Rockhill was not a State Department official in 1903 but director of the International Bureau of American Republics, predecessor of the Pan American Union. On the side, however, he was the Department's Far Eastern expert. Indeed,

---

[20] Allen Diary, June 5–22, 1903.
[21] Allen Diary, September 30, 1903; memorandum by Allen, 1905 or later, in the Allen MSS.

he had been brought to Washington for just that purpose. Roosevelt, Lodge, and others had worked to have him appointed Librarian of Congress. Failing in that, they had obtained the Pan American position for him in 1899, which provided a handsome salary and leisure time for the advising work. Hay and McKinley had trusted Rockhill, as is shown by the part he played in the Open Door negotiations; and Roosevelt continued the relationship when taking office in 1901. In that year the new executive asked Allen "very kindly, to tell Rockhill everything and he would dole it out to him as he could use it." More; Roosevelt then later told Allen that Rockhill was "the author of and sponsor for our Asiatic policy."[22]

Rockhill, of course, was the man to see; but the interview gave Allen little satisfaction. The doctor was convinced that the United States should aid the Russians, in Manchuria at any rate; Rockhill was just as sure that the Japanese should be supported, should be allowed to swallow Chosen and should be helped to check the Tsarist drive to get Manchuria.

Disappointed, Allen went to Roosevelt "and told him he was making a mistake regarding Russia."[23] Had the minister seen Rockhill, asked the chief executive. Yes, Allen had. Then all must get together, said the president, be at the White House at nine-thirty in the evening.

Toothaches are likely to come at inconvenient times. One came to Allen on that last day of September as he waited for the evening to arrive. Already uneasy at the thought of facing Roosevelt, he became extremely restless. Hour by hour his nervousness and irritation grew beyond the point of self-control.

The result was just what might have been expected. Roosevelt's "trip-hammer queries" rattled Allen, as did the chief executive's attempts to twist the doctor's words to form

[22] Allen to Rockhill, January 4, 1904, and to E. V. Morgan, September 2, 1902, March 6, 1903, in the Allen MSS.
[23] Allen Diary, September 30, 1903, on which the account that follows is based.

a Rooseveltian pattern. Whereupon the conversation took on a tone of violence, with the president insisting and Allen crying out, "I didn't say anything of the kind."[24]

Before the fireworks started, Allen outlined his Russophile position, centering on the vital question of Manchuria. Roosevelt had erred, the doctor said, in opposing Russian occupation and acceptance of the Open Door. Because of trade, for one thing. Russia had opened up a "great commercial field" in pacifying Manchuria and constructing roads and railroads there; and "75% of this great and growing trade [was] coming to us." Would the president desire to sacrifice such gains?

Unwise commercially, the Rockhill-Roosevelt outlook was also pointless. Allen thought it foolish to suggest that Russia would yield hard-won supremacy; "there was no more likelihood of her voluntarily evacuating Manchuria than there was that we should evacuate Texas or to make the example better Hawaii."

Finally, Allen believed that the administration attitude made the United States the cats-paw of Britain and Japan. In fighting Russia, America appeared to be "getting the chestnuts out of the fire" for this imperial pair. If Roosevelt continued on this line, he "would undoubtedly lead Japan to count upon assistance from us which would lead her to adopt a too bellicose attitude towards Russia." After that, reluctantly or willingly, "we would simply be forced into more or less of an alliance with England & Japan."

Roosevelt took issue with the doctor on every point; and Rockhill backed up his chief in most impressive fashion. On trade affairs Rockhill accused Allen of "simply advocating a time serving policy in the interests of commerce." Such a policy was improper, all the more so since it was unnecessary. Anti-Russian action would not impair our chances in Manchuria, "the Russian Governm't had fully sanctioned all our attempts to secure the 'Open Door' and . . . they favored our getting the open ports." With everything assured, a shift in

[24] Memorandum by Allen, 1905, or later, in the Allen MSS.

policy would show inconsistency, "would simply 'stultify' ourselves and injure our standing."

Answering, Allen suggested that Russia might meet opposition from America with an attack upon the trade of the United States. No, snapped Roosevelt in his sharpest tone, the government had assurances on that point; and he had Rockhill say the same.

The chief executive also attacked Allen's claim that Japan would expect support. He had Rockhill "endorse him in saying that Japan had given the greatest assurance that she must under no consideration count on anything of the kind." Well, stated Allen, both Tokyo and St. Petersburg would know that moral aid was there; for a year G. Hayashi in Seoul had said "that the U.S. and England were friends and both were very strong friends of Japan and that the United States was almost the same as in the Japan-English Alliance." A good blow, the doctor thought, but Roosevelt and Rockhill "had full swing" and the minister to Chosen could get nowhere.[25]

Allen had called the Roosevelt position pointless. How so, the aggressive president seems to have asked; who would win if Russia and Japan should meet in war? Japan on the sea, asserted Allen, perhaps also on land. Well then, why back a loser? Simply because Russia "wanted us to have all her trade we could handle," insisted the envoy to Korea, while "Japan was just the opposite and would make us increasing trouble until we might have to cross swords with her."[26]

But it was useless, absolutely useless, to try to convert

[25] Allen Diary, September 30, 1903. The following, though they add little to the basic account, are also relevant: Allen, *Things Korean,* 251–252; memoranda by Allen, February 26, 1904, 1905 or later, 1924, Allen to Morse, February 27, 1904, and to Everett, November 10, 1904, in the Allen MSS. Hayashi's statement is taken from Allen's letter of April 6, 1902, to E. V. Morgan, in the Allen MSS.

[26] This part of the interview is not covered by Allen's diary entry of September 30, 1903. It is given after the fact in Allen to Nash, May 4, 1904, address to the Naval War College in 1905, and memorandum of 1905 or later, in the Allen MSS, and in Allen, *Things Korean,* 251.

Roosevelt. The president could not stand interference, saw only what he wanted to see, "like the Kaiser could not be crossed." Allen could do nothing but retire, expressing his regret that he had made so poor a showing, that he had reached his conclusions after a tour through the Russian empire and had stated them "as a duty."[27]

So far, so good. Rockhill rightly censured Allen for excess of zeal, for being far too blunt with his country's chief of state. The matter might have ended there. But Allen smarted under what he took to be ill treatment, itched to appeal from Roosevelt to the people of America. Thus was he betrayed into insubordination. On his way back to Korea, the doctor gave a "careful interview" to Edward Rittenhouse, then editor of the *Daily Telegraph* of Colorado Springs. The Associated Press snapped up the statement and it was broadcast throughout the land, in sharp defiance of the State Department and the president of the United States.[28]

The interview restated the arguments that had been used on Roosevelt. Bandits and the lack of transportation facilities had kept Manchuria out of the stream of international trade until Russia had come, enforcing order, constructing railroads, making Manchuria "a splendid and growing field for American commerce." In consequence, America should avoid supporting Japan in Russo-Japanese disputes, should remain aloof lest Russia turn against American traders.

Press reaction was not unfavorable to this position. The *Washington Post,* for example, was glad to be informed about a region from which "many of the press telegrams show unmistakable signs of inaccuracy and sentimentalism." Sounding a note of Anglophobia, it hoped that Roosevelt and the State Department would "for the future consult its official representatives in that part of the world rather than

[27] Allen Diary, September 30, 1903; memorandum of 1905 or later, memorandum of 1924, in the Allen MSS. On a similar point, see Sands, *Undiplomatic Memories,* 237.

[28] Allen Diary, October 16, 1903, entry made on October 20; memorandum of 1905 or later, in the Allen MSS.

the mischievous and alarming gossip that comes by way of London"; but it feared that Allen would be reprimanded for his action.[29]

That he was. The Department was distressed and Roosevelt angered by the "inexcusable" publication of anti-administration views. There was even talk of a dismissal; rumor had it that John Hay headed off the president on that. In lieu of discharge, a telegram of censure was dispatched.[30] The reprimand reached Allen as he was passing through Japan. He answered humbly and evasively: "Will comply with your instructions. Reporters whom I did not see have reported an interview." But he was late with compliance, late with evasion, late with humility. Never again was he to work in harmony with his superiors in Washington.

[29] *Washington Post*, October 21, 1903, clipping in the Allen MSS.
[30] Allen Diary, November 16, 1904; Allen to Everett, September 3, 1904, and to Bostwick, February 20, 1907, Morse to Allen, January 22, 1904, note by Allen in the Allen MSS; Allen to the Secretary of State, November 11, 1903, Dispatches, State Department Archives. See, however, Rockhill to Allen, June 30, 1904, in the Rockhill MSS.

18

I Fell With Korea

"WHY sleep?" asked a Korean when he saw an acquaintance dozing in a public place.

"It's uneasy I am," replied the friend, "that's why I sleep."

So did the politicians of Chosen meet their problems in the dying days of Korean independence. Trembling with fright and recognition of impotence, they hardly dared to speculate on a future certain to be disastrous.[1]

They had ground for their fears. When Allen spoke to Roosevelt in October, 1903, the clouds were getting darker every day. Russia, dominated by imperialists, had become defiant in Manchuria and was pushing into the Yalu region of Korea. Japan was countering by making ready for the conflict in which she was to call a halt to the Tsarist operations. Japanese merchants in Seoul called in their loans; their government strengthened its control over the line from Fusan to the capital and brought large quantities of military stores into Chosen.

Back at his post, Allen watched the Japanese moves with great interest. He watched the Russians, too, whose in-

[1] James S. Gale, "Korea in War Time," *Outlook*, 77 (1904):453–456. For the diplomatic background, see Asakawa, *Russo-Japanese Conflict*, 273–322.

efficiency contrasted sharply with the careful preparations of
Japan. Pavloff was still busy with his gay young wife, who
"set the town by the ears" that winter. When he did turn
to work, the Russian representative laughed off the threat
from Tokyo. Let conflict come, he cried, Japan would have
her fill if she chose war. He took no steps to gain protection
for the Russian ships at Chemulpo, nor did he stop the
Russian navy from storing fifteen hundred tons of coal on
unprotected Roze Island (off Chemulpo) as late as February
2, 1904.[2]

One week later there was war. Like others, Allen had
expected it, had called marines as early as December, 1903.
Then he had waited, listened to rumors: Japan was coming,
Russian troops were near the border, war was certain, war
would be postponed. The best source was the American
minister to Japan, Lloyd Griscom, who wrote from Tokyo
that Japan would not abandon her Manchurian ventures.
that she had "practically decided for war," that her citizens
would greet peace news with disappointment. Then, finally,
the guns did sound; the Allens heard the rumble of the first
engagement, the naval battle of Chemulpo.[3]

As usual in a crisis, Allen's influence increased. The worried emperor sought him out, going so far as to ask asylum
in the United States legation. Knowing his superiors, Allen
did not feel free to offer that. But he did almost as much,
granted His Majesty's request that American marines act
"as a sort of guard to him." On leaving the Russian legation
in 1898, the monarch had moved into a palace close to
Allen's residence. After April, 1904, he came closer still.
When the palace was burned, he moved into a library building adjoining the American legation and "quite surrounded

[2] Hulbert, *Passing of Korea*, 187–193; Allen, *Things Korean*, 248; address to the Naval War College, in the Allen MSS.

[3] Allen to the Secretary of State, December 18, 1903, January 5,
February 2, 1904, Dispatches, State Department Archives; Allen to his
sons, January 5, February 9, 1904, Griscom to Allen, January 2, 26, 1904,
address to the Naval War College, memorandum by Allen, and manu-

by American property." Each day His Majesty walked on
United States legation property (a path behind his library);
and the timid ruler did his best to create the general impression that he was under Allen's care. American marines contributed to the illusion by standing guard at the legation and
before the missionary houses, giving the "unfortunate" appearance of furnishing protection to the emperor.[4]

With this the strength of Allen soared. He insisted that he
had not sought this position and would try "not to seem to
turn it to our own profit." He even sent away seventy-five of
his one hundred marines "to show that I am not in the protecting business." He closed the rear legation path and told
the emperor that he must not expect asylum. Still, he was
obliged to admit that he appeared to have the preponder-
ating influence. Although Japan was in control of Seoul,
her envoy now approached the Korean emperor through
Allen.[5]

Under some circumstances, Allen's power might have
meant a lot. He might have used it to work for neutralization
of Chosen. He might have increased the importance of
America in Seoul. He might have helped choose a future
overlord for the Korean state. As it was, the power came too
late. Neutralization was a dead proposal. Japan and Russia

script report by Brigadier General Henry T. Allen, in the Allen MSS;
Allen, *Things Korean*, 234.

[4] Allen to the Secretary of State, October 13, 1897, enclosing map,
March 8, 1898, enclosing statement from the *New York Herald*, January
27, 1897, April 14, 16, 22, 1904, E. V. Morgan to the Secretary of State,
October 17, 1905, Dispatches, State Department Archives; Allen to
Ellinwood, April 26, 1897, to E. V. Morgan, May 29, 1903, to his sons,
January 4, February 8, 1904, to Rockhill, April 19, 1904, to Jennie
Everett, April 23, 1904, and to Wilson, November 13, 1906, in the
Allen MSS; E. V. Morgan to Rockhill, June 4, 1904, in the Rockhill
MSS; "The Burning of the Palace," *Korea Review*, 4 (1904):155–163.

[5] Allen to the Secretary of State, April 16, 22, 1904, Dispatches, State
Department Archives; E. V. Morgan to Rockhill, June 4, 1904, in the
Rockhill MSS; Allen to E. V. Morgan, March 11, 1904, to his sisters and
brother, April 23, 1904, and to General Wilson, November 13, 1906, in
the Allen MSS.

had both favored it in the years of Chinese domination. So had Chosen. Back in 1890 the Korean foreign minister had told Allen that "he thought the only relief was to be found in an agreement of the nations to protect Korea in her Independence and allow her to proceed unmollested in her development." Going further, he had asked Allen to have America lead the way, combining with France, Italy, Germany, and Japan and later asking China, Russia, and Great Britain to cooperate. Again in 1899 Korea had made such a move, the emperor requesting Allen to approach McKinley. The doctor had done so, interviewing the president and Secretary of State Hay at Lake Champlain; but McKinley had said no. A year later, apparently at Japanese request, the Korean minister to Japan had made the same proposal. It had been forwarded to Washington by Minister Buck, but neither there nor in Japan had it received much attention. Russia seems to have toyed with the idea then and later, but without result, and no one could have revived it in 1904.[6]

It was the same with the possibility of aid from the United States. Allen was in no position to persuade his superiors to take on any task. The State Department had little use for the doctor after his debate with Roosevelt. Assistant Secretary of State Alvey A. Adee ridiculed him in the public press for requesting a new legation building. In defending his petition, the minister had cited his height with hat to show how low the eaves and ceilings were. "Well," cracked Adee and the reporters whom he addressed, "he shouldn't wear his hat in

[6] On neutralization, Allen to Ellinwood, October 28, 1886, and memorandum by Allen, November 17, 1890, and on interview with President of Korean Foreign Office, Allen to Fassett, November 3, 1900, in the Allen MSS; Allen to the Secretary of State, August 31, September 10, October 3, 1900, January 30, 1904, Dispatches, State Department Archives; Dennett, *Roosevelt and the Russo-Japanese War*, 104, note; Isvolski, Russian envoy in Japan, to Russian Minister of Foreign Affairs, January 4, 1901, in *Chinese Social and Political Science Review*, 18 (1934):573; Sands to the author, May 28, 1939; Treat, *Diplomatic Relations between the United States and Japan*, 3:129, 164–166; Sands, *Undiplomatic Memories*, 123.

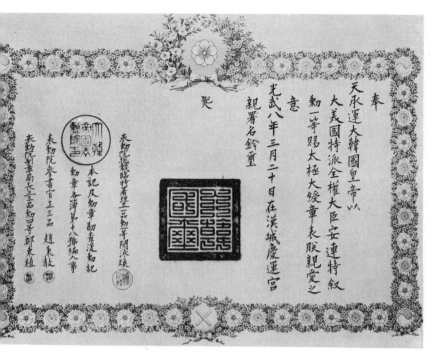

**Imperial Korean Decree Conferring on Allen
the Decoration of Tai Kook**

Allen was four times decorated by the monarch of Chosen. This, his fourth
decoration, which he received in 1904 shortly before his return to the
United States, was the highest that might be conferred upon any person
who was not of royal blood.

the house anyway." Like other jokes about those in authority, this spread all through the country.[7]

Again in December, 1903, on the question of Korean ports. Instructed to insist on having the north Korean port of Wiju opened to world commerce, Allen struck for the near-by city of Yongampo as well and failed to get a thing. In the process he misread instructions; and when the State Department wished to be officially ignorant of Russian opposition persuaded Pavloff to admit that he was fighting the Americans. That was too much for Rockhill and Adee. The former spoke sourly of "our distinguished Minister in Korea" and doubted the merit of his "bull in a china shop" technique. Adee distrusted Allen so completely that when war came he would not credit the doctor's statement of the news. "I fight shy of giving *Allen's* reports to the Press," he told John Hay.[8]

Even if the doctor had possessed influence in Washington, he still could have done nothing. Roosevelt made sure of that. Pro-Japanese, the chief executive was most contemptuous of Chosen and was perfectly willing to have the region ruled from Tokyo. "I cannot see any possibility of this Government using its influence 'to bolster up the Empire of Korea in its independence,' " said Rockhill in outlining what both he and Roosevelt believed. "I fancy that the Japanese will settle this question when the present war is finished. The annexation of Korea to Japan seems to be absolutely indicated as the

[7] Clippings in the Allen MSS from the *New York World* of December 20, 1903, the *Carbondale* [Pennsylvania] *Leader* of February 27, 1902, and other papers. That the legation was in need of repair is indicated by letters of Sill to the Secretary of State, January 7, 1895, June 10, 1897, and Allen to the Secretary of State, September 20, 1897, Dispatches, State Department Archives.

[8] Secretary of State Hay to Allen, November 7, 12, 16, 19, December 11, 1903, January 2, 1904, Assistant Secretary Loomis to Allen, January 26, 1904, Instructions, State Department Archives; Allen to the Secretary of State, November 17, 1899, November 18, 19, December 5, 6, 8, 9, 11, 23, 1903, January 2, 3, 10, March 30, 1904, January 8, 1905, Sands to the Secretary of State, August 10, 1899, Dispatches, State Department Archives (the dispatches of November 17, 1899, December 5, 11, 23, 1903, March 30, 1904, and January 8, 1905, were annotated by Rockhill and

one great and final[!] step westward of the extension of the Japanese Empire. I think when this comes about it will be better for the Korean people and also for the peace in the Far East." When the Korean envoy in Washington told Hay that his country was "in serious straits" and wanted "some assistance" from the United States, the secretary of state replied in "carefully guarded phrases, expressing our friendship and good wishes for Korea, but added that our interests were rather commercial than political."[9]

It appeared, then, that there would be no chance to neutralize Korea, none to bring in the United States, none to help the Russians, whom Allen saw as better than the Japanese. All this was discouraging. Privately the doctor could cry out against the "yellow peril," could say that England and America "may very well repent later on" for having helped Japan. But Roosevelt, of course, would not consider Allen's views; the president represented the general American sympathy for Japan. Allen's friend Morse expressed this view when he called the Russians "rotten to the core . . . unprincipled, tyrannical and brutal, and I hope the Japanese will knock their heads off."[10]

Allen was amazed at the speed and ease with which Japan gained triumph. He had spoken of the "red tape forms" of Tokyo, but after watching a debarkation was forced to admit the islanders' efficiency. It was astounding, a "steady stream

Adee); Allen to Rockhill, January 4, 1904, April 19, 1904, in the Rockhill MSS; Allen to E. V. Morgan, January 15, February 26, 1904, in the Allen MSS. For Rockhill's early interest in Wiju, see Rockhill to the Assistant Secretary of State, March 28, 1887, Consular Dispatches, State Department Archives.

[9] Rockhill to Allen, February 20, 1904, Allen to Rockhill, January 4, 1904, in the Rockhill MSS. See also the statements of Roosevelt quoted in Dennett, *Roosevelt and the Russo-Japanese War*, 110–113, 161. Eleanor Tupper and George E. McReynolds, *Japan in American Public Opinion* (New York, 1937), 6–17, shows the favorable attitude of Roosevelt and the American public toward Japan.

[10] Allen to Everett, February 27, 1904, Mrs. W. W. Rockhill to Allen, June 30, 1904, Morse to Allen, April 15, 1904, in the Allen MSS.

of quiet determined men came off like molasses running out of a barrel in summer. No noise or friction."[11]

Nor was there noise or friction when Japan took over in Seoul. In theory Korea was not in the conflict, had announced neutrality a full fortnight before the declaration of hostilities. Actually, however, war inevitably brought Japanese soldiers to Chosen. In a few days' time the Japanese had the palace and the capital completely under their control and had forced the emperor to accept a "very strong" protectorate agreement. Quite naturally, Japan broke up the pro-Russian pedlars' guild and ousted the Russophile Koreans from office. Out went Pavloff, too. Allen went to see him leave, "on a cold gray morning with a pall of snow hanging over the city and falling gently upon us." It was a sight to be remembered. Allen had disliked Pavloff, had listed the envoy's "silly and provoking" opposition to the opening of Wiju as one of the chief immediate causes of war.[12] Still, he was impressed by the sight of the Russian minister with his young wife and legation staff, all under military escort of Japan. Au revoir, called Pavloff, bravely as he could; and then his train chugged off to Chemulpo, leaving Japan in complete control of the empire of Korea.[13]

News of Russian losses soon indicated that Japan had come to stay. Only a diplomatic combination could force her to withdraw and prevent eventual absorption of Korea. Clutching at straws, the emperor bid for that combination. He

[11] Allen to his sons, February 17, 1904, in the Allen MSS.

[12] Allen to the Secretary of State, March 24, 1904, Dispatches, State Department Archives; Allen to Rockhill, April 19, May 6, 1904, Rockhill to Allen, February 20, 1904, in the Rockhill MSS; Allen to Captain C. S. Sperry, April, 1904, in the Allen MSS.

[13] See Allen, *Things Korean*, 248, on the departure of Pavloff. The Japanese policies were foretold by Allen in a letter to the Secretary of State, January 1, 1904, Dispatches, State Department Archives. Lloyd Griscom, American minister to Japan, stated during the war that "there is no concealment of the intention to make Korea into a Japanese province if Japanese arms are victorious." Quoted in Treat, *Diplomatic Relations between the United States and Japan*, 3:196.

turned to all the powers, counting most on the United States. For had not Allen (when concession-hunting) said that America was "his friend," that the Americans were "the only people who could speak a strong and disinterested word for him in his prospective trouble"? Besides, there was the Korean-American treaty of 1882. Its good office clause was mild enough, but when given "a very free and favorable translation" it seemed to guarantee that America would intervene to save Korea. Consequently, His Majesty in 1904 believed the United States would "do something for him . . . to retain as much of his independence as . . . possible."[14]

But that was not to be. Allen knew it, and by 1904 he did not care. For, at long last, he had come to feel that Korea was beyond salvation, "impossible," "simply abominable and getting worse all the while." Morning Calm was out of date, he said, Chosen should be entitled the Land of the Cold Gray Calm of the Morning After. The people "cannot govern themselves . . . They must have an overlord as they have had for all time." Once he had thought the emperor had possibilities; now he found him "an awful blight and curse to this country," a ruler who spent his time "playing with dancing girls, like Nero fiddling while Rome burned." Natural resources and a population with potentialities gave some promise for the future, *if* the government was changed. That is, a war would be a "good thing" for the natives, "and they deserve to be absorbed by someone who would give the people a little liberty and keep in check these rapacious and inhuman officials." Again, at the outbreak of war: "I hope that whatever may be the outcome, Korea will go outright to one or the other of the contestants."[15]

[14] Allen to the Secretary of State, April 14, 1904, Dispatches, State Department Archives; Allen Diary, June 1, 1903; Allen to Hunt, April 13, 1900, and to Morse, September 30, 1904, in the Allen MSS.
[15] The situation is well described in Allen to the Secretary of State, May 31, 1902, Dispatches, State Department Archives; Allen to Ellinwood, April 26, 1897, to his sons, April 6, 1902, to Everett, June 2, 1902, to E. V. Morgan, June 25, 1902, February 14, 1904, to John Hay, No-

Obviously it would be Japan. Unhappy thought, for with Japan in power Allen thought it would be "increasingly difficult to properly protect and advance American interests." A month after the war began, the Japanese were talking of the white menace. "The countries of Asia must stand together as brothers," Ito told the Korean emperor, "otherwise the Western Powers would devour them." Chosen, in other words, "must lean upon Japan alone," must stop issuing concessions to Americans and must regret that an American flag flew over the waterworks headquarters, the "most commanding building [in Seoul] and over what should be Korean property," Japanese-protected.[16] Unpleasant, that. It made Allen wish he had not helped Japan get the Seoul-Fusan railroad grant nor aided that pro-Japanese official, McLeavy Brown.

Yet, since it was inevitable, the doctor was prepared to have it so. Japan would help the common people of Korea. Perhaps the doctor could save something for his concessionaire acquaintances. "We will be protected in our vested rights," he thought, and might be able to supply the Japanese with capital they lacked. Wherefore it was advisable to talk in favor of Japan, whatever were one's private views. It was politic to write Rockhill, "I have favored the Japanese entirely—after Korea herself and the United States." "I have all along held that Japan should have the paramount influence [in Korea]."[17]

Allen knew that the rise of Japan imperiled his own job.

vember 21, 1902, to E. E. Rittenhouse, January 20, 1903, to Rockhill, February 28, 1901, January 4, 1904, to Morse, June 7, 1904, and Townsend to Allen, November 30, 1905, in the Allen MSS; Hamilton, *Korea*, 52–55; Gale, "Korea in War Time," *Outlook*, 77 (1904):453–456; and Sands to the Secretary of State, August 10, 1899, Dispatches, State Department Archives.

[16] Allen to the Secretary of State, March 27, 1904, Dispatches, State Department Archives. Allen refers to the Pan Asia movement in his diary entry for June 19, 1885. See also Hayashi, *Secret Memoirs*, 64–65.

[17] Allen to E. V. Morgan, December 23, 1903, March 2, 1904, to Morse, January 22, 1904, and to Rockhill, January 4, 1904, and memorandum

Ministers are seldom sent to colonies and as Chosen was "now to be more under the control of Japan than Egypt is under that of England, I think that an Agent and Consul General will soon be more fitting for our representation here than an Envoy Extraordinary." Allen "might be transferred or dropped out entirely."[18] Preferably the former. The latter would be sad, although recall would have its compensations. Allen was "not in love" with Korea, "this insignificant hole." He would be glad when he could leave. There were more comforts than there had been when he and Fannie arrived, but even so all was not perfect. The legation was an ugly building even in the rare years when it was in repair. Quarrels with business men and missionaries were as common as before and social obligations far heavier. Fannie was ill, the boys were off at college; it might be pleasant to get back to America.[19]

It seemed likely that Allen would be thrown out anyway, for insubordination or in the political shakeup sure to follow the election of 1904. If the Democrats came in, he would go "out 'with honors.'" If Roosevelt stayed in, "I may have to go out anyway as I am a McKinley man and he has kept me long enough." True, the Americans in Chosen got "cold

by Allen, February 26, 1904, in the Allen MSS. For an interesting and similar statement by Walter D. Townsend, see Ladd, *In Korea*, 116–119.

[18] Allen to Rockhill, January 4, 1904, to E. V. Morgan, February 26, 1904, to Hebe Allen, October 15, 1904, to E. E. Rittenhouse, October 18, 1904, and to John Hay, December 24, 1904, in the Allen MSS. Allen, in a letter to Foraker dated March 29, 1916, in the Allen MSS, says Foraker proposed in 1903 that Allen be given the Tokyo mission, but was defeated by Mark Hanna, who favored Griscom.

[19] Allen to Rockhill, January 30, 1898, March 13, 1901, D. W. Stevens to Rockhill, February 6, 1905, in the Rockhill MSS; Allen to Heard, August 15, December 13, 1890, to Min Chong Mok, Korean minister of foreign affairs, January 12, 1891, to Adee, February 10, 1891, to Everett, November 29, 1897, to his mother, February 13, 1898, and to his sisters, May 17, 1904, in the Allen MSS; letters to the Secretary of State from Foulk, July 28, 1885, from Rockhill, December 15, 1886, March 5, 1887, from Heard, August 15, December 1, 1890, from Allen, August 15, 1890, September 20, 1897, November 10, 1904, and from Sill, January 7, 1895, June 10, 1897, Dispatches, State Department Archives.

shivers" when he spoke of leaving, and the doctor "had hoped to remain here to the end of things, having been here almost at the beginning."[20] But fate was fate.

All that was very philosophical. In practice, the doctor could not be so calm. He flared with anger in March, 1905, when Roosevelt turned him out in just the way he had expected. The dismissal could be called a routine matter. Roosevelt was sure "eight years was long enough for any man in office," the "very limit that one of our Ministers should reside at any foreign court." When recalled, Allen had served as minister for seven and three-quarters years. Had the chief executive been attached to his Seoul agent, tenure might have been extended for a while—possibly until December, when the United States withdrew its legation from Korea. But Allen drew no spark of love from Roosevelt's great heart, the president was glad to see the doctor go. The more so, doubtless, in that Allen would be followed by Edwin V. Morgan, who was a friend of Roosevelt and daughter Alice, and was not likely to ape Allen's insubordination tactics.[21]

Routine or not, the dismissal hit its victim without warning. Allen's friends in the United States expected him to be retained. Officials in Washington—Hay, Japanese Minister Takahira, even Rockhill, had little notice of the move. It was "one of the President's own impetuous acts." There was a telegram from Rockhill, then a summary dispatch from the Department; and Allen was a diplomat no more.[22]

Caught by surprise, the doctor was deeply shocked. He

[20] Allen to Everett, February 27, 1904, to Rockhill, April 19, 1904, to Morse, June 7, 1904, and to his sister Georgia, July 10, 1904, in the Allen MSS.

[21] Dennett, *Roosevelt and the Russo-Japanese War*, 302–303; Allen to Huntington Wilson, July 9, 1906, quoting Roosevelt through Captain John Weeks, in the Allen MSS; Treat, *Diplomatic Relations between the United States and Japan*, 3:254. The difference in attitude may be seen from E. V. Morgan's letters to the Secretary of State, September 9, October 13, 17, 1905, Dispatches, State Department Archives.

[22] Letters to Allen from Rockhill, June 30, 1904, from Morse, April 15, 1904, and from Charles W. Needham, April 6, 1905, and Allen to

forgot that he had called American diplomatic representation
in Seoul "superfluous" considering Japanese ascendancy. He
forgot that he had written, "if the Administration really has
lost confidence in me, whether I merit it or not, they had
better relieve me and send one in whom they have full confidence." Recollection of those words was blotted out by the
sting of the removal. "I can scarcely realize it." ":It . . . seems
an ungrateful thing for the government to do considering all
I have done here."[23] Friends made the matter worse. Allen
spoke of "tears I have seen strong men shed over this news."
The European diplomats," he said, "seem to think our Govmt
'mad.' " Business men expressed their sorrow, missionaries
wrote home to their boards and drew up a petition in the
doctor's favor. The emperor told Roosevelt he was "greatly
grieved."[24]

Smarting the more when he had picked up all this sympathy, Allen looked for individuals to blame. The president
of course was the key villain, but there was room for others.
For a time the doctor erroneously thought that Hunt, Fassett,
Foraker, and the Presbyterian board had opposed or failed to
help him, though they had done nothing of the kind. Ray-
mond Krumm, a personal enemy, drew some of Allen's cen-

Collbran, March 9, April 18, 1905, to Lloyd Griscom, April 18, 1905,
to William E. Griffis, May 24, 1905, and to Huntington Wilson, July 9,
1906, in the Allen MSS. See, however, Allen to Collbran, December 18,
26, 1904, and to John Hay, December 24, 1904, in the Allen MSS.
Rockhill, in a letter of March 21, 1905, to D. W. Stevens, in the Rockhill MSS, stated that Hay respected Rockhill's belief that a change was
inexpedient and Roosevelt "would have waited" had Hay not been ill.

[23] Allen to McKinley, September 14, 1896, to Morse and Hunt, July
3, 1897, to E. V. Morgan, February 26, 1904, to Arthur J. Brown, October
17, 1904, to Everett, March 20, 1905, to Rockhill, March 21, 1905, and
to his sons, March 26, 1905, in the Allen MSS. A calmer note is seen in
Allen's letter of March 31, 1905, to F. E. Butcher, in the Allen MSS.
For sharp criticism of Rockhill, see Thomas F. Millard to James H.
Wilson, September 10, 1906, in the Allen MSS.

[24] Letters to Allen from Morse, March 20, 1905, from William B.
Scranton, March 21, 1905, from O. R. Avison, March 23, 1905, from
Griscom, March 31, 1905, from E. E. Rittenhouse, April 25, 1905, from
George Heber Jones, April 28, 1905, from Charles W. Needham (of the

sure. And E. V. Morgan, surely he was partially responsible. Allen had befriended and trained this man, had thought him "most capable," a "jewel," a "gentleman and a scholar." To be succeeded by him was "like a stab from one of my family." "It seems ungrateful on his part," was among the milder comments Allen let himself deliver. More frequently he labelled his presumed opponent "rich and ambitious," pompous, hypocritical, "a contemptible character." Morgan was wise to avoid the doctor in the months to follow; had they met there would have been a scene.[25]

But personalities were not enough. Allen came to feel that there was much beneath the surface, that he had been relieved because he was a friend of Chosen. "I can only account for it all on the supposition that this Legation is shortly to be removed," he wrote in April, "and it might be just as well not to have a man here to whom intimate relations

Korean legation in Washington), April 6, 1905, from T. C. Thompson, June 8, 1905, and from Bostwick, February 14, 1907; Rittenhouse to P. B. Stewart, April 25, 1905, and to Bostwick, April 28, 1905; Allen to Rockhill, March 21, 1905, to his sons, March 26, April 23, 1905, to Morse, April 26, 1905, and to Arthur J. Brown, April 30, 1905; original of petition held back at Allen's request; copy of Bostwick to Roosevelt, March 22, May 23, 1905. All these documents are in the Allen MSS. Pertinent official documents are E. V. Morgan to the Secretary of State, June 26, 1905, Dispatches, State Department Archives, and the Emperor of Korea to Roosevelt, March 25, 1905, Notes from the Korean Legation, State Department Archives.

[25] Letters from Allen to his mother, June 2, 1900, to Morse, May 20, 1902, to John Hay, May 20, December 2, 1902, to E. V. Morgan, August 15, 1902, to Collbran, March 9, 1905, to his sons, March 20, 1905, to Bostwick, March 24, 1905, to Arthur J. Brown, April 30, 1905, to D. W. Stevens, November 29, 1905, to Homer Hulbert, December 2, 1905, to Scranton, December 8, 1905, to Townsend, June 28, 1905, to Bostwick, February 20, 1907, and to Foraker, March 29, 1916, Bostwick to Allen, February 14, 1907, memoranda and notes by Allen, and clipping from the *Seattle Times*, July 20, 1905, in the Allen MSS; Allen to Rockhill, March 13, 21, 1905, E. V. Morgan to Rockhill, June 4, 1904, July 12, 1905, and Lloyd Griscom to Rockhill, June 23, 1905, in the Rockhill MSS. Allen to the Secretary of State, May 20, August 18, December 2, 13, 1902, June 21, 1904, March 21, 1905, Dispatches, State Department Archives, the last annotated by L. B. Loomis.

with the Korean Government would make such a step one of more or less awkwardness."[26] This explanation fell short of truth. Allen himself had said a dozen times that the end of Chosen was at hand, had expressed his pleasure that the country was going under. Yet now he saw himself as the defender of Korean liberties, dismissed because he wished to save the region from Japan.

Time did not make the doctor see the contradictions there revealed. Rather he forgot his "down with Korea" period and maintained he had always served as champion of Chosen. If the emperor had followed him in 1903, he said, if the court had opened Wiju and Yongampo, the land might have been saved. If Roosevelt had only listened that night in the White House—but the chief executive had "to hand over Korea to Japan in order to stop the fight he had egged on" and had to "have someone in Seoul who would not be too friendly with the Koreans as to be unable to do his bidding."[27]

The Allens were back in the United States when Chosen went down. That was in November and December, 1905, when Japan established a formal protectorate over Korea and the United States withdrew its minister. Annexation, though five years delayed, was plainly in the cards. "Sad and depressing," Allen thought; "I confess it simply sickens me." With a Korean friend he granted that nothing "else could be expected from such a reign of corruption, imbecility and vanity as you and I have known during the past twenty years." He even felt it would "prove better in the end to have responsible rule in the Palace," that "the condition of

[26] Letters from Allen to Lloyd Griscom, April 7, 1905, to Scranton, December 8, 1905, and to Homer Hulbert, December 12, 1905, and note by Allen, 1924, in the Allen MSS; Brown, *Mastery of the Far East,* 199; McKenzie, *Tragedy of Korea,* 117; McKenzie, *Korea's Fight for Freedom,* 87; Tupper and McReynolds, *Japan in American Public Opinion,* 95.

[27] Allen to Ye Ha Yong, November 30, 1905, to Pak Chung Yang, November 30, 1905, and to Scranton, December 8, 1905, manuscript articles by Allen, written in 1905, and note by Allen, 1924, in the Allen MSS.

the common people will doubtless be improved. The rights of property will be respected, and your Korean officials will be paid adequately for their services." But all the same, it was unfortunate that the United States had led the way to recognition of the domination of Japan. "This blotting out of the independent rights of such an ancient and kind people is most sad and regretable," he wrote his old acquaintance Pak Chung Yang, "and Mrs. Allen has shed many tears over the fate of Korea, while tears have been in my own heart."[28]

Jobless as he wrote those words, Allen feared he had "gone down with Korea."[29] It was not as bad as that. He was through with his diplomacy, through as a public figure. But he still had his medical degree. With that he set up in Toledo and soon had quite a practice there.

The emperor was far less fortunate in attempts to reestablish his shattered fortunes. Vainly did the monarch write to Allen enclosing ten thousand dollars to be used in the Korean cause. Vainly did the Koreans in America keep dogging Allen's footsteps, begging aid. The doctor wrote around, secured cooperation from General Wilson, Olney, Choate, Moorfield Storey, and Wayne MacVeagh. But who

[28] Letters from Allen to George K. Nash, May 4, 1904, to Pak Chung Yang, September 30, November 30, 1905, to Ye Ha Yong, September 30, 1905, to Yun Chi Ho, November 30, 1905, and to Scranton, December 8, 1905, address to the Naval War College, and clipping from the *Toledo Bee*, February 23, 1916, in the Allen MSS. As E. V. Morgan noted in his letters to the Secretary of State, November 10, 17, 18, 20, 22, 28, 1905 (Dispatches, State Department Archives), the Korean cabinet "cannot be considered to have acted entirely as free agents." See also Tupper and McReynolds, *Japan in American Public Opinion*, 91-95. Even D. W. Stevens, pro-Japanese American adviser to Japan, admitted to Allen in a letter of January 10, 1906, that "you know and I know that the Emperor would not have yielded willingly." A pro-Korean view is presented in E. A. Elliot's letter of December 10, 1905, to Allen. "I suppose it could not be otherwise," Allen wrote Stevens on January 29, 1905, "but I certainly do like those people." These three letters are in the Allen MSS.

[29] Letters from Allen to Ye Ha Yong, November 30, 1905, to Yun Chi Ho, November 30, 1905, and to Bostwick, December 1, 1905, in the Allen MSS. Writing Yun Chi Ho, Allen said, "they left the whole thing

could move the Roosevelt administration? Allen returned the ten thousand, concluding that all was over for Korea.[30]

Mixed emotions crowded Allen's heart and mind as he watched the later history of the land where he had lived so long. Sometimes he recognized gains made under the Japanese overlordship. Before his departure he had made up a Korean *Who's Who* for D. W. Stevens, American adviser in Japanese employ. Later he was pleased to see that the men he had endorsed were given high positions, made puppet rulers in Seoul. Equally pleasant was the steady growth of Christian missions ("the missionary marvel of the age") and the apparent prosperity of American concessionaries.[31]

Even so, the doctor was not sure. He always felt that Roosevelt had erred in backing the Japanese. Occasionally he saw the Japanese rule in Korea as a "double tyranny and a dual anarchy." And he was ever apprehensive for the future. Dying on December 11, 1932, he did not survive to hear of

to me until they decided they would turn it over to Japan and then they saw they must get rid of me so I fell with Korea." E. A. Elliot to Allen, December 10, 1905, Bostwick to Allen, December 10, 1905, January 6, 19, 1906, Allen to Bostwick, December 16, 18, 1905, January 25, 26, 1906, Allen to James H. Wilson, December 14, 1905, D. W. Stevens to Allen, January 10, 1906, in the Allen MSS.

[30] Notes by Allen and letters of Allen to Homer Hulbert, December 12, 1905, and to Choate, December 18, 1905, with reply of January 20, 1906; James H. Wilson to Allen, December 15, 22, 1905 (with criticism of Allen), Allen to Huntington Wilson, July 9, 1906, in the Allen MSS. For similar efforts of Hulbert, see Dennett, *Roosevelt and the Russo-Japanese War*, 304–306; E. V. Morgan to the Secretary of State, October 19, 1905, with note by Loomis, Dispatches, State Department Archives; Adee to Root, December 7, 1905, filed with Notes from the Korean Legation, State Department Archives; and Bostwick to Allen, January 19, 1906, in the Allen MSS ("I know you dislike Hulbert as much as I do"). Allen tried to avoid Koreans who sought him out, remarking to Townsend, January 8, 1906 (Allen MSS): "I am sorry for them of course, but Gee Whiz, I am not running any asylums just yet." According to a memorandum of February 12, 1906, in the Allen MSS, Allen kept five hundred dollars of the Korean money "to cover travelling expenses, and minor expenditures."

[31] Notes by Allen, 1905 and 1924, and "Who's Who in Korea," in the Allen MSS; Ladd, *In Korea*, 288–289. See also Allen to Collbran, February 26, 1904, to Morse, February 26, 27, 1904, and to D. W. Stevens,

the withdrawal of the Oriental Consolidated Mining Company, largest of the firms he had made possible. Neither did he see the Japanese assault on Christian missions. But had he lived to see those things, he would have said, "I told you so." And so he had, in 1905, in 1903, way back in 1898.

Allen's views had never been consistent; they had shifted with the changing colors of the court kaleidoscope in Seoul. But even when he favored letting Japan have Korea, Allen had maintained that he was not pro-Japanese.[32] Generally he had claimed that Japan triumphant would cripple the American enterprises which he had built up with loving care. Cripple them, swing shut the open door. Roosevelt had not paid heed, Rockhill had insisted that Korean annexation would be the "final step westward" for the Empire of the Rising Sun. But Allen, who had seen the yellow islanders in action, thought their advance would not be stopped with the acquisition of Chosen. Rather the Japanese would seek an Asia for the Asiatics, an Asia for Japan. And in the years to come each Western nation would be forced to yield its interests in the Orient, or to cross swords with the Japanese.[33]

April 8, 1906, in the Allen MSS; Allen to the Secretary of State, February 27, 1904, Dispatches, State Department Archives; and Tupper and McReynolds, *Japan in American Public Opinion*, 95. D. W. Stevens, in writing Allen on January 10, 1906 (Allen MSS), stated that Allen's old ally Ye Wan Yong made possible the protectorate treaty of 1905. Allen's pro-Japanese attitude at this point may have been associated with his efforts to secure a sugar beet concession for George P. Morgan. See Allen to George Morgan, March 18, 23, 1905, and Morgan to Allen, March 30, May 8, 1905, in the Allen MSS. Allen stopped writing Stevens after the collapse of the Morgan project. Allen to Bostwick, October 4, 1907, in the Allen MSS.

[32] Address to the Naval War College, 1905, notes and manuscript articles by Allen, 1905 and 1924, Allen to Rockhill, January 4, 1904, in the Allen MSS.

[33] Allen, *Things Korean*, 251; Rockhill to Allen, February 20, 1904, in the Rockhill MSS; Allen to Everett, February 27, 1904, memorandum and notes, 1905 and 1924, in the Allen MSS. For a similar view see General James H. Wilson to Allen, January 26, 1906, in the Allen MSS: "It is becoming every day more evident that victory means 'Asia for the Asiatics' and that Japan is to be the hegemon of all the Asiatic nations. It means also that all Western powers will have to take a back seat."

Bibliography

Bibliography

MANUSCRIPTS AND PRINTED DOCUMENTS

The chief sources for this work are the Horace N. Allen Manuscripts, in the New York Public Library, and the archives of the Department of State, in the National Archives in Washington, D.C. The Allen Manuscripts contain letters to Allen, letterpress, carbon, and other copies of letters written by him, copies of petitions, missionary resolutions, and franchise agreements, photographs, translations from Korean newspapers, and a file of the Seoul *Daily Independent*. In the State Department collections, I have examined all the diplomatic and consular instructions sent to our representatives in Korea during the entire period of American diplomatic relations with that kingdom (1883–1905); all the diplomatic and consular dispatches received from our representatives there during the same period; the correspondence between the Department of State and the Korean diplomats in Washington; and the Seoul legation archives, which include miscellaneous letters, the correspondence of the United States legation with Korean officials, with other legations in Seoul, and with American naval officers in the Far East.

The George C. Foulk Manuscripts, in the New York Public Library, and the W. W. Rockhill Manuscripts, now deposited in the Yale University Library, were also consulted. For access to the latter I am indebted to Mrs. W. W. Rockhill and to Professor A. Whitney Griswold of Yale University.

William Franklin Sands of Washington, D.C., Philip Jaisohn of Media, Pennsylvania, and Miss Alice Appenzeller of Seoul, Korea, have written me interesting and important letters of recollection, and Mrs. Bessie Beal, Associate Alumni Secretary, has provided me with material from the alumni files of Allen's alma mater, Ohio Wesleyan University.

I have examined two manuscript dissertations: Harold J. Noble's

Bibliography

Korea and Her Relations with the United States before 1895, dated 1931, deposited in the library of the University of California, and Hong Sub Yoon's Korea in International Far Eastern Relations, dated 1935, deposited in the American University Library.

The published documents are disappointing. There is little on Korea in the English collections (*Parliamentary Papers; British Documents on the Origins of the War, 1898–1914*) or in the French (*Documents diplomatiques: Documents diplomatiques français, 1871–1914*). The monumental German series, *Die Grosse Politik der Europäischen Kabinette, 1871–1914*, likewise has less material than might be expected. There is rather more in the Russian *Krasnyi Arkhiv*, pertinent Far Eastern documents being available in English translation in the *Chinese Social and Political Science Review*, 17 (1933–34):480–515, 632–670; 18 (1934–35): 572–594; 19 (1935–36):125–145, 234–267. *Foreign Relations of the United States, 1884–1905*, contains a considerable amount of Korean material, especially for the years 1884–88 and 1894. There has been some editing, but the texts are generally sound. I have, however, checked back to the original documents in preparing this work. *Commercial Relations of the United States, 1884–1905*, is less valuable, although the volumes include some of the consular reports from Seoul.

The *Annual Reports* of the foreign missionary bodies of the Presbyterian and Methodist churches, 1884–1905, contain material of importance.

BOOKS AND ARTICLES

ALLEN, HORACE N. "An Acquaintance with Yuan Shi Kai," *North American Review*, 196 (1912):109–117.

————. *Korea: Fact and Fancy: Being a Republication of Two Books Entitled "Korean Tales" and "A Chronological Index."* Seoul, 1904. The "Chronological Index" contains lists of diplomats and Korean officials and a fairly accurate day-by-day summary of events in Chosen.

————. *Things Korean: A Collection of Sketches Missionary and Diplomatic.* New York, 1908. Interesting but none too revealing.

ARIGA, NAGAO. Chapter on "Diplomacy," in Stead, ed., *Japan by the Japanese*, which see.

ASAKAWA, KANICHI. *The Russo-Japanese Conflict.* Boston, 1904. An excellent Japanese study which sheds light on Korean developments from 1898 to 1904.

BEE, MINGE C. "Origins of German Far Eastern Policy." *Chinese Social and Political Science Review*, 21 (1937):65–97.

BEMIS, SAMUEL F., ed. *American Secretaries of State and Their Diplomacy*, Vols. 7, 8, and 9. New York, 1928.

BERNADOU, J. B. "Korea and the Koreans." *National Geographic*, 2 (1890):232–242.

BISHOP, ISABELLA L. *Korea and Her Neighbours: A Narrative of Travel with an Account of the Recent Vicissitudes and Present Condition*

Bibliography

of the Country. 2 vols. London, 1898. Good for 1894–97; based in considerable part on the *Korean Repository.*

BLAND, J. O. P. *Li Hung Chang.* London, 1917.

BOURDARET, EMILE. *En Corée.* Paris, 1904.

BRANDT, MAX VON. *Dreiunddreissig Jahre in Ost-Asien,* vol. 3. Leipzig, 1901.

————. *Drei Jahre ostasiatischer Politik, 1894–1897.* Stuttgart, 1897. By a well-informed German diplomat who married a daughter of Augustine Heard. Contains a good section on Korea.

BROWN, ARTHUR J. *The Foreign Missionary: An Incarnation of a World Movement.* New York, 1907. An important contribution by a Presbyterian board member.

————. *The Mastery of the Far East: The Story of Korea's Transformation and Japan's Supremacy in the Orient.* New York, 1919. Largely on Korea; gives the missionary point of view.

————. *One Hundred Years: A History of the Foreign Misssionary Work of the Presbyterian Church in the U.S.A.* New York, 1936. Contains an excellent summary of the Korean situation, covering all sects.

————. "A Reading Journey through Korea." *Chautauquan,* 41 (1905):491–578. Similar to the preceding.

CARLES, W. R. *Life in Corea.* London and New York, 1888. By a British vice-consul.

CHAILLÉ-LONG, CHARLES. *My Life on Four Continents.* London, 1912. Interesting but wildly inaccurate recollections of Allen's predecessor as secretary of legation in Seoul.

CHANG, CHUNG-FU. *The Anglo-Japanese Alliance.* Baltimore, 1931.

CHIROL, VALENTINE. *The Far Eastern Question.* London, 1896.

CHUNG, HENRY. *The Case for Korea.* New York, 1921.

Church at Home and Abroad, 1887–1905. A Presbyterian organ.

CLARK, CHARLES A. *The Korean Church and the Nevius Method.* New York, 1930. Contains much historical material.

CLYDE, PAUL H. *International Rivalries in Manchuria, 1889–1922.* Columbus, 1926.

COLQUHOUN, ARCHIBALD R. *English Policy in the Far East.* London, 1885.

CORDIER, HENRI. *Histoire des relations de la Chine avec les puissances occidentales, 1860–1900,* Vols. 2 and 3. Paris, 1902. Useful.

COURANT, MAURICE. *Bibliographie Coréene.* 3 vols. Paris, 1895.

CROLY, HERBERT D. *Willard Straight.* New York, 1924.

CURZON, GEORGE N. *Problems of the Far East: Japan–Korea–China.* London, 1894. Curzon visited Korea in 1892.

DALLET, CHARLES. *Histoire de l'église de Corée.* 2 vols. Paris, 1874. The standard work for Catholic missions.

DAVID, HEINRICH. *Zur Politik der Grossmächte im Fernen Osten, 1894–1902.* Zurich, 1932. Little on Korea.

Bibliography

DENNETT, TYLER. *Americans in Eastern Asia: A Critical Study of the Policy of the United States with Reference to China, Japan and Korea in the 19th Century.* New York, 1922. Valuable for missions and commerce as well as for diplomacy.

DENNETT, TYLER. "Early American Policy in Korea, 1883–7: The Services of Lieutenant Geo. C. Foulk." *Political Science Quarterly,* 38 (1923): 82–103. A good study, based on the Foulk papers.

————. *John Hay: From Poetry to Politics.* New York, 1933.

————. *Roosevelt and the Russo-Japanese War: A Critical Study of American Policy in Eastern Asia in 1920–5, Based Primarily upon the Private Papers of Theodore Roosevelt.* Garden City and New York, 1925.

DENNIS, ALFRED L. P. *Adventures in American Diplomacy, 1896–1906, from Unpublished Documents.* New York, 1928.

DENNY, O. N. "China and Korea." *Congressional Record,* 50 Congress, 1 session (1888), 8135–8140. A good description of the methods of Yuan Shih Kai.

DICKINS, FREDERICK V., and STANLEY LANE-POOLE. *The Life of Sir Harry Parkes,* Vol. 2. London and New York, 1894.

Foreign Missionary, 1884–1886. Organ of the Presbyterian Board of Foreign Missions and an important source on early mission efforts. Was succeeded by *Church at Home and Abroad.*

FRANKE, OTTO. *Die Grossmächte in Ostasien von 1894 bis 1914.* Hamburg, 1923. An excellent general study.

GALE, JAMES S. "Korea in War Time." *Outlook,* 77 (1904):453–456.

————. *Korean Sketches.* Edinburgh and London, 1898.

————. *Korea in Transition.* New York, 1909.

GAPANOVICH, J. J. "Sino-Russian Relations in Manchuria, 1892–1896." *Chinese Social and Political Science Review,* 17 (1933):283–306, 457–479. A summary and review of B. A. Romanov, *Rossia v Manchzhurii, 1892–1906.* Good on Russian activity in Korea.

GIFFORD, DANIEL L. *Every-Day Life in Korea.* New York, 1898.

GILMORE, GEORGE W. *Korea from Its Capital, with a Chapter on Missions.* Philadelphia, 1892. Gilmore was one of the American clergymen hired to teach in the Korean schools.

GRAVES, LOUIS. "Willard Straight at the Legation in Korea." *Asia,* 20 (1920):1079–1086. This and other articles were reprinted in 1922 in a book entitled *Willard Straight in the Orient.*

GRIFFIS, WILLIAM E. *Corea, the Hermit Nation.* New York, 1907.

————. *A Modern Pioneer in Korea: The Life Story of Henry G. Appenzeller.* New York, 1912.

GRISCOM, LLOYD C. *Diplomatically Speaking.* Boston, 1940.

GRISWOLD, A. WHITNEY. *The Far Eastern Policy of the United States.* New York, 1938.

HADDO, GORDON. "The Rise and Fall of the Progressive Party of Korea." *Chautauquan,* 16 (1892):46–49. Based on Japanese sources.

HAMADA, KENGI. *Prince Ito.* London, 1937.

Bibliography

HAMILTON, ANGUS. *Korea.* New York, 1904. An informative but not altogether trustworthy account by an English journalist.

HAYASHI, TADASU. *The Secret Memoirs of Count Tadasu Hayashi,* edited by A. M. Pooley. New York and London, 1915.

HEARD, AUGUSTINE. "China and Japan in Korea." *North American Review,* 159 (1894):300–308. Pro-Chinese statement of a former American minister to Korea.

HISHIDA, SEIJI G. *The International Position of Japan as a Great Power.* New York, 1905. A Japanese study which includes an examination of the Korean question.

HOUGH, WALTER. "The Bernadou, Allen, and Jouy Korean Collections." *Report of the U.S. National Museum,* 1891, pp. 429–488.

HSÜ, SHUHSI. *China and Her Political Entity: A Study of China's Foreign Policy with Reference to Korea, Manchuria and Mongolia.* New York, 1926. A Chinese study which may be set against the preceding.

HULBERT, HOMER B. *The History of Korea.* 2 vols. Seoul, 1905. This standard work, by an American missionary, makes its chief contribution in the earlier period.

————. *The Passing of Korea.* New York, 1906. Contains a useful summary of later Korean history.

JONES, FRANCIS C. "Foreign Diplomacy in Korea, 1866–1894." *Summary of Theses, Harvard University,* 1935, pp. 163–166. Indicates use of British as well as American documents.

JOSEPH, PHILIP. *Foreign Diplomacy in China, 1894–1900: A Study in Political and Economic Relations with China.* London, 1928.

KERNER, ROBERT J., ed. *Northeastern Asia: A Selected Bibliography.* 2 vols. Berkeley, 1939. The best guide available. Has an excellent section on Korea.

Korean Repository, 1892, 1895–1899. Indispensable for an understanding of Korean history and problems. The Methodist missionaries who edited this magazine included in it news features and articles by men who knew Korea and Korean history at first hand.

Korea Review, 1901–1905. Less important than the preceding; largely the personal organ of Homer B. Hulbert.

KRAHMER. *Die Beziehungen Russlands zu Japan mit besonders Berücksichtigung Koreas.* Leipzig, 1904.

LADD, GEORGE T. *In Korea with Marquis Ito.* New York, 1908. Strongly pro-Japanese account by an American professor who visited Korea in 1906.

LANGER, WILLIAM L. *The Diplomacy of Imperialism, 1890–1912.* New York and London, 1935. The best general background study.

LAUNAY, ADRIEN. *La Corée et les missionaires français.* Tours, 1899. Serves as a supplement to Dallet.

LIN, T. C. "Li Hung Chang: His Korean Policies, 1870–1885." *Chinese Social and Political Science Review,* 19 (1935):202–233. Based on Chinese documents.

343

Bibliography

LOBANOV–ROSTOVSKY, PRINCE. *Russia and Asia.* New York, 1933.

LOWELL, PERCIVAL. "A Korean Coup d'Etat." *Atlantic,* 58 (1886): 599–618. A pro-Japanese account of the émeute of 1884.

LOWELL, PERCIVAL. *Chosen, The Land of Morning Calm: A Sketch of Korea.* Boston, 1888.

MARC, PIERRE [B. B. GLINSKII]. *Quelques années de politique internationale: antécédents de la guerre russo-japonaise.* Leipzig, 1914. Excellent treatment of Russian policy. Based on Russian materials.

McCORDOCK, R. STANLEY. *British Far Eastern Policy, 1894–1900.* New York, 1931.

McKENZIE, F. A. *Korea's Fight for Freedom.* New York, 1920. By an English journalist. Valuable because of information obtained from Philip Jaisohn.

——————. *The Tragedy of Korea.* New York, 1908.

MOELLENDORFF, ROSALIE VON. *P. G. von Moellendorff: Ein Lebensbild.* Leipzig, 1930. The author, Moellendorff's widow, incorporates in this volume much material by her husband.

MORSE, HOSEA B. *The International Relations of the Chinese Empire,* Vol. 3. London, 1918.

NOBLE, HAROLD J. "The Korean Mission to the United States in 1883, the First Embassy Sent by Korea to an Occidental Nation." *Transactions of the Korea Branch of the Royal Asiatic Society,* 18 (1929):1–21.

——————. "The United States and Sino-Korean Relations, 1885–1887." *Pacific Historical Quarterly,* 2 (1933):292–304. Based on the American legation archives in Seoul.

NORMAN, HENRY. *The Peoples and Politics of the Far East.* New York, 1895.

PAIK, L. GEORGE. *The History of Protestant Missions in Korea, 1832–1910.* Pyeng Yang, Korea, 1929. Excellent survey by a Korean Methodist.

PAN, STEPHEN C. Y. *American Diplomacy Concerning Manchuria.* Washington, 1938.

PAULLIN, CHARLES O. *Diplomatic Negotiations of American Naval Officers, 1778–1883.* Baltimore, 1912.

POLLARD, ROBERT T. "American Relations with Korea, 1882–1895." *Chinese Social and Political Science Review,* 16 (1932):425–471. Based on *Foreign Relations.*

PRICE, ALLEN T. "American Missions and American Diplomacy in China, 1830–1900." *Summary of Theses, Harvard University,* 1934, pp. 174–177.

Re-Thinking Missions. 7 vols. New York and London, 1932–1933. Although it does not bear directly on Korea, this work of the Laymen's Foreign Mission Inquiry is helpful.

RHODES, HARRY A. *History of the Korea Mission, Presbyterian Church, U.S.A., 1884–1934.* Seoul [1935]. Excellent for details, especially of the later period.

Bibliography

ROCKHILL, WILLIAM W. *China's Intercourse with Korea from the XVth Century to 1895.* London, 1895.

ROSEN, BARON. *Forty Years of Diplomacy.* 2 vols. New York, 1922.

SANDS, WILLIAM F. *Undiplomatic Memories.* New York, 1930. Interesting and important recollections of a man who served as Allen's legation secretary and later as adviser to Korea.

————. "Korea and the Korean Emperor." *Century,* 69 (1905): 577–584.

SAVAGE-LANDOR, A. H. "A Visit to Corea." *Fortnightly Review,* 62 (1894):184–190.

Seoul *Daily Independent,* 1896–1898. In English and Korean. Edited by Philip Jaisohn. Excellent material on Korean politics and foreign relations from the viewpoint of the leader of the Independence movement.

SPEER, ROBERT E. *Missions and Modern History: A Study of the Missionary Aspects of Some Great Movements of the Nineteenth Century.* Vol. 2. New York, 1904. For the Tong Haks.

————. *Missions and Politics in Asia.* New York, 1898.

STEAD, ALFRED, ed. *Japan by the Japanese: A Survey by Its Highest Authorities.* New York and London, 1904. The chapter on "Diplomacy," by Nagao Ariga, pp. 142–218, is an outstanding source for Japanese material on the Korean question.

STEINMANN, FRIEDRICH VON. *Russlands Politik im Fernen Osten und der Staatssekretär Bezobrazov.* Leipzig, 1931. Indispensable for a study of Russia's economic activity in Korea after 1896. Based on Russian archives.

STEVENS, D. W. "China and Japan in Korea." *North American Review,* 159 (1894):308–316. The Japanese viewpoint by an American adviser in Japan.

TANSILL, CHARLES C. *The Foreign Policy of Thomas F. Bayard, 1885–1897.* New York, 1940. Important, particularly for materials from the Bayard MSS.

TREAT, PAYSON J. "China and Korea, 1885–1894." *Political Science Quarterly,* 49 (1933):506–543. An important indictment of Chinese policy, based on unpublished American diplomatic correspondence.

————. *Diplomatic Relations between the United States and Japan, 1853–1895.* 3 vols. Stanford University, 1932–38. A standard work, based on a careful examination of the American diplomatic archives. Contains much on Korea.

TRUBETZKOI, G. *Russland als Grossmacht.* Berlin, 1917.

TSIANG, T. F. "Sino-Japanese Diplomatic Relations, 1870–1894." *Chinese Social and Political Science Review,* 17 (1933):1–106. A valuable work, emphasizing Korea. Is based on Chinese materials.

TUPPER, ELEANOR, and GEORGE E. McREYNOLDS. *Japan in American Public Opinion.* New York, 1937.

UNDERWOOD, HORACE G. *The Call of Korea, Political–Social–Religious.* New York, 1908. By a leading Presbyterian missionary.

Bibliography

UNDERWOOD, HORACE H. "Occidental Literature on Korea." *Transactions of the Korea Branch of the Royal Asiatic Society*, 20 (1931): 1–185. A useful bibliography by a second-generation missionary in Korea.

UNDERWOOD, LILLIAS H. *Fifteen Years among the Top-Knots or Life in Korea*. Boston, 1904. By a woman missionary, the wife of Horace G. and the mother of Horace H. Underwood.

————. *Underwood of Korea*. New York, 1908. A biography of Horace G. Underwood.

VAGTS, ALFRED. "Der Chinesisch-Japanische Krieg, 1894–95." *Europäische Gespräche*, 9 (1931):234–252, 285–302. An excellent account, emphasizing Korea. Uses unpublished American diplomatic correspondence.

"VLADIMIR" [Z. VOLPICELLI]. *The China-Japan War*. London, 1896. By an Italian who performed diplomatic service in Korea.

VONLIARLIARSKY, V. M. "Why Russia Went to War with Japan: The Story of the Yalu Concession." *Fortnightly Review*, 93 (1910):816–831, 1030–1044. An important account.

WHIGHAM, HENRY J. *Manchuria and Korea*. London, 1904. By an English journalist who visited Korea.

WILKINSON, WILLIAM H. *The Corean Government: Constitutional Changes, July 1894 to October 1895, with an Appendix on Subsequent Enactments to 30th June 1896*. Shanghai, 1897. Wilkinson was a British consular officer in Korea.

WRISTON, HENRY M. *Executive Agents in American Foreign Relations*. Baltimore, 1929.

YAKHONTOFF, VICTOR A. *Russia and the Soviet Union in the Far East*. New York, 1933.

YARMOLINSKY, ABRAHAM, ed. *The Memoirs of Count Witte*. New York, 1921.

ZÜHLKE, HERBERT. *Die Rolle des Fernen Ostens in den Politischen Beziehungen der Mächte, 1895–1905*. Berlin, 1929.

Index

Index

Index

Allen, Dr. Horace N.—*continued*
aid of, 309–310, 320–321; recalled, 327–332; tries to help Korea in United States, 332–335; later career and death, 333–334
Allen, Maurice (son of Horace N.), 57
American Bible Institute, 86
American Korean Electric Company, 198n
American Korean Mining Company, 198n
"American party" at Korean court, led by Allen, 145; and concessions, 154–157, 165, 174, 188, 196; Allen gives asylum, 276; in Korean cabinet, 292–293; criticized by Speyer, 297–299; decline, 306; serves Japan, 334
American Trading Company, 56, 150, 200; timber-cutting grant for Dagelet Island, 128; yields right to Russians, 173; buying agent for king of Korea, 128; and mine grant, 131n; and sale of railroad equipment, 170, 179–181; out of Korea, 200. *See also* James R. Morse
Americans in Korea, 195n, 252n
Anglican missionary work in Korea, 88, 94, 109
Anglo-Japanese alliance, Allen notes background in *1899*, 306; relation of Allen to, 310 and note; and the United States, 315, 316
Appenzeller, Alice, 68
Appenzeller, Henry G., 49; active missionary, 68, 69, 76; criticized for rashness, 79, 90, 109
Arsenal, king offers grant to Allen, 129
Arthur, President Chester A., on Korean trade, 126
Aston, William G., British consul, 22, 23, 27, 32, 38, 43
Asylum, granted Japanese by American legation in *1884*, 28, 32; given Koreans by Sill and Allen, *1894–95*, 257, 276, 281–282, 286; State Department disapproves, 281; Russian legation gives to king, 288–293; American legation offers, then refuses, to king, 257, 299, 321

Avison, Dr. O. R., and hospital, 95; protects king, 284–285

Banking and currency, 188, 299
Baptist missionary work in Korea, 88
Bayard, Secretary of State Thomas F., promises to support concessionaires, 134; opposes political interference in Korea, 212, 225, 236, 237
Belgian capitalists, seek concessions, 192, 194
Bernadou, John B., 129
Blaine, Secretary of State James G., Korean policy, 134–135; loses interest, 246
Bostwick, Harry, *see* Collbran and Bostwick
Boxer revolt, 105, 112, 114, 139
Bradley, William D., 142n
Brice, Calvin S., 177
British, number of, in Korea, 252n
Brown, Arthur J., 109, 121
Brown, McLeavy, British adviser to Korea, opposes Americans, 189–190, 296, 327; influence, 292–293; effort to remove, 306
Brown, Sevelon, 142, 143, 236
Buck, American minister to Japan, 322
Buddhism, 10, 105, 109
Budler, German Consul Hermann, fights missions, 48
Bull, William C., 161
Bunker, Reverend Daniel A., 49, 76

Catholic missionary work in Korea, 7, 11–12, 44–45, 61, 86, 94; conflict with Protestant work, 51–53, 88–90, 115–117
Cemetery rights, 95
Chai Chung Won, *see* Hospital, royal
Chaillé-Long, Charles, 97n, 135
Chance, British capitalist, 193, 194n
Chemulpo, Japanese influence in, 3; missionary work at, 10, 86–87, 142; trade at, 149; foreigners in, 252n; in Sino-Japanese war, 256; battle of, in Russo-Japanese war, 320. *See also* Roze Island
Chen Shu Tang, 22
China, influence in Korea, *1884*, 3, 14–18, 20–21; in émeute of *1884*, 21–

350

Index

Index

Index

Index

Index

Okamoto, Japanese adviser in Korea, and murder of queen, 268

Okuma, Count Shigenobu, and American railroad equipment, 180–181; and Tong Hak, 250

Olney, Secretary of State Richard, policy in Korea, 171, 279–281, 333

Omaha, U. S. S., 232

Open Door, in Manchuria, 314–315

Oriental Consolidated Mining Company, 144, 335; organization, 161; English interest, 161n; profits, 166; sells out to Japan, 167

Orthodox missionary work, and Russian legation, 109, 304

Ossipee, U. S. S., 217–218, 220

Paddock, Gordon, American legation secretary, defends Allen, 159; urges pressure on Korea, 191; defends street car company, 196

Pak Chung Yang, 333; lack of ability, 154n, 228, 236–237; appointed Korean minister to United States, 229–232; relies on Allen, 234-235; ignores orders from China 236–238; is punished, 238; in American society, 238–239; smuggling activities, 136, 240–241, 333; appointed prime minister, *1895,* 154, 261–262

Pak Yong Hyo, Korean progressive, in émeute of *1884,* 22, 28–29; in exile, 39, 78; blocks Un-san grant, 156; deserts Japan to help queen, 260–261, 265

Paper mill, Japanese, 146, 169–170

Parker, William, American minister, pro-missionary, 51; dipsomaniac, 206–208, 216; dismissed, 219

Parkes, Sir Harry, 58–59

Pavloff, A., Russian diplomat in Korea, opposes Americans, 165, 323; expansionist, 303; disliked by Allen, 311; inefficiency of, 320; leaves Korea, 325

Pavloff, Mrs. A., 311, 320

Pearl fishery, 128

Peng Yang province, gold mines in, 144. *See also* Un-san mines

Perkins, Henry C., 161

Phelps, *see* Dodge Phelps

Phyong-an-do province, gold mines in, 130

Pierce, Willard Ide, mining expert, 140–141

Plancy, V. Collin de, French diplomat, and Wilhelm case, 117–118

Port Arthur, 290, 300

Port Hamilton, considered for American naval base, 135, 190–191, 191n, 209n; English seizure of, 208–209

Port Lazareff, Russian interest in, 209, 213–214

Powder mill, offered to Americans, 128–129

Presbyterian Board of Foreign Missions, decides to work in Korea, 8; to furnish physicians for hospital, 45–48; on missionary quarrels, 74; on opening of Fusan, 81, 85–86; orders Allen to Seoul, 87; Allen maintains contact with, as diplomat, 85, 104; requested by Allen to supply military advisers, 220; and Allen's recall, 330

Presbyterian missionary work in Korea, starts, 8; connection with hospital, 45–48, 96; quarrels in mission colony, 72–84; work in interior, 79; program of decentralization, 86; growth, 86, 88, 119–120; emphasis on common man, 90–91; Allen aids, 93–96

Pyeng Yang, growth of missionary work, 113–114

Quay, Matthew, 224

Queen Dowager Cho, 16, 41, 244

Queen of Korea (Queen Min), character, 16, 264–265, 272; fights progressives in *1884,* 16, 20–21; and émeute of *1884,* 28; relies on and aids Allen, 41, 62–63, 153m, 156, 265; declines in power, *1894,* 257; resists Japan, *1895,* 260; safety of, assured by Japanese, 261–262; murder of, by Japanese, 168, 266–271, and consequences, 278, 284, 287; degradation after death, 274–275, and repeal, 279

Quelpart Island, massacre, 116; Japanese active on, 248

358

Index

Index

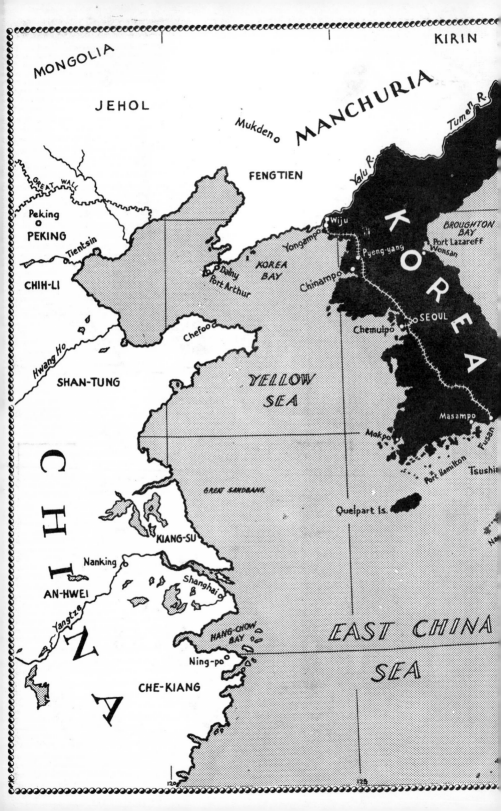